D1796861

THE MEDIEVAL MANUSCRIPTS AT MAYNOOTH

The Russell Library, oil on canvas painted by Thomas Ryan RHA, s.xx^{med}.

The Medieval Manuscripts at Maynooth

Explorations in the Unknown

Peter J. Lucas

<small>AND</small>

Angela M. Lucas

<small>FOUR COURTS PRESS</small>

Typeset in 10.5 pt on 13 pt Garamond by
Carrigboy Typesetting Services for
FOUR COURTS PRESS LTD
7 Malpas Street, Dublin 8, Ireland
www.fourcourtspress.ie
and in North America for
FOUR COURTS PRESS
c/o ISBS, 920 NE 58th Avenue, Suite 300, Portland, OR 97213.

© the authors and Four Courts Press 2014

A catalogue record for this title is available
from the British Library.

ISBN 978–1–84682–534–7

All rights reserved.
Without limiting the rights under copyright
reserved alone, no part of this publication may be
reproduced, stored in or introduced into a retrieval system,
or transmitted, in any form or by any means (electronic, mechanical,
photocopying, recording or otherwise), without the prior
written permission of both the copyright owner and
publisher of this book.

Printed in Spain
by Castuera, Pamplona

To the memory of our parents

Rose and Victor Lucas
Angela and Walter Tyrrell

Curavimus volentibus legere [2 Macc 2.26]
'We have taken care for those who are willing to read'

Contents

Foreword

IN THE MIDDLE AGES, when the catalogue of a library was a hand-list of its manuscripts, the entries were generally minimal: *Horae* for a Book of Hours, or *Commentarius in Exodum*, a commentary on the Book of Exodus. Nothing more. Thus in a medieval catalogue these two items, which are to be found in this book, would have taken two lines! So much more can be said. There was often no information on who wrote the commentary, and certainly it was rarely stated where and when a manuscript was copied out and decorated. It is therefore a serious challenge to determine these elements. As the authors explain, there can also be false trails, as happened with one of ours, where the fifteenth-century prior stated unambiguously that a fine substantial commentary on Psalm 118 was by Alexander of Hales and later, the binder, taking a lead from this, stamped the name of the thirteenth-century Franciscan theologian accordingly, in gold on the spine. It was only through a careful examination of the text that the true author came to light in the person of Englebert of Admont. Again, it was common practice to bind up several works together, with only the title of the first on the binding. So our earliest manuscript from the eleventh century, a record of conciliar events in the diocese of Reims in 991, is tucked away at the end of a volume that contains eight separate booklets, spans three centuries and begins with a thirteenth-century hand copying a work thought then to be by St Augustine – and with only his name on the spine. A love of detection work is an essential qualification for cataloguing medieval manuscripts. Today, there are still medieval manuscripts in libraries that are one-liners in the catalogue or are not in a catalogue at all.

We have been most fortunate, and grateful, that the authors have gone to great trouble to describe in detail the medieval manuscripts in Maynooth. It began with a conversation over a glass of wine at a Christmas party in the 1990s. It came to light that we had a collection of medieval manuscripts which, tantalizingly, were almost unknown to scholars as no list had ever been published: they were hooked, what might they find! The two authors began a very detailed description of each of our Latin manuscripts. The Russell Library staff devoted much time in assisting them in different ways, glad to see the manuscripts in their care receiving the attention they deserved. We are particularly indebted to Penny Woods for devoting her expertise and knowledge to the process for many years. After the authors moved to Cambridge, they were able to maintain progress by many visits to the library and through transmission of images from the manuscripts.

When the catalogue of our library's large collection of manuscripts in the Irish language was published, the contents became widely known thereby and more easily accessible for consultation. As a result, there were regular visits and enquiries from our own departments, and from readers elsewhere in Ireland and abroad, seeking to examine and research the manuscripts in greater detail. Resulting publications from these researches cite the manuscripts and open their contents still further to readers. Publication of *The medieval manuscripts at Maynooth: explorations in the unknown* will bring our holdings to the notice of medievalists worldwide and each manuscript will become part of the corpus of surviving recensions of its text.

The contents of each manuscript have been carefully noted and a detailed physical description given. This will make the book invaluable to students of codicology, learning how medieval books are put together. The authors also made use of the library's 'Unique to the Book' project which was devised after they expressed a desire to include manuscript fragments incorporated in the older printed books. As part of the project's remit, therefore, books in the printed collection were recorded where early binders had used cut-up scraps of vellum manuscripts with fragments of text or sometimes musical notation as part of the bindings. Sixty per cent of the Russell Library collection had been examined by the time of writing, beginning with theology, as that area was known to have many of the earliest bindings. Photographs of these fragments with bibliographical details of the books have been included in this book to tempt further research by other scholars.

The book explores sixteen medieval Latin manuscripts, some of which are composite – one contains eight separate booklets. They range in date from the eleventh century to 1529. There are three further illuminated single-leaf items, each extracted at some stage from a liturgical manuscript or Book of Hours. Because they were decorated, it seems it was a common practice to break up such manuscripts and sell leaves individually as 'pictures'. Bibliographical details are given of nineteen books ranging in date from 1491 to 1694, each containing scraps of manuscript in its binding. Two of the manuscripts are known to have belonged to Laurence Renehan, President of Maynooth (1845–57), an energetic collector of books and manuscripts.

Almost all the manuscripts are very naturally associated with the Church. There are five manuscripts that came from Liège, four of them from the Benedictine abbey of St Jacques whose collections were auctioned in 1788. The authors were able to track down others from the same sale, now in other libraries throughout Europe. There is a very finely decorated Benedictional that had belonged to a fourteenth-century archbishop of Aix-en-Provence. The authors visited that city and, with what must have been great excitement, examined a companion Pontifical in the same ornate style. There are three Books of Hours, with some deftly painted miniatures. While the manuscripts are essentially all in Latin, there is some French, Italian and Dutch present also.

This volume is the culmination of many years of work and we have been fortunate enough to get an occasional glimpse of the fruits of that labour over the past decade. The authors previously published two articles in the journal *Scriptorium*, on six of the manuscripts (Tome LVIII, 1 (2004), pp 83–99 on the five Liège manuscripts; and Tome LXIV, 1 (2010), pp 119–26 on the Benedictional from Aix-en-Provence). The information there has been incorporated and greatly expanded. Peter Lucas also gave a memorable public lecture on the medieval manuscripts on 19 February 2008 in the Russell Library.

This is a book whose importance cannot be overstated. It will be an essential tool for a broad spectrum of scholars and researchers. We are not aware of any other Irish libraries that have a whole book devoted to such detailed descriptions of all their medieval Latin manuscripts. We are delighted that the medieval manuscripts held at Maynooth have received the attention they deserve and congratulate the authors and all who made this possible.

Revd Monsignor Hugh Connolly   Cathal McCauley
President   Librarian
St Patrick's College Maynooth   Maynooth University and
                                                   St Patrick's College Maynooth

September 2014

Preface and acknowledgments

THE LIBRARY OF THE NATIONAL UNIVERSITY OF IRELAND MAYNOOTH includes the collections of St Patrick's College, largely kept as special collections in the Russell Library. It reflects the status of the parent college as National Seminary and Pontifical University, and the now separately constituted National University of Ireland Maynooth. The two institutions are privileged to have a heritage building, designed by Augustus Welby Pugin, reserved for the purpose of preserving the library's bibliographical treasures, drawing scholars and visitors in to what was until the 1960s largely a closed institution. For the first time we here provide descriptions of the medieval manuscripts in Maynooth. Since they have never been catalogued, in most cases the works contained in them have not hitherto been identified. This material has lain mostly unknown for up to two hundred years. No account has been given before now of the collection as a whole and how its make-up may to some extent reflect the history and character of the institution in which it was built up.

Many libraries with collections of medieval manuscripts have over the years (centuries in some cases) gathered together information on each of their manuscripts, sometimes garnered from visiting readers and scholars. Where there is no catalogue, such information can be informal, such as letters or slips of paper with notes of manuscript contents, often kept in a folder. In the case of the medieval manuscripts at Maynooth College no such information was available to us. In 1973 Sir John Ainsworth wrote a report on the afternoon he spent examining the non-Gaelic manuscripts in Maynooth College. There was a useful overview of the collection by Penelope Woods published in 1995, but only one manuscript (RB52) had received serious attention in the form of a published article by Clotilde Soave-Bowe and Christine Meek, for both of which we are grateful. Most of the the manuscripts were not even foliated or paginated. Describing virgin manuscripts – ones that have never been studied before – is a challenge. It is coal-face research. While some issues are resolved easily, others can prove resistant. We have treated each manuscript individually and provided the information that we considered would be most helpful to the reader, sometimes erring on the side of giving more information than would be possible for a larger collection. For liturgical books we have been guided by Abbé Victor Leroquais, whose descriptions are particularly full, and of course by the manuscript itself. No scholar, not even two scholars, can know everything, so there will inevitably be matters on which we have been unable to throw light. This book will provide a platform for others to make further advances in studying this fine collection of manuscripts, and to make revisions where appropriate. Further scope for research also resides in a small archive of legal documents held by the Russell Library, two or three of which are medieval; this collection, where the majority of documents are early modern, would be best dealt with together as a whole and is outside the scope of the present study, which deals with the medieval manuscripts up to 1530. Another possible area for future research lies with the papers of the Revd Dr Laurence Renehan, president of St Patrick's College Maynooth from 1845 to 1857; he was probably the most ardent book and manuscript collector of all those in high office in the college during the nineteenth century, and did a great deal for the library. Further research is also required on the early printed books in which fragments of manuscript material have been found in the bindings. What we say about them is necessarily provisional, not least because searching the remaining books for such material remains to be done. A full analytical study of all the early printed books in the library and their provenance is a desideratum; several are unique copies in these islands.

We have great pleasure in thanking the many friends and colleagues who have helped, supported and advised us while working for over fifteen years on the project. For suggesting readings or corrections in the Latin texts we thank Graham Anderson (Kent), Declan Lawell (Liverpool), David Money (Cambridge), Maeve O'Brien (Maynooth), Hans Sauer (Munich), Patrick Zutshi (Cambridge) and especially Raymond and Sheila Astbury (Dublin). For advice on specific matters we thank Gerard Crotty (who analysed the heraldic devices; Co. Cork), Mary Dove (re. the *Glossa Ordinaria* commentary on the "Song of Songs"; Sussex), Mirjam Foot (re. decorative bindings; London), Joan Greatrex (re. all things Benedictine; Cambridge), Evelyn Mullally (re. Paris; Belfast), Aoibheann Nic Dhonnchadha (re. the binding of SPCM Irish MS C110; Dublin Institute of Advanced Studies), Tadhg Ó Dúshláine (re. Irish manuscripts; Maynooth), Philip Oldfield (re. book-stamps; Toronto), Susan Reed (re. German booksellers; London, British Library), Richard Sharpe (re. auctions of manuscripts in Ireland s.xix; Oxford) and Hendrik Vervliet (re. typography; Antwerp). For advice on manuscript script and dating we thank Ian Doyle (Durham), David Rundle (Oxford), Andrew Watson (Oxford), Teresa Webber (Cambridge) and Patrick Zutshi (Cambridge). For advice on manuscript decoration and illumination we thank Christopher De Hamel (Cambridge), Nigel Morgan (Cambridge), Stella Panayotova (Cambridge) and especially Catherine Yvard (London). Valuable advice and information was given to us about binding materials by the two conservators who work in the Russell Library, Paul Hoary and Louise Walsworth Bell. Library staff have been immensely helpful and supportive, including Mary Brien (Maynooth), I. Bröning (Darmstadt), Sophie Evans (Dublin, Royal Irish Academy), Philippe Ferrand (Aix-en-Provence), Rachel Hynes (Maynooth), Thomas Kabdebo (former librarian, Maynooth), Aisling Lockart (Dublin, TCD), Cathal McCauley (librarian, Maynooth), Agnes Neligan (former librarian, Maynooth), Etaín Ó Siocháin (Maynooth), Carmélia Opsomer (Liège), Regina Whelan Richardson (Maynooth), Valerie Seymour (former special collections librarian, Maynooth), David Sheehy (formerly of Dublin Diocesan Archives), Nicholas Smith (formerly of Cambridge University Library) plus other members of the special collections team in the Russell Library. Any remaining errors and omissions are our own responsibility. We would like especially to pay tribute to the two people who sustained us most in the Russell Library, Penelope Woods, former librarian there, for her enthusiastic support and passionate devotion to the collections in the Russell Library, and for kindly reading an earlier draft of our text, and Celia Kehoe, whose quiet efficiency and steady production of quality digital images greatly facilitated our study of the manuscripts in conjunction with research aids available in other libraries. Their successors, Barbara McCormack (special collections librarian) and Audrey Kinch, have also been exceptionally helpful and supportive.

For support and advice in processing the images we thank Haroon Ahmed (Cambridge), Mick Cafferkey (PandIS, Cambridge), Gavin Lucas (London) and Chris Quy (UCS, Cambridge). For advice on publication we wish to thank Ian Doyle (Durham), Michael Dunne (who also read a draft version of the text, Maynooth), Conrad Guettler (Cambridge), Ruth Hegarty (Dublin, Royal Irish Academy), Gavin Lucas (London), David McKitterick (Cambridge), Revd Hugh Shilson-Thomas (Cambridge) and Frances Willmoth (Cambridge). We are also grateful to the editor of *Scriptorium* for allowing some textual material to be reused, albeit mostly in adapted form, and to all who took the photographic images that adorn this book, including Frédéric Prémartin (Aix-en-Provence), Paul Hoary, Louise Walsworth Bell, Stuart McNamara and, especially, Celia Kehoe. Because it is absolutely necessary to conserve manuscripts carefully even as they are being used, heavy rope cords or transparent slips have sometimes been used to hold pages in place when they were photographed. Most of the manuscripts are membrane, a material that is often stiff or crinkled. These features are inevitably and rightly shown in a photographic reproduction, even if the result may look unaesthetic. Photographic images of the manuscript at Aix-en-Provence (pls 15.2, 15.3) are reproduced by courtesy of the librarian of the Bibliothèque Municipale Méjanes. Material from the collections of St Patrick's College held in the Russell Library is reproduced by permission of the librarian, National University of Ireland Maynooth. We are grateful to Thomas Ryan RHA for his courtesy in allowing his painting of the Russell Library to be reproduced as the frontispiece. For generous financial assistance that has made publication possible, we are most grateful to the Reverend Monsignor Hugh Connolly, president, St Patrick's College Maynooth, and Cathal McCauley, librarian, National University of Ireland Maynooth. We are also extremely grateful to have been awarded a generous grant-in-aid towards the costs of preparing and reproducing the illustrations by the Trustees of the Neil Ker Memorial Fund under the auspices of the British Academy (London). We are indebted to an anonymous reader for some amendments. Finally we thank Four Courts Press for their positive approach to our book. And we would like to make special mention of Michael Potterton at Four Courts Press, who has guided the book through the publication process.

We undertook this project during the last nine years of our working lives while we were still in post in Dublin and Maynooth. Without the support of an academic home subsequently provided by Wolfson College, Cambridge, the completion of this work would have been much more difficult; we express our profound thanks.

As we were nearing completion of this book we learnt with great sadness of the death of Malcolm Parkes, teacher, friend and professor of palaeography *extraordinaire*. We are confident that he would have appreciated the merits of our work and told us frankly of any faults.

Peter and Angela Lucas
Cambridge
17 March 2014

Illustrations

Fragments in bindings of printed books

Abbreviations

Acta SS	Joannes Bollandus, *Acta Sanctorum*, 68 vols (Antwerp, 1643–1940)
AH	*Analecta Hymnica*, ed. Dreves et al. 1886–1978
attrib.	attributed (to)
BHL	Bibliotheca Hagiographica Latina (by the Bollandists)
BL	British Library, London
BLG	*Catalogue of books printed in the German-speaking countries and of German books printed in other countries from 1601 to 1700 now in the British Library.* 5 vols (London, British Library 1994)
BN	Bibliothèque Nationale, Paris
bp	bishop
BT	Glorieux, Geneviève, *Belgica Typograpica 1541–1600*. 4 vols (Nieuwkoop, B. de Graaf 1968–94)
c.	*circa*
CCCM	Corpus Christianorum, Continuatio Mediaevalis
CCSL	Corpus Christianorum, Series Latina
cf.	*confer* 'compare (like with like)'
CLC	*The Cathedral Libraries catalogue*, ed. Margaret S.G. McLeod, Karen I. James and David J. Shaw. 3 vols (London, British Library 1984–98)
CO	*Corpus Orationum*, ed. Eugenius Moeller, Joannes Clément and Bertrandus Wallant, CCSL 160 (1993)
cod.	codex
col.	column
cp.	compare (with other)
CSEL	Corpus Scriptorum Ecclesiasticorum Latinorum
DIAS	Dublin Institute of Advanced Studies
erron.	erroneous(ly)
fd	feast-day
fl.	*floruit* 'flourished'
fo(s)	folio(s)
ISTC	Incunabula Short Title Catalogue
L	Latin
MCA	Maynooth College Archives (catalogued by Patrick J. Corish 2007)
MGH	Monumenta Germaniae Historica
n.d.	no date
n.s.	new series
NUIM	National University of Ireland Maynooth
OBL	Oxford Bodleian Library
ODNB	*Oxford dictionary of national biography*

PL	Patrologia Latina, cursus completus, ed. J.-P. Migne
pl./pls	plate/plates
Ps	Psalm (cited by its number in the Vulgate Bible)
Ps.	Pseudo [followed by name, as Ps.Bede = Pseudo-Bede]
RB	*Révue Bénédictine*
repr.	reprint; reprinted in
RTAM	*Recherches de Théologie ancienne et médiévale*
s.n.	*sub nomine* 'under the name'
SofS	Song of Songs
SPCM	St Patrick's College, Maynooth
TCD	Trinity College Dublin
USTC	Universal Short Title Catalogue

Form of entries

ACH MANUSCRIPT is an individual hand-made artefact, but as far as is practicable the description of each one follows the form of entry set out below.

HEADING

Each manuscript entry is assigned its own number in the catalogue, and begins with the library class-mark – for example, RB47 – followed by a brief indication of the contents, normally in Latin because that is the language of most of the manuscripts, but occasionally in English, as Book of Hours. In the case of the fragments, textual identification often being impossible, a briefer practice is followed; if the fragment is preserved in a printed book, the bibliographical details of that printed book are also given.

HISTORY

This section begins with a brief description of the manuscript in terms of its origin (if known) or its likely origin on the basis of the date and localization of the script (as far as possible). It includes what is known about the manuscript's external history together with an indication of any internal notes, inscriptions etc. that might point to a particular origin or provenance. If anything in a calendar points to a particular date or place of origin, this is included here. What is known about the history of the manuscript, including when and how it came to Maynooth (if known) is also included. The binding is described and related to the history of the manuscript where possible.

Dates: if an exact year of writing is known it is stated, as 1529. Where a date is based on the style of writing it is given approximately in the form, s.xii, i.e., twelfth century. Refinements here include:

s.xii^{in}	beginning of the twelfth century
s.xii^{1}	first quarter of the twelfth century
s.xii^{2}	second quarter of the twelfth century
s.xii^{med}	middle of the twelfth century
s.xii^{3}	third quarter of the twelfth century
s.xii^{4}	last quarter of the twelfth century
s.xii^{ex}	end of the twelfth century
s.xii/xiii	turn of the twelfth into the thirteenth century
s.xii$^{1/2}$	first half of the twelfth century

CODICOLOGICAL DESCRIPTION

This section begins with the physical make-up of the manuscript, as fos ii + 100 + ii, where the roman numbers refer to endleaves and the arabic number records the number of folios, and includes a full description of the pricking, ruling, quality of membrane, hair/flesh sides (HF), and anything else pertinent to the collation. Dimensions of leaves and written areas are given in milimetres. If not already dealt with under 'history', the main hand will be characterized and assigned a date and country or region of writing, thus filling out as appropriate what has been summarized above; where appropriate a separate section designated *Script* or *Scribes and script* will give further details. The illustrations and decoration (including colour) are also described as forming an integral part of the manuscript, and indeed in devotional books such as Books of Hours they may be considered more important than the text. For the titles of illustrations (given in *italics*) we have been guided where convenient by Réau (1955–9), but have otherwise followed the guidance of the illustration itself or the text accompanying it.

COLLATION

Given in the abbreviated form, as I^8 (fos 1–8), including a note of any singletons or other irregularity in the make-up of each quire. Quire signatures and catchwords (if any) are noted below the collation.

CONTENTS

A full list of the contents is given, item by item in the manuscript, listed by folio and line, as fo 21r/a/16 means folio 21 recto, column a, line 16, with references to the most recent or best printed version(s) of the texts concerned when possible. Any text heading or "title" is given between double inverted commas, followed by the 'incipit' between single inverted commas, and (unless the text is very short) the 'last words of text' and 'explicit'. Bold type is used to represent red ink (rubrics, shaded capitals etc.). If we have noticed a lacuna in a text it is indicated, normally by giving the last words where the text breaks off and the first words where it resumes. In the transcriptions <diamond brackets> indicate abbreviations or contractions, and a vertical stroke | marks a line division, while a double vertical stroke || marks a page division. \Angled strokes/ indicate suprascript letters, written or inserted above the main line of writing. [Square brackets] are used for material (words or letters) that is supplied. Medieval orthographical practice often used e where classical Latin would have ae, as in 'emuli' for classical Latin 'aemuli' (RB47H).

BIBLIOGRAPHY

The bibliography for each manuscript is included in the bibliography for the whole book, with an indication where appropriate of which manuscript(s) a particular item in the bibliography refers to.

Introduction

THE ROYAL COLLEGE OF ST PATRICK, Maynooth, Co. Kildare, Ireland, was founded in 1795. Its foundation was part of a movement to improve the education of Catholics in late eighteenth-century Ireland, and took place against the backdrop of major historical events in other countries, most importantly the French Revolution, which Theobald Wolfe Tone, the great Irish patriot of the period, called the 'morning star of Liberty in Ireland'.[1] Prior to 1795 Irishmen wishing to become priests had to study abroad. Clergy and politicians alike at the end of the eighteenth century were worried about the danger of Catholic priests, newly ordained on the Continent, bringing what was dubbed 'the contagion of sedition and infidelity' and the 'pernicious maxims of a licentious philosophy' back to Ireland.[2] The Irish Catholic hierarchy, led by John Thomas Troy OP, archbishop of Dublin (1786–1823),[3] not only complained in a pastoral letter about 'the idolatrous French, the chief enemies of our ... country',[4] but was also concerned that there should be an education for future priests once the French colleges were closed because of the revolution there. So there were two socio-political pressures that combined to lead to the foundation of the college.[5]

After a series of complex negotiations in London and in Dublin, a college 'for the education exclusively of persons professing the Roman Catholic Religion' was established by Act of Parliament in May 1795, and royal assent was given by King George III on 5 June 1795. Trustees were appointed, prominent among them the archbishop of Dublin, Dr Troy.[6] By July of that same year a site at Maynooth 'in the very centre of a beautiful, healthy and plentiful country' had been chosen. Its first house was that of Mr Stoyte, land agent of the duke of Leinster, whose magnificent estate of Carton lay close by. The college opened on 6 October 1795 with forty students.

To celebrate its centenary in 1895, the college at Maynooth became a Pontifical University, gaining approval from Rome of its statutes for the three faculties of Theology, Philosophy and Canon Law in 1900.[7] On 25 February 1910, backdated

---

1 T.W. Moody, R.B. McDowell and C.J. Woods, *The writings of Theobald Wolfe Tone*, 1 (Oxford, 1998), p. 105. Cited by John Healy, *Maynooth College: its centenary history* (Dublin, 1895), p. 88. 2 These quotations appeared first in *An humble address to our most gracious sovereign King George III: from the Roman Catholic prelates of Ireland* (London, 1794), p. 19. 3 On Troy, see Dáire Keogh, s.n. Troy, John Thomas in H.C.G. Matthew and Brian Harrison (eds), *Oxford dictionary of national biography*, 61 vols (Oxford, 2004), vol. 55, pp 450–2. 4 ESTC t226700, cited by Hugh Fenning OP, 'Dublin imprints of Catholic interest, 1796–1799', *Collectanea Hibernica* 48 (2006), 67–108 at 108. 5 For a good account of the founding of the college, see P.J. Corish, *Maynooth College, 1795–1995* (Dublin, 1995), pp 6–13. This book and that by Healy (*Maynooth College*) supply most of the information about the college summarized here. 6 35 Geo.III, c. 21. See Healy, *Maynooth College*, Appendix I, pp 657–8 and Appendix VI, pp 666–8. 7 Corish, *Maynooth College*, p. 240.

to November 1909, St Patrick's College Maynooth, Seminary and Pontifical University, became a Recognized College of the newly established National University of Ireland (1908) in respect of its three faculties of Arts, Philosophy and Celtic Studies. That status was confirmed four years later with the addition of a Faculty of Science.[8]

In 1966 the Maynooth trustees, their number drawn from among the Irish Catholic bishops, declared their intention to develop Maynooth as a centre of higher educational studies, opening its doors to brothers, nuns, and the laity.[9] By 1971 the first full-time lay members of staff were appointed. By the 1990s the lay students and staff had grown to such large numbers that the decision was made to separate formally the university from the Seminary and Pontifical University of St Patrick, and so in 1997, by act of the Irish Parliament, Dáil Éireann, the National University of Ireland Maynooth was born. The Seminary and Pontifical University of St Patrick continue on the same site. At the time of writing, the National University of Ireland Maynooth has a large mainly lay academic staff and more than nine thousand students.

THE LIBRARY

The Catholic Seminary of Maynooth had a library from 1800 onwards.[10] The first librarian was Revd Andrew Dunne, appointed in 1800. A priest of the diocese of Dublin, he was educated at Bordeaux, and subsequently became the third president of Maynooth College.[11] Fr Dunne's books, later bought by the college, formed the foundation of the library's collection, and the collection continued to be built up through purchases, donations and bequests.[12] In the years to come, the position of librarian was invariably held in conjunction with some other office, notably that of prefect of the Dunboyne establishment for postgraduates. Only the most recent six librarians have been full time. The first catalogue, really just an inventory, was made in the 1820s.[13]

THE LIBRARY HOUSING

The first proper library building came as part of a new range of buildings designed by Augustus Welby Pugin (1812–52),[14] who has usually been credited as one of

8 Ibid., pp 263–5.   9 Ibid., p. 365.   10 Agnes Neligan, 'The library looking back, 1995–1800' in Agnes Neligan, *Maynooth Library: treasures from the collections of Saint Patrick's College* (Dublin, 1995), pp 3–28 at p. 4; for an account of the college library at the end of its first century, see Healy, *Maynooth College*, pp 645–50.   11 Healy, *Maynooth College*, Appendix XI, pp 698–9; Neligan, 'The library looking back', p. 18.   12 Neligan, 'The library looking back', p. 9.   13 On the first and subsequent Library catalogues, see Neligan, 'The library looking back', pp 20–5. See also Corish, *Maynooth College*, pp 225, 323.   14 See Jeanne Meldon and Caroline Gallagher, *Pugin at Maynooth:*

or at least moral, is a 'Commissione' given by the Doge of Venice to a captain of the fleet that guarded the Adriatic; it is the only one that had received detailed study before we began the present work (RB52).[17]

LANGUAGES

Most of the texts in the manuscripts are in Latin. French occurs with Latin in the Books of Hours (RB37, 38, 39), Italian with Latin in the 'Commissione' (RB52), and Dutch with Latin in the Psalter with Canticles (RB519). There is nothing in English.[18]

DATES

Very few manuscripts record when they were written. Mostly the dating has to be worked out from the style of handwriting, or script. The earliest manuscript is eleventh century, a record of conciliar events in the diocese of Reims during 991 (RB47/18). The latest is a Missal from Liège, which does actually state its date of writing: 1529 (RB54). In between these earliest and latest dates, the *Glossa Ordinaria* for "Exodus" (RB45) and Bruno of Segni on "Exodus" (RB46) are both twelfth century. From the thirteenth century there are the *Glossa Ordinaria* for the "Song of Songs" (RB47/8), Ambrose *De Conflictu Vitiorum et Virtutum* (RB47/2), the *Summula Raymundi Versificata* (an abbreviated version in verse of the *Summa* of Raymund de Peñafort OP = RB47/12–13), a formulary of papal letters relating to Margaret countess of Flanders and Hainault (RB47/14), and several works by Augustine (RB71). Dating from the thirteenth/fourteenth centuries (*c.*1300) there is an extract from Vincent of Beauvais on the *Vision of Tundale* (RB47/5), Seneca *Ad Lucilium epistulae Morales* (extracts = RB47/17), and a Bible (RB53). From the fourteenth century comes Engelbert of Admont's Commentary on Psalm 118 (RB16), and the Benedictional of Armand de Narcès can be dated precisely between 1329 and 1348 (RB74), the only instance in the collection of a manuscript datable from external historical evidence. The Psalter (RB36) dates from the fourteenth/fifteenth centuries (*c.*1400). Several manuscripts date from the second half of, or late in, the fifteenth century: the Breviary (RB31), two Books of Hours (RB37 and RB38), the Canon Law manuscript (RB29), and the 'Commissione' (RB52). The Psalter with Canticles (RB519) dates from the

17 Clotilde Soave-Bowe and Christine Meek, 'A voyage to Barbary in the fifteenth century', *Hermathena* 124 (1978), 24–41.   18 Equally there is nothing in Irish. For Irish manuscripts, see Paul Walsh, *Catalogue of Irish manuscripts in Maynooth College Library*, pt 1 (Maynooth, 1943); Pádraig Ó Fiannachta, *Lámhscríbhinní Gaeilge Choláiste Phádraig, Má Nuad*, fasc. 2–8 (Maynooth, 1965–73). Details are available on the website for Irish Script on Screen at www.isos.dias.ie.

first quarter of the sixteenth century, and the Book of Hours that is printed (with hand-painted illuminations) dates from 1526 (RB39).

Only rarely does a manuscript have some indication of where it was written. The place of origin has to be worked out from features such as the script, or if there is a calendar or litany, from the mention of specific saints with a local significance. For example the Missal of 1529 (RB54) thrice mentions St Lambert, who gave his name to the cathedral at Liège until it was suppressed in 1794 in the French Revolution, once for his translation (31 May), once for his feast-day (17 Sept.) and again for his octave (24 Sept.); this evidence confirms that the manuscript was written at Liège. One of the Books of Hours (RB38) features the double appearance of St Geneviève in the calendar, both on her feast-day of 3 January (fo 1r) and on the anniversary of the procession of her relics to save Paris from ergot-sickness on 26 November 1129 (fo 6r), as well as displaying a full-page picture of her on fo 46v. The manuscript was almost certainly a Paris production. The largest proportion of manuscripts was written in France. With regard to the *Glossa Ordinaria* texts, the "Song of Songs" comes from the north (RB47/8) and "Exodus" from the north-east (RB45). Also from northern France come the *Summula Raymundi Versificata* and the formulary of papal letters relating to Margaret of Hainault (RB47/12–14). The record of conciliar events at Reims 991 comes from north-east France or the Rhineland (RB47/18). The Bible is from France, written by a scribe from the south (RB53), and the Benedictional was written in the south-east of France, if not in Aix-en-Provence itself (RB74). The Book of Hours that is printed comes from Paris (RB39). After France the area most represented is the Low Countries. Bruno of Segni on "Exodus" is from there (RB46), as are the Missal (RB54) and the Breviary (RB31), another Book of Hours is from Bruges (RB37), and the Psalter with Canticles (RB519) is probably from the Maastricht area. Two manuscripts were written in Italy: the Seneca (RB47/17) and the 'Commissione' (RB52). So all of the manuscripts are continental; none of the manuscripts was written in these islands.

Only two manuscripts yield information pertinent to the question of what caused the manuscripts to be written. The 'Commissione' (RB52) was written by a single hand at Venice in 1481, being the *copia di pregio*, i.e., a fair copy prepared to order for preservation in a noble family. It was given by the Doge of Venice to Niccolò da Pesaro, Captain of the Venetian Fleet in the Adriatic. Members of the Pesaro family were leading naval commanders at the time.[19] The other manuscript that yields information on the circumstances that led to it being written is the Benedictional, perhaps the most important manuscript in the collection (RB74).[20] This Benedictional is based on the collection of episcopal blessings brought together and organized by Guillaume Durand (bishop of Mende, 1285–96). It was written almost certainly in south-east France, probably in Aix-en-Provence, and is datable by external criteria between 1329 and 1348. According to the inscription on fo 1ᵛ, it was the Benedictional used by Armand de Narcès, archbishop of Aix-en-Provence (1329–48).[21] He was a canon lawyer by training who had a collection of some seventy books.[22] His will, surviving in the Vatican, records that he left this book together with two others, a Bible and a Pontifical, all three written in the same hand, to the chapter of the cathedral of St Sauveur at Aix.[23] Together, the manuscripts would have provided the archbishop with a set of well-organized books pertaining to the duties of his office. The Benedictional probably stayed at St Sauveur's Cathedral in Aix until the French Revolution, when the goods belonging to the cathedral chapter were 'nationalized', and in this case at least probably sold. The Bible is now lost, but the Pontifical is still in Aix, no longer the property of the cathedral chapter, but in the municipal library, Aix-en-Provence, Bibliothèque Méjanes, cod. 13 (Rey 75).[24] The history of the Benedictional until it came to Maynooth in the nineteenth century is unknown.[25] The college is privileged to possess a manuscript whose circumstances of origin are well attested, written at the express wish of an archbishop, with a surviving sister manuscript written in the same hand, which is still in the same city where both were probably made and certainly used.

---

19 See Soave-Bowe and Meek, 'A voyage to Barbary', 24–41.   **20** See P.J. Lucas, 'Un nouveau manuscrit daté : le Bénédictionnaire d'Armand de Narcès, archevêque d'Aix-en-Provence (1329–48), retrouvé à Maynooth en Irlande', *Scriptorium* 64 (2010), 120–6.   **21** J.H. Albanés, *Gallia Christiana Novissima: histoire des archevêchés, évêchés & abbayes de France*, 1 (Montbéliard, 1899), 83–6; Marie-Henriette Jullien de Pomerol, *Bibliothèques ecclésiastiques au temps de la papauté d'Avignon*, 2, Documents, Études et Répertoires publiés par l'Institut de Recherche et d'Histoire des Textes 61 (Paris, 2001), no. 348.54, pp 247–54 at p. 247.   **22** J.H. Albanés, 'Deux archevêques d'Aix qui n'en font qu'un seul et un autre archevêque qui en fait deux', *Bulletin du Comité des Travaux Historiques et Scientifiques* (Section Histoire et Archéologie) (1883), 87–132 at 122–5; Noël Coulet, 'Bibliothèques aixoises du XVe siècle (1433–88)' in *Livres et Bibliothèques (XIII–XVe Siècle)*, Cahiers de Fanjeaux 31 (Toulouse, 1996), pp 209–39 at p. 211; Marie-Henriette Jullien de Pomerol, 'Les livres dans les Dépouilles des Prélats Méridionaux' in *Livres et Bibliothèques (XIIIe–XVe siècle)*, Cahiers de Fanjeaux 31 (Toulouse, 1996), pp 285–314 at p. 314; Jullien de Pomerol, *Bibliothèques ecclésiastiques*, pp 248–54.   **23** Albanés, 'Deux archevêques d'Aix', 120; Jullien de Pomerol, *Bibliothèques ecclésiastiques*, p. 248, whose labelling is adopted in square brackets.   **24** For a description, see V. Leroquais, *Les pontificaux manuscrits des bibliothèques publiques de France*, 1 (Paris, 1937), pp 3–7; Michel Andrieu, *Le pontifical romain au moyen-age* 3 : *Le pontifical de Guillaume Durand*, Studi e Testi 88 (Città del Vaticano, 1940), pp 23–35; and, for a facsimile of part of fo 27, see Charles Samaran and Robert Marichal, *Catalogue des manuscrits en écriture latine portant des indications de date, de lieu ou de copiste*, 6 (Paris, 1968), pl. xlviii (with a notice at p. 7).   **25** See further below, pp 182–5.

The history of the manuscripts since they were written is the area we know least about. We can work out from the script (occasionally the illustrations) and aspects of the contents where and when manuscripts were written, not with absolute precision of course, but in what area or region and in what period of about fifty years. And we know that the manuscripts are in Maynooth now, and that in the case of the Augustine (RB71) it belonged to Frederick Conway in Dublin for at least twenty years before it came to Maynooth. Where were the manuscripts in between? Five of them were in Liège, four in the Benedictine abbey of St Jacques (RB16, 45, 46, 47), and one, the Missal (RB54), at St Leonard's, originally a cell of St Jacques. We know this because, as well as their bindings by Philippe Fisen (precentor at the abbey of St Jacques, Liège, s.xviii[1]), the four show the class-marks of St Jacques, and these class-marks conform to those in a catalogue of St Jacques preserved in Brussels, also because some of them include the handwriting of Philippe d'Othée, prior of St Jacques from 1404 to 1426, who did a great deal of work to put the contents of the library there in order. This information does not completely plug the gap between the making of the manuscripts and their arrival in Maynooth, but in some cases, such as the eleventh-century account of conciliar events at Reims (RB47/18), it seems unlikely that the manuscript moved very far from the place where it was made to Liège, and there it probably rested for the best part of seven hundred years, after which it probably came directly to Maynooth in the early nineteenth century. In most cases, the history is much less clear. Only one manuscript shows signs of having come to Ireland via England. The Breviary (RB31) apparently belonged to a member of the Webster family who were based in Chester, and it looks likely that this manuscript was sold at an auction in England in 1828 before becoming the property of Dr Laurence Renehan, president of Maynooth College from 1845 to 1857.

THE MANUSCRIPTS IN IRELAND

What happened to the manuscripts when they came to Ireland and how did they come to Maynooth? As far as the five manuscripts from Liège (RB16, 45, 46, 47, 54) are concerned, nothing at all happened to them. This is good. Other manuscripts from the big Liège sale in 1788 made their way into other libraries. The few received by the British Museum, for example, were immediately provided with new British Museum-style bindings, which destroyed the evidence of the bindings done in Liège around 1720. These Liège bindings of the early eighteenth century by Philippe Fisen, the librarian/precentor, are well preserved in the manuscripts here (pl. A). One of them, the Miscellany (RB47) has the Liège number 'MS B 61' on the spine (pl. 4.2). When we first saw this manuscript it

had a twentieth-century sticky label over this part of the spine,[26] but since we were suspicious that it was hiding something valuable, Paul Hoary, one of the Russell Library conservators, very skilfully removed the offending label, and the

26 For a similar label that is still in position on the spine of another manuscript (RB53), see pl. C.

A Five books with spines decorated with gold tooling by Philippe Fisen of the abbey of St Jacques, Liège, c.1721. Note the variety of tooling used.

B Red goatskin morocco binding by James Adams of Dublin s.xix[2] on RB71, the Augustine owned by James Conway.

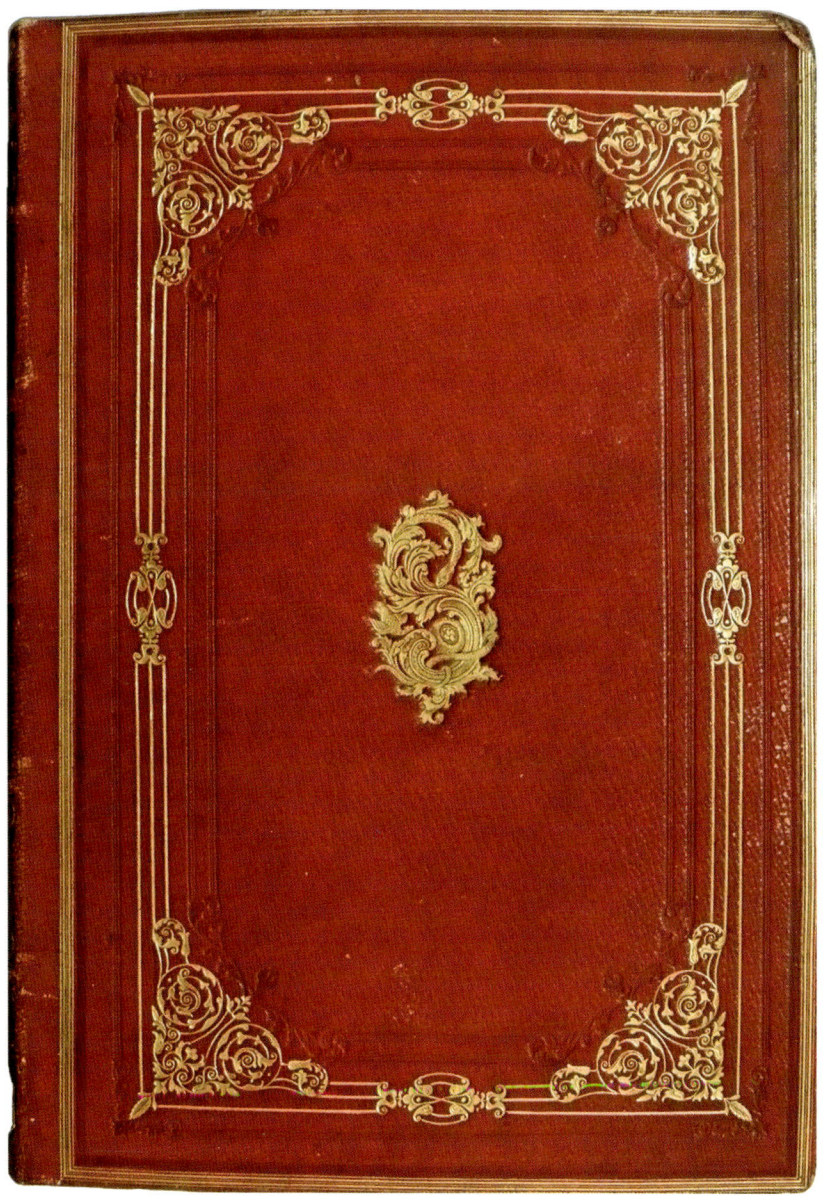

Liège number was revealed. And the presence and retention of these Liège bindings suggests that the manuscripts came more or less directly from Liège to Maynooth, without the 'interference' of any intermediary. At least six of the Maynooth manuscripts have nineteenth-century Irish bindings, including some good-quality ones. The Augustine manuscript (RB71) was bound in 1834 in red goatskin morocco with gold tooled ornament and gilt edging to the leaves by James Adams of Dublin for Frederick W. Conway (1782–1853), the Irish bibliophile and founder of the *Dublin Political Review* (pl. B). It was sold to Maynooth College at the auction of Conway's books in 1854 for 13*s*.[27] Two manuscripts – the Bible written by a scribe from the south of France (RB53) and the Benedictional from Aix-en-Provence (RB74) – have mid-nineteenth-century bindings by Gerald Bellew of Dublin,[28] both signed at the bottom of the inside of the front cover. The Bible is in red sheepskin with gold tooling and gilt edging to the leaves (pl. C), and the Benedictional is in white vellum with blind-stamped covers, some gold tooling, notably on the spine, and gilt edging to the leaves. From an inscription on fo 1r we know that the Bible was given to the college by the Revd Dr Laurence Renehan, president from 1845 to 1857. It is possible that he commissioned the binding, and that of the Benedictional too. The spine of the Benedictional is stamped at the base 'M.S. | A.D. 1348'. Other bindings have similar stamps. The Psalter is entitled on the spine 'PSALTERIUM | DAVIDIS' and marked at the bottom 'M. S. | SÆC. XIV.' The Breviary is entitled on the spine 'BREVIARIUM | ROMANUM', and below 'MS | SÆC. XV.', and, more importantly, added in slightly larger lettering below that 'O'RENEHAN | MSS.'. This last manuscript did indeed come to the library from Dr Renehan *c*.1857, and it is difficult to avoid the conclusion that he was responsible at least for the added lettering if not in some of the other cases for the binding itself, as the binding of the Breviary, stamped with the Webster arms and motto, must have been in place when Renehan acquired the manuscript. He is probably responsible for the presence of these manuscripts in the library. Certainly he was active in this respect, as is shown by his papers, now in the college archives. Those related to book buying and bookbinding include a letter dated 24 November 1847 from the Cologne bookselling firm of J.M. Heberle (Antiquargeschäft mit Auktionanstalt) offering two illuminated manuscripts of possible interest to Renehan.[29] Unfortunately neither can be matched with any of the manuscripts known to have come to the college library from Renehan.[30] In his will Renehan left manuscripts up to the value of £200 to the college library, to be selected by Dr Russell, then professor of ecclesiastical history;[31] not all of these manuscripts were medieval of course.

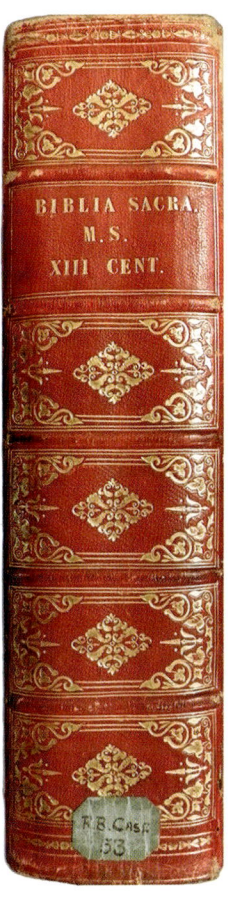

C Spine of binding by Gerald Bellew of Dublin s.xix[mid] on RB53, the Bible owned by Laurence Renehan, president of St Patrick's College, Maynooth. The octagonal blue library label stems from when the rare books were first classified s.xx[2].

27 As noted by Penelope Woods, 'Books rich, rare and curious' in Neligan, *Maynooth Library*, pp 29–63 at p. 31, and p. 58, n. 9. Woods notes a similar binding for Dublin, Trinity College MS 42, an English Bible of the second half of the thirteenth century (M.L. Colker, *Trinity College Library Dublin, descriptive catalogue of the mediaeval and Renaissance Latin manuscripts*, 2 vols (Aldershot, for TCD Library, 1991), vol. 1, 73–5). 28 Charles Ramsden, 'Bookbinders of the United Kingdom (outside London), 1780–1840' (privately printed, 1954), p. 28 gives two addresses: 21 S. King St., and 79 Grafton St. 29 MCA, Box 8, Folder 31, §5. The firm, founded by Johann Matthias Heberle (d. 1840) and carried on by his employee Heinrich Lempertz, still exists as an auction house today: www.lempertz.com/ueberuns.html. 30 Further investigation of his correspondence might be worthwhile, especially to throw light on Dr Renehan's passion for building a manuscript and printed book collection, and especially if the successors of Dr Renehan's correspondents have preserved their dealings with him in their business papers. 31 Woods, 'Books rich, rare and curious', p. 58, n. 10. See Appendix below, p. 235.

Of the other two manuscripts with nineteenth-century bindings, the Canon Law manuscript (RB29) probably arrived through some other source or sources. And the Italian 'Commissione' (RB52) was given to St Patrick's College, Maynooth, by Dr Daniel McCarthy, professor of scripture (Hebrew) and vice-president of Maynooth College (1854–, 1872–81) on 17 March 1871 (St Patrick's Day), as recorded on fo 27v.

CONCLUSION

During the nineteenth century Ireland was politically tied to Great Britain by the Act of Union of 1800. Yet the associations of these manuscripts are almost entirely continental. This association is in keeping with the strong links between the Irish Catholic Church and continental Europe. Those who worked to acquire the manuscripts and those who donated them were expressing their belief in the importance of Maynooth College's position in Ireland and in Ireland's place within the wider European tradition. The college and university have every right to be proud of this collection of manuscripts as a vital part of their heritage.

THE MANUSCRIPTS

The Liège connection

A S MENTIONED ABOVE IN THE INTRODUCTION (p. 8), five of the manuscripts described below were at Liège before they came to Maynooth early in the nineteenth century. Four (nos 1–4) were at the Benedictine abbey of St Jacques, and one (no. 5) at St Léonard, originally a cell of St Jacques. Five manuscripts from one place out of a total of sixteen form a significant group. We here give some account of the library at St Jacques so that the features of the manuscripts in Maynooth that reflect their previous provenance in Liège can be the better understood.

The Benedictine abbey of St Jacques at Liège, founded in 1015, became an important monastic centre. By the fourteenth century, having taken a leading role in spiritual reform in its region and beyond, it contained an important growing collection of manuscripts. In accordance with the library regulations modified under the influence of the Dominicans, as promulgated by their fifth master-general, Humbert of Romans (1254–63),[1] books were held more closely than before (when borrowing in return for a pledge was allowed) and curses on those who removed books became fashionable once more,[2] as illustrated by the curse added after 1419 to RB16 (see below and pl. 1.1). The monastery continued to be a leading example of spiritual devotion and discipline through the sixteenth and seventeenth centuries. When they visited in 1718, the Maurists Edmond Martène and Ursin Durand remarked upon the rich contents of the library.[3]

For the present purposes, five phases in the history of the library at St Jacques are of particular importance:

(1) In the fifteenth century a great deal of work to put the library in order, adding lists of contents and rubrics to indicate contents, was done by Philippe d'Othée, prior from 1404 to 1426. He frequently wrote in manuscripts statements such as 'Hu<n>c libru<m> co<n>tulit mo<na>st<er>io s<an>c<t>i Iacobi leodien<sis>'.[4] He also showed great zeal for enhancing the library holdings.[5] Annotations in his hand are noted quite frequently in the descriptions of the relevant manuscripts below.

---

1 Paulus Volk OSB, *Der liber ordinarius des Lütticher St Jakobs-Klosters*, Beiträge zur Geschichte des alten Mönchtums und des Bendiktinerordens 10 (Münster, 1923), pp lxxi, 44–5. On the history of the library, see Sylvain Balau, 'La bibliothèque de l'abbaye de Saint-Jacques, à Liège', *Bulletin de la Commission Royale d'Histoire de Belgique* 71 (1902), 1–61, 226. 2 See P.J. Lucas, 'Borrowing and reference: access to libraries in the late Middle Ages' in Elisabeth Leedham-Green and Teresa Webber (eds), *Cambridge history of libraries in Britain and Ireland*, 1: *To 1640* (Cambridge, 2006), pp 242–62. 3 *Voyage littéraire* (Paris, 1717–24), II.172–5, esp. 173. 4 BL, Additional MS 16608, fo 1r. 'This book belongs to the monastery of St Jacques at Liège'. 5 See Balau, 'La bibliothèque de l'abbaye de Saint-Jacques', 11–22.

(2) Around 1667 the manuscripts were catalogued by Nicolas Bouxhon (abbot 1695–1703).[6] Each manuscript was classed under a letter of the alphabet, A–M, depending on its subject matter, and then given a number. Under A were biblical commentaries, under B fathers of the Church and major theologians, C canon and civil law, D biblical texts, E books on morality, F works of spiritual guidance, G sermons, H philosophy, I ecclesiastical history, L books on the quadrivium, including medicine, M books on the trivium. For example, a commentary on Psalm 118 (no. 1, RB16 below) has the class-mark A.90. For convenience, the Bouxhon class-marks are normally used as a basis for classification.

(3) Bouxhon (d. 1703) also presided over the building of a new *salle* for the library,[7] no doubt the 'grande salle voutée' seen by Martène and Durand in 1718,[8] and it appears that a new (post-Bouxhon) classification of the collection was put in place to provide for the rearrangement of the books.[9] It is characteristic of books from St Jacques that they show their Bouxhon class-mark crossed through and another later one usually added in a paler ink. For example, MS A.90 has this class-mark crossed through, as A̶9̶0̶, and the later class-mark D.5 added (see pl. 1.2).

(4) Perhaps in connection with this re-arrangement, during the abbacy of Nicholas IV Jacquet (1709–41) many of the manuscripts were bound in brown calf with spines decorated in gold leaf by, or under the supervision of, the then precentor/librarian, Philippe Fisen.[10] He dutifully recorded his good deed in several of the relevant books, as 'hunc librum religauit d[ominus] Philippus Fisen hujus Monasterii Religiosus et Cantor 1721'.[11] Other bindings in a similar style, in brown calf with gold tooling on the spine (but without the inscription inside the book) also survive.[12] All five of the Maynooth

---

6 Nicolas Bouxhon, 'Summa Omnium quae in Inferiori Bibliotheca Sti Jacobi continentur ordine quidem alphabetico', unpublished handwritten catalogue of books *c.*1667 from St Jacques, Liège, in: Brussels, Bibliothèque Royale, Collection Générale, MS no. 13993.   7 Liège, Bibliothèque de l'Université (LBU), MS 1682B, p. 390.   8 *Voyage Littéraire*, II.173.   9 We have not been able to find the source of this new classification. It was not that of Basile Ernotte, whose 'Index Manuscriptorum' of 1731 survives in LBU MS 1432C; his list of 323 manuscripts (without shelf-marks) attempts to arrange them in order of date. Another catalogue by Romain Marnette (1743) has not survived: see Christine Mortiaux-Denoël (with Étienne Guillaume), 'Le fonds des manuscrits de l'abbaye (de) Saint-Jacques de Liège', *RB*, 101 (1991), 154–91, and 107 (1997), 352–80 at 162. The post-Bouxhon catalogue was presumably earlier than these, perhaps *c.*1710.   10 For example, Darmstadt, Landes- und Hochschulbibliothek, MS 756 (IV.114). Six such bindings with the inscription inside the book are recorded as surviving in Darmstadt: see Kurt H. Staub and Hermann Knaus, *Die Handschriften der Hessischen Landes- und Hochschulbibliothek Darmstadt*, 4 (Wiesbaden, 1979), p. 11. For an example, see below, pls 2.1, 3.1.   11 BL, Additional MS 17743, fo 4r; the binding itself was replaced by one for the British Museum in the nineteenth century. Such an inscription was recorded by Balau, 'La bibliothèque de l'abbaye de Saint-Jacques', 40, n. 1, from one of the manuscripts formerly at Louvain but now 'disappeared'. 'Dom Philippe Fisen, religious and cantor of this monastery, bound this book'.   12 For example, Darmstadt, Landes- und Hochschulbibliothek, MSS 330, 502, 510, 511, 716, 736, 183, 523, 524, 747, 766, 789, 1489, 2777, as mentioned by Staub and Knaus in their catalogue: vol. 4, nos 7, 12, 13, 14, 21, 22, 48, 86, 87, 108, 117, 122, 149, 172; also MS 315, as mentioned in K.H. Staub, *Die Handschriften der Hessischen Landes- und Hochschulbibliothek Damstadt*, vol. 5.1 (Wiesbaden, 2001), p. 29. See further A.M.

manuscripts from Liège have bindings that date from when they were there (pl. A). The four St Jacques manuscripts (and the one from St Leonard's (no. 13, RB54, below), whose spine has been superimposed with gold tooling from the workshop of Philippe Fisen of St Jacques) therefore stand out on account of their retention of bindings from the first third of the eighteenth century.

(5) From about the middle of the eighteenth century the spiritual life of the monastery declined, and from 1765 the monks demanded their secularization, which they obtained in 1785.[13] In 1787 a catalogue of the St Jacques books by Jean-Noël Paquot was printed (but not published),[14] and in 1788 the contents of the library were sold. The sale was a big one, widely advertised, certainly as far away as Rome. The Paquot catalogue, annotated with details of to whom the books were sold, provides important evidence for those trying to ascertain the subsequent whereabouts of the manuscripts.

A survey of the St Jacques manuscripts by Christine Mortiaux-Denoël (with Étienne Guillaume), published in 1991/7, shows that there were 192 surviving, 63 disappeared and 357 untraced manuscripts (a total of 612). At the sale of 1788 there were two principal buyers. One of these was Gabriel-François de Laruelle, professor of philosophy at the seminary in Liège,[15] who bought 189 manuscripts, most of which are now untraced.[16] The other, Baron Hüpsch of Cologne, bought seventy-eight manuscripts, and this group of manuscripts, most of which are now at Darmstadt, constitutes the largest collection of surviving manuscripts from St Jacques.[17] Many of the St Jacques manuscripts (and printed books) were on the market in the decades following the 1788 sale. For example, the seven St Jacques

Lucas and P.J. Lucas, 'Lost and found: some manuscripts from Liège now in Maynooth', *Scriptorium* 58 (2004), 83–99 at 98–9. There are likely to be more such bindings in other libraries we have not visited. A full study of all these bindings as a group is a desideratum. A selection of spines decorated in the workshop of Philippe Fisen are currently shown in an image available on the Darmstadt website: www.ulb.tu-darmstadt.de (Sammlungen/Hüpsch). **13** Dom Ursmer Berlière, 'La sécularisation de l'abbaye de Saint-Jacques a Liège (1785)', *RB*, 34 (1922), 46–66, 109–18, with an account of the sale of the books at pp 55–61. **14** Jean-Noël Paquot, 'Catalogue de livres de la bibliothèque de la célèbre ex-abbaye de St-Jacques à Liège, dont la vente se fera publiquement au plus offrant, sur les cloitres de ladite ex-abbaye, le 3 mars 1788 et jours suivans, à 2 heures précises de relevée', unpublished printed sale catalogue prepared prior to sale of books from St Jacques, Liège, beginning 3 Mar. 1788, in: Brussels, Bibliothèque Royale, Fonds Van Hulthem, MS no. 22595. For some account of Paquot, see Comte de Becdelièvre, *Biographie Liégeoise*, 2 vols (Liège, Imprimerie de Jeunehomme Frères, 1836–7), vol. 2, pp 562–70. **15** For a brief notice of Laruelle, see Joseph Daris, *Notices sur les églises du diocèse de Liège*, 4:2 (Liège, 1871), p. 196. J. Hoyaux, *Inventaire des manuscrits de la bibliothèque de l'université de Liège. Manuscrits acquis de 1886 à 1960* (Liège, 1970), vol. 1, p. 127, no. 899, records that Laruelle was 'examinateur synodal' in 1761 for a thesis by one Noël Jamotte. **16** See *Catalogue des livres de la bibliothèque de feu G.-F. Laruelle chanoine et chantre de St-Barthélemy, et Professeur en Philosophie au Séminaire de Liège* (Liège, [1804]), pp 247–60; the sale began 18 February 1805. The copy at the University of Liège (LBU, XIV.119.39) has cross-references by Adrien Wittert (1823–1903) to his copy of Paquot, which is bound with it, and notes items with St Jacques provenance. Many of Laruelle's books went to what is now the Bibliothèque Municipale Jacques Prévert at Cherbourg-Octeville. **17** See Paulus Volk OSB, 'Baron Hüpsch und der Verkauf der Lütticher St. Jakobsbibliothek (1788)', *Zentralblatt für Bibliothekswesen* 42 (1925), 201–17. Thirty-three of them are catalogued to date in *Die Handschriften der Hessischen Landes- und Hochschulbibliothek Darmstadt*, vol. 2 by Leo Eizenhöfer and Hermann Knaus

manuscripts now in the British Library in London were acquired by the then British Museum between 1836 and 1856.[18] In 1919 a group of fifty-nine St Jacques manuscripts, formerly in the possession of the counts of Fürstenberg, who gave them to the Academy at Paderborn, were ceded to Belgium as First World War reparations under the terms of the Treaty of Versailles. They were deposited in the library of the University of Louvain/Leuven, which had been destroyed in the First World War. There, in the Second World War, there was a repeat performance and the St Jacques manuscripts disappeared in flames with the rest of the library. These form the bulk of the manuscripts that are classified as 'Disappeared'. Even so, well over half of the St Jacques manuscripts listed by Paquot in 1787 are still untraced.

From our researches in Maynooth, we have been able to reduce that number by four, so leaving 357 minus 4 = 353 untraced manuscripts, and therefore increase the list of surviving manuscripts by the same number, making 192 plus 4 = 196 surviving manuscripts. There is some correspondence of Dr Troy in the Dublin Diocesan Archives about the possibility of the college acquiring books in the period immediately after its foundation.[19] The books at Liège were sold just before the French Revolution. There are three letters dating from 1802/3 in the Troy correspondence from Jenico Preston, a member of the well-known Gormanstown family, who was provost of the church of St Paul in Liège. In the first letter, Jenico Preston is offering to buy books on behalf of Maynooth College. He is expecting to attend the sale of the library of a Professor Laruelle, late of the seminary at Liège, who had purchased the largest number of manuscripts at the recent sale of the Benedictine abbey of St Jacques in the city. The second letter to Troy from Jenico Preston indicates that it is a reply to one from Troy, and suggests that Troy had expressed interest in the Laruelle sale. The third letter, while listing books from yet another library, indicates that purchases have already been made on

(Wiesbaden, 1968), nos 45 (MS 839), 65 (MS 934), and vol. 4 by Staub and Knaus (Wiesbaden, 1979), nos 7 (MS 330), 12 (MS 502), 13 (MS 510), 14 (MS 511), 15 (MS 532), 21 (MS 716), 22 (MS 736), (?)40 (MS 3150), 41 (MS 14), 48 (MS 183), 53 (MS 314), 58 (MS 344), 59 (MS 345), 86 (MS 523), 87 (MS 524), 94 (MS 549), 95 (MS 622), 100 (MS 681), 106 (MS 725), 108 (MS 747), 114 (MS 756), 117 (MS 766), 122 (MS 789), 149 (MS 1489), 151 (MS 1955), 157 (MS 2284), 167 (MS 2666), 172 (MS 2777), and vol. 5.1 by Staub (Wiesbaden, 2001), MSS 315, 434 and 676. See also Hermann Schnitzler, *Die Sammlungen des Baron von Hüpsch Ein Kölner Kunstkabinet um 1800* (Cologne, 1964).   **18** BL, Additional MS 10019, Petrarch etc. (Bouxhon class-mark E71, Mortiaux-Denoël no. 164) was acquired by the BM in 1836; BL, Additional MS 15254–15258, Bible in 5 vols (Bouxhon class-mark D45, Mortiaux-Denoël no. 165) in 1843; BL, Additional MS 16608, Anselm etc. (Bouxhon class-mark F130, Mortiaux-Denoël no. 166) in 1847; BL, Additional MS 17743, William of Brittany (Bouxhon class-mark A34, Mortiaux-Denoël no. 167) in 1849; BL, Additional MS 18217, Walter of Châtillon (Bouxhon class-mark I122, Mortiaux-Denoël no. 168) in 1850; BL, Additional MS 20009, Alexander de Villa Dei etc. (Bouxhon class-mark D8, Mortiaux-Denoël no. 169) in 1854; BL, Additional MS 21244, Liber de diversis ordinibus (Mortiaux-Denoël no. 170, where they give the Bouxhon class-mark E100) in 1856. BL, Additional MS 22278, attributed to St Jacques by Mortiaux-Denoël, no. 171, and identified as no. A.25, shows no indication of Liège provenance; on the contrary, it is attributed to St Lambert, Liesse in Hainault, on the inside of the front cover. The mistake perhaps originated with the *Catalogue of additions to the manuscripts in the British Museum in the years MDCCCLIV–MDCCCLX* (London, 1875), pp 622–3, where the manuscript is attributed to 'St Lambert at Liége [*sic*]'.   **19** Troy Papers, Dublin Diocesan Archives,

D Bookplate of John Thomas Troy, archbishop of Dublin (1786–1823), showing his heraldic device and motto in an architectural frame of books.

Troy's behalf, and goes into some detail about packaging arrangements and how the money was to be transferred. Whether these purchases were for Troy's own collection, which was considerable,[20] or for Maynooth, is moot. Troy chose an armorial book-plate in what is termed the 'bookpile' style,[21] architecturally framed with books and featuring the motto 'Laudat Tentat Vincit' (He praises, He strives, He conquers),[22] which suggests his desire to create a centre of learning where books were an integral part of the structure; see pl. D. It is disappointing that only the three letters survive from what was evidently a considerable correspondence, and that Archbishop Troy did not keep copies of his own letters to Preston. But it is a fact that five of the sixteen manuscripts now in the college came from Liège.[23] These manuscripts must have been some of the first medieval manuscripts acquired by the library (RB16, 45, 46, 47, 54). Although the college library's inventory of the 1820s is incomplete, it does contain a reference to one of these manuscripts (RB16, see below, p. 22).[24] It is impossible to say whether the five manuscripts from Liège now at Maynooth were purchased as a result of the activities of someone like Jenico Preston, or were donated by one of the early professors (see above, pp 3–4). None of the four manuscripts from St Jacques bears witness to having been in any other library between leaving Liège and appearing in Maynooth. They seem to be much as they must have been when sold from St Jacques in 1788, and this state of preservation is a bonus (see above, pp 16–17).

AB/29/9/2, letters 7, 53, 57; also Woods, 'Books rich, rare and curious', esp. p. 29. **20** On his death, Troy's books were auctioned 25 June 1823. There is no evidence that any manuscripts came to Maynooth College either by gift from Dr Troy or as a result of the sale of his books. A copy of the very rare auction catalogue of Troy's books is held by the Royal Irish Academy at the temporary shelf-mark of MR14/AC/Box 27: *Catalogue of the very choice and valuable library of the late Most Rev. Doctor Troy, Roman Catholic archbishop of Dublin ... catalogues may be had of ... Charles Sharpe, auctioneer, 33 Anglesea Street* (Dublin, Richard Grace [1823]). No manuscripts whatsoever feature among the 1,092 lots. **21** For the 'bookpile' style, see David Pearson, *Provenance research in book history: a handbook* (London, 1994), p. 64. **22** It is shown as plate 22 in William Griggs, *147 examples of armorial book plates: from various collections*, 2nd ser. (London, 1892). **23** See further Lucas and Lucas, 'Lost and found', 83–99. **24** On this catalogue, see Neligan, 'The library looking back', pp 20–4, with illustration.

Engelbert (Poetsch) of Admont OSB (formerly erron. attrib. Alexander of Hales), *Commentarius in Psalmum CXVIII* (*c*.1320)

HISTORY

A HANDSOME MANUSCRIPT WRITTEN s.xiv in a textualis script by a single hand with corrections by the scribe, e.g., by insertion on fos 47, 91r, 111r etc., and by writing over an erasure on fo 56v. This manuscript was at Liège (see above, pp 15–19).

At the top of fo ii^v there occurs in the hand of Philippe d'Othée, prior of St Jacques, Liège, from 1404 to 1426: 'liber monasterii s[ancti iacobi] leodiensis. | et e‹st› alexa‹n›d‹er› h[alesiensis] auctor ei‹us›', and the later statement 'Expositio psalmi centesimi decimi octaui. Qui i‹n›cipit. Beati i‹m›maculati | in veteri volumine.', but the attribution to Alexander of Hales (*c*.1186–1245) is erroneous. At the end of fo 232v/b/35ff in a hand of s.xv 'Hu‹n›c libru‹m› contulit Monasterio S‹an›c‹t›i Ia|cobi leodien‹sis› ordinis b‹ea›ti Benedicti D‹omin›us | Joha‹n›nes dictus de Wallenrode ep‹iscop›us leodien‹sis› | vt or‹ati›onu‹m› Fratru‹m› eiusd‹em› mo‹na›sterii mere‹re›tur fore | p‹ar›ticeps ta‹m› in vita q‹uam› in morte

Ad claustrum	sancti Jacobi	spectat liber iste
Si quis eum	ferat hi‹n›c alibi	te vindice ‹Chr›iste
Grande malum	patiare sibi	succrescere iuste'.

(The lord called Johannes de Wallenrode, bishop of Liège, bestowed this book on the abbey of St Jacques of the order of the blessed Benedict at Liège in order that he will have been deserving as a partaker of the prayers of the Fathers in death as much as in life. This book belongs to the cloister of St Jacques. If anyone bears it from here to somewhere else, with you Christ as avenger, may you justly allow great woe to pile up for him); see pl. 1.1. The three verses scan as hexameters. Johann von Wallenrode (previously archbishop of Riga, 1393–1418), was bishop of Liège in 1418–19 (Eubel 1913: I, 302, Jähnig 1970: 140–5), and the book passed to the abbey of St Jacques after he died in 1419. The manuscript was evidently at Liège in St Jacques, and remained there until the sale of the abbey's books in 1788 (Paquot no. 27). On fo 1r near the top right-hand corner there occur the St Jacques class-marks A9c and D.5, this second mark written just below

1.1 RB16, fo 232v, the end of the text and the 'curse' inscription of s.xv.

the first in a slightly paler ink (pl. 1.2). Mortiaux-Denoël (1991: 167, no. A.90) assigned the new no. 297 and it was listed (Mortiaux-Denoël 1997: 378) as among 'manuscrits non retrouvés'. The binding is of s.xviii¹, probably done at or for St Jacques, in brown calf on thick cardboard with gold tooling on the spine (pl. 1.4), on which there is an identification saying 'ALEXANDER DE ALES | SUPER | PSALMUM CXVIII.', which is probably derived from the mistaken attribution of s.xv on fo ii. Although the tooling on the spines is not the same, there are similar bindings on RB45 and RB46, and, being contemporary with those claimed by Philippe Fisen, this binding must be attributed to him or his workshop, and is very finely tooled. For the centrepiece composed of four fleurons in each compartment of the spine cf. that in the top compartment of the spine of RB54; see below, pp 56–8.

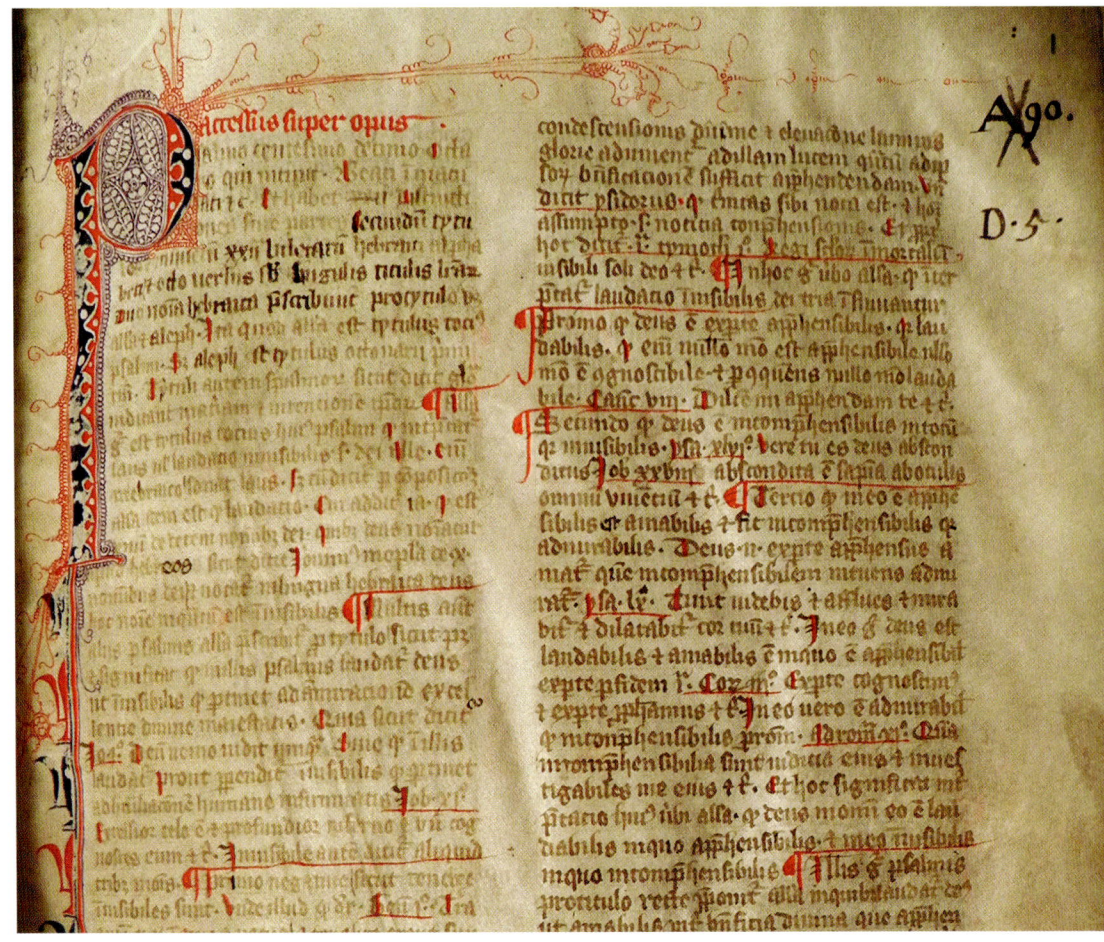

1.2 RB16, fo 1r, the beginning of the text with calligraphic capitals and vine-stem border, and the Liège St Jacques class-marks. Actual page dimensions 355 x 240mm.

Acquired by St Patrick's College, Maynooth, s.xix[in]. In the library catalogue of the 1820s (a ledger) under S.Scripture, letter D, the third entry reads 'De[H]ales, Alexander, super Psalmum a ms on vellum', which must refer to this manuscript (see pl. 1.3).

Modern foliation in pencil in top right-hand corner of recto pages was entered in 1998.

Secundo folio: 'at tribulati erepcione'.

1.3 Extract from the 1820s Maynooth Library catalogue showing the entry for RB16 with its former attribution to Alexander of Hales.

CODICOLOGICAL DESCRIPTION

Fos ii + 232, membrane, + ii paper endleaves, the first of which shows an unidentified watermark of two interlinked horseshoes 30 x 31mm, one with its open end upwards, the other with its open end downwards. Leaves measure 355 x 240mm, written area 255 (rising to 277 towards the end of the manuscript) x 177mm. There are regular quires of twelve (**I–XVIII**) until the last quire (**XIX**), where the scribe apparently calculated that sixteen leaves would be sufficient to complete the work, but then found that he had to add another singleton leaf (fo 231) before the last to make sufficient space to receive all of the text. The text is disposed in two columns with a void dividing margin in the middle measuring 7mm across, but the layout changes subtly as the manuscript progresses. The handwriting gradually gets larger, and the depth of the lines increases so that towards the end there are fewer lines on the page than at the beginning even though the depth of the written area increases slightly. The number of lines per page varies slightly as if the scribe was constantly trying to adjust while following an exemplar with a similar layout more or less page by page. On fos 65v–69r, 80v, 82v–84r, the bottom line of the ruled frame has been erased (and there is no text on it), and in the last six quires (**XIV–XIX**) the number of lines per page settles to a narrower band of variation (40–2).

Pricking: This was done to facilitate the arrangements described above. Four prick-marks were made at the top and bottom of leaves for the vertical rules, one for the outer boundaries of each column, and there are 47–51 prick-marks at the outer edges of leaves (clear throughout Quire **VI**, for example) for the horizontal lines, but in many quires (**I, XII–XIX**) they have disappeared since the binder cropped them. On fos 23–4, the last two in Quire **II**, the bottom three lines show another set of prick-marks on the inside of the main set, and on fo 36 there is another set of prick-marks down the outer frame rule. Fo 46 has been pricked twice for the horizontal lines.

Ruling: Frame rule in fine ink with outer lines ruled to the edge of the leaf. The ruling was done by quire, opening by opening, as is clear, for example, on fos 27v/28r (48 lines as against forty-nine lines on fos 28v/29r) and on fos 12/13, with fifty-one lines on 12r, fifty-two on 12v and forty-eight on 13r (the first leaf of Quire **II**). There is no writing on the top line of the frame, and the number of lines written varies between forty-eight and fifty-two in Quires **I–IX**, but between forty-one and forty-five in Quires **X–XIX**. In Quires **I–II** the top and second from the top, and the bottom and second from the bottom, two horizontal lines are ruled to the inner and outer edges (and this feature occurs occasionally later in the manuscript, as on fos 49v/50r, 79v/80r), but in subsequent quires the lines third from the top and the bottom are usually so ruled; occasionally the fourth line from the bottom is so ruled, as on fos 41v/42r, 42v/43r, 47v/48r. In

Quire **II** there are forty-eight prick-marks (visible on fo 21), forty-eight lines of writing on fo 13r (the first leaf), but two more lines of writing at the top, giving fifty elsewhere.

Hair/Flesh: All quires HFHFHF except Quires **I** HFHFHH; **IV** HFHHHF; **VII** HFFHFH; **XIV** HFFHFH; **XV** HFHHFH. Catchwords on fos 12v, 24v, 36v, 48v, 60v, 72v, 84v, 96v, 108v, 119v, 131v, 143v, 155v, 167v, 179v, 191v (slightly cropped at the bottom), 203v, 215v.

Colour: Calligraphic capitals in red and blue on fos 1r (with rectilinear border in red and blue down the left side and across the bottom, and a vine stem with tendrils across the top in red; see pl. 1.2), and divided by bracket motifs on fos 2r, 2v, 7v etc.; there is an alternating scheme of blue capitals with red flourishing, as on fos 10v, 12v, 14r etc., and red capitals with blue flourishing, as on fos 11v, 13v, 14v etc., but the scheme is not carried out with complete consistency.

COLLATION

Two membrane endleaves (fos i–ii), the first pasted on to a paper backing with the membrane on the verso.
I¹² (fos 1–12), II¹² (fos 13–24), III¹² (fos 25–36), IV¹² (fos 37–48), V¹² (fos 49–60), VI¹² (fos 61–72), VII¹² (fos 73–84), VIII¹² (fos 85–96), IX¹² (fos 97–108), X¹² (fos 109–19; lacks 11), XI¹² (fos 120–31), XII¹² (fos 132–43), XIII¹² (fos 144–55), XIV¹² (fos 156–67), XV¹² (fos 168–79), XVI¹² (fos 180–91), XVII¹² (fos 192–203), XVIII¹² (fos 204–15), XIX¹⁷ (fos 216–32; 16 is a singleton). Two paper endleaves.

Note 1: In Quire **X** there is a leaf missing in the second half of the quire, although no stub can be seen: from the pattern of H/F sides and the apparent textual discontinuity it is presumed to be missing between fos 118/119.
Note 2: In Quire **XIX** the sewing occurs between fos 223/224 and the pattern of HF sides indicates that leaf 16 (fo 231) is a singleton, although no stub can be seen; no loss of text is apparent.

QUIRE SIGNATURES

Quire I has rudimentary quire signatures in the form of dots on leaves 2–6 (that on leaf 1, together possibly with something below the dots, presumably lost through the binder's cropping). Quire II has rudimentary quire signatures in the form of vertical strokes visible on leaves 1, 2 and 6, these and those presumably lost on leaves 3–5 suffering from cropping by the binder. Quire IV has the first

1.4 RB16, spine of binding by Philippe Fisen (Liège), c. 1721, showing centrepiece fleurons.

six leaves (fos 37–42) numbered (not by the scribe) at the bottom centre on the recto 'i', 'ii', 'iii', 'iiii', 'iiiii', 'iiiiii'. Quire V has the first six leaves (fos 49–54) numbered (not by the scribe) at the bottom centre on the recto 'i', 'ii', 'iii', 'iiii', 'iiiii', 'iiiiii'. Quire VI has very faint quire signatures (by the scribe?) on the first six leaves (fos 61–6) at the bottom centre on the recto, 'bi', 'bij', 'biij', 'biiij', 'bv', 'bvi'. Quire VII has very faint quire signatures (by the scribe?) on the first six leaves (fos 73–8) at the bottom centre on the recto, 'ci', 'cij', 'ciij', 'ciiij', 'cv', 'cvi'. Quire VIII has very faint quire signatures (by the scribe?) on the first six leaves (fos 85–90) at the bottom centre on the recto, 'dj', 'dij', 'diij', 'diiij', 'Dv', 'Dvi'. Quire IX has very faint quire signatures (by the scribe?) on the first six leaves (fos 97–102) at the bottom centre on the recto, 'Ej', 'Eij', 'Eiij', 'Eiiij', 'Ev', 'Evi'. Quire X has very faint quire signatures (by the scribe?) on the first six leaves (fos 109–14) at the bottom centre on the recto, 'fi', 'fii', 'fiij', 'fiiij', 'fv', 'fvi'. Quire XI has very faint quire signatures (by the scribe?) in red ink on the first six leaves (fos 120–5) at the bottom centre on the recto, 'gi' (largely cropped), 'gij', 'giij', 'giiij', 'gv', 'gvj'; also 'g' in brown ink on leaf 7 (fo 126r) in the bottom right corner. Quire XII has very faint quire signatures (by the scribe?) in red ink on the first six leaves (fos 132–7) at the bottom centre on the recto, '4i' (largely cropped), '4ij', '4iij', '4iiij', '4v', '4vi'. Quire XIII has very faint quire signatures (by the scribe?) in red ink on the first six leaves (fos 144–9) at the bottom centre on the recto, '5i' (largely cropped), '5ij', '5iij', '5iiij', '5v', '5vi'. Quire XIV has very faint quire signatures (probably not by the scribe) on the first six leaves (fos 156–61) at the bottom centre on the recto, 'fi' (largely cropped), 'fij', 'fiij', 'fiiij', 'fv', 'fvi'. Quire XV has very faint quire signatures (probably not by the scribe) on the first six leaves (fos 168–73) at the bottom centre on the recto, 'Gi', 'Gij', 'Giij', 'Giiij', 'Gv', 'Gvi'. Quire XVI has very faint quire signatures (probably not by the scribe) on the first six leaves (fos 180–5) at the bottom centre on the recto, 'hi', 'hij', 'hiij', 'hiiij', 'hv', 'hvi'. Quire XVII has very faint quire signatures (probably not by the scribe) on the first six leaves (fos 192–7) at the bottom centre on the recto, 'ki', 'kij', 'kiij', 'kiiij', 'kv', 'kvi'. Quire XVIII has very faint quire signatures (probably not by the scribe) on the first six leaves (fos 204–9) at the bottom centre on the recto, 'mi', 'mij', 'miij', 'miiij', 'mv', 'mvi'. Quire XIX has very faint quire signatures (probably not by the scribe) on the first six leaves (fos 216–21) at the bottom centre on the recto, 'Ni', 'Nij', 'Niij', 'Niiij', 'Nv', 'Nvi'.

CONTENTS

1. Fos 1r/a/1 to 232v/b/31 Engelbert (Poetsch) of Admont OSB (1250–1331, abbot of Egmont 1297–1327), *Commentarius in Psalmum CXVIII* (*c.*1320), lacks Dedicatory Preface (for which see Fowler 1962) and Epilogue (incipit and explicit given by Fowler 1954: 485).

(a) Fo 1r/a/1–5 [Introduction] 'accessus super opus. | Psalmo centesimo decimo Octa|uo qui incipit. Beati i<m>macu|lati &c. Et habet xxii distincti|ones siue partes' (see pl. 1.2). [This form of the incipit is very similar to that given as a variant by Stegmüller II: 296, no. 2241 from Berlin, Staatsbibliothek, Theol. fo 236, written in 1427, on which see Rose 1901.] Ends fo 7v/b/13 'morali<ter> <et> doctrinali<ter> incipit dicens | Beati i<m>maculati i<n> uia &c.'.

(b) Fo 7v/b/15 'beati i<m>maculati i<n> via qui a<m>bulant | in lege d<omi>ni. IN capite libri sc<ri>ptum e<st> de capite <Christ>o. be|atus uir qui non abiit in consilio impio<rum>'.

Commentary proceeds one verse or half-verse at a time, with the text written in red and the commentary beginning with a calligraphic capital. There is a lacuna between fos 118 and 119; part of the commentary to verse 100 is missing. Fo 118v ends 'Queri etia<m> p<otes>t quare; fo 119r begins 'Dauit int<er> tet<r>a dona magis'. Ends fo 232v/b/20–31 'Vt in co<n>fessione <et> or<ati>one <et> satis|factione i<n>nuat<ur> sua p<er>f<e>c<t>a consu<m>mac<i>o. ¶D<omin>us noster ih<es>us <Christ>us pastor bonus | nos oues suas in p<e>cc<at>is n<ost>ris ab el<ec>tis | <et> assu<m>ptis suis gregibus aberra<n>tes | i<n> uia hui<us> vite miserabilis dignet<ur> | filia[li]ter corrigere mise<ri>cordit<er> reuoca|re secure <con>ducere. et felicit<er> perduc<er>e | ad <com>p<re>hendendu<m> brauiu<m> <et> attingendu<m> | <con>sortiu<m> b<ea>titudinis et<er>ne. Qui cu<m> p<at>re | et sp<irit>u s<an>c<t>o. viuit et regnat vnus deus | p<er> omnia secula seculorum. AmeN.' [This explicit agrees with that given by Stegmüller II: 296, no. 2241, and Fowler 1947: 202, and 1954: 485.]

Fo 232v/b/34 'Finito libro sit laus <et> gl<ori>a <Christ>o Amen' (see pl. 1.1).

Unprinted, except for the Dedicatory Preface (not in this MS), of which there are two versions extant, the second (shorter) version first printed by Pe[t]z and Hueber 1729: pt III, pp 6–8, item ix, and by Wichner 1892: 46–7, the first (longer) version, including the shorter version, printed by Fowler 1962: 307–12.

Stegmüller 1940–80, no. 2241: he lists eight other manuscripts of this work at II.296. As erroneously attributed to Alexander of Hales (from the note on fo ii^v), the work also appears as Stegmüller no. 1127 (Ps 118: Leodii, Bibl. S. Iacobi) and the reference is evidently to this manuscript from Liège, and another (A.89: Mortiaux-Denoël 1991: 167, no. 296), but the attribution is probably an error (the same error probably applies to A.89, also listed among those 'non retrouvés'), and there is no evidence that Alexander of Hales ever wrote a work of this title (cf. Herscher 1945): Stegmüller no. 1127 should probably be deleted.

"Exodus", Latin Bible text accompanied by the
Glossa Ordinaria

HISTORY

A VERY REGULAR MANUSCRIPT arranged in quires of eight, and written in a late caroline minuscule by a single hand of s.xii^{med} probably in north-east France. The text begins with a colourful initial **H** in Franco-Saxon style (pl. 2.1). The scribe writes both text and gloss/commentary above the top ruled line (cf. de Hamel 1984: 30). Some corrections by the scribe, e.g., fos 72v–73r, 95r, 129r. An annotation on fo 37v is probably in a contemporary hand. Some other annotations occur on fos 36–7r, 43–6 etc., but they are extremely pale. The first leaf, probably blank as there is no loss of text, is missing, and the last leaf, fo 159, is much soiled on the (blank) verso. The book was attacked by worms front and back, wormholes in Quire **I** penetrating to the first leaf of Quire **II** (fo 8), and the last leaf (fo 159) shows a number of wormholes, some penetrating into the last quire (**XX**) as far back as fo 155.

The manuscript was evidently at Liège in the Benedictine abbey of St Jacques (see above, pp 15–19) from 1412 until the sale of the abbey's books in 1788 (Paquot no. 14). On fo 159r at the end of the text (pl. 2.2) is a note in d'Othée's hand of the manuscript's purchase by Monsignor Philippe d'Othée 'prior of this place [i.e., St Jacques, Liège, 1404–26] 19 June 1412': 'hu<n>c libru<m> emit Mon<signorus> philipp<us> de Otheij | p<ri>or hui<us> loci. Anno d<omi>ni M°.CCCC°.xij°. | die geruasij <et> p<ro>thasij cui<us> a<n>i<m>a per | misericordia<m> dei req<ui>escat i<n> pace Ame<n> | Anno p<ri>orat<us> sui nono.': on d'Othée and his zeal for enhancing the library holdings at St Jacques, see Balau 1902: 11–22.

On fo 1r near the top right-hand corner there occur the St Jacques class-marks D̶z̶4̶ (Bouxhon) and C.52 (post-Bouxhon) written beside it in a paler ink (pl. 2.1); it is no. 340 in Mortiaux-Denoël and Guillaume 1991/7.

Binding in brown calf of 1721 with gold-tooled spine containing a stamp showing a heraldic motif of a pair of compasses and three stars with the text 'Constanter ad Astra' (pl. 2.3), the motto of Nicholas IV Jacquet, abbot of St Jacques, Liège (1709–41; Lèpine 1973: 11; Sammarthanus 1725: 988). At the bottom of fo 1r (pl. 2.1) there occurs the statement 'hunc librum religauit D: Philippus | Fisen hujus Monasterii Religiosus | et Cantor 1721'. [Dom Philippe Fisen, precentor of this abbey (St Jacques, Liège), bound this book 1721]. There

2.1 RB45, fo 1r, the
beginning of the
text with Franco-
Saxon style initial **H**,
the statement of
Philippe Fisen's
binding 1721, and
the Liège St Jacques
class-marks. Actual
page dimensions
257 x 168mm.

is an almost identical inscription in RB46, and also in another St Jacques manuscript
formerly at Louvain as recorded by Balau 1902, p. 40, n. 1. The paper endleaves
that belong with the binding show a watermark 'CM' in ligature. There are similar
bindings on RB16 and RB46, but the tooling on the spines does not match. Some

cropping by the binder has resulted in the loss of some annotations, e.g., fo 30v. Acquired by St Patrick's College, Maynooth, probably s.xix[in].

Secundo folio: 'om<ne>s reges egyptio<rum>'.

CODICOLOGICAL DESCRIPTION

Fos i + 159 + i, membrane, except for the paper endleaves, measuring 257 x 168mm, written area 180 x 130mm, with one paper endleaf front and back belonging with the binding of 1721. The text is disposed in three columns with the Bible text in the centre in larger script (suprascript glosses smaller) and the commentaries on either side.

Pricking: To facilitate this arrangement the pricking was done as follows. At top and bottom (clear in Quire **IX**, fos 64–71) there are six prick-marks, one either side to mark the outer bounds and two sets of two to mark the divisions either side of the central column for text. At the outer margins of the leaves there are thirty-five prick-marks for the horizontal lines, mostly preserved but some (partially) cropped (again clear throughout Quire **IX**).

Ruling: In fine crayon. It has apparently been executed page by page, perhaps with the guidance of an exemplar. There are generally single bounding lines for the frame, but on fo 6r the outer vertical rule is double, probably reflecting an adjustment outwards in anticipation of a need to accommodate more text; the written area is 135mm wide. After fo 1v the rules to mark the vertical divisions of the written space are placed according to convenience and often do not conform to the position of the prick-marks. Sometimes, e.g., fos 33v, 34v, 35v, 36v, 56v–57r, 69v, 70v, 71rv, 87–88r, verticals are ruled only part of the way up or down to fit in with the requirements of the text, so presumably the ruling was done by the scribe as he proceeded with his copying. Usually some horizontal lines are ruled to the outer edge, e.g., the top two and the bottom two lines, but the practice is inconsistent, fos 2–4, for example, having four such lines at the top ruled to the outer edge but fo 6 only three. Vertical rules generally extend to the outer edges of the leaves. From time to time the scribe goes outside his ruled boundaries. On fo 127 there is an extra line of biblical text below the ruled frame. On fo 130r there is an extra line of text in the central column below the ruled frame. On fo 125v the scribe has ruled an extra line for the central column to accommodate text and gloss suprascript. On fo 113v the scribe has ruled an extra five lines below the ruled frame to accommodate commentary at the end of a section; the written area on this page is 205mm deep. On fos 141v and 144r there is an extra line of commentary in the outer column and an extra line of text in the inner column. On fo 140r the scribe has written an extra two lines below the ruled frame. On fo 150v there is an extra ruled line to accommodate the last sentence of a section

2.2 RB45, fo 159r, the end of the text with a note added in the hand of Prior Philippe d'Othée of St Jacques, Liège, s.xv[1].

in the commentary. On fo 124r some commentary in the right-hand column is squashed in in very cramped writing with up to two lines of writing for every ruled line and four lines extending below the ruled frame.

Fos 21, 26, 130, 138 have one or more small holes in the membrane, which the scribe has worked around. Fos 80–82 are stained at the top by some liquid.

Modern foliation in pencil in top right-hand corner of recto pages entered 1997.

Colour: Initial **H** in Franco-Saxon style on fo 1r in blue, green, gold, red, with alternating red and green letters for **EC S<un>T** following at the beginning of the biblical text in the central column (pl. 2.1). The only colour thereafter is the marking of chapter numbers in gold capitals (supplied to guide letters) in the outer margin on fos 5r (II), 9r (III), 11v (IIII), 15v (V), 18v (VI); thereafter there are guide numbers on fos 20v (vij), 24r (viij), but none on fos 28r and 32r for chs 9 and 10 respectively, while those on fos 35v (xi), 37r (xij), 44r (xiij), 46v (xiiij), 50r (xv), have probably been added later.

2.3 RB45, binding showing the heraldic motif of Nicholas IV Jacquet, abbot of St Jacques, Liège s.xviii[1/2].

Guide letters for capitals, e.g., fo 1ᵛ 'e' for 'Erant' (Ex 1.5) etc., entered near the edge of the leaves, but the capitals were never executed.

Hair/Flesh: All quires HFHF except quire **XIV** (fos 104–111) which is HFFF.

COLLATION

I⁸ (fos 1–7; lacks 1), **II**⁸ (fos 8–15), **III**⁸ (fos 16–23), **IV**⁸ (fos 24–31), **V**⁸ (fos 32–9), **VI**⁸ (fos 40–7), **VII**⁸ (fos 48–55), **VIII**⁸ (fos 56–63), **IX**⁸ (fos 64–71), **X**⁸ (fos 72–9), **XI**⁸ (fos 80–7), **XII**⁸ (fos 88–95), **XIII**⁸ (fos 96–103), **XIV**⁸ (fos 104–11), **XV**⁸ (fos 112–19), **XVI**⁸ (fos 120–7), **XVII**⁸ (fos 128–35), **XVIII**⁸ (fos 136–43), **XIX**⁸ (fos 144–51), **XX**⁸ (fos 152–9).

The quires are numbered by the scribe at the bottom centre of the verso of the last leaf: '.I.' on fo 7v, '.II.' on fo 15v, '.III.' on fo 23v, '.IIII.' on fo 31v, '.V.' on fo 39v, '.VI.' on fo 47v, '.VII.' on fo 55v, '.VIII.' on fo 63v, '.VIIII.' on fo 71v, '.x.' on fo 79v, 'xj.' on fo 87v, '.xii.' on fo 95v, '.xiij.' on fo 103v, '.xiiii.' on fo 111v, '.xv.' on fo 119v, '.xvi.' on fo 127v, '.xvij.' on fo 135v, '.xviii.' on fo 143v, '.xix.' on fo 151v.

CONTENTS

1. Fos 1r/1–159r/32 "Exodus", biblical text, accompanied by the *Glossa Ordinaria* (or 'Normal Tongue'), the standard medieval biblical commentary, in the form of (b) suprascript glosses to the text and (c) commentary to the left and (d) the right, a work attributed to Walafridus Strabo (*c*.808–49), but *recte* the product of the school of Anselm of Laon (s.xii¹); the Gloss to the Pentateuch was probably compiled by Gilbert of Auxerre 'the Universal', who was bishop of London, 1128–34 (Smalley 1935/6).

(a) Text begins with the heading ". lib<er> exodus .", then 'H|EC S<un>T | nomina filio<rum> isr<ae>l' (Ex 1.1; pl. 2.1).

　　Ends with Ex 40.36 'Nubes q<ui>ppe d<omi>ni i<n>cubabat | p<er> die<m> tab<er>nac<u>lo . <et> ignis i<n> nocte . [v]id<e>ntib<us> p<o>p<u>l<i>s isr<ae>l p<er> cu<n>ctas ma<n>sio|nes suas; explicit;.' (pl. 2.2).

(b) Suprascript glosses begin: '¶Que sc‹ri›pta s‹un›t in celo', including some glosses not in the facsimile of the 1480/1 printed edition.

(c) Commentary on left begins: 'Exodus | exitus uel | g‹re›ssus latine.'

(d) Commentary on right begins: '¶Rab' In pe‹n›|tatheuco ex|cellit exodus. | in quo pene | omnia sacram‹en›|ta quib‹us› eccl‹es›ia | instruit‹ur› fig‹ur›a|liter exp‹ri›mu‹n›|tur . p‹er› corp‹or›a|lem.' Ends 'nubes p‹er› diem. fla‹m›ma p‹er› nocte‹m›.' (as Migne, col. 294, penultimate line). Lacks concluding paragraphs.

As Migne, PL 113, 183–296, who prints only (d) the commentary on the right; for reproduction of the 1480/1 printed edition, see Froehlich and Gibson 1992: I.112–208 (and for a critique of Migne's edition I, xxv–xxvi). Cp. Darmstadt, Hessisches Land- und Hochschulbibliothek, MS IV.14. Stegmüller 1940–80, IX.468–9, no. 11782. Smalley 1952: 46–66.

3 RB46
Bruno of Segni (d. 1123), *Commentarius in Exodum*

HISTORY

A VERY REGULAR MANUSCRIPT in quires of eight until the last two quires, with thirty-one lines per leaf throughout and the text apparently ending on the last line of the last leaf of the last quire. Some poor-quality and second-hand membrane used, also some half-sheets, especially towards the end. The last two quires are of ten rather than eight leaves, presumably to enable inclusion of all of the text without having to use a reduced-size quire at the end for the last part of the text. Written in the Low Countries by a single hand of the twelfth century, except that the commentary (not the text in red) on fo 1r has been written over by a hand of the fourteenth/fifteenth century using a textualis script (pl. 3.1). Some corrections by the scribe, e.g., on fos 3v, 5v, 7r, 8v etc., and 94r, 110r, 113r etc., with the triple point to mark the place of insertion in reverse colour from the text, i.e., in red where the text is black/brown, and in black/brown where the text is red, but not on fos 72v (red with red), 77v, 105v (black/brown with black/brown).

The manuscript was evidently at Liège in the Benedictine abbey of St Jacques (see above, pp 15–19), almost certainly until the sale of the abbey's books in 1788 (Paquot no. 15). On fo 1r near the top right-hand corner there occur the St Jacques class-marks A69 (Bouxhon) and another, the post-Bouxhon class-mark C.63, written in a paler ink (pl. 3.1), which also occurs on the verso of the front paper endleaf; it is no. 294 in Mortiaux-Denoël (with Guillaume) 1991/7.

Binding in brown calf of 1721 with gold-tooled spine containing a stamp showing a heraldic motif of a pair of compasses and three stars with the text 'Constanter ad Astra' (cf. pl. 2.3), the motto of Nicholas IV Jacquet, abbot of St Jacques, Liège (1709–41; Lèpine 1973: 11; Sammarthanus 1725: 988); for the tooling on the spine, cf. Darmstadt, Landes- und Hochschulbibliothek, MS 510 (Knaus, IV.13 on p. 39). At the bottom of fo 1r there occurs 'hunc librum religauit | D:Philippus Fisen | hujus Monasterii religiosus | et Cantor | 1721' [Dom Philippe Fisen, precentor of this abbey (St Jacques, Liège), bound this book 1721]; pl. 3.1. There is a similar inscription on its companion volume, RB45, and also in other St Jacques manuscripts, e.g., the one previously at Louvain recorded by Balau 1902, p. 40, n. 1. Nos 1 and 2 (RB16, RB45) have very similar bindings, but the gold tooling is different. The paper endleaves that belong with the binding show watermarks: at the front a fleur-de-lys in a crowned frame; and at the back 'CM' in ligature.

3.1 RB46, fo 1r, initial **L** with intricate vinescroll work in Low Countries style of s.xii, the statement of Philippe Fisen's binding 1721, and the Liège St Jacques class-marks. Text written over s.xv. Actual page dimensions 230 x 140mm.

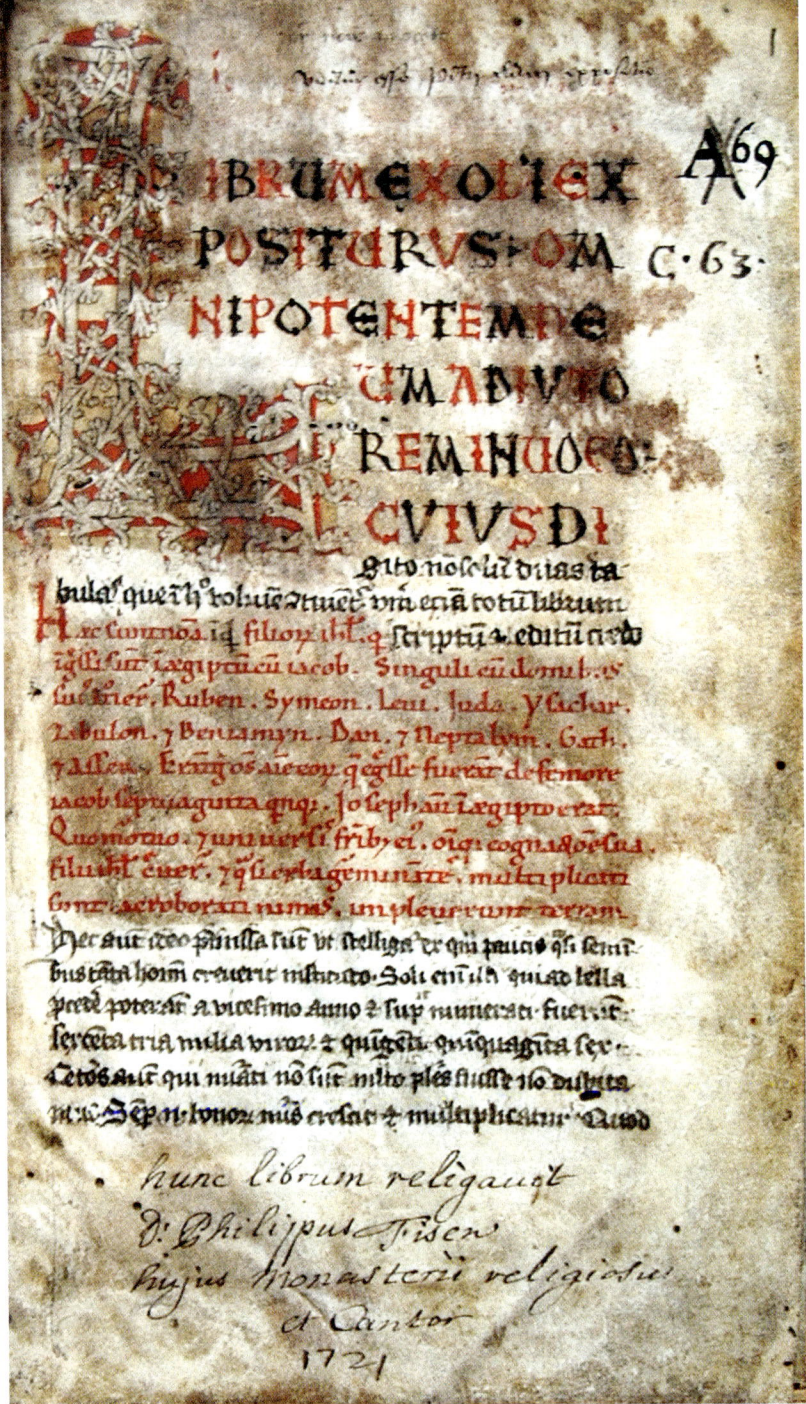

Foliation in ink on fos 2–102 (fos 25, 26 misnumbered 15, 16) in the top right-hand corner of the recto page, otherwise entered in pencil 1998. Acquired by St Patrick's College, Maynooth, probably s.xix[in].

Secundo folio: 'S<ed> p<er> h<oc> uidet<ur>'.

CODICOLOGICAL DESCRIPTION

Fos 140, membrane, measuring 230 x 140mm, written area 170 x 94mm, with one paper endleaf front and back belonging with the binding.

Pricking: Single prick-marks to mark the vertical bounds of the frame rule are visible at the top and bottom of the leaves, together with thirty-one prick-marks for the horizontal lines visible towards the outer edges of leaves. The prick-marks are double for parts of the vertical run on fos 8 (lines 8–14), 72 (lines 1–11), and for the whole vertical run on fos 100–4, 116–17, and 123 (a half-sheet); on fo 128 there are triple prick-marks on the whole of the vertical run, but one set is probably from an earlier pricking as an earlier ruling appears below the written area.

Ruling: Ruling on the hairsides is in hardpoint with vertical frame rules extending to the outer edges of leaves and the horizontal ruled lines for writing extending to the hinge. Writing occurs above the top ruled horizontal line. All quires HFHF(H). There is a large hole at the centre of fos 67/70 and some other smaller holes but no apparent loss of text. Holes also within the written area on fos 16, 26, 66, 98/103 (i.e., the sheet comprising fos 98, 103), 99, 122/129, 124/127, 135/6, 139, 140. As for fos 66/71, 74/79, 75/78, 82/87, 83/86, 90/95, 91/94, 98/103, 99/102, 105–6/111–12, 108–9, 114/119, 115, 122/129, 124/127, 128, 133/138, 134, 135/136 and 137, they were apparently ruled and partially written on (subsequently more or less erased: 'OREMUS' legible upside down on fo 99v, and 'i<n> ap<osto>l<orum>' in red on fo 134r) before receiving the present text.

Colour: Initial **L** on fo 1r in gold, red, with intricate vinescroll work (Low Countries, s.xii; cf. Lapière 1981: esp. ch. 2), with alternating red and green letters for the following opening words of the text (pl. 3.1). Biblical text in red alternates with commentary in black/brown ink throughout (pl. 3.2).

COLLATION

I[8] (fos 1–8), II[8] (fos 9–16), III[8] (fos 17–24), IV[8] (fos 25–32; 3 and 6 are half-sheets), V[8] (fos 33–40), VI[8] (fos 41–8), VII[8] (fos 49–56), VIII[8] (fos 57–64), IX[8] (fos 65–72), X[8] (fos 73–80), XI[8] (fos 81–8; 3 and 6 are half-sheets), XII[8] (fos 89–96), XIII[8] (fos 97–104; 3 and 6 are half-sheets), XIV[8] (fos 105–12; 2 and 7

3.2 RB46, fo 130v, text with alternating red for the Bible itself (Ex 25.20) and brown for the commentary.

are half-sheets), **XV**[8] (fos 113–20; 3 and 6 are half-sheets), **XVI**[10] (fos 121–30; 3 and 8 are half-sheets), **XVII**[10] (fos 131–40; 2, 4, 7 and 9 are half-sheets).

The quires are identified by letter by the scribe at the bottom centre of the verso of the last leaf (lower-case or capital letters indicating how they appear in the manuscript): 'B' on fo 8v, 'C' on fo 16v, 'd' on fo 24v, 'e' on fo 32v, 'F' on fo 40v, 'G' on fo 48v, 'h' on fo 56v, 'I' on fo 64v, 'k' on fo 72v, 'l' on fo 80v, 'm' on fo 88v, 'n' on fo 96v, 'o' on fo 104v, 'p' on fo 112v, 'Q' on fo 120v, 'R' on fo 130v.

CONTENTS

1. Fos 1r/1–140v/31: Bruno of Segni (1049–1123), *Commentarius in Exodum.* "**LIBRUM EXODI EX|POSITURUS: OM|NIPOTENTEM DE|UM ADIVTO | REM IN UOCO: | CVIVS DI**|gito no‹n› solu‹m› duas ta|bulas que i‹n› h‹oc› volu‹mi›ne ‹con›tine‹n›t‹ur›. v‹eru›m etia‹m› totu‹m› librum | scriptu‹m› ‹et› editu‹m› credo" (pl. 3.1).

(a) Fo 1r/9: Biblical text in red begins '**Hæc sunt no‹min›a filio‹rum› i‹sra›h‹e›l›.**' (Ex 1.1).
(b) Fo 1r/18: Commentary begins in brown/black 'Hec aut‹em› ideo p‹re›missa su‹n›t vt i‹n›telligat‹ur› ex q‹uoru›m paucis q‹ua›si se‹m›ini|bus ta‹n›ta ho‹m›i‹nu›m creuerit m‹u›ltitudo.'

Fo 140v/18: Biblical text in red ends 'p‹er› c‹unc›ta‹s› man|siones suaS.' (Ex 40.36).

Fo 140v/31: Commentary in brown/black ends apparently complete (the page is much rubbed and the text is partially undecipherable) '[…] celsu‹m› asc‹e›nde'. As Migne, PL 164, 233–378, but his edition ends at Ex 35.3 [= this manuscript fo 129r/31], claiming, presumably erroneously, that the commentary ends here, omitting the last five chapters, and Stegmüller, no. 1843, cites the close of the work as in Migne. Migne's text is notably less full than that in this manuscript, e.g., Migne's first paragraph (col. 233) ends 'fuere septuaginta animæ' but this manuscript has 'fuere septuaginta quinq‹ue›' (fo 1v/14) followed by over a page of additional commentary before Ex 1.8 'Surrexit interea rex' (fo 2r/20). Further work is required to establish the text of Bruno's commentary on Exodus, with or without subsequent additions.

4 RB47
Miscellaneous works

Ps.Augustine: *De spiritu et anima* • Ambrose: *De Conflictu vitiorum
et virtutum* • Ps.Bonaventure, *Instructio Sacerdotis ad se praeparandum
ad celebrandum Missam* • Vincent of Beauvais on the *Vision of Tundale*
(extract) • "Song of Songs" accompanied by the *Glossa Ordinaria* • *Cantica
Canticorum [Beate Marie] Versificata* • *Summula Raymundi Versificata*
(excerpt) • Papal letters relating to Margaret, countess of Flanders and
Hainault (excerpts) • Seneca: *Ad Lucilium Epistulae Morales* (excerpt)
• Record of conciliar events in the diocese of Reims 991

HISTORY

A COMPOSITE MANUSCRIPT COMPRISING eight booklets (A–H), the earliest
dating from s.xi (H), brought together s.xv[1]. The hand that wrote the list
of contents on fo 1[v] is that of Philippe d'Othée, prior of the Benedictine abbey
of St Jacques, Liège, 1404–26 (see above, pp 15–19), evidently the compiler; he
has also written folio numbers in the top left-hand corners of verso leaves (up to
fo 114v) and sometimes titles at the head of individual works, e.g., fos 25r, 41v,
49v (in margin), 50r, 78v, 80r, 84v, 88r, 92v (in margin), 93v, 94v (endnote), 95r,
99r. The manuscript was evidently at Liège in St Jacques, as indicated by d'Othée's
inscriptions on fos 1[v] (Booklet A), 43r (Booklet C; pl. 4.4, below) and 99r (Booklet
H; pl. 4.9, below): 'Liber Sancti Jacobi in Leodio'), where 'Leodium' = Liège,
and remained there until the sale of the abbey's books in 1788 (Paquot no. 123).
Cf. below, under Contents, items 1–2.

At the top of fo 2r (pl. 4.1) there occur the St Jacques class-marks 'B5' and
'B.61'. Mortiaux-Denoël (1991: 167) cites the manuscript as no. B.5, and assigns
it the new no. 300; it is listed by her as among 'manuscrits non retrouvés' (1997:
378).

Binding in brown calf of s.xviii[1] with gold-tooled spine showing a title in red
'D AUGUSTI | DE GRATIA | ET SPIRITU | ET OPUSCU' done at or for
St Jacques in the workshop of Philippe Fisen. At the base of the spine in gold is
the classification number 'MS B 61', a reference to its post-Bouxhon class-mark
at St Jacques (pl. 4.2). Compare the bindings of RB16, RB45, RB46, but the
paper endleaves show no watermark. For the tooling on the spine, cf. Darmstadt,
Landes- und Hochschulbibliothek, MS 524 (Knaus, IV.87 on p. 144). Acquired
by St Patrick's College, Maynooth, s.xix[in].

Secundo folio: 'Incipit liber aug<us>tini'. But before the addition of fo 1 the relevant
reading was: 'p<at>ris <et> filij <et> sp<iritus> s<an>c<t>i'.

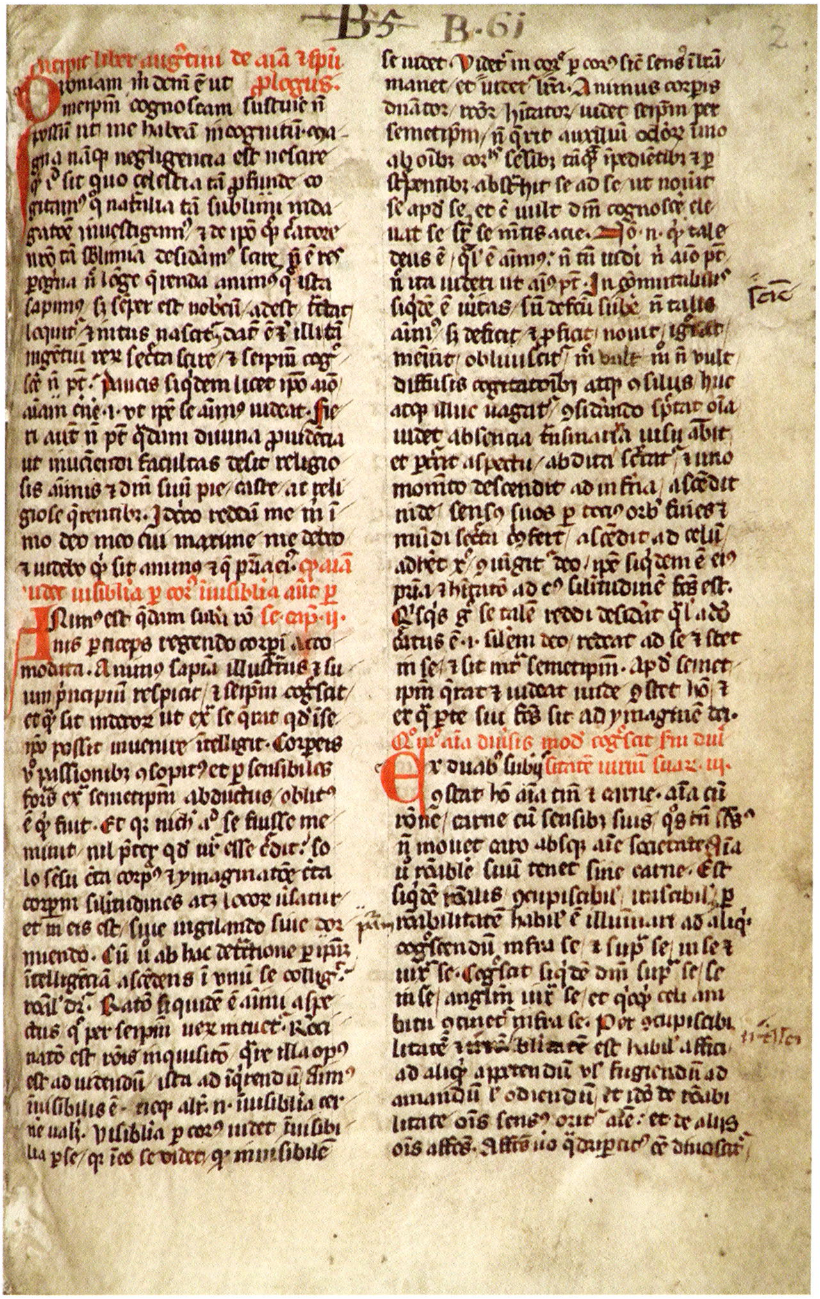

4.1 RB47, fo 2r, the first page of the text of *De spiritu et anima*, with the Liège St Jacques class-marks. Actual page dimensions 209 x 145mm.

4.2 RB47, spine of binding by Philippe Fisen, precentor of the abbey of St Jacques, Liège, c.1721, showing the Liège class-mark (post-Bouxhon) 'MS B 61'.

CODICOLOGICAL DESCRIPTION

Fos i + 152 + i, membrane, except for the single paper endleaves (part of the binding) front and back, measuring 209 x 145mm.

Booklet A (Quires **I–III**): Fos 24, written area 176 x 115mm in double columns, each column being 53mm wide. No pricking or ruling on fo 1. On fos 2–9 prick-marks for the double column frame rule are visible at top and bottom for the vertical frame rules, with the holes apparently pricked twice in close proximity, one each side and two in the centre, and forty-five prick-marks for the horizontal lines near the outer edges of the leaves (some lost on some leaves towards the bottom on account of cropping by the binder), with forty-four lines written. Ruling in fine crayon, with the verticals, and (usually) the top two horizontals and the bottom horizontal, extended to the edge of the leaf (clear on fo 22v). Quire **I** FHFH, **II** HHFH, **III** FHFH.

Booklet B (Quires **IV–V**): Fos 18, written area 150 x 102mm in double columns, each column being 45/46mm wide. Prick-marks for the double column frame rule are visible at top and bottom for the vertical frame rules, one each side and two in the centre, except that on fo 25 two prick-marks about 4mm apart are visible in the top inner corner, presumably to facilitate the artwork border linked to the initial capital; no prick-marks for the thirty-one horizontal lines are visible but there are vestiges of them on fo 32. Ruling in fine crayon, with the verticals extending to the edge of the leaves, and on fo 32 the top and penultimate horizontals extend in the same way. The ruling pattern is the same throughout with the scribes of items 2, 3 and 4 all using it. Quire **IV** FHHF, **V** FHFHFH.

Booklet C (Quire **VI**): Fos 7, written area 171 x 118mm in double columns, each column being 55/56mm wide. Prick-marks for the double column frame rule are visible at the top for the vertical frame rules, one each side and two in the centre, and those at the bottom can occasionally be seen, e.g., the outer ones on fos 47, 49. No prick-marks for the forty-three horizontal lines are visible. Ruling in fine crayon, with the verticals extending to the outer edge of the leaves, and the horizontals ruled right across the central column. Quire **VI**: FHFH.

Booklet D (Quires **VII–X**): Fos 30, written area 150 x 105mm usually in triple columns, biblical text in centre 16/17mm wide (but sometimes exceeded) and columns to left and right (each 41mm wide) for commentary. Prick-marks for the triple column frame rule are (usually) visible at top and bottom for the vertical frame rules, with two marks for each, those for the outer frame lines allowing for paraphs on the left of the written page, and those for the central column allowing for space (3mm) between the columns; prick-marks for the horizontal lines are (usually) visible at the outer (not the inner) margin of the leaves, there being thirty-four in Quire **VII** (fo 50 showing a double line of prick-marks, the inner one apparently not penetrating to the other folios), thirty-eight in Quire **VIII**, not fully visible in Quire **IX** (some on fo 73) but thirty-eight lines written, forty in Quire **X** (visible on fos 77–9). The ruling, very faint in hardpoint (probably done one sheet at a time), shows an extra vertical (for which there are no prick-marks) in the outer margin (inside the line of prick-marks), which is used to guide an added gloss (e.g., fo 65v = Dove 257/25–8, gloss 116 to SofS 4.12); horizontal lines are not generally ruled, but some are drawn right across the outer margin as far as the additional vertical, in Quire **VII** lines 1, a line above it (not indicated with a prick-mark), and 31, in Quire **VIII** lines 1, 2, 35 and 38 (clear on fo 61), in Quire **IX** lines 1 and 2 (clear on fo 71), and in Quire **X** not visible. The layout conforms to Ker's stage 3 with text below and gloss above the top line of the frame (De Hamel 1984: 30), which is compatible with a late twelfth-century date. Quires **VII–IX** HFHF.

Booklet E (Quire **XI**): Fos 8, written area 155–61 x 105–11mm in double columns, each column being approximately 50mm wide. Prick-marks for the double-column frame rule are visible at the top and bottom for the vertical frame rules, two each side and two in the centre, allowance being made for the initials beginning each verse line. No prick-marks for the 32–37 horizontal lines are visible. Ruling in fine crayon, with the verticals (where visible), and on fos 82–7 the top two horizontals, extending to the outer edge of the leaves, and the horizontals ruled right across the central column; no horizontal ruling visible on fos 80–1. Quire **XI**: FHFH.

Booklet F (Quire **XII**): Fos 88–92 written area 157–62 x 115mm (narrowing to 110mm on fo 92) in single long lines; there is a later addition on fo 92v. No prick-marks for the vertical frame rules are visible. Prick-marks for the forty-four horizontal long lines are visible near the outer edges of fos 88–9 (and partially on fo 94), the top prick-mark having no line of writing corresponding to it. Ruling in fine crayon visible for the verticals on fos 89–91, and for some horizontals on fo 89v, where they go in to the gutter of the hinge. Quire **XII**: FHFH. At one time this quire was a folded booklet with fo 88 on the inside of the fold, clearly visible across the middle of that folio, and progressively less sharply throughout the quire; on folded booklets, see Bischoff 1966–81. Nevertheless, fo 88r is much soiled, as is fo 94v, though to a lesser extent.

Fos 93v–94 written area 190–3 x 125–35mm added later than when the membrane was originally prepared to receive the text found on fos 88–92.

Booklet G (Quire **XIII**): Fos 4, written area 160 (reducing on fo 98v to 155) x 114mm in double columns, each column being approximately 50mm wide. Prick-marks for the double column frame rule are visible at the top for the vertical frame rules, two each side and two in the centre. No prick-marks for the thirty-six horizontal lines (32 on fo 98v) are visible. Ruling in fine crayon, with the verticals (where visible), and on fos 96 and 98 the top horizontal, extending to the outer edge of the leaves, and the horizontals ruled right across the central column. No writing on the top line. Quire **XIII**: FH.

Booklet H (Quires **XIV–XIX**): Fos 54, written area 145–50 x 116/111mm (outer/inner) in single long lines. Prick-marks for the vertical double frame lines are occasionally visible, e.g., fo 106 (top inner), fo 107 (bottom inner, done twice), and those for the twenty-two horizontal long lines are often visible at least in part, e.g., fo 106. In Quire **XIV** only (the first in this booklet and numbered 'I') there are additional prick-marks for a double vertical rule 18/23mm in from the outer edge of the inner written area. Ruling in hardpoint, scored so deeply that the membrane is partially cut on some leaves, e.g., fos 99, 127. The vertical frame lines are ruled to the outer edges. In most quires the top two horizontal lines and the bottom two horizontal lines are ruled to both the inner and the outer edges of the leaf, but in Quire **XV** (II) these lines are ruled to the inner edge only. There is writing on the top ruled line. In this Booklet the quires are numbered by the scribe at the centre of the bottom margin of the recto leaf, 'I' on fo 99r, 'II' on fo 107r, also on fo 114v, 'III' on fo 115r, 'IIII' on fo 124r, 'V' on fo 134r, 'VI' on fo 142r. Quire **XIV** (I) has a binding strip about 5cm long inserted at the bottom around leaves 2/7 to provide extra strength. Quire **XV** (II) has similar strips attached to the inside of leaves 1/8, 2/7, 3/6, 4/5. In Quire **XIX** (VI) a strip of membrane has been attached at the bottom of fo 152 (the last leaf, much damaged) and wrapped around to the front of fo 143 (the first leaf). Quires **XIV–XV**, **XVIII**: HFHF; Quires **XVI–XVII**, **XIX**: HFHFH.

Foliation in ink in roman numerals in top left-hand corner of verso leaves probably by d'Othée: the number 'xxiii' occurs twice, and the sequence ends at '.cxv.' on fo 114v, the last leaf of Quire **XV**. Modern foliation in pencil in top right-hand corner of recto pages entered 1997. Catchwords occur on fos 32v (Booklet B), and 98v (last leaf of Booklet G, but the original leaf with which it agreed is not present).

COLLATION

Booklet A: **I**[1+8] (fos 1–9), **II**[8] (fos 10–17), **III**[8] (fos 18–24; lacks 1);
Booklet B: **IV**[8] (fos 25–32), **V**[12] (fos 33–42; lacks 10, 11);
Booklet C: **VI**[8] (fos 43–9; lacks 8);
Booklet D: **VII**[8] (fos 50–7), **VIII**[8] (fos 58–65), **IX**[8] (fos 66–73), **X**[6] (fos 74–9);
Booklet E: **XI**[8] (fos 80–7);
Booklet F: **XII**[8] (fos 88–94; lacks 8);
Booklet G: **XIII**[4] (fos 95–8);
Booklet H: **XIV**[8] (fos 99–106), **XV**[8] (fos 107–14), **XVI**[10] (fos 115–24), **XVII**[10] (fos 125–34), **XVIII**[8] (fos 135–42), **XIX**[8] (fos 143–52).

CONTENTS

Booklet A (fos 1–24):

Fo 1r blank.

In a hand of s.xv[1]:

Fo 1v list of contents. 'liber mo‹na›sterij s‹an›c‹t›i jacobi leodien‹sis› . In quo co‹n›tine‹n›tur p‹ri›mo.'. Ends 'Ite‹m› lib‹er› synodo‹rum› ac co‹n›cilio-‹rum› i‹n› remensi t‹er›ritorio celeb‹ra›to‹rum›. Quere. [fo] ic.'.

In a university book hand of s.xiii (pl. 4.1):

1. Fos 2r/a/1 to 24v/a/40: Ps.Augustine, *De spiritu et anima*. "**Incipit liber aug‹us›tini de a‹n›i‹m›a ‹et› sp‹irit›u | p‹ro›logus.**" 'Qvoniam m‹ihi› d‹i›c‹tu›m e‹st› ut | me ip‹su›m cognoscam | sustin‹er›e n‹on› | possu‹m›'. Ends 'et gl‹or›i|ficet et port‹et› d‹eu›m in corp‹or›e suo . et | sectetur pacem.' 'Explic‹it› liber b‹ea›ti aug‹us›tini de a‹n›i‹m›a | et spiritu.'. As Migne, PL 40, 779–832. Not found in Dekkers.

Possibly to be identified with the item listed from St Jacques, Liège, by Montfaucon 1739, II, 1350, col. b, item 9, 'De anima & Spiritu'.

Fo 24v/a/41 to 24v/b/44 blank apart from a later annotation on fo 24v/b/13.

Booklet B (fos 25–42):

In a hand of s.xiii[1] (pl. 4.3):

2. Fos 25r/a/1 to 36r/b/22: Ambrose, here erron. attrib. Gregory, *De Conflictu vitiorum et virtutum*. '**Incipit liber s‹an›c‹t›i Greg‹orii› p‹a›p‹e› de ‹con›flictu uitio‹rum› ‹et› machina v‹ir›tutu‹m›** | Apostolica uox clamat per orbem at|q‹ue› in procinctu fi|dei positis. ne securitate torpeant dicit.'. Ends incomplete, lacking chs 27–8: 'Tu aut‹em› homo | dei. uigilanti studio. Atte‹n›|de que dico. ‹et› me adhuc ma|gis stipendia. u‹e›l stupenda | narrante fide‹m› p‹re›beto.' [= ed. Weber, end of ch. 26 on p. 929] plus six more lines now erased; note the scribe's uncertainty in copying 'stipendia. u‹e›l stupenda', *recte* 'stupenda'. As Weber 1979: 909–31; Migne, PL 40, 1091–1106, and compare also Migne, PL 83, 1131–44. Not in Dekkers.

Compare the item listed from St Jacques, Liège, by Montfaucon 1739, II, 1349, col. b, item 51, 'De conflictu virtutum & vitiorum'.

Fo 36r/b/22 (end) to 28 shows an erasure, fo 36r/b/29–31 blank.

In a hand of s.xv showing some humanistic influence:

3. Fos 36v/a/1 to 41r/b/19: Ps.Bonaventure, *Instructio Sacerdotis ad se praeparandum ad celebrandum Missam*. '**Quom‹odo› se debeat sac‹er›dos p‹re›p‹ar›are | int‹er›iori medit[ati]o‹n›e ad missa‹m› celebra‹n›|dam**'. 'Ad missam celebranda‹m› sex | consid‹er›at‹i›o‹n›es su‹n›t utiles et dispositio ad p‹re›p‹ar›at‹i›o‹n›em. Prima | est rat‹i›o‹n›is discretio'. Ends 'Videam

4.3 RB47, fo 25r, the opening page of
Ambrose, *De Conflictu vitiorum et virtutum*.
Actual page dimensions 209 x 145mm.

te sicut ‹tu› es cu‹m› eodem | p‹at›re ‹et› sp‹irit›u s‹an›c‹t›o per infinita saeculorum | bened‹i›c‹tu›s deus. AmeN.' As Little 1904: 124.
Fo 41b/20–30 blank.

Added on a blank leaf s.xv:
4. Fo 41v/a/1–41v/b/20: On the Ten Commandments. "De dec‹em› p‹rae›ceptis decalogi". '[P]Rimu‹m› ma‹n›datu‹m› e‹st› decl‹aratio› | en‹im› vnius dei v‹idelicet› n‹on› adores | deos alienos'. Ends 'no‹n› s‹er›uu‹m›. et vnu|u‹er›sa [recte vniv‹er›sa] q‹uae› illi‹us› s‹unt›. Explicit.'
Fo 42 blank.

Booklet C (fos 43–49) written in a hand of s.xiii/xiv (pl. 4.4):
5. Fos 43r/a/1 to 49v/a/29: Heading 'liber s‹an›c‹t›i iacobi i‹n› leodio.' added s.xv¹.
Extract from Vincent of Beauvais on the *Vision of Tundale*. "**Incipiu‹n›t quaedam ex‹tra›cta a xxviii° lib‹ro› spec‹u›li | historialiu‹m› de raptu a‹n›i‹m›e tundali ‹et› | eius uisione**".
Fo 43r/a/4–23: List of chapters.
Fo 43r/a/24 'ANno domini m° c° xlix° qui fu|it annus ij‹us›. expeditionis ‹hier›oso|limo‹rum› conradi regis romano‹rum›'. Ends: '**auctor** Hec | aut‹em› uisio ‹et› huic si‹mi›les apud doctores | n‹ost›ros calu‹m›pnia‹m› patiu‹n›tur nullum | penitus locu‹m› u‹e›l statu‹m› a‹n›i‹m›a‹rum› e‹ss›e pone‹n›|tes mediu‹m› int‹er› purgatoriu‹m› ‹et› p‹ar›adisu‹m› | q‹uam›uis beatus bernadus i‹n› quoda‹m› s‹er›mo|ne ‹contra›ria innu‹er›e uideantur. Explicit uisio tundali. am‹en› am‹en›'. As Vincent of Beauvais, *Speculum Historiale* (1494), sig. 2CS8r/b–2CT2v/a, fos 364r/b–366v/a, Bks 27/8, chs 188–204; also *Speculum Maius* (1591), IV, sig. 3C6r–3C8v = fos 390r–392v, Bk 27, chs 88–104.

6. Fo 49v/a/30–41: Heading "De ebrietate" added s.xv. Twelve lines of verse beginning: 'Nunc attendans q‹uid› sit stat‹us› eb‹ri›etatis'.

7. Fo 49v/b/1–23 Prayers based on biblical/liturgical formulae: 'Deus misereatur n‹ost›ri et b‹e›n‹e›dicat | nobis. illuminet uultu‹m› . ‹et› c‹etera›. [= Ps 66.2] | Gloria p‹at›ri. Fac mecu‹m› signu‹m› i‹n› bono | ut uideant qui me oderu‹n›t ‹et› co‹n›fun|dantur. [= Ps 85.17] Signatu‹m› e‹st› sup‹er› nos lum‹en› vul|tus tui d‹omi›ne. Dedisti letitia‹m› i‹n› corde | meo. [= Ps 4.7] OremuS.' Ends 'dominu‹m› n‹ostr›u‹m› ih‹esu›m ‹Christu›m filiu‹m› tuu‹m› | qui tecu‹m› uiuit ‹et› regnat deus. P‹er› o‹mn›ia | secula seculo‹rum›. AmeN. D‹omi›ne exau|di uocem meam. Et clamor meus | ad te ueniat [= Ps 101.2] B‹e›n‹e›dicamus domino | Deo gracias ...' Partly overwritten in darker ink.
Booklet D (fos 50–79):

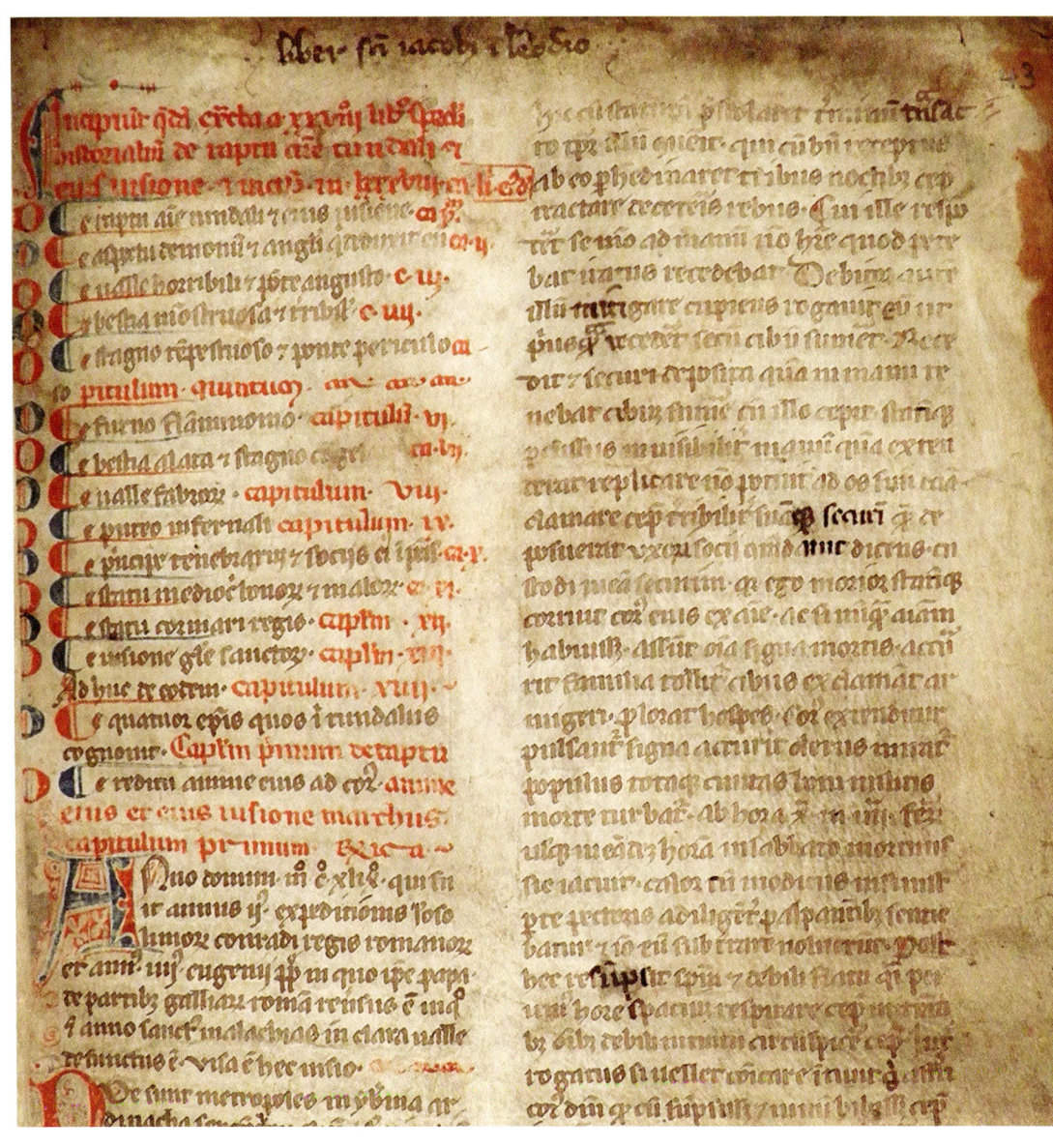

4.4 RB47, fo 43r, the opening page of the *Vision of Tundale*. Actual page dimensions 209 x 145mm.

In a hand of s.xiii[in] probably written in northern France (pl. 4.5):
8. Fos 50r/1–78r/26 "Song of Songs", biblical text in central column (b), accompanied by the *Glossa Ordinaria* (or 'Normal Tongue'), the standard medieval biblical commentary, in the form of suprascript glosses to the text and commentary to the left (col. a) and the right (col. c), a work attributed to Walafridus Strabo

4.5 *(opposite)* RB47, fo 50r, the beginning of the Glossa Ordinaria on the "Song of Songs".

Salomon .i. pacificus qr i regno eis pax .p. qem futura pax ecce figura bat. ydida .i. dilects. 7 sue illum ded dr. specios forma p̃ filii ho. p. b. redeus met. Exo̅ter i. ecionat̃. 7 sue illum q vonabilr erat allocutus 7 ggregatus ec eciam. iuxta numer. vocabulox. qx fecit libros plura i quo libro docet puulos non ta etate qm sapia de eorum querisacoe in mdo. s. quali posst licite uti qalibus; Exo̅ter iq instruit hoies puectois eta tis ad gteptum caducox. Cantica cantico. in q uirum gstimarit docet de solo amore di. ut refescat inte brachia sponsi vn. 7 cantic canticox dr. sua dignitate ota alia excellere. p̃ illa cantica ota uicia uitant. cantetur hoibs. p̃ ista locupletari creturb; dno gmungim. Sili oedinie 7 phy istrute l suas porte. primum ethica do cent dea physicam ut q in his pfecisse uidet. ad theoricam us pducant.

Si uis ascende ad canticum canticorum necesse est egdi de egypto ut post tusitum maris rubri subiisse unicis primum posst canie canticuox. Cantemin dno Glose .iq. ic. S; qr adhs longe es a cã tico canticox. p amibla trram desti spualr 7 gsiqur iordanis ad ripam gstitui sedin canere canas. audite celi q loquar ic. 7 t unuisa terris. ad altiora gscendes. possis aia derota cum sponso uih canie canticuox canticox .q;.

Quattuor in uih ope uideor inuenisse s. Sponsum .1 Sodales ipsius. Sposam

71 adolescentulas ē ea. alia a sponso alia dr. a sponsa. uii ista annuenclis; qdã a sodalib; sponsi. Congruum qpe est ut i nuptiis sit adolescentiu uitudo coy sponsa. iuuenum. ǣba. ē sponso. Spon sum. xpm intellige. Sponsa. ecce sine macla .1 ruga. anglos u. reos q puenire iuyrum pfem intellige amicos sponsi. adolescentule st. sponsarum incipientiu. ǣbe iuxta modu quidam salutem adep te. Et h aut libro gentiles. s. epytalami um uendicauere .1 nuptul g̅n̅s carmen assuptum est.

Docandium qd sponsa semp in do mo l. in lectulo l. in alio i uentu loco c sponso manere geiperet qd mulierib; quenit. Ipse qd masclox est ad foruisdea uineat l. ad hi opa amicam euocat. qr iuuntru ecce si si posst. in tranquilitate pacis dno sobole educare desidat. at ipe in pseuti ea cretis psecutoib; gercet. quo muudioe ad eria puenuat. ve si ipsa gtingat incolatu psentis exilii delectata. mi nus ad celestem suspiret patam.

Omnes aie mociones uniusitati conditor ds creauit ad bonum s; usu uro sepe fit ut res q bone st p pdi ditu male his abutuntur. nos ad pee ded ucantu. vnus ex aie motibz; amor est q bn utimur si sapiam uertra rem amem. Male aut si carnem aut sanguinem tu q ut spualiat audi spua liter amatoria uerba cantari. 7 disce mo tum aie tue. 7 illis amoris incendium (*c*.808–49), but *recte* the product of the school of Anselm of Laon (s.xii¹): see Smalley 1952: 46–66; compare RB45. The version here has some characteristics of post-1170 manuscript versions: at SofS 1.1 glosses 6–9 (post-1170) are absent, but gloss 15 has the post-1170 reading 'adiuuans est <et> finis uita eterna' (Dove 1997: 85–7). It lacks the prefatory material added post-1170, as listed by Dove 1997: p. 7, n. 13, and p. 43, n. 86.

(a) Fo 50r begins with the heading "Cantica Cantico<rum> Glo<ssa>ta". Biblical text begins fo 50v beside col. c/7: 'O|scule|tur | me os|culo o|ris sue [*corrected to* sui] (= SofS 1.1). Ends fo 78r/b/11 'assim<i>la|re capree. | hyn[n]uloq<ue> | ceruorum | super | montes | aromatum;. | **Explicit**;.' (= SofS 8.14).
(b) Commentary begins with Preface no. v on fo 50r/1 'Salomon. i<d est> pacificus q<uia> i<n> regno eiu<s> | pax? p<er> q<ua>m futura pax ecc<lesi>e figura|batur' (= ed., p. 79, line 66, followed by the other prefaces in the order iv, ii, i, iii, vi). Ends fo 78r/c/22–6 '¶ Non optando loq<ui>tur. | quis eni<m> optet eu<m> q<ue>m | diligit fugere? s<ed> me|mor sue conditionis illj|us uoluntati co<n>sentit;.' (= ed., p. 413, line 3). Lacks final paragraphs (ed. VIII.127–32).

As Dove 1997: 73–413 (to which reference is made); also Migne, PL 113, 1125–68, who prints only the commentary on the right; and, for reproduction of the 1480/1 printed edition, Froehlich and Gibson 1992: II, 707–23. Trans. Dove 2004. Stegmüller IX.499–501, no. 11804.

In another hand added s.xiii¹:
9. Fo 78r/27–44: Further commentary on the "Song of Songs": '¶ Oleu<m> effusu<m> n<omen> t<uum> [SofS 1.2]. h<abet> iuda ol<eu>m | ini<mi>cu<m> die<m> notitie.' Not listed by Stegmüller.

Possibly by the same hand (s.xiii^in) as item 8:
10. Fos 78v/a/1 to 79r/a/35: Anon. "Cantica Cantico<rum> [Beate Marie] Versificata", a poem in rhyming hexameters on the "Song of Songs" (based on the late 12c *Aurora* by Peter Riga). '[S]ponsu<m> c<um> sponsa salamo<n>is ca<n>tica regis | alti<us> extollu<n>t sup<er> om<n>ia cantica legis' [= lines 1–2]. As Beichner 1959 from OBL Laud misc. 576; here lines 1–91 only, with an extra line, 48bis, Per sex exteriores signat<ur> opus pietatis, omitting verses from Song of Songs and some initial capitals. Stegmüller IX.447, no. 10073.1.
By the same hand as item 9:
11. Fo 79r/a/36 to 79v/b/6: Further commentary on the "Song of Songs": 'Sic<ut> uitta coc &c. [SofS 4.3] Labia spo<n>se sic<ut> uitte s<unt> | q<uia> exhort[ati]o<n>e s<an>c<t>e e<cclesi>e'. Not listed by Stegmüller.
Fo 79v/b/7–41 blank.

Booklet E (fos 80–7) written in a hand of s.xiii[1] probably in northern France (pl. 4.6), annotated later by another hand s.xiii:

12. Fos 80r/a/1 to 84v/a/14: Excerpt from the *Summula Raymundi Versificata*, an abridged version in verse of the *Summa* of St Raymund de Peñafort OP (on whose writings, see Kuttner 1937: 438–52), by (?)Adam of Adersback (Alderspacensis), headed by d'Othée "Libellus de officio diuino versificat<us>". 'Non ex subtili sed uili scribere stilo | eloquio; placet; hec sociis q<uia> magna stu<den>\di/'. Lines 1–9 as [Adam of Adersback, *c.*1500], sig. b1 (fo vi). Line 10: 'ORdo sac<er>dotu<m> cantandi siue legendi | Talis erit q<ua>lis me<tri>c<e> describit<ur> isto'. Fo 84v/a/15–34 blank.

13. Fos 84v/b/1 to 87v/b/29:
Headed by d'Othée "Su<m>ma romoldi v<er>sificata … folia."
Excerpt from the *Summula Raymundi Versificata*, an abridged version in verse of the *Summa* of St Raymund de Peñafort OP, by (?)Adam of Adersback (Alderspacensis); see Hauréau 1890: II, 209–11. 'Quando paras calice<m> t<un>c vinu<m> p<ur>ius illi | Infundas'. Begins as [Adam of Adersback, *c.*1500], sig. c5r (fo xvi).

Booklet F (fos 88–94):
In a hand of s.xiii[4] probably written in northern France (pl. 4.7):
14. Fos 88r/1 to 92v/30: Excerpts from a formulary of papal letters headed by d'Othée "Quedam dictamina". The letters focus on correspondence between Margaret of Constantinople, countess of Flanders and Hainault (1202–80), together with her son, Guy, and popes Gregory X and Innocent V, and so originally date from *c.*1271–6. Because they are apparently unpublished, a fuller description is provided.
Incomplete at the beginning: 'diebus int<er>medijs nuptias celebrare. Nos vero c<er>tificat<i>one sup<er> p<er>missis a | vobis habita <et> recepta'.

Fo 88r/4: "lit<er>a su<m>mo po<n>tifici sup<er> negocio allema<n>nie". 'Sanctissimo pat<ri> Sup<er> hijs q<ui> v<est>ra s<an>c<t>a | benignitas p<er> d<omin>um'.

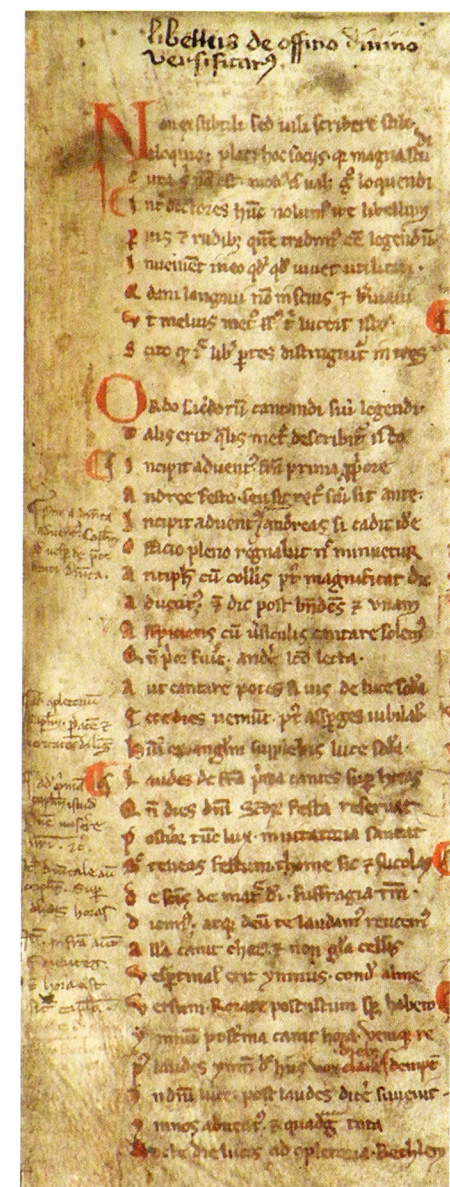

4.6 RB47, fo 80r, the beginning of the excerpt from the *Summula Raymundi Versificata*.

4.7 RB47, fo 88r, the beginning of the excerpts from papal letters.

Fo 88r/24: "**Sup‹er› eode‹m› Cardina|libus**". 'Cum nos dil‹e›c‹tu›m capellanu‹m› n‹ost›r‹u›m d‹omin›um'.

Fo 88v/5: "**Sup‹er› eode‹m› neg‹oci›o Regi sycilie**". 'Excellentissimo d‹omi›no suo consang‹ui›neo karissimo .k. dei gra‹tia› Regi Sycilie | Ducat‹ui› apulie ‹et› p‹ri›ncipatui Capue alme vrbis Senatori ... Quonia‹m› consid‹er›at‹i›o‹n›e p‹ro›uida hoc anno'.

Fo 88v/41: "**litt‹er›a p‹ro› or‹ati›o‹n›ib‹us› i‹m›perand‹is› p‹ro› Rege ludouico defu‹n›cto**". 'Margar‹eta› fland‹rum› | & hay‹nonensis› Comitissa ven<er>ab<i>lib<us> & Religiosis viris in <Christ>o sibi k<arissi>mis v|niu<er>sis abbatib<us> abbatissis p<ræ>positis. Decanis.'

Fo 89r/42: "**litt<er>as su<m>mo po<n>tifici Greg<orii> | sup<er> reg<num> co<mmun>e gra<tiarum> impe<n>sa<rum> d<omi>no .R. dom<ino> flandr<um> & p<re>p<o>sito Brugen<sis>**" [Gregory X, pope, 1271–6]. (fo 89v/1) 'Sanctissimo patri &c'. m. fland<rum> & hayn<onensis> &c'. Ex continuatis v<est>re sereni|tatis b<e>n<e>ficiis p<ri>mo. R. de flandr<um> nepoti u<est>ro karissimo.'

Fo 89v/11: "**litt<er>a p<ro> pe<n>sione conf<er>enda**". 'Nos Margar<eta> &c'. q<ui> nos ven<erabili> viri k<arissi>mi u<est>ri in <Christ>o Mag<ist>ri yzembardi [papal notary] d<omi>ni'.

Fo 89v/19: "**litt<er>a reg<num> co<mmun>is d<omi>no p<a>p<æ> sup<er> neg<oti>o casleten<sis>**". 'Sanctissimo p<at>ri ac d<omi>no .G. diuina &c'. Margar<eta> &c'. & guido eius fili<us> | &c'. sup<er> plerisq<ue> gracijs & honorib<us> quib<us> hoc a<n>no nos & u<est>ros'.

Fo 90r/5 "**litt<er>a sup<er> obligat<i>o<n>e facie<n>da ex p<ar>te d<omi>ne & comitis p<ro> neg<oci>o allema<n>nie | regni**". 'Cum nos tales & tales n<ost>ros nu<n>cios speciales mittam<us> ad partes allema<n>nie'.

Fo 90r/15: "**litt<er>a | p<ro> co<n>fessore impet<r>anda**". 'Pro Elizabet tali inclusa ad d<omi>ni | voluntate<m> infirmitates tribulat<i>o<n>es & miserias sustinente'. (fo 90r/25) 'Excellentissimo d<omi>no suo. P<hi>l<ippo> dei gr<ati>a | franco<rum> Regi magnifico fidelis eius & consa<n>guinea Margar<eta> flandr<um> | & hayn<onensis> comitissa salute<m> & cu<m> promptitudine'.

Fo 90v/11: "**litt<er>a vt sciat<ur> Orat<us> & rumo<rum> i<n>timat<i>o sup<er> c<re>at<ion>æ su<m>mi | po<n>tificis**". 'Magnifice ac potenti d<omi>ne nobis in <Christ>o k<arissi>me M. flandr<um> | & hayn<onensis> Comitisse. Guill<elm>us miserat<i>one diuina c<er>t<um> s<an>c<t>i marchi sac<ro>s<an>c<t>e | eccl<es>ie p<res>b<yte>r Cardinal' Salute<m> & cu<m> sincero affectu parata<m>'.

Fo 90v/31: "**litt<er>a p<ro> or<ati>o<n>ib<us> p<ro>cura<n>|dis**". 'Margar<eta> flandr<um> & hayn<onensis> Comitissa religiosis viris | sibi in <Christ>o k<arissi>mis ministro cet<er>isq<ue> ministris & fratrib<us>| ac diffinitorib<us> gen<er>alis Capituli ordinis s<an>c<t>e t<ri>nitatis'.

Fo 91r/19: "**litt<er>a sup<er> <con>stitut<i>o<n>e Ballini & receptoris**". 'Iohannes filius Comit<isse> flandr<um> p<ræ>positus Burgen<sis> & Cancellar<ius> | flandr<um> vniu<er>sis &c'.

Fo 91r/32: "**exe<m>pto' & j<m>muni|tas sup<er> feodo**". 'Nos Margar<eta> qui nos n<ost>r<u>m p<ro>bemus assentu<m> | ad id q<uod> talis .N. ex viginti & octo'.

4.8 RB47, fo 95r, the
beginning of Seneca,
*Ad Lucilium Epistulae
Morales* (excerpt).

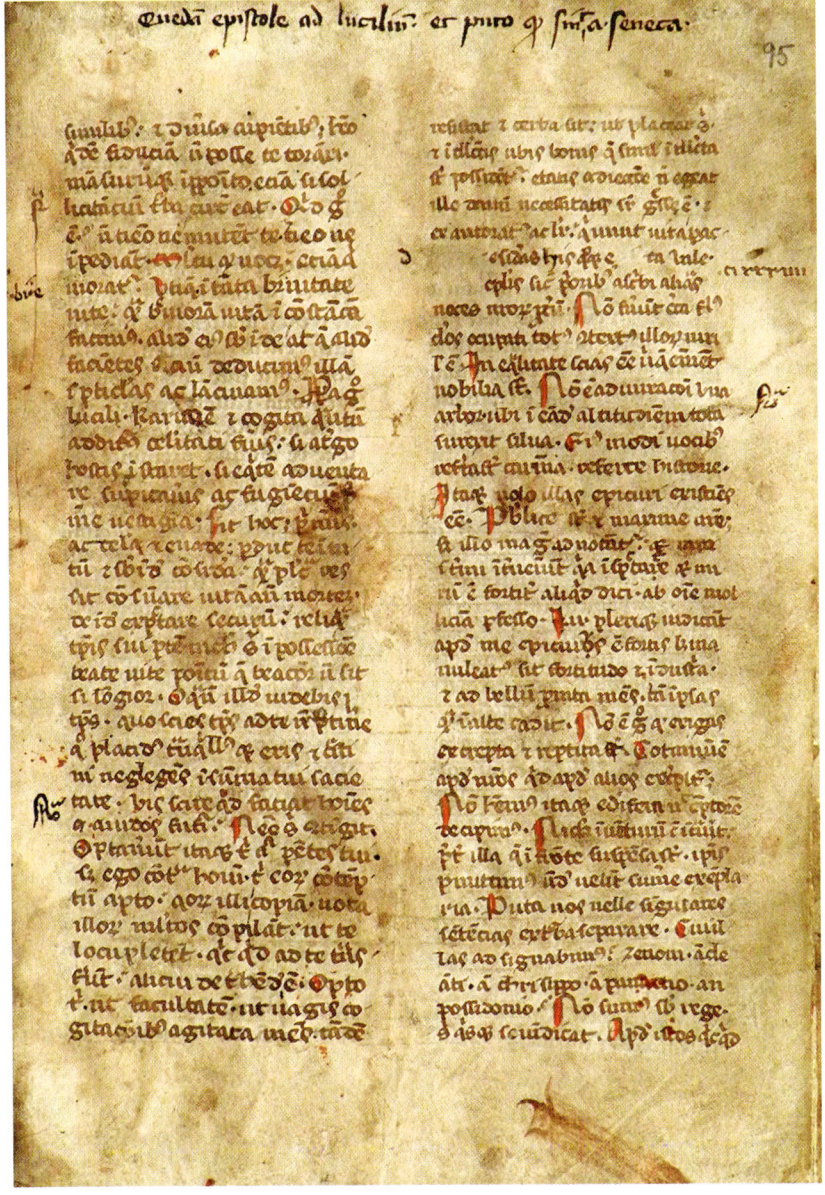

Fo 91v/3: "litt<er>a sup<er> resignat<i>o<n>e b<e>n<e>ficij". 'Ego talis notu<m>
facio vniu<er>sis q<uod> ego dilecto amico meo tali'. Compare Barraclough
1934: 164–5, no. 52.

Fo 91v/13: "Cam<er>acen<sis> Ep<is>c<opus> sc<ri>b<it> d<omi>ne comitisse".
'Nouerit v<est>ra dominatio in t<er>ra u<est>ra sub u<est>ro d<omi>nio accidisse'.

Fo 91v/26: "**litt‹er›a ‹con›tine‹n›s f‹a›c‹tu›m Ganden‹sis›**". 'Excellentissimo suo d‹omi›no | Ph‹ilippo› Dei gr‹ati›a franco‹rum› regi illustrissimo ville Ganden‹sis› co‹m›munitas'.

Fo 92v/11: "**litt‹er›a directa d‹omi›no Inoc‹entio› su‹m›mo po‹n›tifici**". 'Sanctissimo pat‹ri› ac d‹omi›no Innoce‹n›tio diuina p‹ro›uidencia sac‹ro›s‹an›c‹t›e | &c'. Auditis v‹est›re s‹an›c‹t›e creat‹i›onis rumorib‹us› qui cu‹n›ctis'. [Innocent V, pope, 1276]

Added in a hand of s.xv:
15. Fo 92v/31–44: Notes (from another formulary?) for the reception of each monk of two, headed by d'Othée in the margin "copia re|cept[i]o‹n›is vtri‹us› mo‹na›chi". 'Ven‹erando› ac religioso in ‹Christ›o p‹at›ri ac d‹omi›no ... d‹omi›no [...] de diuina prouidentia'. Ends: 'V‹ere› u‹t› valeatis in ‹Christo›'.

Fo 93r blank, except for a heading at the top: 'In no‹m›i‹n›e s‹an›c‹t›e trinitatis Incip‹it› exp‹er›im‹enta› mag‹istr›i Pillissi[?] p‹atri›'.

In another hand of s.xiii:
16. Fos 93v/1–94v/20: Recipe headed by d'Othée 'Experime‹n›ta q‹uae›da‹m› seu docume‹n›ta medicine'. 'Ad raucitate‹m› Juniperu‹m› ‹con›tunde diligent‹er› cu‹m› vino ‹et› coq‹ue› us‹que› ad medietate‹m›'.

16a. Fo 94v/21–3: a note by d'Othée (much faded and on creased membrane, making it difficult to read) beginning: 'De c‹er›ta co‹n›sid‹er›at‹i›o‹n›e. Id e‹st› veri‹ta›s circa salutifera‹m› d‹omi›nj cruce‹m› ‹et› passione‹m›'.

Booklet G (fos 95–8):
In a hand of s.xiii/xiv, probably written in Italy (pl. 4.8):
17. Fos 95r/a/1 to 98v/b/32: Seneca, *Ad Lucilium Epistulae Morales* (excerpt) headed by d'Othée "Quedam epistola ad luciliu‹m› et puto q‹uod› sin‹t› a seneca". Begins imperfectly '[dis]similib‹us›. ‹et› diu‹er›sa cupie‹n›tib‹us›. H‹ab›eo | q‹ui›de‹m› fiducia‹m› n‹on› posse te' (= Epistula 32.2). Ends incomplete 'In g‹rae›cis ha‹n›c li|ce‹n›ciam tuleris. Nos etia‹m› cum [catchword] scribimus' (= Epistula 40.11). As Reynolds 1965: I.92/11–107/6. From the imperfect beginning and incomplete ending marked by a catchword it is evident that this booklet was originally part of a larger manuscript unit.

Booklet H (fos 99–152):
In several hands of s.xi written in north-east France or Rhineland (pl. 4.9):
18. Fos 99r/1–152r/9: Record of conciliar events in the diocese of Reims 991, attrib. Gerbert, bishop of Reims, 991–8, later Pope Sylvester II, headed by d'Othée s.xv "Liber Sijnodorum et conciliorum | in Reme‹n›si territorio celebrato‹rum›'".

... sci iacobi in leodio. liber synodos ac maior ...
... remens ... ...

Incip pr r. p...o logus

Lucæ emuli mei dentes in me exacuant. dictis meis
et facta pscindere parent. qi iustam amicoꝭ obsede
qua inuidor odio pmoueor. Sanctum ubi nerat timor
timere didici. nec amicoꝭ i secta relinquere nego

Accurati igit et sūmariū qde genera causarū i
mensi concilio exposita breuit attinga. ut
gestaꝭ ueritas inorescat. æque aliimiuris retce
tası agnoscant. sero aut abbiard sacramentis
platis. siqd mei graue ut parū copiu expssero
iisue iuurie ieti mea ꝑ adscribi ignorantie. Ab au
ditoribꝯ quoqꝫ nemo aliena ut parū discuss se de
rotent. Si qde triplici genere uit pretatio
nis utendū fore censeo. scilicet ut oud dā aduer
bii explicata i illā transfenmū lingua. Inqbusdā
aut sententiarū grantas et eloqii dignitas di
core genere esormeit. Porro in aliis una dir
tio occasione facit ad abdita inuestiganem
lucq plos affectus manifeste ꝑferri. Liue e sine
plenū assequi nꝑotuit ero. Instam modis poetissi mex
beqniū sententias cantator unt ꝑtan. Sed earū
enpli et canones. digressiones. et siqua eius modi si.

liber synodos
     euagelio

'Lic<et> emuli mei dentes in me exacuant dictaq<ue> | et facta p<ro>scindere parent'. Ends 'Eos uero sacrilegos | urbisq<ue> p<ro>ditores qui nec sponte nec ui ad satisfactione<m> | uenerant iterato anathemate da<m>pna\n/t· Post hec conciliu<m> | solle<m>pniter determinatur.'. As Pertz 1839: 658–86. Some damage to fos 151–2 with loss of text on fo 151.

Fo 152r/10–22 blank; fo 152v blank except for later addition 'lib<er> synodo<rum> <et> <con>silio<rum>'.

4.9 (*opposite*) RB47, fo 99r, the beginning of the record of the diocesan Council of Reims 991, the oldest manuscript in the collection (s.xi). Actual page dimensions 209 x 145mm.

5 RB54
Missal 1529

WRITTEN BY PETRUS VENLONENSIS (Pieter van Venlo, near Maastricht), priest of St Léonard's (abbey of Augustinian Canons, previously a cell of St Jacques), Liège, dated 17 March (fd St Gertrude of Nivelles) 1529, as indicated by the inscription on fo 262r. Illuminated capitals are used to mark important places in the text (pl. 5.1). Corrections in the main hand on fos 60v (trimmed by the binder) and 63r. The sanctorale part of the manuscript at least was evidently copied from an exemplar of almost identical layout, as there are forward references, e.g., on fo 165r/a/29 to fo 226r (numbered by the scribe 'ccxvi'), and on many others, indicated below. A change in the depth of colour in the ink at fos 11r, 55v/b, 122v/b/21 and 129r indicates the end of one scribal stint and the beginning of another. A larger script on fos 132–7 is reserved for the Canon of the Mass.

The paper used for most of the manuscript shows a gap between chain marks of 27/29mm. The watermark visible on fos 5, 6, 10, 36 shows a gothic **p** similar to Briquet no. 8532 (assigned among other places to Antwerp, 1490–1).

Contemporary binding of brown calf blind-stamped on wooden boards later re-backed at the spine (see below). The insides of the boards are covered with fragments from L texts of s.xv. On the rear inside cover (upside down), an inscription reads 'Liber Canonicoru<m> Regulariu<m> S<an>cti Leonardi prope Leodium'. On the front inside cover endleaf there is a printed slip pasted on saying: 'EX BIBLIOTHECA | EDMUNDI-SEBASTIANI-JOSEPHI DE | STOUPY, Perillustris Ecclesiæ Ca|thedralis Leodiensis Canonici, Abbatis | Commendatarii Abbatiarum S. Petri in | Chalons-sur-Saone, & S. Petri in | Airvaux. | N°. [none]'. Edmond Sebastien de Stoupy (abbot of St Pierre de Chalons; on whom see Peremans 1972) was a lecturer in divinity ('Theologal') at St Paul's, Liège, in 1740 (Liège, Bibliothèque de l'Université, MS 1662B, fo 62r), whose books were posthumously listed in the *Catalogue des Livres de la Bibliothèque de feu M. de Stoupi* (Liège, 1786). In a copy at Cambridge University Library, class-mark 7880.c.94², the prices have been written in, and that for this Missal is relatively low at '1,,10'. On p. ix of this *Catalogue*, the names of two Dublin booksellers, Thomas Ewing and William Wilson (*fl.* 1777–86), are given among 'Noms de Messieurs les Libraires, chez qui l'on peut s'adresser pour remettre les Commissions'; for these booksellers, see Kennedy 2006, p. 374.

The spine of the binding (pl. 5.2) has been superimposed with gold tooling from the workshop of Philippe Fisen of St Jacques, Liège (*c.*1721); the centrepiece comprising four fleurons in the top compartment matches that used on RB16 (see above, pls A, 1.4 and pp 16–17, 21), and the corner-pieces used vertically in

the third and fourth compartments match those used horizontally in all the compartments except the second on the spine of RB16. The application of these designs is slightly inferior to that on RB16, perhaps because the tools were being struck onto leather of a different quality already in place for a hundred years. For this feature (superimposition of gold tooling on the spine of an earlier binding), cf. Darmstadt, Landes- und Hochschulbibliothek, MS 622 (IV.95). The spine is inscribed 'MISSALÆ ANTIQUUM MUNSEP.', and at the bottom 'M.S. 1529', the bottom inscription being probably a later addition. Possibly Stoupy was responsible for the addition of the bottom inscription, or it might have been done in Ireland s.xix. Foliation in pencil at top right-hand corner of recto pages provided in 1999.

Secundo folio: 'Co<m>ple<n>da. | Beatissime spiritus'.
Secundo folio of the main part of the manuscript (fo 5): '[ce]loru<m>. Hic est eni<m>'.

CODICOLOGICAL DESCRIPTION

Fos i + 262 + i, mostly paper, but the following folios are membrane: fos 4/11 (outer sheet of Quire **II**), 112–37 (Quires **XV–XVII**), 162/169 (outer sheet of Quire **XXI**), 226 (singleton first leaf of Quire **XXIX**), 247/254 (outer sheet of Quire **XXXII**). Leaves measure 263 x 186mm, written space 210 x 148/151mm (except on fos 132–7 where it is 195 x 144mm), disposed in two columns of text.

Pricking: No prick-marks are visible.

Ruling: In fine crayon (often scarcely visible) dividing the page into two columns, each 69mm wide with a central column 17mm wide. In Quire **I** fos 4/11 (outer membrane sheet) shows narrower columns (65mm) and thirty-two lines to the page; fo 5 also has thirty-two lines to the page, but fos 6–10 show twenty-nine. In Quire **II** fo 12 shows the vertical frame rules drawn twice and the column width is again the narrower 65mm. The number of lines per page continues to vary. For example, at the end of Quire **VI** fo 45v shows thirty-two lines, but at the beginning of Quire **VII** fo 46r shows twenty-nine lines: despite the change of layout over a quire division, the text runs on.

Fos 4–246 (omitting 130–7, which contain the Canon of the Mass) show roman numbers in red (by the scribe) at the top centre of recto pages: i–ccxxxviii, omitting no. cxvii (after fo 119). Between nos cxxvii (fo 129) and cxxviii (fo 138), Quire **XVII** (fos 130–7) has been inserted after the bulk of the manuscript (Quires **II–XVI**, **XVIII–XXXI**) was written; there are also no such numbers in Quires **XXXII–XXXIII**, the later part of the manuscript (fos 247–62, containing a separate section of special prayers of masses arranged according to the liturgical year, plus the common of the saints), so these quires were probably an afterthought added at the end of what was first thought of as sufficiently complete in itself.

5.2 RB54, spine (s.xvi²) superimposed with decorative gold tooling by Philippe Fisen (Liège, c.1721).

Colour: Illuminated capital **A** on fo 4r in blue with gold surround and magenta infill decorated with gold filigree swirls to mark the beginning of the Proper of the Time (pl. 5.1). Illuminated capital **D** in blue, with red, green, yellow and pink colouring on fo 162r to mark the beginning of the Proper of the Saints. Illuminated capital **E** in red, with turquoise, green, yellow and silver colouring on fo 226r to mark the beginning of the Votive Masses. Blue calligraphic initials (often with mauve flourishing) on fos 12r (Christmas), 89v (Easter), 103v (Ascension), 105r (Pentecost), 111v (Trinity Sunday), 112v (Corpus Christi), 138r, 170v, 189r (fd SS Peter and Paul), 190v (Visitation of the Blessed Virgin Mary), 195r (Anne, mother of the Blessed Virgin Mary), 201r (Assumption of the Blessed Virgin Mary), 203v (St Augustine), 205v (Birthday of the Blessed Virgin Mary), 208r (St Lambert), 217r (All Saints), 218r (St Léonard), 220v (St Elizabeth), 221r (Presentation of the Blessed Virgin Mary), 223r (Dedication of a Church), 224v (Compassion of the Blessed Virgin Mary), 234v, 239r, 241v, 243v. Blue secondary initials on fos 206v (SS Protus and Hyacinth), 210v (St Michael the Archangel), 214v (11,000 virgins), 216r (SS Simon and Jude), 219v (St Martin), 222r (St Chrysogonus), 229v, 233r, 238v. Red is used for secondary initial capitals (guide-letters usually visible), section headings and rubrication (red shading of capitals etc.); on fo 15v/b/15 a red **D** occurs erroneously instead of **P**. Red underlining of a rubric occurs on fos 15v/b/7–14, 17r/a/13–6, 18v/a/15–20. Metallic red occurs in headings etc., e.g., on fos 7v, 8r, 10v, 11v, 12r, 71r, 71v, 73v, 92v, 98v. In Quire **XVII** a red and blue illuminated initial **T** occurs on fo 132r, the beginning of the Canon of the Mass. Alternating red and blue secondary initial capitals on fos 132–7. Purple secondary initial on fo 170v/b/1 to mark the beginning of the mass for the Purification of the Blessed Virgin Mary.

COLLATION

I¹⁺¹⁺¹ fos 1–3 (1–3 are singletons joined by strips pasted on at the hinge; 1 pasted to binding endleaf), **II**⁸ fos 4–11, **III**⁸ fos 12–19, **IV**⁸ fos 20–7, **V**¹⁰ fos 28–37, **VI**⁸ fos 38–45, **VII**⁸ fos 46–53, **VIII**⁸ fos 54–61, **IX**⁸ fos 62–9, **X**⁸ fos 70–7, **XI**⁸ fos 78–85, **XII**⁸ fos 86–93, **XIII**⁸ fos 94–101, **XIV**⁸ fos 102–11, **XV**⁸ fos 112–19, **XVI**¹⁰ fos 120–9, **XVII**¹⁰ fos 130–7 (lacks 3, 4), **XVIII**⁸ fos 138–45 (sheets 2 and 3 in reverse order: correct order is 138, 140, 139, 141–2, 144, 143, 145), **XIX**⁸ fos 146–53, **XX**⁸ fos 154–61, **XXI**⁸ fos 162–9, **XXII**⁸ fos 170–7, **XXIII**⁸ fos 178–85, **XXIV**⁸ fos 186–93, **XXV**⁸ fos 194–201, **XXVI**⁸ fos 202–9, **XXVII**⁸ fos 210–17, **XXVIII**⁸ fos 218–25, **XXIX**⁸ fos 226–33 (1 and 8 singletons), **XXX**⁶ fos 234–9, **XXXI**⁸ fos 240–6 (lacks 8), **XXXII**⁸ fos 247–54, **XXXIII**⁸ fos 255–62 (8 pasted to binding endleaf).

Note: the text carries on from fo 239v to fo 240r 'a verbo || mendacii.' (Ecclus 51.7).

CONTENTS

Fo 1 blank.

1. Fo 2r/a/1–2v/b/10 "Exorcismus . Salis." 'Adiutorium n<ost>r<u>m in no<m>i<n>e domini'. 'Exorcizo te crea|tura salis per | deum'.

Fo 3r/b/1–14 [to follow on from fo 3v/b] "Co<m>ple<n>da". 'Beatissime spiritus per | quem Condita sunt'.

Fo 3v/a/1–34: "¶ Pro nauigan|tibus." 'DEus, qui tra<n>stu|listi patres no|stros per mare Rubru<m>'.

Fo 3v/b/1–33: "¶ Pro una pregna<n>te". 'EXaudi clementissi|me pater deprecatio|ne<m> serui tui'. Another hand writing in an italic style takes over at line 11 and continues on the previous page.

2. Proper of the Time

Fo 4r/a/1–5r/b/32 [First Sunday of Advent] 'A|D te leuaui a<n>i<m>a<m> mea<m>' (pl. 5.1).

Fo 5v/a/1–6v/b/6 [Second Sunday of Advent] "Do<min>ica s<e>c<un>da". 'POpulus syo<n> ecce d<omin>us | veniet'.

Fo 6v/b/7–10v/b/17 [Third Sunday in Advent] "Do<min>ica tercia." 'GAudete in d<omi>no semp<er>'.

Fo 10v/b/18–11v/a/8 [Fourth Sunday in Advent] "Do<min>ica quarta." 'MEme<n>to n<ost>ri d<omi>ne i<n> benepla|cito p<o>p<u>li tui' [Ps 105.4].

Fo 11v/a/10–12r/b/8 [Christmas Eve] "In vigilia natiuitat<is> <Christ>i". 'HOdie sciet<is> q<ui>a ve<n>i|et d<omin>us'.

Fo 12r/b/9–13r/b/27 [Christmas Day] "In die s<an>c<t>o". 'PUer natus est | nob<is>'.

Fo 13r/b/29–14r/b/14 [St Stephen's Day] "Stephani prothom<artir>is". 'ET eni<m> sederu<n>t p<ri>nci|pes et aduersu<m> me loq<ue>|bant<ur>'.

Fo 14r/b/15–14v/b/29 [Feast of St John the Evangelist] "Joha<n>nis ap<osto>li | et eua<n>gelis[t]ᵉ". 'IN medio | ecclesie aperuit os | eius'.

Fo 14v/b/31–15v/b/6 [Feast of Holy Innocents] "In die s<an>c<t>o<rum> i<n>nocentiu<m>". 'Ex ore i<n>fanciu<m> deus et lactenciu<m>'.

Fo 15v/b/6–16v/a/9 [Octave of the Nativity of Our Lord] "Do<min>ic<a> infra oct<avo>". 'No<n> q<uod> seque<n>s officiu<m>' underlined in red. At line 15 'Puer nat<us>'.

Fo 16v/a/10–17r/a/16 [Feast of Circumcision] "In die circu<m>ci|sionis." 'PUer nat<us> est nob<is>'.

Fo 17r/a/17–17v/a/27 [Epiphany Eve] "**In vigilia ep\<ip\>h\<an\>ie**". 'VOx fulgebit hodie | sup\<er\> nos'.

Fo 17v/a/28–18v/b/10 [Epiphany] "**In die s\<an\>c\<t\>o.**" 'ECce adue\<n\>it d\<omi\>nator d\<omin\>us et regnu\<m\>'.

Fo 18v/b/11–19v/a/10 [Octave of Epiphany] "**In oct\<avo\> ep\<ip\>h\<an\>ie.**" 'O\<mn\>ia sic\<ut\> in die p\<rae\>ter'. Line 12: 'DEus cui\<us\> vnige\<n\>it\<us\> in | substa\<n\>cia'.

Fo 19v/a/10–20r/b/12: [First Sunday after the Octave of Epiphany] "**Do\<mini\>c\<a\> pri\<m\>a p\<ost\> oct\<avo\> ep\<ip\>h\<an\>ie**". 'IN excel|so throno vidi sede\<re\> viru\<m\> | que\<m\> adorat'.

Fos 20r/b/13–21r/a/27: [Second Sunday after Epiphany] "**Do\<mi\>nica s\<e\>c\<un\>da**". 'OMnis t\<er\>ra | adoret te deus'.

Fos 21r/1/28–22r/a/2: [Third Sunday after Epiphany] "**D\<omi\>nica tercia**". 'Adorate deu\<m\> om|nes angeli'.

Fos 22r/a/3–22r/b/21: [Fourth Sunday after Epiphany] "**Do\<min\>ica q\<ua\>rta**". 'Adorate deu\<m\> p\<er\> totu\<m\>.

Fos 22r/b/22–23r/a/8: [Fifth Sunday after Epiphany] "**Do\<mi\>nica q\<ui\>nt\<a\>**". 'Adorate deu\<m\> p\<er\> totu\<m\>.

Fos 23r/a/8–24v/b/23: [Septuagesima] "**Do\<mi\>nica in lxxᵃ**". 'Circundederu\<n\>t [*sic*] me | gemit\<us\> mortis'.

Fos 24v/b/24–27r/a/32: [Sexagesima] "**Do\<min\>ica in sexagesima**". 'Exurge quare ob|dormis d\<omi\>ne'.

Fos 27r/b/1–28r/a/12: [Quinquagesima] "**D\<omin\>ica in qui\<n\>quagesima Int\<imati\>o**". 'Esto michi in deum | protectore\<m\>'.

Fos 28r/a/12–29r/b/24: [Quadragesima, Sunday before Ash Wednesday] "**In capite ieiunij | Introit\<us\>**". 'MIsereris om\<n\>i\<um\> | d\<omi\>ne et nichil odisti'.

Fos 29r/b/25–30r/a/1: [Thursday after Ash Wednesday] "**Feria q\<ui\>n|ta.**". 'DUm clamare\<m\> ad | d\<omin\>um'.

Fos 30r/a/2–31r/a/13: [Friday after Ash Wednesday] "**Fe\<r\>ia sexta**". 'Audiuit d\<omin\>us | et misert\<us\> est michi'.

Fos 31r/a/14–31v/b/14: [Saturday after Ash Wednesday] "**Sabbato**". 'Esto michi p\<er\> to|tu\<m\> ut s\<upra\>'. Line 16: 'Adesto d\<omi\>ne suppli|cacionib\<us\> n\<ost\>ris:'.

Fos 31v/b/14–33r/a/5: [First Sunday in Lent] "**Do\<mi\>nica i\<n\> \<quadragesima\>**". 'Inuocauit me'.

Fos 33r/a/6–34r/a/13: [Monday, first week in Lent] "**feria secunda**". 'Sicut oc\<u\>li | seruoru\<m\>'.

Fos 34r/a/14–34v/b/19: [Tuesday, first week in Lent] **"feria tercia".** 'DOmine | refugiu<m> f<a>c<t>us es'.

Fos 34v/b/20–36r/b/21: [Ember Wednesday] **"fe<r>ia quarta q<ua>tuor tp<oru>m Int<imati>o".** 'REminiscere misera|tionu<m> tuaru<m>'.

Fos 36r/b/21–37v/b/4: [Thursday, first week in Lent] **"feria qui<n>ta Introit<us>".** 'COnfessio et p<u>lchri|tudo in co<n>spectu eius'.

Fos 37v/b/6–38v/b/29: [Ember Friday] **"Feria sexta quatuor tem|porum Introitus—:√".** 'DE necessita|tibus meis | eripe me do|mine'.

Fos 38v/b/30–40v/b/7: [Ember Saturday] **"Sabbato quatuor tp<oru>m√".** 'INtret oracio mea'.

Fos 40v/b/8–41v/a/12: [Second Sunday in Lent] **"Do<mi>nica s<e>c<un>da√".** 'REminiscere miseratio|nu<m> tuaru<m>'.

Fos 41v/a/13–42r/b/19: [Monday, second week in Lent] **"feria s<e>c<un>da√".** 'REdime me'.

Fos 42r/b/20–43r/b/2: [Tuesday, second week in Lent] **"feria tercia Int<imati>o".** 'Tibi dixit cor meu<m>'.

Fos 43r/b/3–44r/a/14: [Wednesday, second week in Lent] **"feria quarta".** 'NE derelinquas me'.

Fos 44r/a/15–45r/a/13: [Thursday, second week in Lent] **"feria v.".** 'DEus in adiu|toriu<m> meu<m>'.

Fos 45r/a/14–46r/b/5: [Friday, second week in Lent] **"fe<r>ia sexta".** 'Ego aute<m> | cum iusticia'.

Fos 46r/b/6–48r/b/2: [Saturday, second week in Lent] **"Sabbato".** 'LEx d<omi>ni'.

Fos 48r/b/3–49r/b/6: [Third Sunday in Lent] **"Do<min>ica t<er>cia".** 'Oculi mei semp<er>'.

Fos 49r/b/7–50r/b/26: [Monday, third week in Lent] **"feria s<e>c<un>da√".** 'IN deo laudabo'.

Fos 50r/b/27–51r/b/5: [Tuesday, third week in Lent] **"feria tercia√".** 'Ego clamaui q<uonia>m exau|disti me'.

Fos 51r/b/5–52r/b/15: [Wednesday, third week in Lent] **"feria quarta√".** 'EGo aute<m> in d<omi>no spe|raui'.

Fos 52r/b/16–53r/a/23: [Thursday, third week in Lent] **"feria <quint>a".** 'SAlus p<o>p<u>li ego | su<m>'.

Fos 53r/a/24–54v/b/16: [Friday, third week in Lent] **"feria <sext>a".** 'FAc mecu<m>'.

Fos 54v/b/17–57r/a/4: [Saturday, third week in Lent] **"Sabbato√".** 'VErba mea auribus | p<er>cipe'.

Fos 57r/a/5–58r/a/5: [Fourth Sunday in Lent] "**Do‹min›ica quarta**". 'LEtare ih‹e›r‹usa›l‹e›m'.

Fos 58r/a/6–59r/a/25: [Monday, fourth week in Lent] "**feria secunda Intro[itus]**". 'DEus in no‹m›i‹n›e tuo'.

Fos 59r/a/26–60r/b/12: [Tuesday, fourth week in Lent] "**feria tercia√**". 'Exaudi deus or‹ati›o‹n›e‹m› mea‹m›'.

Fos 60r/b/13–62r/a/17: [Wednesday, fourth week in Lent] "**feria√ | q‹ua›rta.**". 'DUm s‹an›c‹t›ificatus | fuero in vob‹is›'.

Fos 62r/a/17–63r/b/16: [Thursday, fourth week in Lent] "**feria qui‹n›ta**". 'LEtetur cor quere‹n›ciu‹m›'.

Fos 63r/b/17–65r/a/16: [Friday, fourth week in Lent] "**feria sexta√**". 'MEditacio cordis mei'.

Fos 65r/a/16–65v/b/31: [Saturday, fourth week in Lent] "**Sabbato√**". 'SIcientes venite ad a|quas'.

Fos 65v/b/32–67r/a/11: [Passion Sunday] "**Do‹min›ica in passione Introi[tus]**". 'IUdica me deus'.

Fos 67r/a/12–67v/b/24: [Monday in Passion Week] "**feria s‹e›c‹un›da√**". 'Miserere | michi'.

Fos 67v/b/25–69r/a/16: [Tuesday in Passion Week] "**feria tercia√**". 'Expecta | d‹omin›um viriliter age'.

Fos 69r/a/17–70r/a/23: [Wednesday in Passion Week] "**feria quarta**". 'Liberator meus'.

Fos 70r/a/24–71r/b/19: 'OMnia q‹uae› fecisti nob‹is›'.

Fos 71r/b/20–72r/a/32: [Friday in Passion Week] "**fe‹r›ia sexta√**". 'Miser‹er›e michi'.

Fos 72r/a/32–73v/b/2: [Saturday in Passion Week] "**Sabbato. Int‹imati›o**". 'IUdica me deus'.

Fos 73v/b/3–78v/b/22: [Palm Sunday] "**Do‹min›ica in ramis palmaru‹m›√**". 'Domi‹n›e ne longe facias auxilium tuu‹m›'.

Fos 78v/b/23–80v/b/21: [Monday in Holy Week] "**feria s‹e›c‹un›da√**". 'Iudica d‹omi›ne noce‹n›tes me'.

Fos 80v/b/22–84v/a/25: [Tuesday in Holy Week] "**feria tercia Int‹imati›o√**". 'NOs aute‹m› gloriari | oportet'.

Fos 84v/a/26–89v/a/6: [Wednesday in Holy Week] "**fe‹r›ia quarta**". 'IN no‹m›i‹n›e d‹omi›ni | om‹n›e genu flectatur'.

No provision for Holy Thursday, Good Friday or Holy Saturday.

Fos 89v/a/7–90r/a/29: [Easter Sunday] "**In die sancto pasche Introi[tus]**". 'REsurrexi et | adhuc tecu‹m› su‹m›'.

Fos 90r/a/30–91r/b/21: [Monday in Easter Week] "**feria s‹e›c‹un›da√**". 'Introduxit vos d‹omin›us | in terra‹m›'.

Fos 91r/b/22–92r/b/4: [Tuesday in Easter Week] "**feria tercia Inti‹mati›o**". 'Aqua sapie‹n›cie pota|uit'.

Fos 92r/b/5–93r/a/27: [Wednesday in Easter Week] "**fe‹r›ia | q‹ua›rta**". 'VEnite benedicti | p‹at›ris mei'.

Fos 93r/a/28–94r/b/4: [Thursday in Easter Week] "**fe‹r›ia quinta√**". 'VIctrice‹m› manu‹m› tua‹m›'.

Fo 94r/b/5–94v/b/23: [Friday in Easter Week] "**feria sexta√**". 'Eduxit eos | d‹omin›us in spe'.

Fos 94v/b/24–95v/b/8: [Saturday in Easter Week] "**Sabbato**". 'EDuxit d‹omin›us p‹o›p‹u›l‹u›m suu‹m›'.

Fos 95v/b/9–96r/a/26: [Octave of Easter] "**In oct‹avo› pasche√**". 'Nota q‹uod› | hac die'.

Fos 96r/a/26–97v/a/17: [First Sunday of Easter] "**Do‹min›ica prima | post pascha et d‹ies› p‹er› hebdom‹ada›√**". 'QUasi modo geniti | infantes'.

Separate readings are provided for the Wednesday and Friday of this week at fo 97r/a/14 and fo 97v/a/3 respectively.

Fos 97v/a/18–98v/b/22: [Second Sunday of Easter] "**Do‹min›ica s‹e›c‹un›da | post pascha et d‹ies› p‹er› hebdom‹ada›√**". 'MIsericordia d‹omi›ni ple|na e‹st› terra'.

A separate reading is provided for the Wednesday of this week at fo 98r/a/27.

Fos 98v/b/23–99v/a/30: [Third Sunday of Easter] "**Do‹min›ica t‹er›cia. et d‹ies› p‹er› hebdom‹ada›√**". 'JUbilate | deo'.

Separate readings are provided for the Wednesday and Friday of this week at fo 99v/a/31 and fo 100r/b/9–29 respectively.

Fos 100r/b/30–101v/a/3: [Fourth Sunday of Easter] "**CAntate | d‹omi›no canticu‹m› nouu‹m›**".

Separate readings are provided for the Wednesday and Friday of this week at fo 101r/a/24 and fo 101r/b/18 respectively.

Fos 101v/a/4–102r/a/28: [Fifth Sunday after Easter] "**Do‹min›ica qui‹n›ta√**". 'VOce‹m› iocunditatis an|nu‹n›ciate'.

Fos 102r/a/29–102v/b/31: [Rogation Days] "**Feria s‹e›c‹un›da in ro|gacio‹n›ib‹us›√**". 'Exaudiuit de | templo'.

Fos 102v/b/32–103r/b/31: [Ascension Eve] "**In vigilia ascensionis d‹omi›ni√**". 'OMnes gentes plau|dite'.

Fos 103r/b/32–104v/a/13: [Ascension Day] "**In die sancto Introitus√**". 'VIri galilei'.

A separate reading is provided for the Saturday of this week at fo 104r/b/25.

Fos 104v/a/13–105r/a/20: [Sunday after Ascension] "**Do<mini>c\a/ infra oct<ava>**". 'Exaudi d<omi>ne voce<m> mea<m>'.

No provision for Pentecost Eve.

Fos 105r/a/22–106r/1/10: [Pentecost] "**In die s<an>c<t>o | Pe<n>thecostes√**". 'SPirit<us> d<omi>ni | repleuit orbem'.

Fos 106r/a/10–106v/a/31: [Monday in Pentecost week] "**feria s<e>c<un>da√**". 'CIbauit eos ex adipe | frume<n>ti'.

Fos 106v/a/32–107r/b/15: [Tuesday in Pentecost week] "**feria tercia Introitus√**". 'ACcipite iocunditate<m> | glorie v<est>re'.

Fos 107r/b/16–108r/b/10: [Ember Wednesday] "**fe<r>ia | q<ua>rta | q<ua>tuor tp<oru>m**". 'DEus cu<m> [*sic*] | egredereris cora<m> p<o>p<u>lo | tuo'.

Fos 108r/b/11–108v/a/32: [Thursday in Pentecost week] "**fe<r>ia quinta√**". 'Totu<m> officiu<m> | sicut i<n> die sancto'. 'Illo nos igne'.

Fos 108v/b/1–109v/a/18: [Ember Friday] "**fe<r>ia sexta√**". 'REpleatur | os meu<m> laude tua'.

Fos 109v/a/19–111r/b/29: [Ember Saturday] "**Sabb<at>o | q<ua>tuor tp<oru>m**". 'KAritas dei | diffusa est in cordib<us> | vestris'.

Fos 111r/b/3–111v/b/21: "**In oct<ava> pe<n>thecost<es>**". Additional provisions for Pentecost week.

Fos 111v/b/22–112v/a/2: [Trinity Sunday] "**De sancta trinitate Introit<us>**". 'BEnedicta sit s<an>c<t>a trinitas'.

Fos 112v/a/3–113r/b/1: [Corpus Christi] "**In die venerabil<is> sacrame<n>ti**". 'CIbauit eos ex | adipe frume<n>ti'.

Note: The Proper of the Time resumes after Pentecost at fo 138r.

2 (a). *Prayers including Special Collects for Particular Masses or Seasons*

Fos 113r/b/1–113v/a/32: "**In co<m>|memoracio<n>e sancti spirit<us>√**". 'SPiritus donu<m> | repleuit orbe<m> | terraru<m>'.

Fos 113v/a/32–114r/a/16: "**De s<ancto> sp<irit>u p<rimus> lxx**". 'DUm sanctificat<us> fue<r>o | in vob<is>'.

Fos 114r/a/17–114v/a/17: "**De s<an>c<t>a cruce√**". 'NOs aut gloria<r>i oportet in cruce'.

Fos 114v/a/17–114v/b/30: "**De b<ea>ta v<ir>gine ma<r>ia in | adve<n>tu usq<ue> ad nati<ui>tate<m> d<omi>ni**". 'Rorate celi desup<er> | et nubes pluant'.

Fos 114v/b/31–115r/b/26: "**De b‹ea›ta v‹ir›gine a natiuitate | d‹omi›ni usq‹ue› ad purificacione‹m› √**". 'SAlue s‹an›c‹t›a parens | enixa puerpera | regem'.

Fos 115r/b/27–116r/a/11: "**De b‹ea›ta v‹ir›gine a festo penthe|costes usq‹ue› ad aduentu‹m› d‹omi›ni√ | Et a purificacio‹n›e usq‹ue› ad ‹quadragesimam›**". 'SAlue s‹an›c‹t›a pare‹n›s enixa | puerpera | regem'.

Fo 116r/a/11–116r/b/26: "**De b‹ea›ta | v‹ir›gine a pascha usq‹ue› ad pe‹n›the‹cost›**". 'SAlue s‹an›c‹t›a parens | enixa puerpera | regem'.

Fo 116r/b/26–116v/b/3: "**In co‹m›|me‹m›oracione b‹ea›ti Augustini p‹resbyteri›**" (fd 28 Aug.). 'IN medio ecclesie ape|ruit eu‹m›'.

Fos 116v/b/3–117r/a/32: "**Pro pace√**". 'DA pace‹m› d‹omi›ne susti|nentib‹us› te'.

Fos 117r/a/32–117v/b/11: "**P‹ro› q‹ua›cu‹m›q‹ue› tribulacio‹n›e√**". 'SAlus p‹o›p‹u›li ego sum'.

Fos 117v/b/12–118r/a/26: "**Missa pro p‹e›cc‹at›is√**". 'OMnia que fecisti no|bis d‹omi›ne'.

Fo 118r/a/26–118v/a/9: "**pro infirmo**". 'DE necessitatib‹us› meis | eripe me d‹omi›ne'.

Fo 118v/a/9–118v/b/17: "**Pro infirmo q‹ui› p‹ro›pe est | morti**". 'Om‹ni›p‹oten›s sempit‹er›ne | deus co‹n›seruator a‹n›i‹m›a‹rum›'.

Fos 118v/b/18–119r/a/24: "**De eterna sapi‹ent›ia coll‹ecta›**". 'DEus q‹ui› p‹er› coeterna‹m› ti|bi sapiencia‹m› homine‹m›'.

Fo 119r/a/24–119r/b/15: "**Generalis | collecta de o‹mn›ib‹us› sanct‹is›**". 'COncede q‹uae›s‹umus› om‹ni›p‹oten›s d‹eu›s. | ut sancta dei genitrix ma|ria'.

Fos 119r/b/16–119v/a/5: "**Item g‹e›n‹er›alis collecta**". 'COncede q‹uae›s‹umus› om‹ni›p‹oten›s d‹eu›s: | ut nos i‹n›tercessio sancte dei'.

Fo 119v/a/5–119v/a/25: "**Pro pastore**". 'Deus o‹mn›i‹u›m fideliu‹m› pastor | et rector famulu‹m› tuu‹m› | N‹omen›'.

Fos 119v/a/25–119v/b/17: "**pro rege coll‹ecta›**". 'Quesum‹us› om‹ni›p‹oten›s deus ut famulus tuus .N‹omen›'.

Fos 119v/b/17–120r/a/7: "**Coll‹ecta› | p‹ro› episcopo et pleb‹ibus›**". 'Om‹ni›p‹oten›s | sempit‹er›ne deus q‹ui› fa|cis mirabilia magna sol‹us›'.

Fo 120r/a/7–28: "**Pro semetipso coll‹e›c‹ta›**". 'Om‹ni›p‹oten›s sempit‹er›ne d‹eu›s qui | me peccatore‹m›'.

Fo 120r/a/28–120r/b/14: "**p‹ro› a‹m›ico fideli√**". 'Om‹ni›p‹oten›s sempit‹er›ne d‹eu›s mi|serere famulo tuo .N‹omen›'.

Fo 120r/b/14–120v/a/4: "**Pro pe|nite‹n›te**". 'Deus q‹ui› iustificas | impiu‹m›'.

Fo 120v/a/4–20: "**P‹ro› temptat‹i›o‹ne›**". 'Om‹ni›p‹oten›s mitissime d‹eu›s res|pice p‹ro›picius p‹re›ces n‹ost›ras'.

Fo 120v/a/20–120v/b/5: "**P‹ro› amico in tribu|lacione√**". 'Presta q‹uaesumu›s d‹omi›ne | famulo tuo .N‹omen›'.

Fo 120v/b/5–23: "**P‹ro› ‹con›gregacio‹n›e propria**". 'Familia‹m› hui‹us› cenobij q‹uaesumu›s d‹omi›ne int‹er›cedente'.

Fos 120v/b/23–121r/a/14: "**Pro | familiarib‹us›**". 'Deus qui | caritatis dona'.

Fo 121r/a/14–32: "**Pro fide spe et caritate**". 'Om‹ni›p‹oten›s sempit‹er›ne d‹eu›s qui | iusticia‹m› tue legis'.

Fo 121r/a/32–121r/b/19: "**Pro caritate coll‹ecta›**". 'Deus qui diligentib‹us› te facis cu‹n›cta p‹ro›desse:'.

Fo 121r/b/19–121v/a/3: "**Pro concor|dia fr‹atru›m**". 'Deus largitor | pacis amator cari|tatis:'.

Fo 121v/a/4–26: "**Pro hu‹m›ilitate√**". 'Deus q‹ui› | sup‹er›bis resistis'.

Fo 121v/a/27–121v/b/13: "**Pro castitate√**". 'Ure igne | sancti sp‹irit›us'.

Fos 121v/b/13–122r/a/2: "**Peticio | lac‹ri›ma‹rum›**". 'Om‹ni›p‹oten›s mitissime | deus q‹ui› sicienti populo'.

Fo 122r/a/2–15: "**Pro pluuia col‹lecta›**". 'Deus in | quo viuim‹us›'.

Fo 122r/a/15–122r/b/4: "**Pro serenitate aeris**". 'Ad te d‹omi›ne nos claman|tes'.

Fo 122r/b/4–27: "**P‹ro› iter | agentib‹us›**". 'Adesto d‹omi›ne sup|plicacio‹n›ib‹us› n‹ost›ris:'.

Fo 122r/b/27–122v/a/22: "**P‹ro› benefactorib‹us›**". 'Deus q‹ui› post baptismi | sacramentu‹m›'.

Fo 122v/a/22–122v/b/5: "**Pro aduer|sitatib‹us›**". 'Deus pacis cari|tatisq‹ue› amator et cus|tos√'.

Fo 122v/b/5–22: "**Pro familia p‹ro›pria√**". 'Defende q‹uaesumu›s d‹omi›ne b‹ea›ta ma|ria'.

Fos 122v/b/22–123/a/13: "**Pro deuotis i‹n› tri|bula‹tione›**". 'Rege q‹uaesumu›s d‹omi›ne famu|los tuos'.

Fo 123r/a/13–123r/b/16: "**Pro nimijs p‹re›ssuris**". 'Deus q‹ui› contrito‹rum› non despicis gemitu‹m›'.

Fo 123r/b/17–32: "**Contra mortalitatem**". 'Deus qui non mortem | sed penitencia‹m› desideras'.

Fo 123v/a/1–20: "**Pro salute viuoru‹m› coll‹ecta›**". 'Pretende d‹omi›ne fidelib‹us› tuis | dexteram'.

Fo 123v/a/20–123v/b/15: "**Collecta | Agūalis d‹omi›ni i‹n›noce‹n›cij p‹a›pe**". 'Cu‹n›ctis nos q‹uaesumu›s d‹omi›ne me‹n›|tis et corp‹or›is defende'.

Fos 123v/b/15–124r/a/18: "**Pro vi|uis et defu<n>ctis coll<e>c<ta> b<eati> augus<tini>**". 'O<m>nip<oten>s sempit<er>ne d<eu>s qui viuo<rum>

Fo 124r/a/18–124r/b/29: "**General<is> coll<e>c<t>a**". 'Pietate tua q<uaesumu>s domi<n>e | u<est>ro<rum> solue vincula | delictoru<m>'.

Fos 124r/b/30–128v/b/32: [Masses for the anniversary of a death] "**In a<n>niuersario et exequijs | defunctoru<m> et \in/ presencia fu|neris Introitus:** √". 'Requie<m> eternam | dona eis d<omi>ne et | lux p<er>petua luce|at eis.' At the bottom of fo 124v there is a musical stave with neums for the words 'Hostias ac preces tibi domine offerimus:'.

3. *Ordinary of the Mass (principal parts) in larger script*

Fo 129r/a/1–22: [with neums] 'Gloria i<n> excelsis d<e>o.'

Fo 129r/a/23–129r/b/22: "**De beata uirgine**". 'Gloria i<n> excelsis deo√'.

Fo 129r/b/22–28: [Gradual] "**Sacerdos lecturus eua<n>geliu<m> dicit.**" 'Dominus sit i<n> corde me|o'.

Fo 129v/a/1–129v/b/12: [Creed]. 'Credo in vnu<m> deu<m>'.

Fo 129v/b/13–28: [Offertory] "**Ad abluendas digitos**". 'Lauabo inter i<n>nocentes | manus meas'; 'Quid retribu|am d<omi>no pro om<n>ibus que | retribuit michi Calicem | salutatis accipia<m> et [in] nom<in>e | d<omi>ni i<n>uocabo In spiritu humilitatis'.

Fos 129v/b/28–130r/a/6: "**Benedic vtru<m>q<ue>** √". 'Ueni i<n>uisibilis sancti|ficator'.

Fo 130r/a/6–27: "**Hic inclinet se** √". 'SUscipe s<an>c<t>a trinitas'.

Fo 130r/a/28–130r/b/6: "**Hic v<er>tat se ad populum**". 'Orate pro me p<e>cc<at>ore fr<at>res'.

Fo 130r/b/7–130v/a/10: [Christmas] "**P<re>facio de natiuitate d<omi>ni**". 'PEr o<mn>ia s<æ>c<u>la s[æ]c[u]lo<rum> [...] Vere dignu<m> et iustu<m> e<st>'.

Fo 130v/a/11–130v/b/9: [Epiphany] "**De epyphania do<mini>** √". Vere dignu<m> et iustu<m> | est'.

Fo 130v/b/10–28: [Lent] "**De ieiunio prefa<ci>o** √". 'Vere dignu<m> et iustu<m> e<st>'.

Fos 130v/b/28–131r/b/28: [Easter] "**De resurrect<i>o<n>e**". 'VEre dignu<m> et iustu<us> [*sic*] e<st> equu<m> et salutare. Te quide<m> d<omi>ne'.

Fo 131r/b/28–131v/b/28: [Ascension] "**De ascensio<n>e**". 'VEre dignu<m> et iustu<m> | e<st>'. Ends incomplete 'Thome Iacobi Philippi [Bartholomei Matthei]'.

Fos 132r/a/1–137v/b/17 [in larger script] Canon of the Mass. 'Te igitur cleme<n>tis|sime pater p<er> ih<esu>m | cristu<m> filiu<m> tuum'. Ends:

'Celes|ti benedictio‹n›e be|nedicat nos + | pater et + filius. | et spiritus + sa‹n›|ctus. Amen.' Neums are provided in the bottom margin for 'PEr omnia \secula/ seculorum. PAx C‹hristi› domini.' (fo 135v); 'sit sem+per per vo+ biscum:-' (fo 136r).

2 (b). *Proper of the Time resuming* (from fo 113r) *after Pentecost*

Fo 138r/a/1–138v/b/8: [First Sunday after Pentecost] "**Dominica p‹ri›ma post octa|uas penthecos‹tum›**". 'DOmi‹n›e i‹n› tua | misericordia | speraui'.

Fos 138v/b/8–32, 140r/a/1–140v/a/3: [Second Sunday after Pentecost] "**Do‹min›ica | s‹e›c‹un›da√**". 'FActus est d‹omin›us | protector meus'.

Fos 140v/a/3–140v/b/32, 139r/a/1–139r/b/6: [Third Sunday after Pentecost] "**Do‹mini›cᵃ t‹er›tia**". 'REspice i‹n› me'.

Fos 139r/b/7–139v/b/32, 141r/a/1–8: [Fourth Sunday after Pentecost] "**Do‹min›ica | q‹ua›rta√**". 'DOmin‹us› | illu‹m›inacio mea'.

Fo 141r/a/8–141v/b/20: [Fifth Sunday after Pentecost] "**Do‹min›ica | qui‹n›ta**". 'Exaudi d‹omi›ne voce‹m› mea‹m›'.

Fos 141v/b/20–142v/a/26: [Sixth Sunday after Pentecost] "**Do‹min›ica sexta√**". 'DOmin‹us› fortitudo ple|bis sue'.

Fos 142v/a/26–142v/b/32, 144r/a/1–144r/b/24: [Seventh Sunday after Pentecost] "**Do‹min›ica vijᵃ**" 'OMnes gentes plau|dite manib‹us›'.

Fos 144r/b/25–144v/b/32, 143r/a/1–15: [Eighth Sunday after Pentecost] **Do‹mini›cᵃ viijᵃ**". 'SUscepim‹us› | deus misericordiam | tuam'.

Fo 143r/a/15–143v/b/26: [Ninth Sunday after Pentecost] "**Do‹mini›cᵃ | no|na**". 'ECce deus adiuuat | me'.

Fos 143v/b/26–32, 145r/a/1–145v/a/25: [Tenth Sunday after Pentecost] "**Do‹min›ica | xᵃ**". 'DUm [*sic*] clamare‹m› ad d‹omin›um'.

Fos 145v/a/25–146r/b/26: [Eleventh Sunday after Pentecost] "**Do‹mini›cᵃ vndeci‹m›a**". 'DEus in loco s‹an›cto suo'.

Fos 146r/b/26–147r/a/22: [Twelfth Sunday after Pentecost] "**Do‹mini›cᵃ xijᵃ**". 'DEus i‹n› adiutoriu‹m› me|u‹m› i‹n›tende'.

Fos 147r/a/22–148r/a/23: [Thirteenth Sunday after Pentecost] "**Do‹mini›cᵃ terciadeci‹m›a**". 'REspice d‹omi›ne in testa|mentu‹m› tuu‹m›'.

Fo 148r/a/23–148v/b/22: [Fourteenth Sunday after Pentecost] "**Do‹mini›cᵃ xiiijᵃ**". 'Protector n‹oste›r aspice'.

Fos 148v/b/22–149v/b/18: [Fifteenth Sunday after Pentecost] "**Do‹mini›cᵃ xvᵃ√**". 'INclina d‹omi›ne aurem | tua‹m› ad me'.

Fos 149v/b/18–150v/a/18: [Sixteenth Sunday after Pentecost] "**Do‹min›ica xviᵃ Int‹imati›o**". 'Misere‹re› michi d‹omi›ne q‹uonia›m | ad te clamaui'.

Fos 150v/a/18–151r/b/26: [Seventeenth Sunday after Pentecost] "**Do‹min›ica xvij√**". 'Iustus es d‹omi›ne et rectum | iudiciu‹m› tuu‹m›'.

Fos 151r/b/27–152v/b/16: [Ember Wednesday in Sept.] "**feria q‹ua›rta q‹ua›tuor tempo‹rum›√**". 'EXultate deo adiu|tori n‹ost›ro'.

Fos 152v/b/17–153v/a/20: [Ember Friday in Sept.] "**feria sexta Introit‹us›√**". 'LEtetur cor quere‹n›ciu‹m› | d‹omin›um'.

Fos 153v/a/20–155v/b/26: [Ember Saturday in Sept.] "**Sabbato√**". 'Uenite adorem‹us› deu‹m›'.

Fos 155v/b/26–156v/a/11: [Eighteenth Sunday after Pentecost] "**Do‹mini›c^a xviij^a√**". 'DA pacem d‹omi›ne'.

Fos 156v/a/12–157r/a/30: [Nineteenth Sunday after Pentecost] "**Do‹min›ica xix√**". 'SAlus p‹o›p‹u›li | ego sum'.

Fos 157r/a/31–158r/a/6: [Twentieth Sunday after Pentecost] "**Do‹min›ica xx^a Int‹imati›o√**". 'Omnia que fecisti nob‹is›'.

Fo 158r/a/7–158v/b/8: [Twenty-first Sunday after Pentecost] "**Do‹mini›c^a xxi^a√**". 'IN volu‹n›tate | tua d‹omi›ne'.

Fos 158v/b/8–159v/a/17: [Twenty-second Sunday after Pentecost] "**Do‹mini›c^a xxij^a√**". 'Si iniquitates obser|uaueris d‹omi›ne'.

Fos 159v/a/17–160v/b/11: [Twenty-third Sunday after Pentecost] "**Do‹mini›c^a xxiij^a√ ‹vel› p‹ro›xime ad[ventus]**". 'DIcit d‹omin›us ego cogito co|gitaciones pacis'. With additional readings for extra Sundays after Pentecost depending on the date of the preceding Easter.

Fos 160v/b/12–161v/b/32: [Passion of Our Lord] "**Missa de passione d‹omi›ni et ei‹us› | vulneribus√**". 'HUmiliauit semetip|su‹m› d‹omin›us n‹oste›r ih‹esu›s ‹Christus› | usq‹ue› ad morte‹m›'.

Collect: 'D‹omi›ne ih‹es›u ‹Christe› fili dei viui | qui de celis ad terra‹m›'

Reading: Zacchariah: 'HEc dicit d‹omin›us d‹eu›s. Effu‹n›|dam de sp‹irit›u meo sup‹er› domum | dauid'.

Aue rex n‹oste›r tu sol‹us› n‹ost›ros miseratus errores p‹at›ri | obediens duct‹us› es ad cruce‹m›.

Sequence: 'AUe ih‹es›u ‹Christe› q‹ui› pro hu|mana salute de maria v‹ir›gi‹n›e| nasci voluisti'.

Reading: John: 'IN ill‹o tempore› Sciens ih‹esu›s q‹ui›a ia‹m› o‹mn›ia | co‹n›su‹m›mata era‹n›t'.

Secret: 'D‹omi›ne ih‹es›u ‹Christe› q‹ui› pro mu‹n›di | rede‹m›pcione crucis lignu‹m› asce‹n›|disti'.

Compl‹endum›: 'D‹omi›ne ih‹es›u ‹Christe› fili dei viui | qui hora diei sexta p‹er› r‹e›demp|cione mu‹n›di crucis patibulu‹m› ascendisti'.

4. Proper of the Saints

Fos 162r/a/1–163v/a/32: [St Andrew the apostle, 30 Nov.] 'DOmin‹us› | secus | mare | galilee | vidit du|os fr‹at›res | petru‹m› et | andrea‹m›'.

Fos 163v/b/1–164r/b/26: [St Barbara, 4 Dec.] "**barbare v‹ir›gi‹ne›**√". 'LOque|bar de testimonijs | tuis in co‹n›spectu regu‹m›'.

Fo 164r/b/27–164v/a/18: [Octave of St Andrew, 7 Dec.] "**In oct‹ave› s andree**". 'Domin‹us› secus | mare.'

Fo 164v/a/18–31: [Immaculate Conception of the Blessed Virgin Mary, 8 Dec.] "**In co‹n›cepcione b‹ea›te | ma‹r›ie v‹ir›g‹ine›**". 'Gl‹ori›a i‹n› excelsis d‹eo›'.

Fo 164v/a/32–164v/b/19: [St Damasus, pope, 11 Dec.] "**Damasi pape et co‹n›f‹essione› coll‹e›c‹t›a**". 'MIsericordia‹m› tua‹m› nobis q‹uaesumu›s d‹omi›ne'.

Fos 164v/b/20–165r/a/26: [St Lucy, 13 Dec.] "**lucie v‹ir›ginis**". 'Dilexisti | iusticia‹m› et odisti | iniquitate‹m›'.

Fo 165r/a/27–165v/b/6: [Vigil and feast-day of St Thomas the apostle, 21 Dec.] "**In vigilia s‹an›cti thome ap‹osto›li**√". 'Ego aut‹em› p‹er› totu‹m› sicut i‹n› | vigilia vnius ap‹osto›li√ **ccxvi**', a reference to the introit for masses for any one apostle beginning 'Ego aut‹em› sicut oliua fructificaui', which occurs on fo 226r/a/1, i.e., the leaf numbered 'ccxvi' by the scribe.

Fo 165v/b/7–25: [St Thomas Becket, 29 Dec.] "**Thome ep‹isco›pi et m‹arty›ris collecta**√". 'DEus p‹ro› cui‹us› ecclesia | gloriosus pontifex | thomas'.

Fos 165v/b/26–166r/b/3: [St Silvester, pope, 31 Dec.] "**Siluestri pap^e**". 'SAcerdo|tes tui d‹omi›ne indua‹n›t | iusticia‹m›'.

Fo 166r/b/4–166v/a/6: [St Pontianus, pope, 19 Nov.] "**Ponciani M‹arty›ris**". 'DEus q‹ui› | nos beati ponciani | m‹arty›ris tui co‹n›cedis'. Presumably placed here because his feast-day was (erroneously) thought to be in early January.

Fo 166v/a/6–166v/b/19: [St Marcellus, pope, 16 Jan.] "**Marcelli pa|pe et m‹arty›ris**". 'STatuit ei | d‹omin›us testamentum | pacis'.

Fos 166v/b/19–167r/a/32: [St Prisca, 18 Jan.] "**Prisce | v‹ir›ginis**". 'Loquebar | de testimonijs tuis | in co‹n›spectu regu‹m›'.

Fo 167r/b/1–19: [SS Marius and Martha, 19 Jan.] "**Marij et marthe m‹arty›r‹u›m**". 'Exaudi d‹omi›ne p‹o›p‹u›l‹u›m tuu‹m›'.

Fo 167r/b/20–167v/b/23: [SS Fabian and Sebastian, 20 Jan.] "**fabiani et sebastiani**". 'INtret in co‹n›sp‹e›c‹t›u tuo'.

Fos 167v/b/24–168r/b/8: [St Agnes, 21 Jan.] "**Agnetis v‹ir›g‹inis›**". 'ME expec|taueru‹n›t p‹e›cc‹at›ores'.

Fo 168r/b/9–168v/a/17: [St Vincent, 22 Jan.] "**Vince‹n›cij m‹arty›ris**". 'LEtabit‹ur› | iustus i‹n› d‹omi›no'.

Fo 168v/a/17–168v/b/2: [SS Emerentiana, 23 Jan. and Macarius the Elder, normally 15 Jan.] "**Emere‹n›ciane et | macharij**". 'Maiestati | tue nos d‹omi›ne'.

Fos 168v/b/3–169v/b/31: [Conversion of St Paul, 25 Jan.] "**In co‹n›uersione sancti pauli**". 'SCio cui credidi'.

Fos 169v/b/32–170r/b/13: [Octave of St Agnes, 28 Jan.] "**In octaue s‹an›c‹t›e agnetis int‹troit›o**". 'Uultu‹m› tuu‹m› deprecabunt‹ur›'.

Fo 170r/b/14–170v/a/31: [St Ignatius, 1 Feb.] "**Ignacij e‹pisco›pi et m‹arty›ris√**". 'SAcerdotes tui d‹omi›ne'.

Fos 170v/a/31–171v/a/24: [Purification of the Blessed Virgin Mary = Candlemas, 2 Feb.] "**In purificacione | beate marie virginis. Int‹roit›o**". 'SUscepim‹us› d‹eu›s mi|sericordia‹m› tua‹m›'. Begins with floriated purple S.

Fos 171v/a/24–172r/a/3: [St Blaise, 3 Feb.] "**blasij | m‹arty›ris√**". 'Os iusti medi|tabit‹ur› sapiencia‹m›'.

Fo 172r/a/3–172r/b/18: [St Agatha, 5 Feb.] "**Aghate virginis**". 'Gaudeam‹us› om‹n›es i‹n› d‹omi›no'.

Fos 172r/b/18–172v/a/29: [St Valentine, 14 Feb.] "**Valentini m‹arty›r‹is›**". 'IN virtute tua d‹omi›ne'.

Fos 172v/a/30–173v/a/9: [St Peter's Chair at Antioch, 22 Feb.] "**Cathedra s‹an›c‹t›i petri ap‹osto›li**". 'STatuit ei d‹omin›us testa|mentu‹m› pacis'.

Fos 173v/a/9–174r/b/24: [St Matthias, apostle, 24 Feb.] "**In vigilia s. mathie.**", line 12 "**In die sancto**". 'IUdica‹n›t | sancti gentes'.

Fo 174r/b/25–174v/b/20: [St Gregory the Great, 12 Mar.] "**Gregorij pape Intro**". 'SAcerdotes dei benedicite d‹omi›no'.

Fos 174v/b/20–175r/a/10: [St Gertrude of Nivelles, 17 Mar.] "**Gertrudis v‹ir›g‹inis›**". 'Crescat d‹omine› semp‹er›'.

Fo 175r/a/10–175r/b/26: [St Joseph, 19 Mar.] "**Ioseph nutri|cij d‹omi›ni√**". 'Os iusti medi|tabit‹ur›'.

Fo 175r/b/26–175v/a/32: [St Benedict, 21 Mar.] "**Benedicti abb‹atis›**". 'IUstus ut palma flo|rebit'.

Fos 175v/b/1–176r/b/1: [Annunciation of the Blessed Virgin Mary, 25 Mar.] "**In a‹n›nu‹n›ciacione d‹omi›nica Intro**". 'ROrate celi desu|p‹er› et nubes plu|ant'. Begins with floriated purple R.

Fo 176r/b/1–176v/b/2: [St Ambrose, normally 7 Dec.] "**Ambrosij | e‹pisco›pi et co‹n›f‹essoris›**". 'SAcerdotes dei | benedicite d‹omi›no'.

Fos 176v/b/3–177r/a/10: [SS Tiburtius and Valerian, 14 Apr.] "**Tyburcij et valeriani m‹arty›r‹oru›m**". 'SAncti tui d‹omi›ne b‹e›n‹e›di|cent te'.

Fo 177r/a/11–177r/b/15: [St George, 23 Apr.] "**Georgij m‹arty›ris√ Introi|t‹us›√**". 'Protexisti me deus'.

Fo 177r/b/16–177v/a/20: [St Mark, 25 Apr.] "**Marci eua‹n›geliste Introit‹us›**". 'Protexisti me deus'.

Fos 177v/a/21–178r/a/3: [Translation of St Lambert's remains to Liège, 31 May] "**Translacio sa‹n›cti lamberti√**". 'Protexisti me d‹eu›s.' At some anterior stage this item was probably inserted into an existing Missal, as it is somewhat out of sequence.

Fos 178r/a/3–179r/a/6: [SS Philip and James, apostles, 11 May] "**Philippi et iaco|bi ap‹osto›lo‹rum›√**". 'Exclamauer‹un›t | ad te d‹omi›ne'. This item is also out of sequence.

Fos 179r/a/7–180r/b/1: [Finding of the Holy Cross, normally 3 May] "**In i‹n›uencione sancte crucis√**". 'NOs aut‹em› gloriari | oportet in cruce'. Begins with plain blue **N**.

Fos 180r/b/2–181r/a/20: [St Monica, widow, 4 May] "**In festo s‹an›c‹t›e monice vidue Int‹roit›o**". 'GAudeam‹us› o‹mn›es | in d‹omi›no'.

Fo 181r/a/20–181r/b/28: [St John before the Latin Gate, 6 May] "**Ioha‹n›nis ante por|ta‹m› latina‹m›**'. 'In medio ecclesie | aperuit os eius'.

Fo 181r/b/29–181v/a/32: [SS Gordian and Epimachus, 10 May] "**Gordiani et epymjachi Int‹roit›o√**". 'SAncti tui d‹omi›ne bene|dice‹n›t te'.

Fos 181v/b/1–182r/a/15: [SS Nereus and Achilleus, and Pancras, 12 May] "**Nerei achillei atq‹ue› pancracij**". 'Ecce oculi d‹omi›ni sup‹er› me|tuentes eu‹m›√' (usual reading 'timentes').

Fo 182r/a/15–182v/a/7: [St Servatius, bp of Tongeren, 13 May] "**Seruacij e|piscopi**". 'Protexisti me d‹eu›s'. [celebrated in Tongeren (just north of Liège), Maastricht and Worms]

Fo 182v/a/8–182v/b/27: [St Urban, pope and martyr, 25 May] "**Urbani e‹pisco›pi et m‹arty›ris√**". 'Protexisti me deus'.

Fos 182v/b/28–183r/a/31: [SS Marcellinus and Peter, 2 June, in Paschal Time] "**Marcellini et petri an‹te› pen‹tecoste›**". 'SAncti tui d‹omi›ne bene|dice‹n›t te'.

Fo 183r/a/32–183r/b/24: [SS Marcellinus and Peter, 2 June, out of Paschal Time] "**Marcellini et petri p‹rimus› penth‹ecoste›**". 'Clamaueru‹n›t iusti et do|min‹us› exaudiuit eos√'.

Fo 183r/b/25–183v/b/16: [St Boniface, 5 June] "**¶ Si an‹te› penthecost‹e› vene|rit totu‹m› officiu‹m› ut s‹upra› gordi|ani et epymachi** [= fo 181]". Fo 183r/b/32 "**Post octauas pe‹n›thecostes√**". 'Multi tribulaciones ius|toru‹m›'.

Fos 183v/b/17–184r/a/24: [SS Primus and Felician, 9 June] "**Primi et feliciani Introit<us>**√". 'SApiencia<m> iustoru<m> nar|rant p<o>p<u>li√'.

Fo 184r/a/25–184r/b/31: [St Barnabas, 11 June, in Paschal Time] "**barnabe ap<osto>li an<te> penthecos<te>**". 'Protexisti me deus'.

Fo 184r/b/32–184v/a/23: [St Barnabas, 11 June, out of Paschal Time] "**barnabe ap<osto>li p<rimus> penthecos<te>**". 'Michi aute<m> nimis hono|rati su<n>t'.

Fo 184v/a/23–184v/b/30: [St Odolphus, 12 June] "**Odulphi co<n>f<essoris>**". 'Exaudi d<omi>ne p<re>ces n<ost>ras'.

Fos 184v/b/30–185r/b/10: [SS Vitus and Modestus, 15 June] "**Viti et modesti√**". 'Laudate pueri d<omin>um√'.

Fo 185r/b/11–185v/a/19: [SS Mark and Marcellian, 18 June] "**Marci et marcelliani m<arty>r<u>m**". 'SAlus aut iustoru<m> a | d<omi>no'.

Fo 185v/a/20–185v/b/29: [SS Gervase and Protase, 19 June] "**Geruasij et prothasij m<arty>r<u>m√**". 'Loquetur d<omin>us pacem'.

Fos 185v/b/30–186v/b/18: [Vigil of St John the Baptist, 23 June] "**In vigilia s<an>c<t>i ioh<ann>is bap<tiste>**". 'Ne temeas zacharia'.

Fos 186v/b/19–187v/a/31: [Birthday of St John the Baptist, 24 June] "**In die sancto Int<roit>o**". 'DE ventre m<at>ris | mee vocauit me | d<omin>us'. A blue capital is used for the Post-communion prayer 'SUmat eccl<es>ia tua' at fo 187v/a/26, perhaps in error.

Fos 187v/a/32–188r/a/17: [SS John and Paul, martyrs, 26 June] "**Joha<n>nis et pauli m<arty>r<u>m Int<roit>o**". 'MUlte tribulaciones ius|toru<m>'.

Fos 188r/a/18–189r/a/31: [Vigil of SS Peter and Paul, 28 June] "**In vigilia ap<osto>lo<rum> petri et pauli**". 'Dicit d<omin>us petro'.

Fo 189r/a/32–189v/b/30: [SS Peter and Paul, 29 June] "**In die sancto Introitus√**". 'NUnc scio vere | q<ui>a'. The beginning of this mass is marked by a large blue initial ornamented with purple flourishing.

Fos 189v/b/30–190v/a/15: [Commemoration of St Paul, 30 June] "**In co<m>memoracio<n>e s<an>c<t>i pauli√**". 'Scio cui credidi et certus su<m>√'.

Fos 190v/a/16–191r/b/7: [Octave of St John the Baptist, Visitation of the Blessed Virgin Mary, 2 July] "**In oct<aue> s<an>c<t>i ioha<n>nis√ O<mn>ia sicut | in die√ In visitacio<n>e b<eate> ma<r>ie v<irginis>**". 'GAudeam<us> o<mn>es | in d<omi>no'. This feast was established in 1389. Large purple initial ornamented with purple flourishing to mark the beginning of the mass.

Fos 191r/b/8–192r/a/17: [Translation of St Martin of Tours, 4 July] "**In tranlacio<n>e s<an>c<t>i martini e<pisco<pi | et co<n>fessor<is> Coll<e>c<t>a√** Secreta et Co<m>plenda ut i<n> alio ei<us> festo | **In oct<aue> ap<osto>loru<m> petri et pauli√**" 'SApiencia<m> s<an>c<t>o<ru<m> narra<n>t | p<o>p<u>li√'.

Fo 192r/a/18–192v/a/8: [Seven Holy Brothers, 10 July] "**In oct<aue> visitacio<n>is**√ O<mn>ia sic<ut> | in die√ **Septem fr<atru>m**√". 'LAudate pueri d<omin>um√'.

Fos 192v/a/8–193r/b/11: [St Margaret, 20 July] "**Margarete v<ir>gi<nis>**√". 'Dilexisti iusticia<m> et odis|ti iniq<ui>tate<m>.'

Fo 193r/b/11–29: [St Arnulf, bp of Metz, d. 18 July, fd 19 Aug.] "**Arnulphi e<pisco>pi**√". 'Exaudi q<uaesumu>s d<omi>ne preces | n<ost>ras:'.

Fo 193r/b/29–193v/b/4: [St Praxedes, 21 July] "**Praxedis v<ir>ginis**√". 'LOquebar de testimo|nijs tuis'.

Fos 193v/b/5–194r/a/16: [St Mary Magdalen, 22 July] "**Marie magdalene**√". 'GAudeam<us> om<n>es in do|mino'.

Fo 194r/a/16–194r/b/27: [St Apollinaris, 23 July] "**Appollinaris | martyris**". 'SAcerdotes dei | benedicite d<omi>no√ [*sic*]'.

Fo 194r/b/28–195r/a/20: [St James the Great, 25 July] "**In vigilia sancti iacobi ap<osto>li**√ | Ego aute<m> p<er> totu<m>√ **In die s<an>c<t>o**√". 'Michi aute<m> nimis ho|norati su<n>t'.

Fo 195r/a/21–195v/b/11: [St Anne, mother of the Blessed Virgin Mary, 26 July] "**Anne matris marie Introit<us>**". 'GAudeam<us> om<n>es | in d<omi>no die<m> festu<m> | celebra<n>tes'.

Fo 195v/b/21–35: [St Pantaleon, 27 July] "**Pantha|leonis m<arty>ris**" 'ADesto d<omi>ne supplicationib<us> n<ost>ris:'.

Fos 195v/b/36–196r/b/21: [SS Felix, Simplicius, Faustinus and Beatrice, 29 July] "**felicis simplicij et aliorum**√". 'SAcerdotes eius indua<n>t | salutare'.

Fo 196r/b/22–196v/b/5: [SS Abdon and Sennen, 30 July] "**INtret in co<n>spectu tuo**'.

Fos 196v/b/5–197r/a/27: [St Peter's Chains, 1 Aug.] "**Ad vi<n>cula s. petri**". 'Nvnc scio vere q<ui>a mi|sit d<omin>us angelu<m> suu<m>'.

Fo 197r/a/27–197v/a/6: [St Stephen, pope, 2 Aug.] "**Stephani p<a>pe et m<artyris>**". 'SAcerdotes tui d<omi>ne indu|ant iusticia<m>'.

Fo 197v/a/7: [The finding of the body of St Stephen, 3 Aug.] "**In i<n>uencio<n>e s<an>c<t>i stephani p<ro>th<omartyris>**". [1st martyr]

Fo 197v/a/10–26: [St Dominic, 4 Aug.] "**Dominici confessoris**√". 'Deus qui ecclesia<m> tuam'.

Fo 197v/a/26–198v/a/6: [The Transfiguration of Our Lord, 6 Aug.] "**In transfi|guracio<n>e d<omi>ni**". 'In excelso | throno vidi'.

Fos 198v/a/6–199r/a/16: [St Sixtus, pope and martyr, 6 Aug.] "**Sixti p<a>pe | et m<arty>ris**√". 'SAcerdotes dei | b<e>n<e>dicite d<omi>no'.

Fo 199r/a/16–199v/a/6: [SS Cyriacus, Largus and Smaragdus, 8 Aug.] "**Cyriaci et socio<rum> ei<us>**". 'TImete d<omin>um'.

Fo 199v/a/6–199v/b/14: [Vigil of St Laurence, 9 Aug.] "**In vi|gilia sancti laurencij√**". 'DIsp<er>sit dedit pauperib<us>'.

Fos 199v/b/14–200r/b/8: [St Laurence, 10 Aug.] "**In die sancto√**". 'COnfessio et pulchri|tudo'.

Fo 200r/b/9–200v/a/13: [St Tiburtius, 11 Aug.] "**Tyburcij m<arty>ris Int<ro>it<us>**". 'IUstus ut palma flore|bit sicut cedrus libani'.

Fo 200v/a/14–220v/b/18: [St Hyppolytus, 13 Aug.] "**Ypoliti m<arty>ris et socio<rum> ei<us>**". 'IUsti epulent<ur> et exulte<n>t | in conspectu dei'.

Fos 200v/b/18–201r/b/21: [Vigil of the Assumption of the Blessed Virgin Mary, 14 Aug.] "**In vigi|lia assu<m>pcio<n>is beate marie | virginis√**". 'SAlue sancta parens'.

Fos 201r/b/22–202r/a/18: [Assumption of the Blessed Virgin Mary, 15 Aug.] "**In die sancto√**". 'GAudeam<us> om<n>es | in d<omi>no diem | festu<m> celebran|tes'.

Fo 202r/a/18–202r/b/12: [Octave of St Laurence, 17 Aug.] "**In octa<vi> | s<an>c<t>i laurencij√**". 'Probasti | d<omi>ne cor meu<m>'.

Fo 202r/b/12–202v/a/19: [St Agapitus, 18 Aug.] "**Agapiti m<arty>ris Int<roito>**". 'Lætabitur iustus in d<omi>no'.

Fo 202v/a/19–202v/b/1: [St Magnus of Cuneo, 19 Aug.] "**Magni m<arty>ris√**". 'Adesto d<omi>ne supplicacio|nib<us> n<ost>ris√'.

Fos 202v/b/1–203r/a/9: [St Bernard, 20 Aug.] "**Bernardi ab<bati>**". 'Os iusti meditabitur | sapiencia<m>√".

Fo 203r/a/9–27: [Octave of the Assumption of the Blessed Virgin Mary, 22 Aug.] "**In oct<avo> assu<m>pcionis O<mn>ia sic<ut> | in die√ Eode<m> die collecta√**". 'Auxiliu<m> tuu<m> nob<is> d<omi>ne'.

Fo 203r/a/28–203v/a/29: [St Bartholomew, 24 Aug.] "**In vigilia b<ea>ti barthomomei√ | Ego autem√** p<er> totu<m> ut in vigilia vnius ap<osto>li√ **cc xvi√** [a reference forward to fo 226] **| In die sancto Introitus√**". 'MIchi aute<m> nimis hono|rati su<n>t'.

Fos 203v/a/31–204r/b/25: [St Augustine, 28 Aug.] "**In natali sancti Augustini | episcopi p<at>ris nostri Int<ro>it<us>**". 'IN medio eccl<es>ie | aperuit os eius".

Fos 204r/b/26–205r/b/26: [Beheading of St John the Baptist, 29 Aug.] "**In decollacione s. ioh<ann>is bap<tiste>√**". 'IN v<ir>tute tua d<omi>ne letabitur | iustus√'.

Fo 205r/b/27–205v/b/5: [SS Felix and Adauctus, 30 Aug.] "**felicis et adaucti martyru<m>√**". 'Sapi<enti>am sancto<rum> nar|rant p<o>p<u>li'.

Fo 205v/b/5–6: [Octave of St Augustine, 4 Sept.] "**In oct<avi> | s<an>cti augusti<ni>√**". 'O<mn>ia sic<ut> in die√'.

Fos 205v/b/7–206v/a/21: [Birthday of the Blessed Virgin Mary, 8 Sept.] "**In natiuitate b\<ea\>te marie v\<ir\>g\<inis\>**√". 'GAudeam\<us\> o\<mn\>es | in d\<omi\>no diem | festu\<m\>'.

Fo 206v/a/22–206v/b/26: [St Gorgon, 9 Sept.] "**Gorgonij martyris**√". 'Gloria et ho\<no\>re coronas|ti eu\<m\>√'.

Fos 206v/b/26–207r/a/29: [SS Protus and Hyacinth, 11 Sept.] "**Prothi et iacincti**". 'IUdicant sancti gentes et | d\<omi\>nantur p\<o\>p\<u\>lis√'.

Fo 207r/a/29–207v/b/20: [Exaltation of the Cross, 14 Sept.] "**In exaltacione s. | crucis**√". 'NOs autem | gloriari oportet'.

Fos 207v/b/21–2: [Octave of Birthday of the Blessed Virgin Mary, 15 Sept.] "**In oct\<avi\> b\<ea\>te marie**". 'Om\<n\>ia ut supra in die√'.

Fos 207v/b/23–208r/a/5: [St Nicomedes, 15 Sept.] "**Eodem die nycomedis m\<arty\>ris**". 'Adesto d\<omi\>ne p\<o\>p\<u\>lo tuo:'.

Fo 208r/a/6–208r/b/4: [SS Lucy and Geminianus, 16 Sept.] "**lucie et geminiani coll\<ecta\>**". 'Pr\<aest\>a d\<omi\>ne precib\<us\> n\<ost\>ris'.

Fos 208r/b/5–209v/b/15: [St Lambert, 17 Sept.] "**lamberti e\<pisco\>pi et m\<arty\>ris√ Introit\<us\>**". 'GAudeamus | o\<mn\>es in d\<omi\>no | diem festum'.

Fos 209v/b/15–210r/a/28: [St Maurice and companions, 22 Sept.] "**Mauricij et socio|ru\<m\> ei\<us\>**". 'Multe tribulacio\<n\>es | iustor\<um\>'.

Fo 210r/a/28–9: [Octave of St Lambert, 24 Sept.] "**In oct\<avi\> sancti | lamberti**√". 'Om\<n\>ia ut s\<upra\> in die√'.

Fo 210r/a/30–210v/a/6: [SS Cosmas and Damian, 27 Sept.] "**Cosme et damiani**√". 'Sapiencia\<m\> sancto\<rum\> nar|rant p\<o\>p\<u\>li√'.

Fos 210v/a/7–211r/b/15: [St Michael the Archangel, 29 Sept.] "**Michaelis archangeli Int\<roit\>o**". 'BEnedicite d\<omi\>no o\<m\>|nes angeli'.

Fo 211r/b/15–211v/a/26: [St Jerome, 30 Sept.] "**Jheronimi p\<res\>b\<yte\>ri | et doctoris**√". 'Os iusti | meditabit\<ur\>'.

Fos 211v/a/27–212r/a/4: [St Remigius, 1 Oct.] "**Remigii et aliorum**". 'SAcerdotes dei b\<e\>n\<e\>dicite | d\<omi\>no√'.

Fo 212r/a/4–212r/b/14: [St Leodegar/Leger, 2 Oct.] "**leodegarij e\<pisco\>pi et | m\<arty\>ris**". 'Letabitur iustus | in d\<omi\>no'.

Fo 212r/b/15–30: [St Francis, 4 Oct.] "**francisci co\<n\>fessor\<is\>**". 'DEus | qui eccl\<es\>iam tua\<m\>'.

Fo 212r/b/31–212v/b/23: [St Mark, pope, 7 Oct.] "**Marci p\<a\>pe**√". 'SAcerdotes | dei benedicite d\<omi\>no√'.

Fos 212v/b/23–213r/b/24: [SS Dionysius and companions, 9 Oct.] "**Dyonisij et socio\<rum\> eius**". 'SAlus aute\<m\> iusto\<rum\> a | d\<omi\>no√'.

Fo 213r/b/24–213v/b/1: [St Gereon, 10 Oct.] "**Gereonis victoris et so[cii]**". 'MVlte tribulacio‹n›es ius|tor‹um›√'.

Fo 213v/b/2–4: [Translation of St Augustine] "**In translacio‹n›e s. augustini√**". 'Totu‹m› officiu‹m› sic‹ut› i‹n› natali ei‹us› | folio **c** xciiij√'.

Fo 213v/b/4–214r/a/7: [St Callistus, 14 Oct.] "**Calixti pape**". 'SAcerdotes tui d‹omi›ne in|duant'.

Fo 214r/a/8–24: [St Gall, 16 Oct.] "**Galli abbatis coll‹ec›ta√**". 'DEus qui nos b‹ea›ti galli | confessoris tui'.

Fo 214r/25–214v/a/32: [St Luke, 18 Oct.] "**luce eua‹n›geliste**". 'Os iusti | meditabit‹ur› sapiencia‹m›√'.

Fos 214v/b/1–215r/a/15: [11,000 virgins, 21 Oct.] "**Vndeci‹m› miliu‹m› v‹ir›giniu‹m›**". 'Gaudeam‹us› om‹n›es in | d‹omi›no | diem festum'.

Fo 215r/a/15–215r/b/26: [Severinus Boethius, 23 Oct.] "**Seuerini e‹pisco›pi√**". 'SAcerdotes dei benedicite | d‹omi›no√'.

Fo 215r/b/26–215v/a/32: [SS Crispin and Crispinian, 25 Oct.] "**Crispini et cris|piani m‹arty›r‹ium›**". 'SAlus aute‹m› | iustoru‹m› a | d‹omi›no'.

Fos 215v/a/32–216r/b/20: [SS Simon and Jude, 28 Oct.] "**In vigilia symo‹n›is ‹et› iu[de]**". 'Intret in conspectu tuo d‹omi›ne'. Fo 216r/a/12 "**In die sancto√**". 'MIchi aute‹m› nimis ho|norati su‹n›t'.

Fos 216r/b/20–217v/b/20: [All Saints, 1 Nov.] "**In vigilia om‹n›i s‹an›c‹t›o|rum√**". 'TImete d‹omin›um o‹mn›es s‹an›c‹t›i | eius.' Fo 217r/a/10 "**In die | s‹an›c‹t›o√**". 'GAudeam‹us› | om‹n›es in d‹omi›no | diem festum'.

Fo 217v/b/21–6: [All Souls, 2 Nov.] "**In co‹m›memoracio‹n›e a‹n›i‹m›arum√**". 'Requiem eterna‹m›√'.

Fos 217v/b/27–218r/b/8: [St Hubert, bp of Tongeren-Maastricht, 3 Nov.] "**huberti p‹ri›mi e‹pisco›pi leodi‹um›**". 'SAcerdotes tui d‹omi›ne | induant'.

Fo 218r/b/9–218v/b/26: [St Leonard, 6 Nov.] "**In solempnitate sanctissimi | leonardi confessoris Introi‹tus›**". 'GAudeam‹us› | om‹n›es in | d‹omi›no diem | festu‹m›'. Fo 218v/a/27 "**In co‹m›me‹m›oracione s. leonardi√**". 'Os iusti meditabit‹ur› sapi|encia‹m›'.

Fos 218v/b/27–219r/a/15: [St Willibrord, 7 Nov.] "**Willibrordi e‹pisco›pi et co‹n›fes[soris]**". 'COncede q‹ua›s om‹ni›p‹oten›s deus | beati willibrordi'.

Fo 219r/a/15–219r/b/29: [The Four Crowned Martyrs, 8 Nov.] "**Quatuor coro|nato‹rum›**". 'INtret in consp‹e›c‹t›u | tuo'.

Fo 219r/b/30–219v/b/3: [St Theodore, 10 Nov.] "**Theodori m‹arty›ris**". 'IN v‹ir›tute | tua d‹omi›ne letabit‹ur› iustus' [Ps 20].

Fo 219v/b/4–220r/a/24: [St Martin of Tours, 11 Nov.] "**Martini ep‹iscop›i et confessoris√**". 'STatuit ei d‹omin›us | testamentum | pacis.'

Fo 220r/a/24–220r/b/9: [St Lebuin (Liofwine), 12 Nov.] "**lebuini co‹n›|fessoris col‹lec›ta**". 'DEus qui nos | an‹n›ua b‹ea›ti lebuini | co‹n›|fessoris tui festiuitate letificas:'.

Fo 220r/b/10–11: [Octave of St Leonard, 13 Nov.] "**In octaua sa‹n›cti leonardi√**". 'O‹mn›ia sic‹ut› in die√'.

Fo 220r/b/11–220v/a/18: [St Brice (Brictio), 13 Nov.] "**Brictij co‹n›fessor‹is›**". 'IUstus ut palma florebit' [Ps 91.13].

Fo 220v/a/18–19: [Octave of St Martin, 18 Nov.] "**In octa‹ua› b‹ea›ti martini**". 'Om‹n›ia sic‹ut› i‹n› die√'.

Fo 220v/a/19–221r/a/14: [St Elizabeth, 19 Nov.] "**In sole‹m›pnita|te s‹ancte› elyzabeth√**". 'GAudeamus o‹mn›es | in d‹omi›no diem | festu‹m›'.

Fo 221r/a/15–221r/b/31: [Presentation of the Blessed Virgin Mary, 21 Nov.] "**In presentacio‹n›e b‹ea›te ma‹r›ie v‹ir›g‹inis›**". 'GAudeamus o‹mn›es | in d‹omi›no diem | festu‹m›'.

Fo 221r/b/32–221v/b/7: [St Cecily, 22 Nov.] "**Cecilie virginis et martir‹is›**". 'Loquebar de testimonijs | tuis'.

Fo 221v/b/7–222r/b/7: [St Clement, 23 Nov.] "**Cleme‹n›tis p‹a›pe et m‹artyris›**". 'Dicit d‹omin›us sermones mei'.

Fo 222r/b/7–222v/a/12: [St Chrysogonus, 24 Nov.] "**Crisigoni m‹arty›ris**". 'IUstus non conturbabitur'.

Fo 222v/a/13–222v/b/26: [St Catherine, 25 Nov.] "**katherine v‹ir›gin‹is›**". 'GAudeamus o‹mn›es | in d‹omi›no diem festu‹m›'.

Fo 222v/b/27: [Octave of St Elizabeth, 26 Nov.] "**In oct‹aua› s‹ancte› elyzab‹eth›**". 'O‹mn›ia ut in die'.

Fo 222v/b/28–223r/b/6: [St Linus, normally 23 Sept.] "**lini p‹a›pe et m‹arty›r‹is›**". 'STatuit | ei d‹omin›us testamentu‹m› pa|cis'.

5. *Common of the Saints*

Fos 223r/b/8–224v/a/30: [Dedication of a Church] "**In dedicacione ecclesie Introi‹tus›**" 'TErribilis est | locus iste' [Gen 28.17].

Fos 224v/a/31–225v/a/4: [Compassion of the Blessed Virgin Mary] "**In festo co‹m›passionis beate | marie virginis Introit‹us›√**". 'SAlue sancta | pare‹n›s co‹m›passa | sub cruce ‹Christ›o'.

Fo 225v/a/5–15: "**Post oct‹aua› penthecostes√**". 'Officiu‹m› ut s‹upra› cu‹m› g‹rad›or‹um› et co‹mmun›i se|qu‹en›tib‹us›√'.

Fo 225v/a/15–225v/b/10: "**In co‹m›memorat‹i›o‹n›e s‹an›cti | ioseph nutricij d‹omin›i**". 'O‹mn›ia sicut i‹n› | festo eius√ Folio **clxv**√ [= fo 175r] | Sed'.

Fo 225v/b/11–30: (apparently added later) [St Eligius, 1 Dec.] "**De Eligij ep‹iscop›i et co‹n›fesso‹ri› col‹lecta›**". 'DEus q‹ui› b‹ea›t‹issimu›m eligiu‹m› po‹n›tifi|cali dignitate sublimasti:'.

Fo 225v/b/30–32 no text.

6. *Votive Masses*

Fo 226r/a/1–229r/a/18: [Mass for the Holy Apostles] "**In vigilia | vnius ap‹osto›li**". 'EGo aut‹em› | sicut o|liua fr|uctifica|ui in do|mo d‹omi›ni'. Fo 226v/a/22 "**In die s‹an›c‹t›o vni‹us› ap‹osto›li**". 'MIchi aute‹m› | nimis ho|norati su‹n›t'.

Fo 229r/a/18–229v/a/4: [Mass for a martyr not a bishop] "**De vno | m‹arty›re no‹n› po‹n›tifice**". 'LEtabit‹ur› iustus | i‹n› d‹omi›no'.

Fo 229v/a/5–232r/a/5: [Mass for a bishop martyr] "**De vno m‹arty›re et pontifice√**". 'IN v‹ir›tute tua | d‹omi›ne letabitur | iustus.' [Ps 20].

Fo 232r/a/6–234r/b/5: [Mass for more martyrs] "**Plurimoru‹m› martyru‹m› Int‹roit›o√**". 'MVlte tribulaci|ones iustorum'.

Fo 234r/b/5–234v/a/26: [Mass for a bishop confessor] "**De vno | confessore et po‹n›tifice Introi[to]**". 'STatuit ei d‹omin›us | testamentu‹m› | pacis'.

Fo 234v/a/26–235r/a/13: [Mass for a confessor not a bishop] "**De vno confessore non pontifice√**". 'OS iusti meditabit‹ur› | sap‹ient›iam et li‹n›gua | eius'.

Fo 235r/a/13–235r/b/20: [Mass for an abbot] "**De vno abbate**". 'IUstus ut palma florebit' [Ps 91.13].

Fo 235r/b/21–238v/a/17: [Mass for a confessor] "**De confessorib‹us›√**". 'SAcerdotes eius in|duant salutare | et sancti eius ex|ultacione exultabu‹n›t' [Ps 131.9]

Fo 238v/a/18–239r/a/4: [Mass for a virgin martyr] "**De vna v‹ir›gine et martyre√**". 'LOquebar de tes|timonijs tuis i‹n› | co‹n›spectu regum'.

Fo 239r/a/5–241r/b/16: [Mass for a virgin not a martyr] "**De vno virgine no‹n› m‹arty›re**". 'DIlexisti iusticia‹m› | et odisti iniq‹ui›ta|tem' [Ps 44].

Fo 241r/b/17–32 no text.

7. *Special Masses*

Fo 241v/a/1–242r/b/31: [Midnight mass at Christmas] "**In natiuitate domine n‹ost›ri ih‹es›u | ‹Christ›i√ In gallicantu Introit‹us›**". 'Domin‹us› dixit | ad me filius | meus es tu'.

Fo 242r/b/32–243r/b/24: [Dawn mass at Christmas] "**In aurora√ Introitus√**". 'LUx fulgebit hodie | sup‹er› nos'.

Fo 243r/b/25–27: [Passion of Our Lord] "**Missa de passione domini | et eius vulneribus√**". 'Humiliauit semet√ **cli**√' [= fo 161, *recte* 160v].

Fo 243r/b/28–30: [Compassion of the Blessed Virgin Mary] "**In festo co‹m›passionis beate | marie semp‹er› virginis**√ Int‹roit›o√". 'Salue s‹an›c‹t›a pare‹n›s co‹m›passa√ **ccxv**' [= fo 225, *recte* 224v].

Fo 243r/b/31–2: [St Leonard, patron saint, 6 Nov.] "**In co‹m›me‹m›oracione s‹an›c‹t›i leonardi**". 'Os iusti meditabi‹tur›√ **ccix**√' [= fo 219, *recte* 218v].

Fo 243v/a/1–244r/b/30: [Commemoration of St Anne, mother of the Blessed Virgin Mary] "**In co‹m›e‹m›oracione sanctissi‹m›e | a‹n›ne m‹arty›ris b‹ea›te marie v‹ir›gi‹ne›√**". 'SAlue s‹an›c‹t›a pa|rens genitrix | venera‹n›da ma|rie'. Fo 244r/b/31–2 no text.

Fo 244v/a/1–24: [St Gertrude, 17 Mar.] "**Gertrudis virginis**√". 'Uultu‹m› tuu‹m› deprecabu‹n›t‹ur› | om‹n›es diuites plebis'.

Fo 244v/a/25–246r/a/20: [Name of Jesus, second Sunday after Epiphany] "**Missa de dulcissimo nomi‹n›e | Ihesu**√". "IN no‹m›i‹n›e ih‹es›u | o‹mn›e genu flec|tat‹ur›'. Fo 246r/a/21–246v/b/32 no text.

8. *Special Prayers arranged temporale and sanctorale, together with the Common of the Saints*

Fo 247r/a/1: "**In na|ti‹ui›tate d‹omini›**". 'ORates | nunc | om‹n›es | redda|m‹us› d‹omi›no | deo qui | sua natiuitate nos libera|uit de diabolica potestate.';

Fo 247r/a/13: "**Ad secunda‹m› missa‹m›**". 'Eya recolamus laudib‹us› | pijs digna√';

Fo 247r/b/22: "**Ad | su‹m›ma‹m› missam**". 'NAtus | ante secula dei filius | i‹n›uisibilis intermin‹us›.';

Fo 247v/a/27: "**De s‹an›c‹t›o stephano.**" 'HAnc concordi famu|latu colamus sole‹m›p|nitatem';

Fo 247v/b/25: "**De s‹an›c‹t›o ioh‹ann›e | euangelista.**" 'IOha‹n›nes ih‹es›u | ‹Christ›o multu‹m› dilecte virgo√";

Fo 248r/a/19: "**In e‹pi›ph‹an›ia d‹omi›ni et i‹n› oct‹ave›**" 'Festa ‹Christ›i o‹mn›is ‹christ›iani|tas celebret√;

Fo 248r/b/27: "**In die s‹an›c‹t›o pasche et i‹n› oct‹ave›**√";

Fo 248v/b/32: "**feria secunda et quarta.**" 'LAudes ‹Christ›o redempti | voce modulemur sup|plici';

Fo 249r/b/8: "**feria iij'. v'. vi' et sabbato**√"; 'UIctime paschali lau|des i‹m›molent ‹christ›iani';

Fo 249r/b/28: "**In ascensio‹n›e d‹omi›ni**√" 'Su‹m›mi triu‹m›phu‹m› | regis p‹ro›sequam‹ur› lau|de';

Fo 249v/b/7: "**In die | sancto pe‹n›thecostes et in oct‹ave›**" 'Sancti sp‹irit›us assit no|bis gr‹ati›a';

Fo 250r/a/21: "**De sancto | sp<irit>u p<er> tota<m> hebdom<ada>**√" 'UEni sancte sp<irit>us et e|mitte celitus lucis tue radi|um';

Fo 250r/b/12: "**In festo sacramenti**√" 'LAuda syon saluatore<m> | lauda ducem et pas|torem in y<m>nis et canticis√';

Fo 250v/b/18: "**De sancta trinitate**√" 'BEnedicta semp<er> sancta | sit trinitas deitas';

Fo 251r/a/24: "**De s<ancta> monica | vid<ua>** √" [4 May] 'Augustini magni | patris atq<ue> sue pie | matris laudes';

Fo 251v/a/2: "**In natiuitate s<an>c<t>i ioh<ann>is baptis<te>** [24 June] 'SAncti baptiste <Christ>i pre|conis';

Fo 251v/b/1: "**In die ap<osto>lo<rum> | petri et pauli**√" [29 June] 'PEtre | su<m>me <Christ>i pastor et pau|le genciu<m> doctor';

Fo 251v/b/31: "**In visitacione | beate marie virginis**√" [2 July] 'AVe preclara maris | stella';

Fo 252r/b/31: "**De sancta maria mag|dalena Sequencia:**√" [22 July] 'LAus tibi <Christ>e qui es | creator et redemptor';

Fo 252v/b/21: "**De s<an>cta anna m<at>re | ma<r>ie v<ir>g<inis>**" [26 July] 'GAude cu<n>ctis | venera<n>da a<n>na mat<er>';

Fo 253r/a/24: "**De s<an>c<t>o laurencio m<arty>re**" [10 Aug.] 'LAurenti dauid mag|ni martir milesq<ue> fortis√';

Fo 253r/b/18: "**In assu<m>pcione b<eate> ma<r>ie v<ir>ginis**" [15 Aug.] 'COngaude<n>t angelo<rum> | chori gloriose virgi|ni';

Fo 253v/a/24: "**In natili** [*sic*] **s<ancti> augustini ep<iscop>i**√" [28 Aug.] 'INterni festi gaudia | n<ost>ra sonet armonia';

Fo 254r/a/13: "**In decollacio<n>e s<ancti> ioh<ann>is baptis<te>**" [29 Aug.] 'Psallite regi n<ost>ro psalli|te psallite psallite pru|denter';

Fo 254v/a/1: "**In natiui|tate beate ma<r>ie v<ir>g<inis> et in oct<ave>**" [8 Sept.] 'STirpe maria regia p<ro>|creata regem genera<n>s | ihesum';

Fo 254v/a/25: "**In exaltacione s<an>c<t>e crucis**√" [14 Sept.] 'LAudes crucis attol<a>mus nos qui crucis | exultam<us>';

Fo 255r/a/27: "**De s<an>cto | lamberto**" [17 Sept.] '<Christ>i laudem | predicem<us> <Christ>i quide<m> | qui gaudemus insigniri | no<m>i<n>e';

Fo 255v/a/28: "**De s<an>cto | mychaele**" [29 Sept.] 'Su<m>mi regis | archangele mychael | Intende quesum<us> n<ost>ris | precib<us>';

Fo 255v/b/29: "**In translacio<n>e s<ancti> augustini**√" 'De profundis tenebra<rum> | mu<n>do lumen exit cla|rum et scintillat hodie';

Fo 256r/b/9: "**De o<mn>ib<us> sanct<is>**" [1 Nov.] 'Om<n>es sancti seraphin | cherubin throni quoq<ue> | d<omi>nacionesq<ue>';

Fo 256v/a/3: "**In sole‹m›pnitate s‹an›c‹t›i | leonardi confes‹soris›**" [6 Nov.] 'Omnes | simul iocundemur et | d‹omin›um veneremur guberna‹n›|tem o‹mn›ia';

Fo 256v/b/32: "**De sancto martino ep‹isco›po√**" [11 Nov.] 'SAcerdote‹m› ‹Christ›i martinu‹m› | cuncta p‹er› orbem canat | ecclesia';

Fo 257r/b/11: "**De sancta elyzabeth√**" [19 Nov.] 'GAude syon q‹ui› egress‹us› | a te';

Fo 257v/a/21: "**In festo presentacio‹n›is beate | ma‹r›ie v‹ir›gi‹nis› √**" [21 Nov.] 'Altissima | prouide‹n›te cu‹n›cta recte | dispone‹n›te dei sapie‹n›cia';

Fo 258r/a/12: "**In dedicacio‹n›e ecclesie√**" 'Psallat ecclesia m‹ate›r illi|bata et v‹ir›go sine ru|ga honorem huius ecclesie√';

Fo 258r/b/3: "**De ap‹osto›lis in co‹mmun›i√**" 'Clare sancto‹rum› senatus | ap‹osto›loru‹m› p‹ri›nceps';

Fo 258r/b/28: "**De sanctis martyribus√**" 'O beata beato‹rum› m‹arty‹r‹u›m | solempnia';

Fo 258v/a/22: "**De vno co‹n›fessore√**" 'AD laudes saluatoris | ut mens incitetur humilis';

Fo 258v/b/29: "**De vna virgine√**" 'GAude celestis sponsa su‹m›|mi regis iam templu‹m› ingres|sa';

Fo 259r/a/20: "**In co‹m›memoracio‹n›e b‹ea›te | marie ferijs t‹er›cijs et q‹ua›rtis√**" 'AVe marie gr‹ati›a plena | d‹omin›us tecu‹m› v‹ir›go serena';

Fo 259r/b/23: "**In co‹m›me‹m›oracio‹n›e b‹ea›te marie | ferijs v.ⁱˢ et sabbatis**" 'Uerbu‹m› bonu‹m› et suaue | p‹er›sonemus illud';

Fo 259v/a/13: "**In co‹m›memoracio‹n›e b‹eate› ma‹r›ie | v‹ir›g‹inis› post natiuitate‹m› d‹omi›ni√**" 'Letabundus exultet | fidelis chorus all‹elui›a√';

Fo 259v/b/8: "**In co‹m›memoracio‹n›e b‹ea›te | marie v‹ir›g‹inis› post pasch‹a›**". 'Uirgini marie laudes | intonent ‹christ›iani';

Fo 259v/b/29–30 blank.

Fos 259v/b/31–260v/a/29 (apparently added as an afterthought): "**De sancto Anthonio | de padua confessore:~ || Ad missam introitus**" [13 June] 'IN medio ecclesie ape|ruit os eius:' (fo 260r/a/30–4 blank probably because the paper writing surface was torn);

Fo 260v/a/30–4 and col. b blank; fo 261r blank.

9 (a). Fos 261v/1–262r/7 (in a more cursive script): 'Quicu‹m›q‹ue› sex missas cu‹m› sex Monitio‹n›ib‹us› missis assignatis si‹n›gulis deuota cum | inte‹n›tione pro a‹n›i‹m›a alic‹uius› i‹n› purgatorio existe‹n›te'. Ends: 'co‹m›probatu‹m› | foris dinoscitur√'.

9 (b). Fo 262r (towards the bottom right-hand corner): '**Istud missale p<er>tinet regular|ib<us> monasterij s. leonardi | p<ro>pe leodiu<m>. Scriptu<m> est per | fratrem Petru<m> Venlonense<m> | presbiteru<m> et p<ro>fessu<m> in eode<m> | mo<na>ste<r>io. Anno d<omi>ni M° ccccc° | xxix°. In die s. Gertrudis:** √' [and added in another hand] 'Obijt anno x v' lviii [1558] me<n>sis | □ die □ ex peste | Requiescant in pace:—', where the squares indicate spaces left blank to fill in the details.

Liturgical and devotional books

THE PREVIOUS MANUSCRIPT, a Missal (RB54), was designed for worship, which although it could be private, was commonly public. Many other manuscripts were used for private devotion, either by priests (the Breviary) or for either ecclesiastical or lay persons (Books of Hours, the Psalter, Canticles etc.). The following manuscripts grouped under this category come from a variety of sources, mainly France and the Low Countries.

The Breviary (RB31) is a Franciscan production from the Low Countries, written towards the end of the fifteenth century. The cover shows a book-stamp with the unlikely motto for an ecclesiastic: 'Carpe Diem' ('Seize the day'). This motto belonged to the Webster family of Chester in England, making this the only manuscript in the collection to show evidence of arriving in Ireland via England. Also from the Low Countries, with some rubrics in Dutch, came the Psalter that is accompanied by Canticles and the Office of the Blessed Virgin Mary (RB519). It may also be a Franciscan production, dating from the first quarter of the sixteenth century. Another book from the Low Countries is the Book of Hours (RB37) dating from the middle of the fifteenth century. The second artist has been identified as from the circle of the Masters of Otto van Moerdrecht. It was owned by Martha Hornby, whose bookplate is inscribed with her name and the date 20 September 1860.[1] Another bookplate of hers dated 6 January 1859 occurs in a printed book, a copy of *The Minstrel*, a poem by James Beattie.[2] Whether RB37 came directly from the Hornby family to Maynooth College is moot.

The Psalter (RB36), dating from the third quarter of the fifteenth century, was apparently made for a Benedictine house, presumably in south-west France. Like the Breviary, it was probably acquired for Maynooth College Library by Dr Laurence Renehan, president of the college from 1845 to 1857. RB38 is an attractive Book of Hours probably produced in Paris towards the end of the fifteenth century, with illustrations by two artists. St Geneviève, the patron saint of Paris, makes a double appearance, together with a full-page picture of her. Nevertheless, the main part of this Book of Hours shows the Use of Rennes, and the presence of some specifically Breton saints in the litany suggests that the book was commissioned by or tailored for a nobleman and his wife from Brittany.

---

1 The existence of her bookplate (without any details, other than that it showed a shield, crest and motto) is recorded by Norna Labouchere, *Ladies' book-plates: an illustrated handbook for collectors and book-lovers* (London, 1895), p. 291.   2 James Beattie, *The minstrel*, with 33 designs by Birket Foster, engraved by the Brothers Dalziel (London, 1858). Our attention was drawn to this book by Thomas Rare Books (Suffolk) in March 2014. The inscription reads 'Martha Hornby | from her friend | Mrs Van den Meulem | Jan<uar>y 6th 1859'. The context of these two names together could

These observations suggest that the main part of the manuscript was bought 'off the peg', so to speak, and then personalized. Apparently the manuscript came to Maynooth College towards the end of the nineteenth century, perhaps from the Mackey family in Ireland. The printed Book of Hours (RB39) with hand-painted illuminations also comes from Paris (1526); some of the illustrations are of very good quality.

According to the Library Donations Register (begun 1894) there was a gift recorded in January 1940 by Fr Au(gu)stin Hurley of an 'Illuminated vellum manuscript' but this item cannot be any of those in this section of the descriptions, even though that is where it should belong. Possibly it was one of the fragments described below (nos 17–19). Fr Hurley matriculated at Maynooth in 1896,[3] and was ordained in Maynooth College Chapel on 17 June 1900.[4] His obituary appeared in the *Catholic Herald* for 4 September 1953 at p. 5. At the time of the donation he was apparently serving as a priest in Brockenhurst (Hants).

6.1 RB31, the Webster book-stamp on the binding cover.

be North American.   **3** P.J. Hamell, *Maynooth students and ordinations: index, 1795–1895* (Birr, Co. Offaly, 1982), p. 84.   **4** *Irish Catholic directory and almanac* (Dublin, 1901), p. 358.

6 RB31
Breviary
Latin

WRITTEN IN 1483 or very soon afterwards in the Low Countries, this Breviary is a Franciscan production, as indicated by the way the principal Franciscan personages are given prominence: St Francis himself in the Proper of the Saints at fo 231v (where the text is from his *Legenda Minor* by St Bonaventure OFM), his Translation (25 May) in the Calendar on fo 3r/27 in red, the imprinting of the holy stigmata on him (17 Sept.) in the Calendar on fo 5r/19 in red, his feast-day (4 Oct.) in the Calendar on fo 5v/6 in red, the octave of his feast-day on fo 5v/13 in red; Anthony of Padua 'ordi<ni>s fr<ancisci>' (13 June) in the Calendar on fo 3v/15 in red, as well as his Octave (20 May) on fo 3v/22 (and he occurs in the Proper of the Saints at fo 137r/2); the feast-day (19 Aug.), octave (26 Aug.) and translation (8 Nov.) of St Louis, bishop of Toulouse, venerated only by the Franciscans, on fos 4v/21, 4v/28 and 6r/10, the first and last in red; and the feast-day and translation of St Clare, who founded the order of Franciscan nuns known as the 'Poor Clares', on fos 4v/14 and 5v/4, both in red – she also occurs in the Proper of the Saints at fo 201v/19. Since it includes the name of St Bonaventure OFM, canonized in 1482, in red in the Calendar for 14 July on fo 4r/16, the manuscript cannot date from before that year. The book is very compact in the manner described for Franciscan books by d'Avray 1980.

The binding of s.xix¹ in blue-black leather shows a stamp in gold in the shape of a seal on both the front and the back. It shows the arms of Webster (Chester) impaling (probably) Maynard, achievement with couched shield, closed helmet and crest *en capeline*, and the motto 'CARPE DIEM' (Horace, *Odes*, 1.11) shown as a circumscription outside a close double circle that partly encloses the achievement, all within a circular band of scrolled plant forms (pl. 6.1; for a notice of this stamp, see the British Armorial Bindings Database, *s.n.* Webster (stamp-owner) http://armorial.library.utoronto.ca). Arms: Dexter, A cross patonce between four mullets, the cross charged on the upper arm with a crescent for difference (Webster: see Burke 1884: 1086–7; also St George 1909: 139); Sinister, A chevron between three sinister hands erect, couped at the wrist (prob. Maynard; see Burke 1884: 673, but cf. Papworth 1874: 431). Crest: A dragon's head erased *en capeline* (Webster: see Fairbairn 1968: 496 and pl. 107, cr. 10). Book-stamps enjoyed a renaissance in s.xix, and this one occurs elsewhere in four examples cited by Philip Oldfield of the British Armorial Bindings Database (private communication 10 Mar. 2009). The Webster family was well-to-do in Chester, John Webster being alderman of Chester in 1601 (Burke 1884: 1086), and another

John Webster being sheriff in 1797–8 (Harris, Lewis and Thacker 1987–: vol. 5, pt 2, 317), the latter perhaps the former owner of this book. On the spine the title 'BREVIARIUM | ROMANUM' and below 'MS | SÆC. XV.', and added in slightly larger lettering below that 'O'RENEHAN | MSS.', and below that added again, also in slightly larger lettering, 'VOL. | 42.'. Inside the front cover in the top left-hand corner is the small advertising bookplate of 'J[oseph].C. SCULLY | Bookseller & Stationer | *35 Up.ʳ Ormond Quay* | DUBLIN' (*fl.* 1824–31). At least two other manuscripts with the same bookstamp were sold at the Edwards of Halifax sale (1828), which allows the possibility that this manuscript was Lot 200 in that sale: 'Breviarum Romanum, Manuscript, Sæc. XV. small 4to. *on* | vellum, *with illuminated capitals, russia binding*' (1828: 14), the wording on the spine and this description matching perfectly, suggesting that the wording in the sale catalogue was taken from that already on the spine. According to marginal annotations in the copy of the sale catalogue in Cambridge University Library (Munby.c.152(10)), the lot was sold for one guinea to the bookseller Robert Triphook (*fl.* 1809–33). Presumably Dr Renehan bought the present manuscript from Scully's, who perhaps acted as an intermediary and acquired it for Renehan. Bequeathed to the library at Maynooth by Laurence Renehan, president, St Patrick's College, Maynooth (1845–57); it is no. 42, 'Breviarum Romanum M.S. Saec XV', in the list of 'The O'Renehan MSS' attached to his will (see Appendix, below).

Secundo folio: 'R‹ubri›ca Februari‹us› h‹abet› dies xxviii = luna xxix'.

CODICOLOGICAL DESCRIPTION

Fos i + i + 320 + i + i, membrane except for the outer paper endleaves; all the endleaves were added with the binding, when the manuscript was also cropped. The leaves now measure 126 x 96mm, and the written area 93–5 x 67mm. The membrane is very thin and delicate, and holes occur in the written area (with the text written around the holes) on fos 44, 114, 164 and 207, and in the margins on fos 2, 26, 176, 181, 212 and 273. The top outer corner of fo 214 and some holes on fos 269 and 271 have been repaired.

Pricking: Pricking for the single vertical frame can usually be seen near the top edge of leaves, and in the bottom margin; on some folios the prick-marks have been lost with cropping by the binder. Quire I shows prick-marks for thirty-four horizontal lines of writing at the outer edges of leaves (clear on fo 2). No writing on the top line. For the rest of the manuscript thirty-one prick-marks for the thirty long lines can be seen at the outer edge of many leaves.

Ruling: The frame ruling in fine crayon extends to the outer edge of the leaves at both top and bottom, and the third line from the top and the third line from the bottom also extend to the outer edges of the leaves. Otherwise the horizontal lines are ruled between the vertical frame lines.

Scribes and script: The manuscript is written by a number of scribes. The script used by the main scribe (Booklet A, fos 1–250; pls 6.2, 6.3) is a good set hybrida of the Low Countries or adjacent Germany; the hand suggests a date fairly soon after 1482. One particularly distinctive feature of this scribe is that many r's show a long vertical hairline through the arm (pl. 6.2, lines 29–30; pl. 6.3, line 23 'flores'). An unusual feature is the use of a slightly smaller script in a paler brown for the responses, very clear, e.g., on fos 68v–69r, and see pls 6.2, 6.3. In Booklet B another scribe begins at fo 251r, and a third takes over at fo 302r/10 (pl. 6.3, fo 205r). Scribe 4 begins at fo 311r, the beginning of Quire **XXXIII**, but a fifth scribe takes over on the same page at fo 311r/28. At the end (Item 2) another scribe has added material beginning at fo 319v/18. On fo 176r there is an annotation in the right-hand margin, probably contemporary with the main hand.

Colour and ornament: There is apparently a change of decorating style at fo 205r (compare pls 6.2, 6.3), and probably another at fo 251v.

Decorated capitals occur on fos 9r (**U** in red on a green background, infilled in blue with gold fleurs de lys, and a floral trail on a green stem round three sides of the page with flowers in pink and yellow with gold ornament; pl. 6.2), 24r (**P** in blue on a yellow and brown background with gold ornament, and some floral ornament in the margins at the bottom and right-hand side in green, magenta and blue), 33v (**F** in yellow and brown with a blue centre and green in the ornament, and a flower ornament in blue, yellow/brown and green in the bottom margin of the page), 36v (**O** in yellow and brown on a blue ground, flourished with the same colours plus green), 43r (**P** in green on a yellow and brown ground, flourished in the same colours plus blue, and in the bottom margin a flower ornament in blue, green, brown and yellow), 81v (**M** in yellow and brown on a green ground (with yellow flecks), with flourishing in green and yellow/brown in the outside and bottom margins), 98r (**L** in yellow and brown on a green ground (with yellow flecks), with flourishing in green, blue and yellow in the outside and bottom margins), 108v (**F** in blue with pink flourishing), 130r (**R** in blue on a brown/yellow ground, with elaborate floral trails in blue, green, magenta, yellow and brown, forming a U-shape around the text and trimmed by the binder especially at the top, 174v (P in red/brown/yellow on a green ground (with yellow flecks) and with pink flourishing, and a floral motif in green, blue, pink and red in the bottom margin), 177v (**B** in green on a red ground (flecked with yellow) and pink flourishing, and a floral motif in green, blue, pink and red in the bottom margin), 194v (**P** in green on a red ground (flecked with yellow) and pink flourishing, and a floral motif in green, blue, pink and red in the bottom margin), 202r (**U** in green and blue infilled with red (flecked with yellow), and two floral

6.2 RB31, fo 9r, decorated capital **U** (1st style), and smaller script in a paler brown for the responses, as in lines 29–30. Actual page dimensions 126 × 96mm.

motifs in green, blue, red and pink, one in the outer margin and one in the bottom margin), 205r (**C** in green, blue and grey, infilled with red (flecked with yellow) with pink flourishing, and the lower and outer margins filled with pink swirls containing red and blue dotted flowers, and green leaves added to the swirls; pl. 6.3), 209r (**S** in red and yellow with green infill (flecked with yellow), and pink sprays (surmounted by blue or green mostly dotted floral motifs) issuing from the text at the outer, top and bottom margins), 216r (**O** in blue (flecked with white) on a red ground (flecked with yellow), and pink sprays (surmounted by blue or green mostly dotted floral motifs) issuing from the text at the outer and bottom margins), 231v (**A** in blue and grey infilled with green (flecked with yellow) with red spray and flourishing), 241r (**L** in green (with white flecks) infilled with magenta (flecked with white), and a little red flourishing), 251v (**B** in plain blue on a ground of pink and white foliage, with minimal pink flourishing), 274r (**Q** in dark green (plain but with white flower on either side) on a ground of red and white foliage, with red flourishing), 281r (**S** in dark blue (plain but with a lozenge at the centre) infilled with white on red foliage, and red and green flourishing), 288v (**E** in plain dark green on a ground of white on red foliage, with red flourishing), 295r (**C** in plain dark blue on a ground of white on red foliage, with red flourishing).

Secondary flourished capitals occur on fos 70v (red **U** with pink flourishing), 85r (blue **P** with pink flourishing), 101r (blue **C** with pink flourishing), 102v (red **I** with pink flourishing), 110r (blue **F** with pink flourishing), 110v (red **E** with pink flourishing), 111r (blue **P** with pink flourishing), 119r (blue **P** with pink flourishing), 120r (blue **U** with pink flourishing), 120v (red **D** and blue **O**, both with pink flourishing), 121r (red **U** with pink flourishing), 122v (blue **T** with pink flourishing), 123v (blue **A** with pink flourishing), 125r (blue **E** with pink flourishing), 126v (red **F** with pink flourishing), 127v (red **E** with pink flourishing), 129r (blue **A** with pink flourishing), 129v (blue **U** with pink flourishing), 130v (blue **P** with pink flourishing), 132r (blue **N** with pink flourishing), 147v (red **G** with pink flourishing), 148v (red **U** with pink flourishing), 163v (blue **I** with pink flourishing), 170v (red **P** with pink flourishing), 262r (blue **D** infilled with red and white foliage, and with red flourishing), 269r (red **D** with green on white foliage design, and with some green flourishing), 274v (red **D** on a ground of green on white foliage, with green flourishing).

Small capitals alternate in red and blue on fos 9–229, but from fo 229 to the end they are all in red, except for one in blue on fo 293r.

COLLATION

Booklet A: **I**[8] fos 1–8, **II**[10] fos 9–18, **III**[10] fos 19–28, **IV**[10] fos 29–38, **V**[10] fos 39–48, **VI**[10] fos 49–58, **VII**[10] fos 59–68, **VIII**[10] fos 69–78, **IX**[10] fos 79–88, **X**[10] fos 89–98, **XI**[10] fos 99–108, **XII**[10] fos 109–18, **XIII**[10] fos 119–28, **XIV**[10] fos 129–38, **XV**[10] fos 139–48, **XVI**[10] fos 149–58, **XVII**[10] fos 159–68, **XVIII**[10] fos 169–78, **XIX**[10] fos 179–88, **XX**[10] fos 189–98, **XXI**[10] fos 199–208, **XXII**[10] fos 209–18, **XXIII**[10] fos 219–28, **XXIV**[10] fos 229–38, **XXV**[10] fos 239–48, **XXVI**[2] fos 249–50;

Booklet B: **XXVII**[10] fos 251–60, **XXVIII**[10] fos 261–70, **XXIX**[10] fos 271–80, **XXX**[10] fos 281–90, **XXXI**[10] fos 291–300, **XXXII**[10] fos 301–10, **XXXIII**[10] fos 311–20.

Signatures in red occur in Booklet B in the top right-hand corner of the first five leaves of Quires **XXVII, XXVIII, XXIX** (i–iiii only), **XXX** (i–ii only, in brown). There are no catchwords.

Hair/Flesh: The membrane is well prepared, and sometimes it is difficult to tell the flesh side from the hair side. Apart from Quire I, there is a preference for flesh outside, and generally for flesh rather than hair, as follows: **I** HFHH, **II** FHFHF, **III** FHFHF, **IV** FFFFF, **V** HFFFF, **VI** FHFHF, **VII** FHFHF, **VIII** FHFFF, **IX** FHFFF, **X** FFFFF, **XI** FFFFF, **XII** FHFFF, **XIII** FFHFF, **XIV** FHFFF, **XV** FFFFF, **XVI** FFFFF, **XVII** FFFFF, **XVIII** FHFFH, **XIX** FFHFF, **XX** FFFFF, **XXI** FHFFF, **XXII** FFFHF, **XXIII** FFFFF, **XXIV** FFHHH, **XXV** FHHHH, **XXVI** F, **XXVII** FFFFF, **XXVIII** FFFFF, **XXIX** FFFFF, **XXX** FFFFF, **XXXI** FFFHH, **XXXII** FFFFF, **XXXIII** FHHHH.

CONTENTS

1. Fos 1r/1–319v/17: Breviary.

Booklet A

(i)   (a) Fos 1r/1–6v/33: Calendar.
Begins 'R<ubri>Ca Januari<us> h<abet> dies xxxi luna xxx'. Ends 'A sil Siluestri p<a>pe <et> <con>s<ecrate> xviii xii xxxii k'. Includes the name of St Bonaventure OFM, canonized in 1482, in red in the Calendar for 14 July on fo 4r/16.

(b) fos 7r/1–8v/37: Computistical tables for calculating liturgical dates. Begins 'xc ix viii ii c ... | xci'. Ends 'x pe de cris pau nic niar cel'.

(ii)   fos 9r/1–130r/20: Proper of the Time (including some saints' days). Begins '**In nomi<n>e d<omi>ni m<e>i ih<es>u <Christ>i: Incipit nocturnale. Invitato<rium>.** | Regem venturum dominum. Venite adoremus. **ps<almus>**

Ve<n>ite v<ersus>. Uerbum supernum prodiens a patre olim exiens qui | natus orbi subueni[s] cursu decliui tp<or>is' [Chevalier 1892–1920: no. 21392]. Continues (with selected notices) on fo 9r/19 (pl. 6.2): 'Deus nost<er> manifeste veniet. **lib<er> isaie.** | Uisio isaie filii amos qua<m> vidit | sup<er> iudam et ierusalem in die|bus ozie' [Is 1.1]; fo 16r/28 '**Dominica tercia [Adventum].** **Invitat<orium>.** | Domine prestolamur aduentu<m> tuu<m>.'; fo 23r/21 '¶ **In vigilia natiuitatis domini Invitatoriu<m>.** | Hodie scietis q<ui>a veniet d<omin>us.' [after Ex 16.6]; fo 23v/28 '**In nocte natiui<tatis>** | CRistus natus est nobis [after Is 9.6] Venite adoremus'; fo 26r/2 '¶ **In nocte Steffani.**'; fo 27v/10 '¶ **De s<an>c<t>o** iho<ann>e. [*recte* ioh<ann>e]'; fo 30v/15 '**Thome m<arty>ris.**'; fo 33v/14 '**In circu<mci>sio<n>e d>omi>ni.**'; fo 36v/4, 10 "**In nocte sancta e<pi>ph<an>ye ad mat<utinas>**". 'Om<n>es sicientes ve<n>ite ad aq<ua>s' [Is 55.1]; fo 50v/1 '**Do<min>ica i<n> <septuagesima>**'; fo 52v/7 '**D<omi>nica sexagesima**'; fo 54r/16 '**D<omi>nica in q<ui>nq<ua>|gesi<m>a.**'; fo 57r/13 '**D<omi>nica In quadragesima.**'; fo 60v/9 '**D<omi>nica S<e>c<un>da i<n> xl**'; fo 63v/17 '**D<omi>nica <terti>a i<n>** lx [*recte* xl]'; fo 67r/15 '**D<omi>nica letare**' [= fourth Sunday of Lent]; fo 70r/28 '**Domi<ni>ca in passione.**'; fo 74r/5 '**Dominica** | **in palmis.**'; fo 81v/13, 23: '**In die Sancto pasche.**' "Omelia Sancti g<re>go<ri>i ij pape". 'Multis vobis l<e>c<ti>o<n>ibus fr<atr>es k<arissi>mi p<er> dictatu<m> | loqui <con>sueui' [Gregory, Homily 21, PL 76, 1169C]; fo 87r/7 '**D<omi>nica s<e>c<un>da p<os>t pas|cha[m].**'; fo 93r/29 '**In nocte ascensio<n>is.**'; fo 102r/17 '**Corporis cristi.**'; fo 108r/5: '**In octa<vo> . Corp<or>is <Christ>i.**'; fo 108v/2; 108v/6: '**D<omi>nica p<ri>ma p<ost> pe<n>|tecostes.**' 'Fuit vir vnus de ramatha sophiim d<e> | monte effraim.' [1 Sam 1.1]; fo 121r/24 '**D<omi>nica p<ri>ma mensis Septemb<ri>s** | inponitur liber iob et legitur per duas ebdompdas [*recte* ebdomadas]'; fo 125r/12 '**D<omi>nica p<ri>ma mensis octobris**'. Ends 'Et sit d<ominu>s | deus vobis in testem Tu [autem Domine miserere nobis]. **Explicit. Nocturnale d<omini> <Christi>.**'

(iii) Fos 130r/21–250v/3: Proper of the Saints. "**In no<mi>n<e> d<omi>ni. Incipit Nocturnale de s<an>c<t>is. D<e> s<an>c<t>o Sat<ur>nio.** [29 Nov.]". Begins 'Rome s<ub> nat<a>le s<an>c<t>i saturnini m<arty>ris <et> senis | <et> sisimuj [*sic*] diaconi sub maximi'. Continues (with selected saints) fo 130v/11 '**Andree ap<osto>li** [30 Nov.]'; fo 132r/26 '**Nicolai ep<iscop>i <et> <con>fe<ssoris>** [6 Dec.]; fo 133r/18 **Ambrosii \ep<iscop>i/** [7 Dec.]; fo 133v/23 '**Melchiad<is> p<a>pe** [10 Dec.]'; fo 134r/2 '**Damasi p<a>pe** [11 Dec.]'; fo 134r/17 '**Lucie virginis** [13 Dec.]'; fo 135r/20 '**Thome ap<osto>li** [21 Dec.]'; fo 136r/18 '**Marcelli pape et martiris** [16 Jan.]'; fo 137r/2 '**Anthonij abbatis** [17 Jan.]'; fo 137v/5 '**Marij** [*recte* Marie] **m<a>rthe** [19 Jan.]'; fo 137v/30 '**Fabiani <et> sebastiani** [20 Jan.]'; fo 138v/7 '**Agnetis v<ir>g<in>is** [21 Jan.]'; fo 140r/7 '**Vince<n>tij <et> anast<asii>** [22 Jan.]'; fo 142v/19 '**pu<r>ificatio<n>is mar<i>e** [2 Feb.]'; fo 144v/4 '**Blasii ep<iscop>i** [3 Feb.]'; fo 146v/20 '**Mathie apostoli** [24 Feb.]';

fo 147v/19 'Gregorij pape <con>f<essoris> [12 Mar.]'; fo 148r/7 'Benedicti abbatis [21 Mar.]'; fo 148v/26 'In anu<n>ciatio<n>e marie v<ir>ginis [25 Mar.]'; fo 150r/2 'Annaceti pape [17 Apr.]'; 151v/26 'Georgij \m<arti>ris/ [23 Apr.]'; fo 152v/14 'Marci eva<ngelis>ᵗᵉ [25 Apr.]'; fo 153r/25 'Cleti p<a>pe [26 Apr.]'; fo 154r/3 'philippi <et> iacobi [1 May]'; fo 155r/7 'Inuentio s<an>c<te> | crucis [3 May]'; fo 156v/14 'Alexandri . euen<ti>i . theodoli . Iuuenal<is> [3 May]'; fo 157r/24 'Iho<ha>nis an<te> porta<m> latina<m> [6 May]'; fo 158r/11 'Gordia<n>i <et> epymachi [10 May]'; fo 161r/15 'Petronille [31 May]'; fo 161v/6 'Marcellini pet<ri> atq<ue> e<r>asmi [2 June]'; fo 162v/5 'primi <et> feliciani [9 June]'; fo 163r/11 'barnabe. [11 June]'; fo 163v/10 'Anthonij <con>fess<oris> [13 June]'; fo 167v/30 'Viti [et] modesti [15 June]'; fo 170v/1 'In n<a>t<iuita>te iho<han>is bap<tis>\te/ [24 June]'; fo 174v/2 'In festo ap<osto>lo<rum> pet<ri> <et> pau<li> [29 June] | Invitatoriu<m>.' 'Petrus <et> ioh<ann>es ascendaba<n>t in | templu<m> ad horam or<ati>onis nona<m>.' [Acts 3.1]; fo 177v/10 'Visitatio<n>is ma<r>ie v<ir>g<inis> [2 July]'. 'Bonifacius ep<is>c<opus> s<er>u<us> s<er>uo<rum> d<e>i ad p<er>petua<m> rei me|moria<m>.' [Bull of Bonifatius IX]; fo 183v/26 'Septem fr<ater>ni [10 July]'; fo 185r/17 'praxedis virginis [21 July]'; fo 187v/17 'Cristofori martiris [25 July]'; fo 197r/24 'Sixti felicissimi <et> agapiti m<artirum> [6 Aug.]'; fos 201v/19, 202r/4 'In S<an>c<t>e Clare v<ir>ginis. [12 Aug.]'. 'Uene<r>abilis <Christ>i sponse deoq<ue> dicate v<ir>ginis cla<r>e | nataliam diem fr<atr>es k<arissi>mi hono<r>ificentia de|bita celebrantes sacre vite ip<s>i<us> p<ri>mordia' [Mohan 1978: 477]; fo 205r/7; 205r/14 'Assumpsio<n>is ma<r>ie v<ir>ginis. [15 Aug.]' (pl. 6.3); fo 209r/19 'De Sancto luduico. [25 Aug.]'; fo 216r/6; 216r/9 'In natiuitate ma<r>ie [8 Sept.]'. 'Osculet<ur> me osc<u>lo oris sui q<ui>a me|liora su<n>t vbera tua vino fragra<n>cia vng|wentis optimis.' [SofS 1.1–2]; fo 231v/1, 231v/26 'Francisci <con>fess<oris> [4 Oct.]'. 'Apparuit g<ra>cia d<e>i saluato<r>is n<ost>ri dieb<us> istis | nouissimis s<er>uo suo fra<n>cisco q<uem> pater' [= *Legenda minor Sancti Francisci*, incipit (Bonaventura 1941: 655)]; fos 240v/24, 241r/11 'De om<n>ib<us> Sanct<orum> [1 Nov.]'. 'Legim<us> i<n> ecclesiasticis historiis q<uod> s<an>c<t>us bo|nifaci<us> qui q<ua>rt<us> a b<ea>to grego<r>io romane | vrbis ep<iscop>atu<m> tenebat' [Bede, Homily 71, PL 94, 452D]. Ends 'Nolite ti||mere sed gaudete potius . paratu<m> e<st> e<ni>m vobis r<e>g<num> celo<rum> | Ad glor<i>a<m> o<mn>ipotentis dei Scriptus <et> finitus sexta fe<r>ia infra oct. | corp<or>is <Christ>i.' fo 250v/4–30 blank.

Booklet B

(iv)   Fos 251r/1–319v/17: Psalms for the Daily Office, followed by appropriate Canticles, for the period Epiphany to Advent, with the days for reciting some psalms indicated and other prayers and responses added in between the psalms as appropriate. "Invitato<r>ia subsc<ri>pta dic<un>t<ur> sing<u>la singlis diebus | d<omi>nicis ab octa<uo> epypha<nie> us<que> ad <septuagintam>

[**diem**] **a k‹a›l‹end›is oc|toberis** [*sic*] **C‹apitulum› p‹ri›mum**". 'Venite exultem‹us› d‹omi›no iubile‹mus› | deo salutari n‹ost›ro' [Ps 94.1]; fo 251v/7 "**In pascha**". '**B**eatus uir qui no‹n› abiit | in ‹con›silio impioru‹m›' [Ps 1.1]; continues (with selected notices) fo 274r/18: '**Q**vid | gloriaris ‹in› malicia q‹ui› pote‹n›s | es i‹n› [in]iquitate' [Ps 51.3]; fos 280v/25; 281r/3: "**Feria v**". '**S**aluu‹m› me fac de‹us› q‹uonia›m int‹ra›ueru‹n›t | aque usq‹ue› ad a‹n›i‹m›am mea‹m›' [Ps 68.2]; fo 288v/6: 'Exultate deo adiutori n‹ost›ro' [Ps 80.2]; fo 295r/15: '**C**Antate d‹omi›no canticu‹m› nouu‹m›: quia | mirabilia fecit' [Ps 97.1]; fo 315v/4: '**L**Auda i‹e›r‹usa›l‹e›m d‹omin›um lauda deu‹m› tuu‹m› | syon' [Ps 147.1]; fo 316r/6: '**E**Xultauit cor meu‹m› in d‹omi›no' [1 Sam 2.1; Song of Hannah); fo 317r/17 'Domi‹n›e audiui audit‹i›o‹nem› tua‹m› et timui' [Hab 3.1; Song of Habakkuk]; fo 318r/5: 'Audite celi que loquor' [Deut 32.1; Song of Moses], which ends '‹et› p‹ro›pici‹us› est t‹er›re p‹o›p‹u›li sui A‹me›n'. [Deut 32.43].

2. Fos 319v/18–320r/7: A series of citations relating to the Sermon on the Mount. Begins 'in illo t‹em›p‹or›e videns ih‹es›us turbas asce‹n›dit i‹n› mo‹n›tem | Et cum sedisset accesseru‹n›t ad eu‹m› d‹iscipu›li ei‹us› & cet' [Mt 5.1]. Ends 'Docendis tantis reb‹us› idoneo docet‹ur› i‹n› mo‹n›te.' fo 320r/8–30: blank.

7 RB36
Psalter

Latin

HISTORY

A PSALTER IN LATIN handsomely written by a single scribe and nicely illuminated probably in southern or south-western France s.xv³. Corrections by the scribe occur in the margins of fos 19v, 157v. The Calendar appears to be of French origin, possibly southern French, and contains many references to St Benedict of Nursia, as his feast-day (21 Mar.), the translation of his relics to Fleury (St Benoit sur Loire) (11 July), the octave of his translation 18 July, and others on 4 December (another date for his *translatio* in French custom), and 29 December (*relevatio*), which suggests that the book was made for a Benedictine house. St Bernard (20 Aug.) is a notable omission. Some rarely found saints are included, as Rigomerus (missionary in Poitou, s.vi) 24 August, also in the Litany (fo 173v/12). Some saints have strong southern French associations, as Valerius and Eulalia (at 10 Dec.), both Spanish and associated in France with the south-west, Venantius Fortunatus (14 Dec., also in the Litany, fo 173r/12), whose associations were with Poitiers and further south, and Eutrope, first bishop of Saintes (fo 172v/12).

There are annotations to the Calendar (fos 1–6) by a later hand, and musical annotations in the margins of fos 29v, 31v, 33r, 35v, 38r, 40v and 42r.

Provenance is indicated by what is probably a personal mark 'L[with a swirl-flourish]e', probably s.xvi or s.xvii, on fos 1r (twice) and 178v; unfortunately it has defied identification. At the top right-hand corner of fo 1r 'N°440.' suggests a library number (pl. 7.1).

Binding of s.xix^iii in marbled cloth on card with brown sheepskin back (blind-stamped on the spine) and outer corners, entitled on the spine 'PSALTERIUM | DAVIDIS' and marked at the bottom 'M. S. | SÆC. XIV.'; the paper endleaves belong with the binding. The use of marbled cloth was established by Charles Woolnough in 1853, so the binding must date from after that year. The spine, divided into five compartments by raised bands, shows in compartments 1, 3 and 4 a blind-stamped centrepiece design based on fleurons, evidently imitative of those on RB16 and RB54. The centrepiece is made by striking four fleurons into the leather, but, as noticed by Paul Hoary (Russell Library conservator), this has been done somewhat tentatively and clumsily, particularly in the top and fourth compartments. It follows that the binding was probably done for (someone at) Maynooth, possibly Dr Renehan (d. 1857), or his successor Dr Russell (president, 1857–80), someone inspired by the tooled decoration by Philippe Fisen on

7.1 RB36, fo 1r, the beginning of the Calendar, with the (?)class number in the top right corner and the (?)ownership mark below the text. Actual page dimensions 157 x 110mm.

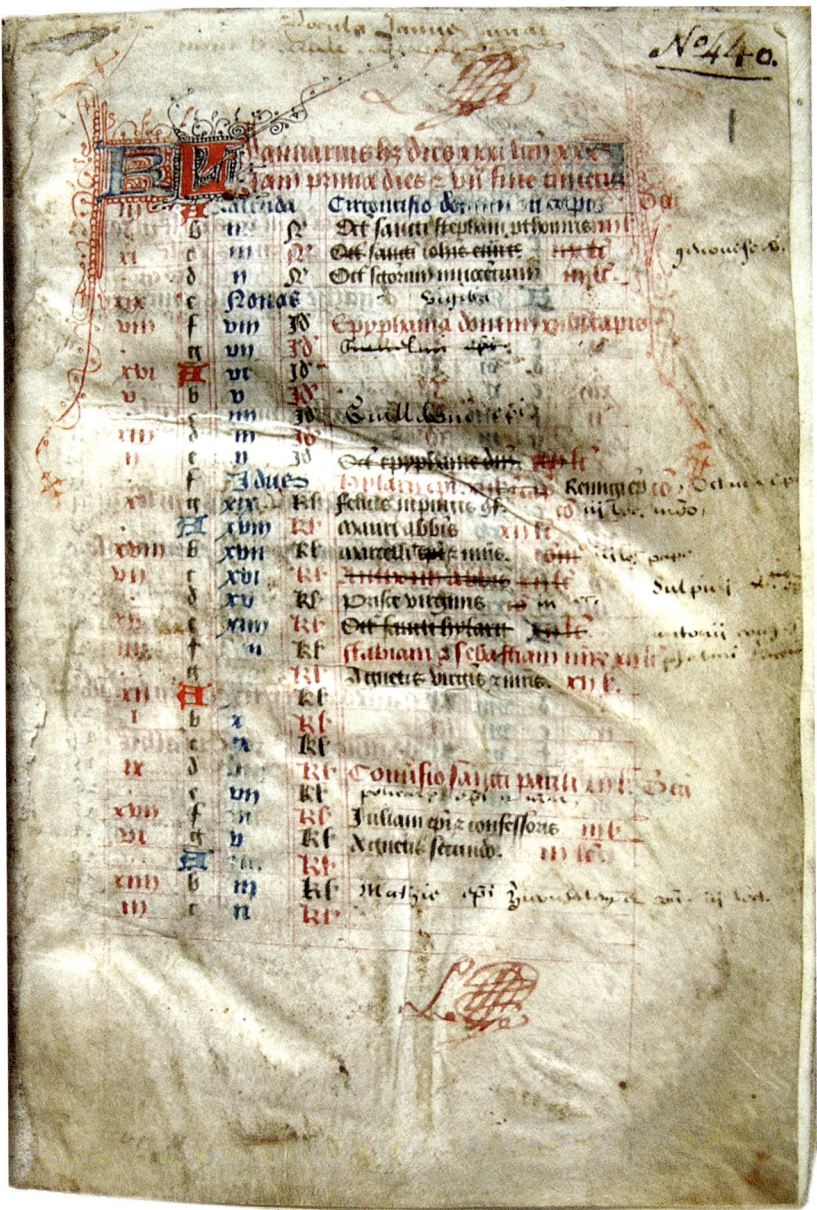

bindings already in the library (see pl. 1.4, above); the design is not an exact copy as the centrepiece on RB36 shows one petal in each quadrant fewer than on RB16 and RB54, and the width of the centrepiece on RB36 is 17.5mm as against 20mm for those on RB16 and RB54. The binding is very tight, making it difficult to hold the book open.

Secundo folio: '**KL** Mensis martii h<abet> dies xxxi lun<am> .xxx.'

CODICOLOGICAL DESCRIPTION

Fos i + 178 + i, membrane except for the paper endleaves, measuring 157 x 110mm, written area generally 96 x 65mm, but in Quire I (the Kalendar) 102 x 68mm with the writing often overflowing beyond the right-hand bounding line.

Pricking: None visible following cropping by a binder.

Ruling: In fine crayon.

(a) Quire I (fos 1–6, the Calendar), evidently ruled leaf by leaf, shows a simple frame with the vertical frame lines usually extending to the outer edges of the leaves, and the top two and bottom horizontal lines sometimes extended to the outer edges of the leaves. The 34–36 horizontal lines for writing are ruled between the vertical frame lines, and the top line does not receive writing.

(b) Quires II–XXII, evidently ruled sheet by sheet, show a simple frame with the vertical frame lines and the top horizontal line usually extending to the outer edges of the leaves. The twenty horizontal lines are ruled between the vertical frame lines, and the top line does not receive writing.

Colour and ornament: On fo 7r there is a three-quarter-page illustration of David with his harp in an arched frame, surrounded at the bottom and on both sides by intricate filigree design forming a pattern in a boxed frame, using blue, gold, brown/black, red and green (pl. 7.2). Similar boxes of filigree design, occupying the top, bottom and inner/outer margins, occur on fos 29v, 44r, 58r, 71v, 89r, 105r and 122v surrounding the page showing the beginning of Psalms 26, 38, 52, 68, 80, 97 and 109 respectively, each marked by an ornamental initial with blue filigree design and blue and red leaf/flower ornament on a gold ground. Lesser ornamented initials of blue with red filigree ornamentation or red with brown/black filigree ornamentation alternate throughout the texts, and psalm verses are distinguished by alternating plain blue and red initials.

COLLATION

I⁶ (fos 1–6), II⁸ (fos 7–14), III⁸ (fos 15–22), IV⁸ (fos 23–30), V⁸ (fos 31–8), VI⁸ (fos 39–46), VII⁸ (fos 47–54), VIII⁸ (fos 55–62), IX⁸ (fos 63–70), X⁸ (fos 71–8), XI⁸ (fos 79–86), XII⁸ (fos 87–94), XIII⁸ (fos 95–102), XIV⁸ (fos 103–10), XV⁸ (fos 111–18), XVI⁸ (fos 119–26), XVII⁶ (fos 127–32), XVIII⁸ (fos 133–40), XIX⁸ (fos 141–8), XX⁶ (fos 149–54), XXI⁸ (fos 155–62), XXII⁸ (fos 163–70), XXIII⁸ (fos 171–8).

Catchwords written vertically (and partially cropped) occur in the bottom right-hand corner of the verso leaf on fos 14, 22 (faint), 30, 38, 46, 54, 62, 70, 78, 86, 94, 102, 110, 118, 126, 132, 140, 148, 154, 162, 170.

Hair/Flesh: (F)HFH throughout.

7.2 RB36, fo 7r, the
beginning of the
Psalter showing *David
with his Lyre*. Actual
page dimensions
157 x 110mm.

CONTENTS

1. Fos 1r/1–6v/33: Calendar of feast-days in Latin arranged one month per page in five columns, showing red, gold, blue, red and gold alternating, followed by a wider column giving the name of the saint, usually in gold, but sometimes in red or blue. Begins 'KL Januarius h<abet> dies xxxi lun<as> xxx.' Ends '**Siluestri p<a>p<ae> et m<arti>ris.**'

2. Fos 7r/1–156v/14: Latin Psalter. Begins 'Beatus vir qui non abiit in | consilio impiorum et in via | peccatorum non stetit:' [Ps 1.1] (pl. 7.2). Ends [Ps 150.5–6] 'laudate eum in cymbalis iubila|cionis omnis spiritus laudet d<omin>um **p<salmu>s d<aui>d**'.

3. Fos 156v/15–178v/4: (continues without a break) Canticles (including one Hymn), Athanasian Creed, Litany and Collects.

(i) Fos 156v/15–169r/9: Ten Canticles and the Hymn *Te Deum*:

  (a) Fo 156v/15: 'Confitebor tibi domine q<uonia>m iratus es | m<ihi> co<n>uersus e<st> furor tu<us> co<n>solat<us> es me | Ecce deus saluator meus: fiducialiter agam et non timebo. [Isa 12.1–6]';

  (b) Fo 158r/10: 'Exultauit cor meum in domino: | et exaltatu<m> est cor<n>u meu<m> i<n> deo meo [I Kgs 2:1–10]';

  (c) Fo 159r/7: 'Ca<n>temus domino gloriose enim | honorificatu<s> est? [Ex 15.1–19]';

  (d) Fo 160v/8: 'Domine audiui? auditum tuum | et timui. [Hab 3:2–19]';

  (e) Fo 162r/17: 'Audite celi que loquor: audiat terra | uerba oris mei [Deut 32.1–21]';

  (f) Fo 164r/6: 'Ignis succcensus est in furore meo: [Deut 32.22–43]';

  (g) Fo 165v/17: 'Benedicite omnia opera d<omi>ni d<omi>no: [Dan 3.57–88]';

  (h) Fo 166v/12: 'Te deum laudam<us> te d<omin>um co<n>fitemur' [liturgical hymn, as Burn 1926: 82–3];

  (j) Fo 167v/14: 'Benedictus dominus deus isr<ae>l: | quia uisitauit et fecit redemp|tionem plebis sue. [Lk 1.68–79]';

  (k) Fo 168v/4: 'Magnificat anima mea d<omi>n<u>m. [Lk 1.46–55]';

  (l) Fo 169r/4: 'Nunc dimittis seruum tuum d<omi>ne: [Lk 2.29–32]'. Ends 'Lumen ad reuelationem gentium: et | gloriam plebis tue israel.'

(ii) Fos 169r/9–171r/19: Athanasian Creed, beginning '**Cimbolum** | Quicumque uult saluus esse: an<te> omnia opus est ut teneat catholicam fidem'. Ends 'Hec est fides catholica: q<ua>m nisi quisq<uis> fideliter firmiter\q<ue>/ cred<id>erit saluus esse non | poterit.' As Kelly 1964: 17–20.

(iii) Fos 171v/1–176v/17: Litany of the Saints, beginning 'Kyri eleison. | <Chr>iste eleison | Kyri eleison.' Ends 'V<ersu>s D<omi>ne exaudi [orationem meam] R<esponsio> Et clamor [meus ad te veniat] V<ersu>s D<omi>n<u>s uobisc<um> | R<esponsio> Et cum spiritu tuo. Oremus.'

(iv) Fo 176v/17–178v/4: Nine Collects headed "**Oratio.**"

  (a) Fo 176v/17: For sinners, 'Deus cui p<ro>prium est misereri semp<er> | et parcere suscipe deprecationem || nostram', as Deshusses 1971: item 851, and no. lxxxi, item 1327;

(b) Fo 177r/3: For monks, 'Omnipotens | sempiterne deus qui facis mira|bilia magna solus pretende super famu|los tuos', as Deshusses 1971: no. lxxiii, item 1308;

(c) Fo 177r/10: For the salvation of the living, 'Pretende domine famulis et | famulabus tuis dexteram cele|stis auxilii:' as Deshusses 1971: no. lxxii, item 1300;

(d) Fo 177r/14: For peace, 'Deus a quo sancta desideria recta | consilia et iusta sunt opera da | seruis tuis', as Deshusses 1971: no. lxxxvi, item 1343;

(e) Fo 177v/2 'Omnipotens sempiterne deus | in cuius manus sunt om<nes> | potestates et omnia iura regnorum', as Deshusses 1971: item 345;

(f) Fo 177v/10: For an abbot, 'Omnipotens sempiterne deus· edificator et custos ih<e>r<usa>l<e>m sup<er>ne | ciuitatis interuentu beate marie | semper uirginis sanctoru<m>q<ue> ap<osto>loru<m> | petri et pauli et beati benedicti', as Andrieu 1938: 76;

(g) Fo 178r/1: For repelling storms, 'A domo tua quesumus domine | spiritales nequitie repellantur.', as Deshusses 1971: no. xcvi, item 1376;

(h) Fo 178r/5: For the dead, 'Absolue domine animas famulo|rum famularumq<ue> tuarum. | ab omni vinculo delictorum:' as Deshusses 1971: item 1016, and no. ciii, item 1404;

(j) Fo 178r/10 'Deus qui es sanctorum tuoru<m> | splendor mirabilis atq<ue> lapso<rum> subleuator'. Ends 'aditum ac defunctorum omniu<m> fideliu<m> | sacri baptismatis unda renatorum | animabus quiete perfrui sempiter|na. Per eundem.' Apparently located elsewhere only in Benevento, Biblioteca Capitolare 44, fo 136r.

Fo 178v/5–19: blank.

Book of Hours

Latin with French addition

HISTORY

WRITTEN BY A SINGLE SCRIBE in a textualis semi-quadrata script of s.xv[med],
this Book of Hours in Latin was probably produced in the Low Countries
(pl. 8.1). It shows illustrations by two hands. The first artist is probably from the
Netherlands (pl. 8.2), and the second has been identified as from the circle of the
Masters of Otto van Moerdrecht (pl. 8.3). Several saints from the Low Countries
are included in the Calendar, as SS Amalberge (10 July), Audegonde (31 Jan.),
Donatien, patron of Bruges (14 Oct.), Gertrude of Nivelles (17 Mar.), Lambert
(17 Sept.), Willibrord (8, *recte* 7 Nov.). It follows the Use of Rome, as indicated,
for example, by the combination of antiphon and capitulum in Prime and None.
A prayer partly in French has been added in another hand (s.xv/xvi). Additions
to the Calendar by a later owner (s.xvi?) include saints connected with Tournai,
as Eleutherius, first bishop of Tournai (20 Feb.), which suggests that the manuscript
was in what is now Belgium before leaving the Continent to come to Ireland.

The binding is French, in red leather, s.xviii, with gold tooling to the spine,
into which the outer stub in the first quire has apparently been absorbed. On the
inside of the front cover there is a bookplate showing a coat of arms surmounted
by a crest (A leopard passant proper) with the motto underneath 'In deo spero'.
The arms are those of Hornby (Dexter, Argent a chevron between three bugle-
horns sable) impaled with those of Bown (Sinister, Azure on a cross or a rose
slipped and leaved). Below is an inscription, 'Martha Hornby | September 20th
1860' (see above, p. 85). Presumably the manuscript came to Maynooth College
around s.xix[ex].

Secundo folio: 'KL februarius h‹abet› dies'.

CODICOLOGICAL DESCRIPTION

Fos ii + 83 + ii, membrane apart from the paper endleaves, measuring 155 x
100mm, written area 105 x 67mm (120 x 80mm in Quire **I**, the Calendar),
disposed in thirteen quires.

Pricking: Mostly not visible or cropped by a binder, but the prick-marks for the
horizontal lines of writing may have been made on the outer bounding line of
the framed area if the marks on fo 23 are anything to go by; unfortunately, the

8.1 RB37, fo 9r, the beginning of the Book of Hours at the Hours of the Holy Spirit. Actual page dimensions 150 x 100mm.

8.1 RB37, fo 9r, the beginning of the Book of Hours at the Hours of the Holy Spirit. Actual page dimensions 150 x 100mm.

ruling of the horizontal lines does not correspond to the position of the prick-marks.

Ruling: Generally a simple frame rule in fine crayon with the two top horizontal lines (or sometimes just the top line) ruled right across the leaf. The other horizontal lines, generally twenty-one, but thirty-four in Quire **I** (the Calendar) are ruled between the vertical bounding lines of the frame. There is no ruling on the leaves showing illustrations.

Colour and ornament: Red is used in the text for headings. Tertiary initial capitals are sometimes in red with blue shading but more often in blue with red shading; sometimes they alternate. Secondary initial capitals, as on fo 9r/13–14 (pl. 8.1), are in brown on a blue ground (with white ornament) with magenta infill (with white ornament), or on a magenta ground with blue infill. The fifteen decorated initials beginning the various sections of the text occur at fos 9r (D; pl. 8.1)), 13r (D), 17r (I), 25r (D), 32r (D), 39r (D), 41r (D), 43r (D), 45r (D), 47r (D), 51r (C), 54r (D), 64r (D), 80v (O) and 82r (O). Apart from the last two, each occurs at or near the top of the page and is set in a brown rectangle, which extends as a frame down the left-hand side of the written area, along the bottom, and up the right-hand side. On several of the folios the brown frame includes blue and pale magenta ornament (fos 9r, 13r, 17r, 25r, 54r, 64r) and on fos 9r (the beginning of the Book of Hours; pl. 8.1) and 25r (the beginning of the Hours of the Blessed Virgin Mary) small gridiron motifs at the two lower corners; on other folios the brown frame is augmented by blue or magenta lines inside it. The letters are drawn in blue (fos 9r, 13r, 25r, 39r, 47r, 54r) or magenta (fos 32r, 41r, 43r, 45r, 51r, 64r) with delicate white ornament, or very thin lines of magenta white and blue (fo 17r), and inside the letters there is filigree work with flower and leaf motifs in magenta, green and blue. The last two decorated initials (fos 80v, 82r) are less elaborate. The rectangle in which the letter is set has a blue upper half and a magenta lower half, each with white ornament, and the brown frame line extends only down the left-hand side of the written area. The letters consist of a solid brown **O**, which is not ornamented. The border of these pages is finely decorated with acanthus stems, flowers and birds or animals, in magenta, blue, green and brown, all on a natural ground filled with filigree wavy lines.

Illustrations: These are by two hands. The first artist, probably from the Netherlands, was responsible for nos 1, 5 and 6 (pl. 8.2). The second artist, who has been identified as from the circle of the Masters of Otto van Moerdrecht (on whom, see Korteweg 1990), was responsible for nos 2, 3 and 4 (pl. 8.3). For commentary on these illustrations and discussion, see Yvard 2005: IV, no. 21, pp 144–5. The borders of the illustrations appear to be by the same hand as each other, probably not the same as the hand that made the borders found on pages with decoration rather than pictures. This observation fits with the fact that all

8.2 RB37, fo 53v, by
the first artist, *Christ
in Majesty*. Actual
page dimensions
150 × 100mm.

the illustrations are on singleton leaves that do not belong to the basic format of
the quires (see Collation below), and generally appear on the verso of the leaves,
features characteristic of the usage of the Low Countries.

1. Fo 8v: *The Descent of the Holy Spirit at Pentecost*

An arch-topped lozenge in a gold/brown frame shows Mary swathed in blue
sitting centre-stage on a raised wooden seat with a purple cushion behind her.
Her hands are clasped diagonally as in prayer and her long auburn hair frames
her face and shoulders. To her left and her right are three men each side dressed

8.3 RB37, fo 24v, by the second artist, *The Annunciation*. Actual page dimensions 150 x 100mm.

in mixed shades of pink, pale green, brown, red and blue; their hands are clasped as in prayer or held up as in giving a blessing. All seven personages are shown with large halos that look like furry hats, presumably here indicating that the Holy Spirit has descended. In front there is a tiled floor with alternating squares of black and pale green. Behind Mary the pink walls of the building and a wooden ceiling taper in to focus on a window revealing a grassy hill surmounted by a single tree surrounded by blue sky, presumably indicating the route by which the Holy Spirit entered. The picture lozenge is framed on the three outer sides by a border of fine trailing stems in brown on a natural ground with flowers and leaves in blue, green, magenta and pale pink.

2. Fo 12v: *The Crucifixion*
A rectangular lozenge in a gold frame shows Christ in a white loin-cloth suspended on the cross (standing on a dark green lawn) with his head (in a fine linear gold crown of thorns) surmounted by a linear halo at the crossbar. He appears against a background of a green park with darker green trees and with a stream going into a lake on which a fisherman plies his sailing-boat, behind which there is a small green hill which points up into a block of gold that stretches right across the picture to form the background to the area above and below the cross-bar of the cross. To Christ's left is the Blessed Virgin Mary in a blue robe over a dark brown undergarment. Between her feet and the base of the cross there is a skull. Behind the Blessed Virgin Mary is Mary Magdalene in red and orange. Both have gold halos. To Christ's right is St John in a red cloak trimmed with brown and ermine, and behind him another figure in blue; there is some damage to this part of the picture. At the top of the lozenge, what looks like a gold handle encompasses the letters 'inri'. The picture lozenge is framed on the three outer sides by a border of fine trailing stems in brown on a natural ground with flowers and leaves in blue, green, orange, gold, magenta and pale pink.

3. Fo 16v: *The Blessed Virgin Mary and Child*
A rectangular lozenge in a gold frame shows the Blessed Virgin Mary in a blue robe over a brown undergarment, with her auburn hair mostly covered by a gold halo, but there is a suggestion of tresses flowing down her left shoulder and upper arm. She holds the Christ-child to her right with her right arm in a position that would have been very uncomfortable if sustained for any length of time. The background is layered. The Blessed Virgin Mary stands on a yellow ground (sand?) and, bordering that, behind her there is what looks like a balustrade in shades of magenta, behind which there is a pale green park with darker green trees merging in the background into darker green hill-forest, which is topped by gold. The picture lozenge is framed on the three outer sides by a border of fine trailing stems in brown on a natural ground with flowers and leaves in blue, green, orange, gold, magenta and pale pink.

4. Fo 24v: *The Annunciation* (pl. 8.3)
An arch-topped lozenge in a gold frame shows Mary in a blue robe over a brown shirt kneeling with her hands resting on a book sloping away from her on a prie-dieu, which is of wood with panelling and is topped with a white cloth/cushion. Her hair is auburn tinged with gold and tresses framing her right shoulder and upper arm. She is kneeling on a yellow dais, of which the grey edging can be seen like a V going into a corner at the front. On the green triangle in front stands a pink vase containing three white lilies symbolizing Mary's virginity. Behind Mary, the angel Gabriel stands semi-crouched wearing a magenta cloak with a brown collar over a white undergarment. His hair is auburn tinged with gold and his very upright wings are white trimmed with bright red. He holds a white scroll, inscribed 'aue gra<tia> plena d<omi>n<u>s [tecum]', which rises up dividing the picture vertically. Behind the two figures there is a grey chest and to the left a green curtain suspended against a gold ground with a deep blue sky above. The picture lozenge is framed on the three outer sides by a border of fine trailing stems in brown on a natural ground with flowers and leaves in blue, green, orange, gold, magenta and pale pink.

5. Fo 53v: *Christ in Majesty at the Last Judgement* (pl. 8.2)
An arch-topped lozenge with a gold frame shows the risen Christ bearded, his pale green and pink robes swirling around him, his feet on a small brown/gold globe, and he is apparently leaning back on a brown and orange rainbow. His wounds are dripping with blood but his hands are opened out as in blessing. The whole figure and the busts of the two figures below are set against a sky in blue with some white clouds, and, above, some angels in dark blue. The two figures below presumably represent the blessed, one on the left in a blue cloak over a pink undergarment, and the other on the right in a blue dress with a bright red cloak. Both figures are kneeling on grass with some bushes at the rear. Two heads, presumably representing the damned, can also be seen on the grass. The picture lozenge is framed on the three outer sides by a border of fine trailing stems in brown on a natural ground with flowers and leaves in blue, green, orange, gold, magenta and pale pink.

6. Fo 63v: *The Vigil of the Dead*
An arch-topped lozenge with a gold frame shows the same architecture as Illustration 1 of the Coming of the Holy Spirit. On a tiled floor with pale green and black squares there is a coffin draped in blue. Behind it on the left two tonsured priests, one in pink on white, and the other in red on white, stand in blessing pose. On the right three monks in black (one in front of the coffin) stand mournfully. Behind, the pink walls of the building and a blue ceiling taper in to focus on a window revealing a lopsided grassy hill with two trees on its right-hand side, surrounded by blue sky, presumably indicating the route by which the

soul makes its exit. The picture lozenge is framed on the three outer sides by a border of fine trailing stems in brown on a natural ground with flowers and leaves in blue, green, orange, gold, magenta and pale pink.

COLLATION

I⁶⁺¹ (fos 1–7; 7 is a singleton for which the stub is not visible but is apparently absorbed into the binding), II⁶⁺¹⁺¹ (fos 8–15; 1 (= fo 8) and 5 (= fo 12) are singletons containing illustrations but no text), III¹⁺⁶ (fos 16–22; 1 (= fo 16) is a singleton containing illustration but no text), IV⁶⁺¹ (fos 23–9; 2 (= fo 24) is a singleton containing illustration but no text), V⁶ (fos 30–5); VI⁶ (fos 36–41), VII⁶ (fos 42–7), VIII⁶⁺¹ (fos 48–54; 5 (= fo 53) is a singleton containing illustration but no text), IX⁶ (fos 55–60), X⁶⁺¹ (fos 61–7; 3 (= fo 63) is a singleton containing illustration but no text), XI⁶ (fos 68–73), XII⁶ (fos 74–9), XIII⁶ (fos 80–3; lacks 5 and 6).

Note 1: The sewing in Quire **X** is not at the centre of the quire (fos 64|65, a bifolium), but between fos 63 and 64.

Note 2: All the illustrations are on singleton leaves that do not belong to the basic format of the quires, and all appear on the verso of the leaf.

CONTENTS

fo 1r blank.

1. Fos 1v/1–7r/34: Calendar, beginning 'KL Ianuarius. habet. dies. | xxxi. luna. xxx.' Ends 'Siluestri pape.' fos 7v–8r blank.

2. Fo 8v: Illustration 1 (full page) of *The Descent of the Holy Spirit at Pentecost*. Fos 9r/1–11r/14: Hours of the Holy Spirit. "**Incipiunt hore de Sancto Spiritu.**" Begins (pl. 8.1) 'Domine labia | mea aperies.'; continues fo 9r/13 'Nobis sancti spiritus | gracia sit data: y<**mnu**>s'; fo 9v/5 'Omnipotens sempiterne | deus da nobis illam | sancti spiritus graciam'; fo 9v/17 'y<**mnu**>s | De uirgine filius ihesus | fuit natus.'; fo 10r/5 'SUum sanctum spiritum | deus delegauit.'; fo 10r/14 'Septiformem [*sic*] graciam tu<n>c | acceptauerunt'; fo 10v/2 'Spiritus paraclitus fuit appel|latus.'; fo 10v/11 'Dextere dei tu digitus.'; fo 11r/1 'SPiritus paraclitus nos uelit | iuuare.'; fo 11r/9 'HAs horas canonicas cum de|uocione.'; ends 'Benedicamus domino. Deo gr<ati>as'. Fos 11r/15–21, 11v and 12r blank.

3. Fo 12v: Illustration 2 (full page) of *The Crucifixion*. Fos 13r/1–15r/7: Hours of the Holy Cross. "**Incipit officium sancte crucis ad ma|tutinas.**" Begins 'DOmine labia mea aperies'; fo 13v/12 'HOra prima ductus est ihesus | ad pylatum.' [*AH* 30: 32, no. 13.2]; fo 13v/20 'CRucifige clamitant

hora ter|ciarum.' [*AH* 30: 32, no. 13.3]; fo 14r/7 'y<m>n<us> | Hora sexta ihesus
est cruci con|clauatus.' [*AH* 30: 33, no. 13.4]; fo 14r/15 'HOra nona dominus
ihesus | expirauit.' [*AH* 30: 33, no. 13.5]; fo 14v/1 'DE cruce deponitur hora
vesper|tina.' [*AH* 30: 33, no. 13.6]; fo 14v/12 'Hympnus. | HOra completorii
datur sepul|ture.' [*AH* 30: 33, no. 13.7] Ends fo 15r/7 'Et anime omnium fidelium
de|functorum per misericordiam dei | sine fine. Requiescant in pace. Ame<n>.'
fo 15r/8–21, fos 15v–16r blank.

4. Fo 16v: Illustration 3 (full page) of *The Blessed Virgin Mary and Child.*
Fos 17r/1–23v/12: Mass for the Blessed Virgin Mary, to precede Item 5, the
Hours of the Blessed Virgin Mary. "**Incipiunt hore b<ea>te marie uirginis. +**".
'INtroibo ad altare | dei. ... Dignare | domine die isto. Si|ne peccato nos cus|todire.'
fo 17r/11 'COnfiteor deo celi beate marie | uirginu<m>'; fo 17v/9 '**Introi|tus
missa.** | Salue sancta | parens'; fo 17v/16 'Kyri eleyson'; fo 17v/19 'GLoria in
excelsis deo.'; fo 18r/14 'COncede nos famulos | tuos quesumus domine deus
noster' [Collect of the Common of the Blessed Virgin Mary]; fo 18v/1 '**lectio
libri sapiencie.** [Ecclus 24.14–16] AB inicio et ante secula crea|ta sum'; fo 18v/12
Gr<aduale> [of the Common of the Blessed Virgin Mary] Benedicta et uene|rabilis
es uirgo maria'; fo 18v/20 '**Inicium s<an>c<t>i | euuangelii. Secundum .lucam.**
[Lk 11.27] || IN illo tempore loquente ihesu ad tur|bas. Extollens uocem
queda<m>.'; fo 19r/7 'y<m>nus. | Credo in unum deum.'; fo 19v/20
'**Offertoriu<m>** | Felix namq<ue> es sacra | uirgo maria'; fo 20r/3 'Sanctus'; fo
20r/8 'Agnus dei'; fo 20r/13 '**Co<m>munio** Beata uiscera | marie uirginis' [*AH*
20: 148, no. 190]; fo 20r/16 '**collecta.** | GRaciam tuam | quesumus domine
men|tibus nostris'; fo 20v/3 'Ite missa est. Deo gracias.' Continues with four
Gospel readings: fo 20v/4 '**Secundum iohannem.** [Jn 1.1] | IN principio erat
verbum.'; fo 21r/14 '**Secundum lucam.** [Lk 1.26] | IN illo tempore. Missus est
angelus | gabriel'; fo 22r/9 '**Secundum matheum.** [Mt 2.1] | IN illo tempore.
Cum natus esset ih<esu>s | in bethleem iude'; fo 23r/7 '**Secundum marcum.**
[Mk 16.14] | IN illo tempore. Recumbentibus | undecim discipulis apparuit illis';
ends 'sequentibus signis. Deo | gracias.' fos 23v/13–21, 24r blank.

5. Fo 24v: Illustration 4 (full page) of *The Annunciation* (pl. 8.3).
Fos 25r/1–31r/15: Hours of the Blessed Virgin Mary. "**Incipiunt hore beate
marie uirginis | secundum consuetudinem romane | ecclesie. Ad matutinas.**"
'DOmine labia | mea aperies.'; fo 25r/15 **Inuitat[orium]** AVe maria gracia ple|na';
fo 25r/16 '**psalmus** [94] | VEnite exultemus domino'; fo 26r/11 'ymnus. QVem
terra ponthus' [*AH* 19: 60, no. 81]; fo 26v/3 '**psalmus.** [8] Domine dominus
n<oste>r quam | admirabile est'; fo 27r/8 [Ps 18] CEli enarrant gloriam dei'; fo
28r/9 '**psalmus.** [23] | DOmini est terra'; fo 29r/2 '**l<e>c<t>io p<ri>ma.** [Ecclus
24.11–13] | IN omnibus requiem'; fo 29r/18 '**lectio .ij.** | [Ecclus. 24:15–16] ET
sic in syon firmata'; fo 29v/13 '**lectio .iij.** [Ecclus 24:17–20] | Quasi cedrus exaltata

sum'; fo 30r/13 '**laus angeloru<m>. TE** deum laudamus'; ends '**uersus. ORa** pro nobis sancta dei geni|trix. Ut digni efficiamur promis|sione <Chr>isti.' fo 31r/16–21, 31v blank (lacks illustration).

6. Fos 32r/1–38r/16: Lauds. "**Ad laudes.**" 'DEus in adiutori|um meum inte<n>|de'; fo 32r/7 '**psalmus.** [92] Dominus regnavit decorem | indutus est'; fo 32v/3 '**p<salmu>s.** [99] Ivbilate deo'; fo 32v/19 '**psalmus.** [62] Deus deus meus ad te de lu|ce uigilo'; fo 33v/3 '**p<salmu>s** [64] Deus misereatur'; fo 34r/1 '**p<salmu>s** [*sic* = canticle of the three children Dan 3.57–88, 56] BEnedicite omnia opera d<omi>ni'; fo 35r/2 '**psalmus.** [148] LAudate dominu<m> de celis.'; fo 35v/8 '**p<salmu>s** [149] Cantate domino canticu<m> no|uu<m>'; fo 36r/6 '**psalmus.** [150] Laudate dominu<m> in sanctis eius'; fo 36r/20 '**capitulum.** [SofS 6.8] Viderunt eam et filie'; fo 36v/3 '**y<m>nus** | O Gloriosa domina. | excelsa supra sydera'; fo 36v/15 '**p<salmu>s d<aui>d** [= Canticle of Zachary, Lk 1.68–79] Benedictus d<omi>n<u>s deus ysrael'; ends 'requie<m> eterna<m> co<n>cede | Per <Christu>m dominu<m> nostru<m> Amen. | Benedicamus domino. Deo gra<tia>s'. Fo 38r/17–21 and 38v blank (lacks illustration).

7. Fos 39r/1–40v/21: Prime. "**Ad primam.**" 'DEus in adiutoriu<m>'; fo 39r/6 '**ymn<us>** | MEmento salutis auctor'; **an<tifon>** 'assumpta est'; fo 39r/15 '**p<salmu>s d<aui>d.** [53] | DEus in nomine tuo saluu<m> me | fac'; fo 39v/9 '**p<salmu>s** [84] Benedixisti d<omi>ne terra<m> tua<m>'; fo 40r/13 '**psalmus.** [116] Laudate d<omi>n<u>m om<ne>s gentes'; fo 40r/19 '**cap<itulum>** [= SofS 6.9] | QVe est ista'; ends 'Et pacem tuam. ut supra.'

8. Fos 41r/1–42v/11: Terce. "**Ad terciam.**" 'DEus in adiutori|um'; fo 41r/8 '**p<salmu>s d<aui>d.** [119] | AD d<omi>n<u>m cum tribularer cla|maui'; fo 41r/20 '**p<salmu>s.** [120] | LEuaui oculos meos'; fo 41v/14 '**p<salmu>s.** [121] | LEtatus sum in hijs'; fo 42r/12 '**Capitulum.** [= Ecclus 24:15] | ET sic in syon firmata su<m>'; ends 'Omnes sancti tui Or<ati>o alia | ET pacem tuam. ut s<upra>.' fo 42v/12–21 blank.

9. Fos 43r/1–44v/4: Sexte. "**Ad sextam**". 'DEus in adiutoriu<m>'; fo 43r/8 '**psalmus dauid.** [122] | 'AD te leuaui oculos meos'; fo 43r/18 '**p<salmu>s.** [123] | 'NIsi quia d<omi>n<u>s erat in nob<is>'; fo 43v/13 '**psalm<us>.** [124] | 'QVi confidunt in d<omi>no'; fo 44r/6 '**cap<itu>l<um>** [Ecclus 24.16] | ET radicaui in populo'; ends 'Omnes sancti tui **Alia** or<ati>o | ET pacem tuam. ut s<upra>.' fo 44v/5–21 blank.

10. Fos 45r/1–46v/9: None. "**Ad nonam.**" 'DEus in adiutori[um]'; fo 45r/7 '**y<m>nus.** | MEmento salutis auctor'; fo 45r/9 '**p<salmu>s d<aui>d.** [125] | 'IN conuertendo d<omi>n<u>s captiuita|tem syon'; fo 45v/1 Psalm 126 'NIsi

d<omi>n<u>s edificauerit domu<m>'; fo 45v/14 'psalmus. [127] BEati om<ne>s
qui time<n>t d<omi>n<u>m'; fo 46r/6 'an<tifon> Pulchra es'; fo 46r/8 'capitulum.
[= Ecclus 24.19] | IN plateis sicut cynamoniu<m> | et balsamu<m> aromatizans
odo|rem dedi'; ends 'Omnes sancti tui Oracio. | ET pacem tuam. ut s<upra>.' fo
46v/10–21 blank.

11. Fos 47r/1–50r/20: Vespers. "Ad uesperas." 'DEus in adiuto|riu<m>'; fo 47r/8
'psalmus. [109]|| DIxit d<omi>n<u>s d<omi>no meo'; fo 47v/4 'p<salmu>s
[112] | LAudate pueri domini'; fo 47v/17 'p<salmu>s [121] | LEtatus su<m>';
fo 48r/15 'psalmus. d<aui>d [126] | 'NIsi d<omi>n<u>s edificauerit domu<m>';
fo 48v/10 'psalmus. d<aui>d [147] | LAuda ih<e>r<usa>l<e>m d<omi>n<u>m';
fo 49r/7 'capitulu<m>. [= Ecclus 24.14] | AB inicio et ante secula creata | sum';
fo 49r/11 'y<m>n<us> | AVe maris stella dei mater'; fo 49v/8 'p<salmu>s [= Lk
1.46] | MAgnificat a<n>i<m>a mea d<omi>n<u>m'; ends 'Omnes sancti tui alia
or<aci>o. | ET pacem tuam. ut s<upra>.' fo 50r/21, 50v blank (lacks illustration).

12. Fos 51r/1–52v/20: Compline. "Ad co<m>pletorium." 'COnuerte nos de|us
salutaris n<oste>r'; fo 51r/9 'p<salmu>s [128] | SEpe expugnaueru<n>t me a |
iuuentute mea'; fo 51v/4 'psalm<us> [130] | DOmine no<n> est exaltatu<m>
cor me|um'; fo 51v/17 'cap<itu>l<u>m. [= Ecclus 24.24] | EGo m<ate>r pulchre
dil<e>ctionis'; fo 52r/1 'NVnc dimittis seruu<m> tuu<m>' [Lk 2.29]; fo 52r/17
blank; fo 52r/18 'Ant<ifon> de domina nostra. | SAlue regina [mater]
misericordie'[*AH* 50: 318, no. 245]; ends 'ab in|stantib<us> malis et a morte
perpetua | liberemur. Per <Christu>m dominum | nostru<m> Amen'. Fos 52v/21,
53r blank.

13. Fo 53v: Illustration 5 (full page) *Christ in Majesty at the Last Judgement*
Fos 54r/1–62r/19: Seven Penitential Psalms and Litany.
(a) Fos 54r/1–59v/19: "Incipiu<n>t septem psalmi penitencial<es>". Begins
    with Ps 6 'DOmine ne in fu|rore'; fo 54v/6 'psalmus. [31] BEati quoru<m>
    remisse su<n>t'; fo 55r/15 'p<salmu>s. [37] DOmine in furore tuo argu|as
    me neq<ue> in ira tua corripias me. | Quoniam sagitte tue'; fo 56v/2
    'p<salmu>s [50] MIserere me deus'; fo 57v/1 'p<salmu>s [101] || DOmine
    exaudi or<ati>onem mea<m> et clamor meus ad te ueniat'; fo 58v/16
    'p<salmu>s. [129] | DE profundis clamaui ad te | d<omi>ne'; fo 59r/9
    'p<salmu>s. [142] | DOmine exaudi or<ati>onem mea<m> | aurib<us>
    percipe obsecracione<m> mea<m>'; ends 'ego ser|uus tuus sum'.
(b) Fos 59v/19–62r/19: "letania." Begins 'Kyri eleiso<n> [3x] | <Christ>e audi
    nos Pater de celis deus'. Ends 'piis supplicacionib<us> | consequantur. P[er]
    <Christu>m dominu<m> nos|trum. amen'. fos 62r/20–21, 62v, 63r blank.

14. Fo 63v: Illustration 6 (full page) of *The Vigil of the Dead*

Fos 64r/1–80v/8: Office of the Dead. "**Incipiu‹n›t uigilie mortuoru‹m›** ∴ **Inc‹ipit›**" | 'Placebo. **p‹salmu›s** [114] | **DI**lexi q‹uonia›m exau|diet d‹omi›n‹u›s uoce‹m›' | orationes [*recte* –nis] mee'; fo 64v/12 **p‹salmu›s** [9] | **CO**nfitebor tibi d‹omi›ne in toto | corde meo'; fo 65r/3 'psalmus. [145] | **LA**uda anima mea d‹omi›n‹u›m'; fo 66v/1 'psalmus [5] || **UE**rba mea aurib‹us› percipe d‹omi›ne'. [7] | **DO**mine deus meus in te spe|raui'; fo 68r/20 'lectio p‹ri›ma. [Job 7.16] | **PA**rce michi d‹omi›ne nichil enim | sunt dies mei.'; fo 68v/20 'lectio .ii. [Job 10.1] | **TE**det a‹n›i‹m›am meam uite mee'; fo 69v/1 'lectio .iii. [Job 10.8] | **MA**nus tue domine. fecerunt me et plasmaueru‹nt› me totum'; fo 69v/19 'p‹salmu›s [22] | **DO**minus regit [me] et nichil m‹ihi› | deerit'; fo 70r/18 'p‹salmu›s. [24] | **AD** te d‹omi›ne leuaui a‹n›i‹m›am mea‹m›'; fo 71r/21 'p‹salmu›s. [26] || **DO**minus illuminacio mea et | salus mea'; fo 72r/21 'l‹e›c‹t›io iiij [Job 13.22/23] || **RE**sponde michi quantas habeo | iniquitates'; fo 72v/17 'l‹e›c‹t›io v. [Job 14.1] **HO**mo natus de mulieri breui | uiuens tempore repletur multis mi|serijs.'; fo 73r/17 'l‹e›c‹t›io .vi. [Job 14.13] | **QV**is michi hoc tribuat'; fo 73v/12 'psalmus. [39] | Expectans expectaui d‹omi‹n‹u›m'; fo 75r/5 'psalmus [40] | **BE**atus qui intelligit sup‹er› egenu‹m› | et paupere‹m›'; fo 75v/20 'p‹salmu›s [41] **QV**emadmodu‹m› desiderat ceru‹us› || ad fontes aquarum'; fo 76v/19 'lectio .vij. [Job 17.1] | Spiritus meus atenuabitur | dies mei breuiabuntur'; fo 77r/19 'l‹e›c‹t›io viij [Job 19.20] | **PE**lli me[e] consumptis carnib‹us› | adhesit os meum'; fo 78r/1 'lectio .ix. [Job 10.18] | **QV**are de uulua eduxisti me'; fo 78v/1 'p‹salmu›s [64] | **TE** decet ymnus deus in syon'; fo 79r/13 'p‹salmu›s [62] | **D**eus deus meus ad te'; fo 79r/14 'psalm‹us› [66] | **D**eus misereatur n‹ost›ri.'; fo 79r/17 'Canticum. [Is 38.10] | **EG**o dixi in dimidio dieru‹m› meo‹rum› | uada‹m› ad portas inferi.'; fo 80r/11 'p‹salmu›s [148] | 'LAudate d‹omi›n‹u›m de celis'; fo 80r/12 'P‹salmu›s [149] | **CA**ntate domino canticu‹m›'; fo 80r/13 'psalm‹us› [150] | **LA**ud‹ate› dominu‹m› in sanctis.' Ends 'Oracio. | **PA**rte‹m› beate resurrexionis optine|a‹n›t anime omniu‹m› fideliu‹m› defunc|toru‹m› uitamq‹ue› eternam habere merea‹n›|tur in celis per te ih‹es›u ‹Ch›riste saluator | mundi rex glorie. Qui uiuis et regnas deus. Per omnia secula seculo‹rum› A‹men›.' fo 80v/9 blank.

15. Fos 80v/10–81v/17: Prayer to the Blessed Virgin Mary formerly attributed to Anselm of Canterbury. "**Oracio ad beatam uirgine‹m› mariam.**" 'O Intemerata et in et‹er›|num benedicta sin|gularis ‹et› inco‹m›parabi|lis uirgo'. Ends 'Et post huius uite cursu‹m› | ad gaudia me ducat electoru‹m› suo‹rum› | benignissimus p‹ar›aclitus. Qui cu‹m› p‹at›re | et filio coeternus et co‹n›substa[ntia]lis cu‹m› eis | et in eis uiuit et regnat omnipote‹n›s | deus in secula seculoru‹m›. Amen.' As Wilmart 1932: 488–90, also PL 158, 959. Fo 81v/18–21 blank.

16. Fos 82r/1–83r/6: "**Item alia oracio de domina n‹ost›ra.**" 'OBsecro te d‹omi›na s‹an›c‹t›a ma|ria mater dei pietate | plenissima'. Ends 'Et hanc or‹ati›o|nem meam supplice‹m› suscipias et exau|dias et uitam eternam michi tribuas | audi et exaudi me dulcissima mater dei | et misericordie. Amen'. fo 83r/7 blank.

Added in another hand (s.xv/xvi)

17. Fo 83r/8–83v/20: Prayer. '❡ Le pape Iehan donna a tous ceulx | qui diront ceste orison qui sensieut cascung jour en sung coer ❡ Et iij | fois le jour nostre dame ❡ cent et | .l. ans de pardons ❡ et le [*sic*] viiᵉ p‹ar›tie | de ses pechies pardonnes ❡ Et se | verra la vierge marie iij fois | deuant sa mort'. Fo 83r/16 'Aue virgo virginum: que portasti filium: creatorem o‹mn›ium: dulcis | mater aue'. Ends 'Jhesus | Et benedicta sit mater tua sancta | anna ex qua sine macula tua | caro processit virginea ❡ Amen'. Chevalier 1892–1920: III, no. 24023.

9 RB38
Book of Hours
Latin and French

A N ATTRACTIVE BOOK OF HOURS probably produced in Paris s.xv^ex, with illustrations by two artists (pls 9.1, 9.2), to which some material from another Book of Hours has been added (Quires **II** and **VI**^bis), also probably Parisian of about the same date or slightly later (pl. 9.3). Since St Nicholas of Tollentino (canonized 1446) and St Bernadino of Siena (canonized 1450) appear in the Calendar (10 Sept. and 20 May respectively), the date of the manuscript must be after 1450, and the style of the bâtarde script suggests it was written even later than that. Specific evidence for Paris comes from (a) the double appearance of St Geneviève in the Calendar, both on her feast-day of 3 January (fo 1r) and on the anniversary of the procession of her relics to save Paris from ergot-sickness on 26 November 1129 (fo 6r), as well as a full-page picture of her on fo 46v; and (b) the twinning of St Leu (Loup) and St Gilles at 1 September in the Calendar (fo 5r), which is exclusive to Paris, where their church still stands on Rue St Denis. Nevertheless, the main part of this Book of Hours shows the Use of Rennes, and the presence of some specifically Breton saints in the litany (fo 56v), viz. SS Corentin (12 Dec.), Hervé (17 June) and Tugdual (30 Nov.), suggests that the Book was commissioned by or tailored for a nobleman and his wife from Brittany who used the motto 'Tenir foy à Dieu ou G[râce à] D[ieu]' (cf. Illustrations 20 and 21 on fos 63r and 77r, and the motto occurs also in the border of Illustration 19 on fo 62v (pl. 9.2), all three of these illustrations being the only ones by the second artist); incidentally, these saints do not occur in the Calendar (fos 1–6). These observations suggest that the main part of the manuscript was bought 'off the peg' so to speak, and then personalized probably in the same workshop with the additional images and motto. The inserted quires by another hand and artist show the Use of Rome. At some stage in its history the manuscript was evidently disbound and some leaves were lost before the surviving parts were reassembled partly in the wrong order, and the additional material was incorporated somewhat clumsily, perhaps because it includes Gospel readings not present in the main part of the manuscript.

The binding of s.xvii/xviii is probably French. It is of white vellum on card with paper endleaves. On the inside of the front cover there is a bookplate showing the arms, crest and motto of Mackay (illustrated in Kennedy 1967: 132). Arms: Azure on a chevron or between three bears's heads couped argent muzzled [gules], a roebuck's head erased between two dexter arms couped at the elbows grasping daggers, the points towards the buck's head all proper. Crest: A dexter arm erect, couped at the elbow, the hand grasping a dagger also erect, proper. Motto, below the shield: 'MANV FORTI', meaning 'With a Strong Hand' (Ex 13.3). These arms are borne in Scotland by Lord Reay, the chief of the clan Mackay. While the undifferenced arms are strictly his alone, the absence of a coronet (and supporters) shows that the bookplate is not his. A branch of the family, which later took the form of the name Mackey or Macky, was established at Belmont, Co. Derry (Burke 1899: 287). Presumably the manuscript came to Maynooth College from some such a source, probably s.xix⁴.

On the recto of the first paper endleaf the French words 'très rare' occur in a hand of s.xix$^{1/2}$, suggesting that the manuscript was then in France.

Secundo folio: 'KL Mars a xxxj iour.'

CODICOLOGICAL DESCRIPTION

Fos ii + 78 + ii, membrane except for the paper endleaves added with the binding of s.xvii/xviii. The leaves measure 164 x 104mm, written area 106 x 62mm, but some illustrations occupy the whole page.

Pricking: None visible.

Ruling: In fine crayon. Quire **I** (Calendar) shows a simple frame ruling with the vertical bounding lines and the top horizontal line occasionally extending to the outer edges of the leaves; there are thirty-three horizontal lines for writing, but no writing on the top line. Quires **II–X** show a similar frame rule with twenty lines ruled for nineteen lines of writing.

Colour and ornament: For the Calendar on fos 1–6 three colours are used – red, blue and gold – the latter being used for the dates and the more important saints. At the top left of each page **KL** is blocked in in blue or red, with gold lettering. In the text there are frequent capitals often in gold on squat blocks of colour, usually red or blue and flecked with gold; some capitals are in blue and white on a red ground flecked with gold, as **V** on fo 9v, or **S** on fo 12v. As well as larger capitals there are even more frequent smaller capitals. Spaces at the end of lines are often filled with bars of colour, red or blue, flecked with gold.

Illustrations: By two main artists, except for nos 1, 8 and 9, which are by the additional artist. The first artist is responsible for nos 2, 3, 4 (pl. 9.1), 5, 6, 7, 10, 11, 12, 13, 14, 15, 16, 17 and 18. The second artist is responsible for nos 19 (pl. 9.2), 20 and 21, the three illustrations that contain the motto 'Tenir foy à Dieu ou G[râce à] D[ieu]', and may have had a closer association with the apparent patrons. The iconographic programme used by the first artist is unusual, introducing Prime of the Blessed Virgin Mary with *St Julian and his Wife ferrying Christ across a River*, Terce with *St Blaise with Crozier and Carding Comb*, Sexte with *Christ in Majesty at the Last Judgement*, Vespers with *Mary Magdalene*, Compline with *Susannah and the Elders*, and the Matins of the Holy Spirit with *St Christopher* (pl. 9.1). In the following analysis, illustrations are by the first artist unless otherwise stated. For commentary on the artists and discussion, see Yvard 2005: IV, no. 22, pp 151–2.

1. Fo 7r: By the additional artist, lozenge of one third of a page showing *St John on the Isle of Patmos* in red and blue and gold, writing his gospel on a white scroll with his eagle in gold by his side against a scenic background in green and blue with gold flowers and sunrays, framed in gold. This lozenge and the text below it are framed by an elaborate border of trailing stems in green, red and blue on a gold ground. The text begins with a capital I in blue with gold ornament on a red ground.

2. Fo 9r: Lozenge of two thirds of a page showing *The Annunciation*. Mary in a blue robe trimmed with gold, and with a purple-brown shirt, holding a book kneeling before a prie-Dieu, and in front of her the angel Gabriel in gold, blue and white, with green wings. Above her is God, holding an orb, at a blue window sending the white dove via rays of gold down towards Mary. Behind is a purple-brown door with a red drape (flecked with gold) above and to the left, and the floor is pink. Below is a decorated initial **D** in purple-brown with green motifs on a gold ground flecked with red, beginning four lines of text. The lozenge and the text are framed by an elaborate border of trailing stems in green, red and blue on a gold ground.

3. Fo 20r: Lozenge of half a page showing *The Crucifixion*. Christ in white loin-cloth suspended low on a tall cross with his head (in a gold crown of thorns) below the crossbar against a background of green land and a blue hill surmounted by a tower below, and pale blue sky above. To Christ's left is the Blessed Virgin Mary in a blue robe trimmed with gold over a purple-brown undergarment; she has a gold halo and is shown weeping. To Christ's right is St John in a red cloak trimmed with gold over a white undergarment; his hair is streaked with gold and he has a gold halo. Above and below are small lozenges of text, the one below showing a decorated initial heart-shaped **D** in red and grey with red and green plant motifs on a gold ground, beginning three lines of text, each one utilizing the initial **D**. The picture and text lozenge is framed by an elaborate border of trailing stems in green and red on a blue ground; there are five gold scrolls containing prayers, reading in clockwise order 'Diev soiet love', 'Adoramvs te <Christ>e', Obsecro te domina', 'Domine miserere nobis', 'Maria mater'.

4. Fo 21r (pl. 9.1): Lozenge of two thirds of a page showing *St Christopher with the Christ Child*. St Christopher is walking through blue water holding his brown staff upright with both hands, with the Christ Child on his left shoulder carrying an orb in his left hand and with two fingers of his right hand raised in blessing. He is dressed in a dark blue tunic and a red and gold cloak. Behind him, emerging from green trees, the bust of a hermit dressed in brown and gold holding a lantern. In front of him there is land in green with dark green bushes. In the background is a blue cliff surmounted by a tower. The picture and text lozenge is framed by an elaborate border of diamond-shaped lozenges in blue and magenta on a cream ground dotted with green stems and blue and magenta petals.

5. Fo 22r: Lozenge of two thirds of a page showing *St Julian and his Wife ferrying Christ across a River*. Christ in a brown robe kneels in the centre of a brown boat on a blue lake with St Julian on the right rowing in a blue jacket and brown scarf and hat and his wife on the left dressed in green with a burgundy hat and holding a lamp. In the foreground is some green land and in the background a landscape green at the water's edge comprising two hills in blue surmounted by twin round towers. The picture and text lozenge is framed by an elaborate border on a cream ground showing intertwined stems in blue, red, green, grey and gold, and a gold scroll inscribed 'SALVE REGINA MATER MISERICORDIE VITA DULCEDO ET SPES NOSTRA SALVE AD [TE CLAMAMUS]' with red and blue alternating from word to word.

6. Fo 25v: Lozenge of half a page showing *St Blaise with Crozier and Carding Comb*. The bishop stands on a pale floor dressed in a white surplice surmounted by a brown tunic and over that a blue chasuble with gold decoration. On his head a white mitre and his right hand holds up a carding comb and his left hand is down holding a crozier. In the background a green rectangular frame with mauve centre. The picture and text lozenge are framed by an elaborate border showing irregular angular shapes in red, blue and gold, with fine stems in green and blue and red flowers on the gold ground, and tracery on the red and blue ground except for a grey swan-like bird on the blue ground in the lower left-hand corner.

7. Fo 28r: Lozenge of half a page showing *Christ in Majesty at the Last Judgement*. Christ, seated on an arc with his feet on a small golden orb, is dressed in a red cloak open at the front to show the wounds of his passion. The figure is on a yellow ground surrounded by orange flames making an oval surrounded by a pale blue oval and then darker blue on either side outside that, except that what look like dark blue tendrils intrude to apparently support the arc. The picture and text lozenge are framed by an elaborate border of trailing stems in green, red and blue on a cream ground.

9.1 RB38, fo 21r, by the first artist, *St Christopher*, with text. Actual page dimensions 164 x 104mm.

9.2 RB38, fo 62v, by the second artist, *St Laurence*, with text and the patron's motto. Actual page dimensions 164 x 104mm.

8. Fo 33r: By the additional artist, lozenge of half a page showing *The Flight into Egypt*. Mary with a red blouse and a blue cloak and hood with gold decoration sits on a brown donkey holding the Christ Child also dressed in blue. Joseph in blue undercoat and red robe and hat walks with his staff on the far side of the donkey. The path is rough with stones and plants, while the background shows a green valley surmounted by flowering shrubs at either side extending to blue sea and sky with golden rays shining down. The picture and text lozenge are framed by an elaborate border showing diagonal stripes of red and blue on a gold ground showing stems with green leaves and blue and red flowers.

9. Fo 37r: By the additional artist, lozenge in a gold border of a third of a page showing *The Coronation of the Virgin*. To the left God the Father in gold and white sits holding an orb in his left hand and his right hand slightly raised in blessing. Before him the Virgin kneels wearing a red robe and a blue cloak with her hair uncovered before a red curtain studded with gold decoration, while behind her an angel places the crown on her head. God is placed in front of a dark blue sky studded with gold stars, while the angel is placed in front of a pale blue sky. The picture and text lozenge are framed by an elaborate border featuring diagonal stripes of gold on a white ground showing stems with green leaves and blue and red flowers on the gold ground and swirls in blue and gold on the white ground.

10. Fo 41r: Lozenge of half a page showing *Mary Magdalene* standing on a pink floor in a green robe over a brown tunic, wearing a brown headdress from which her long brown hair flows down over her shoulders. She holds a pot of ointment in her left hand. Behind is a brown wooden panel surmounted at the top by a crimson curtain that drops to the left with a bench also covered in crimson at the base. To the right there is a window revealing green lawn and blue landscape receding into the distance. The picture and text lozenge are framed by an elaborate border showing swirls of blue and gold on a cream ground interspersed with golden hearts filled with green stems and blue and red flowers, and interspersed also with animal and bird designs in grey.

11. Fo 43r: Lozenge of half a page showing *Susannah and the Elders*. Susannah stands naked in a brown tub containing blue water. The tub is in a green garden with trees lining the background, in which lurk rather conspicuously the two bearded elders, one on the left in red and blue, and the one on the right in brown with a red hat. The picture and text lozenge are framed by an elaborate border showing irregular shapes in red, blue and gold, with fine stems in green, and blue and red flowers on the gold ground, and tracery on the red and blue ground except for two cream-coloured birds on patches of blue ground.

12. Fo 46v: Full-page lozenge showing *St Geneviève with her Taper*. St Geneviève in a blue dress with a gold cloak stands in a green park, with shrubs either side of her, holding a red book in her left hand. Behind her to the left there is a pale brown turreted tower set in trees, to the right a landscape merging from green into blue showing a hill in the distance surmounted by twin towers. In her right hand she holds a taper that goes up towards the blue sky where the devil, dark and insignificant, is extinguishing it, and an angel in red with gold wings is firmly rekindling it. The picture lozenge is framed by an elaborate border showing swirls in blue and gold ornamented with green leaves and red fruit, and two animal/bird motifs in grey.

13. Fo 47r: Lozenge of two thirds of a page showing *David with his Harp*. David, in a brown robe and blue cloak with ermine collar, sits with his golden harp on a throne with a canopy all covered in crimson, with a green drape seen either side of the canopy. The picture and text lozenge are framed by an elaborate border made up of diamonds alternately gold and cream showing blue and gold swirls on the cream ground and green leaves and pink flowers on the gold ground.

14. Fo 59v: Lozenge of one quarter of a page showing *St Michael as Victor over the Devil*. St Michael showing long brown hair and wearing a gold suit of armour stands over a purple-grey devil who is prostrate on the green ground. St Michael's lance surmounted by a cross transfixes the devil at the shoulder. In the background is a blue landscape merging into sky. The border with purple ground shows green stems and leaves with blue and cream flowers and a gold swirling banner (appropriate to St Michael) inscribed in blue (partially erased by rubbing) 'AVE MARIA GRA[TIA PL]ENA DO[M]INVS TECVM BENEDICTA TV I[N MULIE]RIBVS ET BEN[E]DI[CTUS]'.

15. Fo 60r: Lozenge of one quarter of a page showing *John the Baptist with the Lamb*. John stands on a greensward with darker green trees behind. He is dressed in animal skins tinged with gold and holds the smiling lamb with its penant of gold in his left hand and points to it with his right hand. The border on a cream ground with blue and gold tracery swirls shows golden chevrons decorated with green stems and red and blue flowers.

16. Fo 60v: Lozenge of one quarter of a page showing *St Stephen Martyred by Stoning*. St Stephen stands beardless on a greensward dressed in a white undergarment topped by a gold dalmatic appropriate to a deacon. In his right hand across his waist he holds a stone and in his left hand a golden palm. His tonsured head has been struck by another stone and blood drips down his head and his dalmatic, so that the vertical stripes appropriate to the dalmatic look like more blood flowing down. In the background there is a blue rocky hill surmounted

by twin towers. The border on a cream ground with blue and gold tracery swirls shows golden chevrons decorated with green stems and red and blue flowers.

17. Fo 61r: Lozenge of one quarter of a page showing *St Nicholas and the Three Children.* Against a background of a grey door, St Nicholas stands wearing a white undergarment, green robe and gold cloak, and mitre, and in his left hand a crozier. With his right hand he is blessing the three children who are portrayed restored from dismemberment and emerging from a brown brine tub with gold trim. The border is divided into rectangular sections alternating between a cream ground with blue and gold swirling tracery and a gold ground decorated with green-leaved stems with red and blue flowers; in each of two of the segments on a cream ground there is a grey animal or bird.

18. Fo 61v: Lozenge of one quarter of a page showing *St Barbara holding a Tower and Palm.* St Barbara stands in a green garden with a brown area bordered by three green shrubs. In the background there are rocky hills to either side of her, each surmounted by a tower/castle. She is dressed in a red robe with gold trim, and holds a golden three-windowed turret with her right hand (symbolizing the place where she was imprisoned by her father) and a golden palm in her left hand. Her golden hair falls over her shoulders and down below her waist. To her right there are two dark clouds in the sky. The border is divided into rectangular sections alternating between a cream ground with blue and gold swirling tracery and a gold ground decorated with green-leaved stems with red and blue flowers; in each of two of the segments on a cream ground there is a grey animal or bird.

19. Fo 62v (pl. 9.2): By the second artist, lozenge of one quarter of a page showing *St Laurence with Gridiron and Scourge.* St Laurence stands in a green field with bushes behind him and then blue landscape with sky above. He is dressed in a white undergarment surmounted by a red dalmatic appropriate to a deacon. In his right hand he holds a gold scourge and in his left hand his gridiron. Behind him some of the field has gold flames, which also affect his dalmatic. His head is tonsured and surmounted by a thick gold halo. The border is on a gold ground decorated with green-leaved stems with red, blue and white flowers, and showing a blue scroll in three sections with gold lettering each saying 'TENIR FOY A DIEV OV G[râce à] D[ieu].'

20. Fo 63r: By the second artist, lozenge of two thirds of a page showing *The Holy Trinity.* Against a dark blue sky God the Father sits facing forward to the right with the Son to his right, both dressed in crimson robes. On the Father's lap is a golden orb and they hold open a large Bible between them. Between their heads is the Dove, and billowing from both sides of them is the blue smoke of the Holy Spirit which descends to a woman in a brown robe (patroness?) kneeling

at the bottom left of the picture. In front of her there is a green landscape with pale blue sky above. The border is on a gold ground decorated with green-leaved stems with red, blue and white flowers, and showing a blue scroll in three sections with gold lettering each saying 'TENIR FOY A DIEV OV G[râce à] D[ieu].'

21. Fo 77r: By the second artist, lozenge of one quarter of a page showing *St Anne Teaching the Blessed Virgin Mary to Read*. St Anne sits to the left dressed in brown with a red cloak (not the traditional green) draped over her from the head down. On her left thigh sits the Blessed Virgin Mary, also wearing brown but with a blue cloak, shown with a book open in front of her. To the right a background of grey panelling with a Doric column and individual panels in red. In front of this background on a green carpet kneels a man dressed in black (patron?). The border is on a gold ground decorated with green-leaved stems with red, blue and white flowers, also a brown snail, and showing a blue scroll in three sections with gold lettering each saying 'TENIR FOY A DIEV OV G[râce à] D[ieu].'

COLLATION

I⁶ (fos 1–6), **II**² (fos 7–8; lacks matter between fo 7 and fo 8), **III**¹⁰ (fos 9–13; lacks 1 and 10; 3 (= fo 30) has been displaced from its proper position), **IV**¹⁰ (fos 14–23), **V**⁶⁺¹ (fos 24–30; fo 30 is pasted onto fo 29, but properly belongs after fo 9), **VI**¹⁰[⁺⁸] (fos 31–46 (fos 31–2, [33–40], 41–6, lacks 1 and 10, with fos 33–40 constituting a separate quire **VI**ᵇⁱˢ of 8 inserted after leaf 3 of the enclosing quire), **VII**⁸ (fos 47–54), **VIII**⁸ (fos 55–62), **IX**⁸ (fos 63–70); **X**⁸ (fos 71–8).

Note 1: In Quire **II** at least two leaves (which would have included gospel passages from Mt and Lk) are lost between fo 7 and fo 8. Fos 7–8 are by same hand and artist as fos 33–40.

Note 2: In Quire **III** the text on fo 30r follows on from fo 9v.

Note 3: The textual discontinuity between fo 29v and fo 31r (fo 30 belonging after fo 9) is catered for by the loss of leaf 1 in Quire **VI**, and the textual discontinuity between fo 46v and fo 47r is catered for by the loss of leaf 10 in Quire **VI**.

Note 4: In Quire **VI** fos 33–40 constitute a separate quire of 8 (= Vespers (etc.) of the Blessed Virgin Mary according to the Use of Rome), written in a different hand and showing a different illustrator, inserted after leaf 3 of the enclosing quire, possibly in a (clumsy) attempt to provide superior illustration and a fuller text.

Hair/Flesh: **I** FHF, **II** F, **III** FHFH, **IV** HFFFF, **V** HFH, **VI** FHFH, **VI**ᵇⁱˢ FHFH, **VII** FFFF, **VIII** FFFF, **IX** FHFH, **X** FHFH. The arrangement is apparently influenced by the artist's preference for a flesh-side for a large illustration.

CONTENTS

1. Fos 1r/1–6v/31: Calendar in French. Begins 'KL Januier a xxxj iour.' Ends 'viii A Saint siluestre'.

2. Fos 7r/1–8r/19. This bifolium is by the hand and artist of Quire **VI**^{bis} (Item 16 below), and has been added from another Book of Hours; it must be part of a quire originally more substantial.
Fo 7r: Illustration of St John.
(a) Fo 7r/1–7v/19: Gospel Readings headed "Initiu<m> s<an>cti eua<n>gelii s<e>c<un>d<u>m ioh<ann>em." Begins 'In principio erat verbu<m>' (Jn 1.1). Ends 'quasi vnigeniti a p<at>re plenu<m> gr<ati>e | et veritatis. [Jn 1.14] Deo gr<at>i<a>s.'
(b) Fo 8r/1–11: Begins apparently imperfectly 'V<ersus> domine exaudi or<ati>onem meam | R<esponsum> Et clamor meus ad te veniat | Protector in te sperantium | deus sine quo nichil est | validum'. Ends 'sic transeamus per bona temporalia ut | non amittamus eterna. Per | dominum n<ost>r<u>m ih<esu>m <Christu>m filiu<m> tuum qui tecum viuit et reg<na>t.'
Fo 8r/12–19 and fo 8v blank.

3. A leaf is probably missing from Quire **III** before fo 9.
Fo 9r: Illustration of *The Annunciation*
Fos 9r/1–13v/19: Matins of the Blessed Virgin Mary. 'Domine labia m<e>a | aperies Et os me|um annunciabit | laudem tuam || [Ps 69] Deus in adiutoriu<m> meum intende | Domine ad adiuuandum me festi<n>a | Gloria p<at>ri [etc.] | [Ps 94] Venite exultemus domino'. Fo 13r/9 'Te deum laudamus'. Ends incomplete (in *Te Deum*) 'et benedic hereditati tue'.
The apparent lacuna in the text between fos 9v and 10r is supplied by fo 30, fo 9v ending 'coram domino qui fecit' and fo 30r beginning 'nos quia ipse est dominus deus noster | nos autem populus eius', and fo 30v ending 'propter inimicos tuos ut destru' and fo 10r beginning 'as inimicum et ultorem'.

4. Fos 14r/1–20r/2: Lauds of the Blessed Virgin Mary. There is a lacuna between fos 13v (Matins) and 14r (Lauds), which begins imperfectly in Ps 92 '[Dominus regnavit] decorem indutus est indutus e<st> dominus'. Probably the missing folio contained an illustration of the Visitation, which usually accompanied Lauds, and introductory text (antiphon etc.). Ends 'Deus qui corda fidelium | sancti sp<irit>us illustratione | docuisti: da nobis in eodem spiritu rec||ta sapere et de eius semper sancta con|solatione gaudere. Per <Christu>m'.

5. Fo 20r: Illustration of *The Crucifixion*
Fo 20r/3–20v/17: Matins of the Holy Cross. Begins 'Domine labia mea. | Deus in adiutorium | Domine ad adiuua<n>d<um>'. Ends 'et nob<is> | peccatoribus uitam et letitiam sempi|ternam Qui uiuis.'

6. Fo 21r: Illustration of *St Christopher* (pl. 9.1)
Fo 21r/1–21v/14: Matins of the Holy Spirit. Begins 'Domine labia mea | Deus in adiutoriu[m] | Domine ad iuuand<um>'. Continues fo 21v/1 'Nobis sancti spiritus gratia sit | data.' Ends 'in die | sancto penthecostes transmisisti. Qui viuis et regnas deus in secula seculo<rum> | Amen'.

7. Fo 22r: Illustration of *St Julian with his Wife ferrying Christ across a River*
Fos 22r/1–25r/15: Prime of the Blessed Virgin Mary. Begins '[D]eus in adiutorium me|um creator sp<irit>us | mentes tuo<rum> uisita i<m>ple || superna gratia que tu creasti pectora'. Note that the wrong initial, **A**, has been supplied for **D** in [D]eus. Continues fo 22v/9 [Ps 53] **D**Eus in nomine tuo saluu<m> | me fac'; fo 23r/7 [Ps 116] 'Laudate dominum om<ne>s ge<n>tes'; fo 23r/12 [Ps 117] 'Confitemini domino quonia<m> | bonus: q<uonia>m in seculu<m> m<isericord>ia ei<us>. | Dicat nu<n>c Israel quoniam bonus'; fo 24v/14 '**an<tiphona>** O admirabile commercium creator | generis humani'; fo 24v/18 '**capitulum**. | Gaude maria virgo cunctas [= Use of Rennes]. Ends 'ut quib<us> dedi|sti fidem largiaris et pacem [*CO* 1359]. Per'.

8. Fo 25r/15–25v/3: Prime of the Cross. "**de s<ancte> c<ruc>e**". Begins 'Deus in adiutorium me|um int<end>e'. Ends '**a<ntiphon>** Adoramus te criste | Domine iesu criste.'

9. Fo 25v/3–8 Prime of the Holy Spirit. Begins 'Deus in ad<iutorium meum> | De virgine maria cristus fuit na|tus.' Ends 'Et ip<s>is cernentibus [in] celis eleuatus. **an<tifon>** | Veni sancte Omnipotens.'

10. Fo 25v: Illustration of *St Blaise with a Carding Comb*
Fos 25v/9–27v/12: Terce of the Blessed Virgin Mary. Begins 'Deus in adiutorium meum || Veni creator Mater dei sanctissi<m>a | atq<ue> uirgo perpetua [etc.] [Ps 120] LEuaui oculos meos in mo<n>|tes'. Fo 27r/14 [**capitulum**] 'Per te dei genitrix' [= Use of Rennes]. Ends 'ab omnib<us> tueatur | aduersis. Per.'

11. Fo 27v/12–17: Terce of the Holy Cross. Begins 'Deus in adiutori<um meum> | Crucifige clamitant hora terci|arum'. Ends 'ad locu<m> | penarum. Adoramus. **D**<omi>ne ies<u criste>'.

12. Fos 27v/18–28r/4: Terce of the Holy Spirit. Begins 'Deus in adiutoriu<m meum>. **S**uum sa<n>|ctum spiritum deus delegauit.' Ends 'Et de linguis igneis ip<s>os i<n>fla[m]mauit | Relinquere orphanos eos denegauit | Veni sancte. Omnipotens.'

13. Fo 28r: Illustration of *Christ in Majesty at the Last Judgement*
Fos 28r/5–29v/19: Sexte of the Blessed Virgin Mary. Begins 'DEus in adiutorium | Ueni creator sp<irit>us | Domus pudici || pectoris templum [etc.] [Ps 122] Ad te leuaui oculos meos qui | habitas in celis'. Fo 29v/8 [**capitulum**] 'Ego flos campi' [= Use of Rennes]. Ends incomplete '**or<ati>o** | Mentes n<ost>ras quesumus d<omi>ne'.

Fo 30 has been misplaced and belongs properly between fos 9 and 10. A leaf is missing before fo 31; it probably contained Sexte of the Cross, Sexte of the Holy Spirit, an illustration and the beginning of None.

14. Fos 31r/1–32v/2: None of the Blessed Virgin Mary. Begins imperfectly in Ps 125 '[In convertendo Dominus captiui]tatem syon facti sumus sicut consolati | tunc repletum est gaudio os nostrum | et lingua n<ost>ra exultatione'. Fo 32r/3 **Capitulum** | Sicut cynamomum et balsamu<m>' [Ecclus 24.20]. Ends 'et prouidentia guberne|mur: Per.'

15. Fo 32v/2–7: None of the Holy Cross. Begins '**Deus** in adiutorium me<um>'. Ends '**a<ntiphon>** Adoramus Domine ie<su criste>'.

16. Fo 32v/8–14: None of the Holy Spirit. Begins '**Deus** in adiutor<ium meum> Sp<irit>us paracli|tus fuit appellatus'. Ends '**antifo<n>** | Veni sancte spiritus reple tuorum | Omnipotens sempiterne'.

17. Fos 33–40: Added material: Use of Rome. Shows a different hand and a different illustrator (both the same as in Item 2 above) for one quire, which has been inserted.

Fo 33r: Illustration of *The Flight into Egypt* (pl. 9.3)
(a) Fos 33r/1–37r/9: Vespers of the Blessed Virgin Mary. Begins '**Deus** in adiutoriu<m> meu<m> | intende. Domine ad | adiuuandu<m> me festi<n>a | Gloria p<at>ri an<tifon> Dum esset. [= Use of Rome only] **P<salmu>s** [109] | **Dixit** dominus d<omi>no meo | sede a dextris meis:-'. Ends 'et omnib<us> fidelibus | defunctis requiem eterna<m> conce|de. Per d<o>m<i>n<um>'.

Fo 37r: Illustration of *The Coronation of the Virgin*
(b) Fo 37r/9–39v/19: Compline of the Blessed Virgin Mary. Begins '**Ad complecto<rum>** | Co<n> uer|te | nos deus | salutaris | n<oste>r Et | auerte ira<m> | tuam a | nobis'. Fo 37v/2 Ps 128 'Sepe expugnaueru<n>t me a | iuuentute mea dicat | nunc israel'. Fo 40r/1: 'Salue regina [mater] m<isericord>ie vita dul|cedo'. Added material ends at fo 40v/7 'eius pia inter|cessione ad [*recte* ab] instantibus malis | et a morte perpetua atq<ue> subi|tanea liberamur. Per d<omi>n<u>m | n<ost>r<u>m ih<esu>m <Christu>m filium tuu<m>'. fo 40v/8–19 blank.

9.3 RB38, fo 33r, by the additional artist, *The Flight into Egypt*, with text. Actual page dimensions 164 x 104mm.

18. Fo 41r: Illustration of *Mary Magdalene*

Fos 41r/1–42v/15: Vespers of the Blessed Virgin Mary. 'Deus in adiutorium me[um] | Domine ad adiuuandu<m> | **antif[on]** Beata mater. | Letatus sum in hiis que. **psalm‹us›** [121] | **Ad** te leuaui oculos meos **psalm[us** 122] | **Nisi** quia dominus. **psalmus** [123] | **Qui** confidunt in d‹omin›o **psalm‹us›** [124]'. Ends 'Deus qui corda'.

19. Fos 42v/15–43r/1: Vespers of the Holy Cross. Begins 'Deus in adiutor‹ium meum› | **De** cruce deponitur'. Ends 'Ador‹amus› || **Domine** iesu ‹criste›'.

20. Fo 43r/1–6: Vespers of the Holy Spirit. Begins 'Deus in adiutoriu‹m meum› | **Dextre** dei'. Ends 'Sed protegat nutriat foueat s‹u›b alis | Ueni. Omnipotens'.

21. Fo 43r: Illustration of *Susannah and the Elders*
Fos 43r/7–45v/17: Compline of the Blessed Virgin Mary. Begins 'COnuerte nos deus saluta|ris n‹oste›r. Et au‹er›te ira‹m› t[uam] a n[obis].'; continues fo 43v/1: Ps 12 'Vsque quo domine obliuisceris | me in finem'; fo 43v/16 Ps 42 'IUdica me deus et discerne cau|sam meam'; fo 44r/12 Ps 128 'SEpe expugnaueru‹n›t me a | iuuentute mea'; fo 44v/9 Ps 130 'DOmine no‹n› e‹st› exaltatatum cor | meum'; fo 45r/1 [**capitulum**] 'Maria virgo semper letare' [= Use of Rennes]; fo 45v/5 '**an‹tiphon›** tota pulchra es' [= Use of Rennes]. Ends 'et sui roris intima asp‹er›sio‹n›e | fecundet. Per.'

22. Fos 45v/18–46r/8: Compline of the Holy Cross. Begins 'Conuerte nos d‹eu›s | **Deus** in adiutorium meum'. Ends 'solatium in mortis agone | Adoramus. Domine iesu criste'.

23. Fo 46r/9–19: Compline of the Holy Spirit. Begins 'Conuerte nos. **Deus** in adiut‹orium meum› | Spiritus paraclitus nos velit | iuuare.' Ends 'Et viuamus iugiter celi regione. | Dum sancte. **oratio.** | Omnipotens'.

24. Fo 46v: Illustration of *St Geneviève* (full page)
A leaf is missing between fos 46 and 47, as the Collation shows, and some text must be lost, perhaps a prayer to St Geneviève. It would have been most unusual to place two illustrations facing each other.

25. Fo 47r: Illustration of *David with his Harp*
Fo 47r/1–54r/15: Seven penitential psalms beginning with Ps 6 'DOmine ne in furore tu|o arguas me ... Miserere'; fo 48r/2 Ps 31 'Beati quorum remisse s‹un›t i‹n›iquit[at]es'; fo 48v/14 Ps 37 'Domine ne in furore tuo argu|as me ... Quoniam sagitte tue'; fo 50r/10 Ps 50 'Miserere mei deus secundum | magnam m‹iserico›r‹di›am tuam.'; fo 51r/16 Ps 101 'DOmine exaudi or‹ati›one‹m› mea‹m› | ‹et› clamor meus ad te ve‹n›iet.'; fo 53r/2 Ps 129 'DE profundis clamaui ad | te domine'; fo 53r/18 Ps 142 'DOmine exaudi oratione‹m› | meam auribus percipe ob||secrationem meam'; ends 'seruus | tuus sum Gloria p‹at›ri.'

26. Fos 54r/15–59r/9: **"Letania."** Begins 'KYri eleyson. Crist eleyson'. Ends 'optauerunt piis suplicati|onibus consequantur. Qui uiuis'. Includes some specifically Breton saints on fo 56v: Sts Corentin (12 Dec.), Hervé (17 June) and Tugdual (30 Nov.).

Fo 59r/10–19 blank except for '**de monseigneur sanct michel**' on line 16.

27. Fos 59v/1–67r/16: A series of prayers to saints (*suffragia*) with small illustrations and decorated borders around the three outer sides of the page.

(a) Fo 59v/1–19: Illustration of *St Michael*, with text beginning 'Michael ar|changele pa|radisi prepo|site veni in ad|iutorium po|pulo dei.' Ends 'ab hiis i<n> ter|ra uita nostra muniatur. Per'.

(b) Fo 60r/1–17: Illustration of *St John the Baptist*, with text beginning 'Inter natos mu|lierum non sur|rexit maior io|hanne baptista'; ends 'deus in se|cula seculorum amen.'

Fo 60r/18 blank.

Fo 60r/19: '**memoire a monseigneur .s. estienne.**'

(c) Fo 60v/1–18: Illustration of *St Stephen*, with text beginning 'Stephanus | plenus gratia | et fortitudine | faciebat prodi|gia et signa | magna i<n> p<o>p<u>lo.'; ends 'do|minum nostrum iesum cristum | filium tuum.'

Fo 60v/19: '**de sainct nycolas.**'

(d) Fo 61r/1–14: Illustration of *St Nicholas*, with text beginning 'Amicus dei nycho|laus pontificali | decoratus infula | omnibus se ama|bilem exhibuit.'; ends 'incendiis liberemur. Per cristum.'

Fo 61r/15–18 blank.

Fo 61r/19: '**de madamme saincte barbe.**'

(e) Fos 61v/1–62r/18: Illustration of *St Barbara*, with text beginning 'Erude barbara | beata. su<m>me | pollens in doc|trina angeli | misterio. | Gaude virgo | deo gratia.'; ends 'et pu|ram confessionem percipere me|reamur. Qui tecum vivit et re|gnat deus. per o<mn>ia s<e>c<u>la s<ec<u>lo<rum. A<men>.'

(f) Fo 62v/1–18: Illustration of *St Laurence* (pl. 9.2), with text beginning 'Leuita lau|rentius bo|num opus ope|ratus est qui | per signum | crucis cecos | illuminauit.'; ends 'incendia supera|re. Per cristum d<omi>n<u>m n<ost>r<u>m. A<men>.

Fo 62v/19: '**De sanctissima trinitate.**'

(g) Fos 63r/1–67r/16: Illustration of *The Holy Trinity*, with a woman in a brown robe (patroness?) kneeling at the bottom left, with text beginning 'Sancta trinitas Vnus | deus miserere nobis. | Te inuocamus te ado|ramus te laudamus te glorifica|mus o beata trinitas.'; ends 'O crux cristi salua me omnib<us> | diebus vite mee. Amen.'

28. Fos 67r/17–77r/8: A series of prayers to the Blessed Virgin Mary. "**Oratio deuotissima ad bea|tissimam virginem dei geni|tricem mariam.**" Begins 'OBsecro te domina s<an>cta | maria mater dei pietate plenissima'; continues fo 70r/18 'O Intemerata et in | eternum benedicta || singularis et incomparabilis | virgo', as Wilmart 1932: 488–90, also PL 158, 959; fo 72v/1 'Stabat mater dolorosa.'; fo 74r/8 'INterueniat pro no|bis quesumus domine | iesu criste nunc et in hora mor|tis'; fo 74v/2 'AVe cuius conceptio. | Solenni plena gaudio. | Celestia terrestria.'; fo 75r/6 'DEus qui | nos conceptionis nati|uitatis annunciationis puri|ficationis et assumptionis | beata marie virginis'; fo 75v/6 'GAude flore virginali, | Que honore speciali | Transcendis splendiferum. | Angelorum principatum.'; fo 76v/13 'O Domine iesu criste q<ui> | gloriosissima<m> virgine<m> | dulcissimam matrem tuam | mariam'; ends 'ad eterna gaudia feliciter per|uenire mereamur. Per eunde<m> | cristum d<omi>n<u>m n<ost>r<u>m. Amen'.

29. Fo 77r/9–77v/15: "**De sancta anna antipho<n>**". Illustration of *St Anne Teaching the Blessed Virgin Mary to Read*, with a man in black (patron?) kneeling before them, with text beginning 'Celeste | benefici|um i<n>troi|uit in an|nam per | quam no|bis nata | est ma|ria vir|go'; continues fo 77v/3 'DEus qui beate an|ne tantam gratiam | donare dignatus es:'; ends 'ea|rum precib<us> ad celestem glo|riam peruenire valeamus. | Per eundem cristu<m> d<ominum> n<ostrum> A<men>.'

30. Fos 77v/16–78r/14: "**De sancta m<ari>a madgalena a<ntiphon>.**" Begins 'Maria ergo vnxit pedes iesu | et extersit capillis suis'; continues fo 78r/4 'Largire nobis clementis|sime pater q<ui> sicut bea|ta maria magdalena'; ends 'apud tuam mise|ricordiam sempiternam i<m>|petret beatitudinem. Per e|undem cristum dominum | nostrum. Amen.'

Fo 78r/15–19, fo 78v blank.

Note: The contents lack the Office of the Dead, usually found after the Litany.

Printed Book of Hours 1526 with manuscript illuminations

Latin with occasional French

HISTORY

THIS PRINTED BOOK OF HOURS from Paris dated to 1526 shows forty-one hand-painted illustrations as well as decoration, and is printed and painted entirely on membrane (pls 10.1, 10.2). Apparently the same printed book as Bohatta 1924: 44, no. 1111, and Renouard 1985: 298, no. 1021, but these descriptions are not very detailed. A much more detailed description occurs in Lacombe 1907: 202–3, no. 359*bis*, and RB39 is an example of this edition, but shows a different state (see title page below). Apparently each copy of the book was tailored to the client, and this tailoring included the illustrations. Most, if not all, of the illustrations were painted over printed woodcut designs that were incorporated into the printed book. As far as we have been able to discover, no copy of this particular book with the woodcuts unpainted survives, but similar books with unpainted woodcuts do survive and further work with these as a basis would enable more detailed artistic commentary than can be provided here. As an example of how the printed design could be modified, see below under 'Illustrations', no. 1. For comparative work of this kind the following books could be consulted: London, BL C.9.a.32 and C.29.g.2, Paris, Bibliothèque Arsenal MS 6356, and Paris, BN B 27667, Vélins 2942 (these two *ex informatione* Catherine Yvard). Indications of where comparison with unpainted print-designs in BN B 27667 might be profitable are given below (all *ex informatione* Catherine Yvard). The binding is of s.xix in red goatskin with gold on the edges and gold ornamental tooling on the spine including the inscription 'HORÆ | VIRGINIS | MARIÆ | PARIS'. The inside is covered with marbled paper, and there are three paper endleaves front and back. There are no marks of provenance, and it is not known when or how it came to Maynooth.

TITLE PAGE

A1r: The whole page is surrounded by a painted architectural frame in gold. The printer's device has been painted over more or less obliterating the black outlines, and the printer's mark on the shield has almost completely vanished under blue paint. For details of the printed title page device, see below under 'Illustrations'. 'Germain Hardouyn' hand-written on a scroll below the tree.

Title below the printed device: Hore diue virginis Marie secu<n>dum vsu<m> | Romanum cum alijs multis in sequentibus | notatis vna cum figuris Apocalipsis vt mon|strat in calce tabula Nouiter impressis Pari|sius impe<n>sis honesti viri Germani Hardouyn | Co<m>morentis inter duas portas palatij ad inter|signium sancte Marguarete.

Note: A different state from Lacombe 1907: no. 359*bis* is indicated by the absence of the additional word 'vero' between 'impensis' and 'honesti' in RB39, but the setting of the line is otherwise the same.

N4v: Colophon: Finit officium beate Marie virginis se|cundum vsum Romanum. No|uiter impressus per Germa|num Hardouyn. Com|mora<n>te<m> inter duas por|tas Palatij. Ad inter|signiu<m> diue Mar|guarete. Et ibi | venu<m>dantur.

Printer: Hardouyn, Germain, *fl.* Paris, 1500–41.

Date: 1526, as inferred from the almanac on A2v, where that year is the first for which Easter is given.

COLLATION

4° in 8s: A8 B8 C8 D8 E8 F8 H8 I8 K8 L8 M8 N4 [$4 signed (-A1, N4)]. 92 membrane leaves, paginated by hand in pencil s.xx at the top outer corners 1–184, measuring 180 x 111mm, printed area 121 x 63mm showing thirty-two lines of printed text.
Note 1: The signature is preceded by 'Ro' before the folio number except on N3.
Note 2: The signature on N3 is in a different position, only just below the bottom line of print.
Note 3: There is no gathering G, but there is apparently no loss or discontinuity of text.
Note 4: Since the whole book is printed on membrane the hair/flesh arrangement is noted as follows: A–F and H–M FHFH, N FH, i.e., always flesh side outside.

Type: The 'Tholoze' Pica Roman (body size 78mm) found in Paris from 1499 (at the press of Michel Tholoze), for its time a good and well-balanced design, used by many leading printers for the first four decades of the sixteenth century (pl. 10.2). For details, see Vervliet 2005: 24–5, no. 8, repr. Vervliet 2008: I.25, no. 8.
Note: **d** is mostly an alien rotunda, but roman **d** also occurs, e.g., on A1v/27 in 'redemptionis'.

CONTENTS

List: A1r title, A1v the Host, A2r Hardouin's anatomical man, A2v Almanac, A3r–B1r Calendar, B1v–B7r Gospel readings, B7r–C2r Prayers, C2r Hours of

the Blessed Virgin Mary according to the Use of Rome: C2v–D1r Matins, D1v–
D5v Lauds, D6r–D7v Prime, D8r–E1v Terce, E2r–E3v Sexte, E4r–E5v None,
E6r–E8v Vespers, F1r–F5v Compline, F6r–F7r Hours of the Holy Cross, F7v–
F8v Hours of the Holy Spirit, H1r–H3r Office of the Conception of the Blessed
Virgin Mary, H3r–H4r Mass of the Blessed Virgin Mary, H4v–H8v Seven
Penitential Psalms, H8v–I3v Litany, I4r–L2r Vigil of the Dead, L3v–N1v Suffragia,
N2r–N2v Antiphons, verses and prayers to the Blessed Virgin Mary, N2v–N3v
Hours of St Barbara, N3v–N4v List of Contents, N4v Colophon.

Illustrations: Forty-one hand-painted pictures, from full page down to vignettes
showing a depth of six lines of type. The printed book incorporated woodcut
designs that have been painted over (pl. 10.2). Signs of the printing can sometimes
be seen outside the painted area, as with nos 23a, 23g/h/i below, or below the
paint, as with no. 10 below. In no. 23p, for example, the printed outline of St
Barbara's tower can be seen under the paint; cp. no. 24.

1. A1r: Title page showing the printer's device of a tree with green leaves and a
brown trunk against a red ground ornamented with gold arabesques, and standing
on a green lawn. Shadows are painted in to give more depth to the picture. There
is a shield hanging from the tree held by two angelic cherubs, but the coat of arms
on the shield has been painted over in blue. 'Germain Hardouyn' handwritten
on a scroll below the tree. Depth equivalent to twenty-seven lines of type. All in
an architectural gold frame with tassles either side. The printed title-page device
is reproduced in Silvestre 1853–65: fig. 57 on p. 29. It would appear that the
putto in the tree has been painted over, perhaps not unusual as the same apparently
occurs on sig. A1r in the two comparable BL volumes, C.9.a.32 and C.29.g.2.

2. A1v: Lozenge of depth equivalent to 6 lines of type showing a printed host
with Christ on it, heavily painted over with white. The surround is red with gold
rays radiating outwards.

3. A2r: Full page illustration surrounded by a simple gold frame, with the central
section showing planetary man in the form of a skeleton; depth equivalent to
twenty-six lines of type. The device is printed but painted over with the grey
skeleton shown against a blue ground and standing on a green lawn. Eight
philacteries link the planets to the organs. Gothic script is used for the scrolls
and for the indications of when to bleed for the phlegmatic and the melancholic.
Planets are featured as stars except for the sun and moon. The fool has been
painted between the skeleton's legs, with a moustache, wearing a red coat and
green hood, and seems to be talking to the moon. In each corner there is one of
the four humours probably painted over print and showing a depth of 9 lines of
type. Clockwise from the top left they show Choleric, Sanguine, Melancholic,
Phlegmatic, each with his attribute. The bottom four lines of text are handwritten.

4. B1v: *The Martyrdom of St John*, to begin the Gospel reading from St John, in a gold architectural frame with tassles either side. John, rather muscular, with gold hair, stands in a dark green cauldron on a fire, with an arch above him and a garland featuring the head of a cherub suspended across it. A man in a red cloak and blue hat stands to the left as if climbing one step. To the right there sits a bearded soldier in ornate armour holding a bellows. From a window to the right of St John a man in a blue cloak and hat looks out. Depth of picture equivalent to twenty-three lines of type.

5. B2v: Medallion with a depth of nine lines of type showing *St Luke* in a red cloak with green tunic holding a quill in his raised right hand and a calf stands to the left.

6. B3r: Medallion with a depth of eleven lines of type showing *St Matthew* in a blue tunic and red cloak holding a quill with his book open on a stand, and to the right an angel in mauve holding an open book which St Matthew is presumably taking as his model.

7. B3v: Medallion with a depth of eleven lines of type showing *St Mark* in a green tunic and red cloak and wearing a blue hat holding his quill over his open book on the right, with a rather cheerful lion at his feet on the left.

8. B4r: *The Betrayal of Christ* (pl. 10.1), an intricate scene occupying the whole page in a gold architectural frame with tassles either side. Christ is shown in grey in the centre of the composition looking left. A red-haired Judas dressed in green is kissing Him. A hand grasps the front of Christ's tunic but He has His hands behind his back and does not attempt to resist. To the right below is Peter who is brandishing his sword above his head to hit a man in ragged red clothes lying on the ground with a club in his hand. The soldier behind Christ has a big moustache and seems to be tying His hands but this is obscured by Peter. There is a rocky grotto to the right above and a field to the left containing a fenced house between dark blue trees against a pale blue sky.

9. C2v: *Original Sin*, for the beginning of Matins, occupying the whole page, in a gold architectural frame with tassles either side. The tree stands at the centre on a green lawn, with the serpent, blue with red wings flecked with gold, and a human head with gold hair, curled around it. Eve to the left, facing out, with a modesty leaf, holds an apple. Adam to the right of the tree, with fleshy muscles, apparently moving in to the picture, has his left hand out as if to take the apple. The background is white at the centre but with blue sky at the top with gold stars, against which the green leaves of the tree show.

10.1 RB39, sig. B4r,
The Betrayal of Christ.
Actual page dimensions
180 x 111mm.

10. C3r: *The Annunciation*, occupying a depth of twenty-four lines of type, the
whole page in a gold architectural frame with tassles either side. Mary to the right
in a blue cloak sits reading at a prie-dieu, and to the left a large-footed angel
Gabriel arrives in a red cloak with green wings; his right hand is raised and he
holds a staff in his left hand. The floor is in fawn tiles leading to a dark grey

panelled wall, to the right of which, behind Mary, is a canopy with green top and red drapes. The trace of an oval printed underneath shows through in the lower part of the picture.

11. D1v: *The Visitation*, for the beginning of Lauds, occupying a depth of twenty-four lines of type, the whole page in a gold architectural frame with tassles either side. Mary to the left in a mauve tunic and blue cloak in bare feet and ankles, Elizabeth, showing a cleavage, in red emerges to the right from a grey turret to kneel before Mary, touching her belly with her left hand. They are apparently on a greensward that turns into a field as the picture recedes and there are trees and a blue sky above. The scene was apparently painted over a print with an oval frame; this print can be found unpainted in BN B 27667, fo 25r.

12. D6r: *The Nativity*, for Prime, occupying a depth of twenty-three lines of type, the whole page in a gold architectural frame with tassles either side. In front of an arch with columns we see the nativity scene with Joseph in a green tunic and red cloak with both hands raised as if in surprise, and Mary looking much younger to the right in blue with very expressive hands. In front of them the Christ-child is lying on a stone apparently without clothes, to his left three grey steps. Through the arch there is a landscape with green trees and a blue-grey mountain with two leaning rocks. The scene was apparently painted over a print.

13. D8r: *The Annunciation to the Shepherds*, for Terce, occupying a depth of thirty lines of type, the whole page in a gold architectural frame with tassles either side. In the background a splendid walled palace surmounted by gold rays, in front of which, separated by water, is a greensward with some sheep, and what looks like a prostrate horse. From the direction of the palace a shepherdess in blue and brown runs with her arms raised towards two shepherds, one on the left standing with his arms crossed leaning on his staff, dressed in blue and two shades of red, with green stockings, the other on the right seated on the ground with his left hand raised towards the shepherdess; he is bald and is dressed in blue with an ornamental white collar, yellow stockings, with his left foot in a red boot and his right foot unshod.

14. E2r: *The Adoration of the Magi*, for Sexte, occupying a depth of twenty-four lines of type, the whole page in a gold architectural frame with tassles either side. In the background are some ruins, stone to the right where there is an ox chewing hay and an ass braying, and a wooden roof to the left, under which can been seen a landscape with a greensward surmounted by a crag and mountains on the horizon merging into the sky, with some green trees to the right. Mary, looking much older than in the Nativity, veiled, and in blue attire, sits to the right holding the Christ-child on her lap. In front of her kneels an almost bald mage dressed in

pink; he is praying. Behind him a black mage in a blue cloak flecked with gold slashes approaches with his gift, and Mary is apparently looking towards him. To his right and behind stands the third mage in a red cloak and green hood; he is holding a gold chalice in his right hand and talking to the black mage, to whom he gestures with his left hand. Joseph is absent. Probably painted over the print found in BN B 27667, fo 34r.

15. E4r: *The Circumcision*, for None, occupying a depth of twenty-five lines of type, the whole page in a gold architectural frame with tassles either side. In front of a church interior background Mary in blue, veiled, and Joseph in red, holding a taper, stand looking at the scene in front. To the left a priest in blue tunic and green hood holds the squirming Christ-child, while another to the right in a yellow tunic and red hood kneels in front holding a curved knife in his right hand. To the left an assistant holds another taper, and to the right under an arch an onlooker in a blue hood with his red cloak slipping off his shoulder.

16. E6r: *The Flight into Egypt*, for Vespers, occupying a depth of twenty-four lines of type, the whole page in a gold architectural frame with tassles either side. The donkey faces left with Mary in blue and the Christ-child in red seated on it facing front. Joseph, dressed in red with a yellow hood, is situated on the other side of the donkey and leads it along the road. Behind the road a green field stretches back towards a grey-blue walled castle or city, and in a clump of green trees to the left there is another grey castle. The picture has been painted over an oval printed design, clearly visible in the sky of the picture.

17. F1r: *The Coronation of the Virgin*, for Compline, occupying a depth of twenty-four lines of type, the whole page in a gold architectural frame with tassles either side. Mary, dressed in blue, kneels in prayer at the centre on a blue cloud; she has all the youth of the Nativity picture, and her hair is red, edged with gold. To the right God the Father in a green tunic and red cloak with a sceptre in his left hand, and to the left Christ in loin-cloth and loose cloak, which reveals his bleeding wounds, also holding a sceptre in his left hand; both use their right hand to hold a crown above the Virgin against a yellow mandorla. Above the crown there is a dove. To the top right and left are more blue clouds. Probably painted over the print found in BN B 27667, fo 41r.

18. F6r: *The Crucifixion*, for the Hours of the Holy Cross, occupying a depth of twenty-four lines of type, the whole page in a gold architectural frame with tassles either side. The brown Cross (streaked with gold) stands on green ground, with a brown path apparently passing immediately behind it. The green background merges into a blue landscape with sloping mountains and trees, surmounted by a deep blue sky. Jesus in a loincloth is nailed to the cross, his wounds bleeding

red, but the figure is somewhat diminutive. To the left stands Mary, swathed in dark blue, with her hands raised in supplicatory prayer. To the right St John, in a pale blue tunic, with red cloak, stands with his hands raised apart; his right foot is bare.

19. F7v: *Pentecost*, for the Hours of the Holy Spirit, occupying a depth of twenty-five lines of type, the whole page in a gold architectural frame with tassles either side. On a pale blue tiled floor Mary is seated in the middle swathed in dark blue over a mauve tunic. Around her are four apostles, all with raised hands, dressed in green, blue, red and yellow. Above in a yellow mandorla is the white dove radiating gold rays, some straight, some zig-zagged. Note the bare feet of the two apostles at the front. Painted over a print with the oval frame barely visible, probably that found found in BN B 27667, fo 50v.

20. H1r: *The Virgin and Child*, for the Office of the Conception of the Blessed Virgin Mary, occupying a depth of twenty-five lines of type, the whole page in a gold architectural frame with tassles either side. Mary in a red tunic and blue cloak holds the chubby naked Christ-child in her arms in a mandorla of yellow light, which merges into orange at the edge, the whole then surrounded by pale blue (dark blue in the corners).

21. H4v: *David and Bathsheba*, for the Penitential Psalms, occupying a depth of twenty-five lines of type, the whole page in a gold architectural frame with tassles either side. In a courtyard garden a well-endowed naked Bathsheba is sitting on a plank of wood over a pool of water in which her feet are immersed, wearing a diaphanous veil on her thighs, which she holds with her right hand. She has very long untied hair with highlights of gold. With her left hand she takes a piece of red fruit from a plate offered by her maid to the right, wearing a very elegant red dress flecked with gold, with blue sleeves, and showing her décolletage covered with a thin veil. Behind Bathsheba in the corner of the pool is a gold fountain. To the right at the back is David at a window, dressed in blue and gold, and wearing his crown. Around the pool is a green path leading back to a wall with a windowed niche, behind which is a garden with trees and a tall narrow house with a red roof. Probably painted over the print found in BN B 27667, fo 55r.

22. I4r: *Job on his Dungheap*, for the Vigil of the Dead, occupying a depth of twenty-six lines of type, the whole page in a gold architectural frame with tassles either side. At the right a bearded and very healthy-looking Job, naked apart from a diaphanous veil, kneels on his right knee on the golden dungheap (hay?) with his arms crossed looking to the right out of the picture. To his left an old man with a stick and white beard dressed in a red coat flecked with gold, with a blue collar, sleeves and stockings, is holding his right hand out in greeting. Behind

him is a lady (the man's wife?) dressed in mauve with a black headdress and she looks out of the picture towards the left. The setting is a dusty yard flanked by a wall behind and an arch to the right, behind which stretches a vista with a house, two towers and a garden with blue trees merging into the sky. Probably painted over the print found in BN B 27667, fo 63r, although the paint-artist has altered the position of Job.

23a. L2v: *God the Father*, to begin the Prayers to Saints (*Suffragia*), a rectangular vignette occupying a depth of fourteen lines of type. The picture should show the Trinity ('primo de sanctissi|ma Trinitate') but instead corresponds to 'Oratio a deum patrem' at the bottom of the page. God the father is shown in an orange mandorla surrounded by clouds. He is bearded, wearing a red cloak flecked with gold over a green tunic, and on his head a triple crown. In his left hand he holds down a golden orb from which comes a cross (sceptre?), and with his large right hand he offers a two-fingered blessing. The vignette was printed but the painted vignette did not cover the total printed area, so the edges of the print have been erased with a scraper.

23b. L4r: *The Virgin and Child*, to begin the prayers to Our Lady, an oval vignette occupying a depth of twelve lines of type. The Virgin is seated on a green bank dressed in a blue cloak over a red tunic and holding the Christ-child dressed in mauve as he apparently walks on her right thigh. Her hair is brown flecked with gold. Behind there is a red ground with the Virgin's shadow shown in darker red.

23c. L6r: (a) *St Michael*, to begin the prayers to him, an oval vignette occupying a depth of eleven lines of type. Michael, his red hair flecked with gold, stands over the defeated mauve dragon, holding him down with his left foot, on a green lawn. He is dressed in a short blue tunic, gilded brown top armour, and matching cuirasses, with a flowing red cloak. In his right hand he holds aloft a sword; in his left hand a blue shield. The dragon (demon?) is expressive with a red tongue. Behind the lawn there is water and behind that more green surmounted by blue sky. Probably painted over the print found in BN B 27667, fo 81r.

23d. L6r: (b) *St John the Baptist*, to begin the prayers to him, an oval vignette occupying a depth of ten lines of type. On a green lawn merging into white surmounted by blue sky St John the Baptist stands barefoot in a red cloak. In his right hand he holds the lamb with a cross on a blue cushion, while his left hand gestures as if to draw attention to the *agnus dei*. Probably painted over the print found in BN B 27667, fo 81r.

23e. L6v: *SS Peter and Paul*, to begin the prayers to them, an oval vignette occupying a depth of eleven lines of type. St Peter with grey hair and beard is on the right dressed in a blue tunic with purple and mauve cloak, and holds his key in his left hand, gesticulating towards St Paul to the left. St Paul, with brown hair and beard flecked with gold, is dressed in a green tunic and red cloak flecked with gold, and holds a sword upright in his left hand, while his right hand seems to point downwards to their bare feet on a green ground. Behind them at the top is blue sky. Probably painted over the print found in BN B 27667, fo 81v.

23f. L7r: *St Stephen*, to begin the prayers to him, an oval vignette occupying a depth of eleven lines of type. On a green ground a tonsured St Stephen stands wearing a red tunic over a white undergarment. With both hands he holds up part of his tunic, in which nestle some stones. Behind him the green ground merges into pale blue with a green tree to the right and dark blue sky above. Probably painted over the print found in BN B 27667, fo 82r, where a stone is shown on St Stephen's head.

23g. L7v: *St Laurence*, to begin the prayers to him, an oval vignette occupying a depth of twelve lines of type. A tonsured St Laurence stands on a green ground, which is surmounted by a dark blue sky with swirls of gold. He is wearing a red tunic over a white undergarment, holding the gridiron in his right hand and supporting a book with his left arm.

23h. L8r: *St Christopher*, to begin the prayers to him, an oval vignette occupying a depth of twelve lines of type. St Christopher, with the Christ-child on his back, is stepping out of water with his right foot on a rock to the left. He is dressed in a blue tunic with swirling red cloak and holds a staff in his right hand. The Christ-child, seen against the blue sky, has red hair and carries an orb in his left hand and has his right hand raised in two-fingered blessing.

23i. L8v: *St Sebastian*, to begin the prayers to him, an oval vignette occupying a depth of eleven lines of type. St Sebastian, naked except for a loincloth, with long red hair, is tied very awkwardly to a yellow and black tree-trunk at the right (to fit the shape of the oval?). To the left of the tree-trunk is a red background, and to the left of that an even darker red background, against which can be seen the archer, in a short blue tunic, pulling an enormous bow, which actually overlaps the saint's arm! One arrow has already shot him in the thigh. Probably painted over the print found in BN B 27667, fo 83r.

23j. M1v: (a) *St Nicholas and the Three Children*, to begin the prayer to him, a rectangular vignette occupying a depth of twelve lines of type. St Nicholas, in a green mitre and tunic with a red cloak stands on a tiled floor with the three children praying naked in the tub to his right (one has his left leg over the side of the tub). Behind a blue sky with swirls of gold.

fitatibus ad ipfum affluit: & quicunq; eũ pie
ac deuote quefierit defolatus non remanebit
va nobis quefum⁹ domine iufta defideria po
ftulare.vt que iufte poftulauerimus fuis me:
ritis & interceffioe apud te iugiter valeam⁹
obtinere.Qui viuis & regnas deus.Per oĩa
          De fancto anthonio.aña.

nthoni paftor i
clyte: qui cruciatos
reficis :morbos fan
nas& deftruis ignis
calorem extinguis:
pie pater ad do mi:
num ora pro nobis
quefum⁹.ꝟ. Ora ꝑ
nobis btẽ pater an:
thoni.℟.Vt digni efficiamur promiffionib⁹.
Eus qui nos concedis obtẽtu beati an
thoni confefforis tui morbidum ignẽ
extingui & membris egris refrigeria preftari
facnos ipfius meritis & precibus a gehenne
incendiis liberatos integros mente & corpo:
re tibi feliciter in gloria prefentari.Per dñz.
          De fancta ãna.aña
eſefte beneficiuz
introiuit in annã per
quam nobis nata eft
maria virgo.ꝟ.Ora
ꝑ nobis btã ãna dei
genitricis mater.℟.
Vt digni efficiamur
ꝑmiffionib⁹ xp̃i.

Ro.   M.ij.

10.2 RB39, sig. M2r,
showing medallions of
St Anthony and *St Anne*.

23k. M1v: (b) *St Claud*, to begin the prayer to him, a square vignette occupying a depth of nine lines of type. St Claud, in green mitre and red cloak over a white undergarment sits on a wooden chest on a green ground, holding a cross in his left hand and giving a blessing with his right hand. Behind is a dark blue sky with swirls of gold. To the left is a child dressed in white (the garment covering his head also), who prays.

23l. M2r: (a) *St Anthony*, to begin the prayer to him, a medallion occupying a depth of nine lines of type (pl. 10.2). Anthony, in sharp profile facing left, bearded with a bald head, dressed in a blue tunic and red cloak, kneels praying in fire on a greensward. From the left a boar's head indicates its approach. Behind, above the greensward, there is a pale blue sky, and to the right a green tree. Probably painted over the print found in BN B 27667, fo 84v.

23m. M2r: (b) *St Anne*, to begin the prayers to her, a medallion occupying a depth of nine lines of type (pl. 10.2). St Anne, enveloped in a red cloak over a green tunic, sits to the right, with Mary in blue kneeling to the left. Mary's right hand is approaching the book in Anne's left hand, possibly guided by Anne's right hand. Probably painted over the print found in BN B 27667, fo 85r.

23n. M2v: (a) *Mary Magdalene*, to begin the prayer to her, a medallion occupying a depth of nine lines of type. Seated on a greensward Mary is dressed in a blue tunic with a swirling red cloak flecked with gold, showing some décolletage, and wearing a white scarf on her head. She holds a book on her lap with her right hand, and a tall pot (of ointment) in her left hand. The background is grey. Probably painted over the print found in BN B 27667, fo 85r,

23o. M2v (b) *St Catherine*, to begin the prayers to her, a medallion occupying a depth of nine lines of type. St Catherine sits on a greensward wearing a blue tunic showing some décolletage with a swirling red cloak flecked with gold, and a pink and purple turban, from which her long curly hair emerges flecked with gold. Her right hand holds a sword upright, to the left of which can be seen the edge of her wheel. To her left a green tree and behind a pale blue sky. Probably painted over the print found in BN B 27667, fo 85v.

23p. M3r: *St Barbara*, to begin the prayers to her, a medallion occupying a depth of nine lines of type. St Barbara in red and crimson, showing some décolletage, sits on a greensward looking towards the viewer and holding a book in her right hand and a palm in her left. Behind the greensward are some trees, then a pale blue horizon merging into dark blue sky above. To the left of St Barbara the trace of the printed outline of a tower can be seen. Cp. no. 24 (N2v).

23q. M3v: *St Geneviève*, to begin the prayers to her, a square vignette occupying a depth of nine lines of type. St Geneviève sits on a tiled floor dressed in a mauve tunic with a red cloak swirling round her flecked with gold. She holds a tall taper in her right hand and an open book on her lap with the left. Against the dark blue background above there is a red angel with green wings to the left lighting the taper, while to the right a green devil arrives with a bellows to blow it out. Probably painted over the print found in BN B 27667, fo 86r.

23r. M6v: *St Roche*, to begin the prayers to him, a square vignette occupying a depth of ten lines of type. St Roche, bearded, with a pink hat, sits to the right on a greensward with his back to some rocks and his right leg stretched out in front of him; he holds a sword in his right hand which comes straight down to his knee. He is wearing a blue tunic with a swirling red cloak flecked with gold. To the left an angel in mauve with golden wings lifts St Roche's tunic to expose the wounded leg. A dog with bread in its mouth sits to the left looking up. Behind the dog there is a mauve path leading beside green trees on the left to a white cloud in an otherwise blue sky. Probably painted over the print found in BN B 27667, fo 84v.

24. N2v: *St Barbara*, to begin her Hours, a medallion occupying a depth of nine lines of type: cp. no. 23p (M3r). St Barbara in red flecked with gold, showing some décolletage, sits on a greensward looking to the right and holding an open book in her right hand and a palm in her left. Behind the greensward are some trees, then a pale blue horizon merging into blue sky above. To the left of St Barbara there is a grey stone tower with a dark entrance to the left. Probably painted over the print found in BN B 27667, fo 86r.

Colour and ornament: Each page, except those with large illustrations, has a gold border on three sides with a red line border on the hinge side. The outer border is approximately 12mm wide in gold with red, green, white and blue stems, leaves and flowers. Initials in the texts (and KL in the Calendar) are generally in gold on red or blue.

Psalter, Canticles, Litany, Office of the Blessed Virgin Mary

Latin with occasional Dutch rubrics

HISTORY

THIS HANDY BOOK OF DEVOTIONS and offices comes in three booklets no doubt assembled contemporaneously. It was probably written in the Low Countries s.xvi[1] by a single hand, perhaps in the area around Maastricht (pl. 11.1). Rubrics in Dutch occur in Quires **I** and **XLVII–XLVIII**. The inclusion of some saints in the Calendar and Litany suggests a local connection, as Hubert (3 Nov.) and Lambert (17 Sept.) for Liège, Gaugericus (11 Aug.) and Ursmarius (18 Apr.) for Liège and Cambrai, St Gudula (8 Jan.) for Brabant (patron saint of Brussels), St Gertrude of Nivelles (17 Mar.), St Dympna (15 May) for Gheel and Cambrai, St Amalburga (10 July) for Flanders, St Hunegunde (25 Aug.) for Cambrai. Also notable are the number of Scandinavian saints, as St Birgitta (d. 1373, patron saint of Sweden, 23 July or 8 Oct.), Sigfrid (d. 1045, apostle of Sweden, 15 Feb.) and his companion Eskil (s.xi, 12 June), Erik IX (d. 1160, king and patron saint of Sweden, 18 May), Olaf II (d. 1030, king and patron saint of Norway, 29 July), and Canute (Knud) IV (d. 1086, king and patron saint of Denmark, 19 Jan.). Perhaps the texts of the Calendar and Litany were based on ones that circulated through Scandinavia, although the *Passio Olavi* was known in Flanders (Jirouškova 2010: 224), and Knud IV was married to Adela of Flanders, where he spent two short periods. The inclusion of St Francis (4 Oct.) suggests a Franciscan connection.

The manuscript is apparently in its original binding (since repaired, see below) of s.xvi[1] in brown calf on wooden boards much decorated with blind stamps (including medallions of a rose, an eagle and a fleur-de-lys), and the relics of two strap clasps for holding the book closed. The earlier binding has been repaired s.xix by renewing the spine, which shows some blind stamps and the inscription in gold on a red oblong 'LIBER OFFICIORUM DEVOTIONALIS'. At the time of examination the binding was detached from the spine at the front. Nevertheless, the binding is so tight that it is virtually impossible to see the sewing of the quires, making codicological examination difficult: for example, in Quire **XXVII** a leaf is missing, but it is not possible to determine which one. On the inside cover is a printed notice from an auction catalogue s.xix, 'Liber Officiorum Devotionalis, continens Psalterium, Hymnos, | Litaniam, Officium B. Marie Virginis. | 4to., paper and vellum, in a heavy German hand of the 15th cen-|tury, with illuminated capitals. Some of the rubrics at the | end are in Dutch.' This

Beatus vir qui non abiit in consilio impiorum: et in via peccatorum non stetit: et in cathedra pestilencie non sedit. Sed in lege domini voluntas eius: et in lege eius meditabitur die ac nocte. Et erit tamquam lignum quod plantatum est secus decursus aquarum quod fructum suum dabit in tempore suo: Et folium eius non defluet: et omnia quecumque faciet prosperabuntur. Non sic impii non sic: sed tamquam pulvis quem proicit ventus a facie terre Ideo non resurgunt impii in iudicio:

11.1 RB519, fo 8r, the beginning of the Psalter, with ornamental capital **B**. Actual page dimensions 202 x 135mm.

entry corresponds to item 1356 on p. 74 of the sale catalogue of the books of James Henthorn Todd (1805–69; on whom, see Simms 1969), whence it has been cut out and stuck in this book. Todd was active in acquiring manuscripts on the Continent for himself as well as for TCD. The catalogue was probably written by William Reeves (1815–92), later bishop of Down and Connor (on whom, see Thompson 1996 and *ODNB, s.n.*). According to the copy of the sale catalogue (Todd 1859) in the manuscript room at TCD (shelf-mark MSL-1-847), which has prices and buyers written in by hand, the present item was sold for one guinea to 'HF & Co', i.e., Hodges Foster, a forerunner of the present Hodges Figgis, which originated s.xviii[4] in the partnership beween William Gilbert and Robert Hodges (Pollard 2000: 238–9, 291). Its progess from there to Maynooth is unattested, but presumably it came to the college s.xix[3] after 1859. Folio numbers entered in pencil 2008.

Secundo folio: '**KL februarius h‹abe›t dies xxviii. luna xxix**'.

CODICOLOGICAL DESCRIPTION

Fos ii + 319 + i, membrane and paper, with paper endleaves, disposed in fifty-four quires. Most quires consist of a membrane outer bifolium with paper leaves for the internal part of the quire. Leaves measure 202 x 135mm and the written area is generally approx 137 x 87mm, but 144 x 91mm in the Calendar (Quire **I**); however, at Quire **XXXIV** the width diminishes to 82mm. There are holes in the text area of membrane leaves, as fos 114 and 180, and holes in the margin area of fos 106, 169 and 175. Some paper leaves have been repaired, as fos 36, 203, 207, 254, 255, 269, 282 and 289; one damaged leaf, fo 272, is notably unrepaired.

Pricking: Much cropped by the binder. Occasionally prick-marks for the single vertical frame lines can be seen at the bottom of the leaf, as for example on fos 56, 115–16, 155, 242–3 and 319. Prick-marks for the horizontal lines are rarely visible, having been cropped by the binder, but a few can be seen right at the outer edge of the leaf, as on fos 105, 143.

Ruling: In crayon for a simple frame with the bounding lines, horizontal as well as vertical, extending to the edges of the leaves. Generally there are nineteen horizontal lines ruled for writing between the vertical frame lines, except that in Quire **I** (the Calendar) there are thirty-three.

Scribe and script: The scribe employs a set hybrida script of s.xvi[1] using a thick quill. Note the **g** with a short tail and the bottom stroke turned to the left, fairly flat, tapering downwards at the tip. Amendments by the scribe occur occasionally, as on fo 20r, and notes of liturgical occasions appropriate for the use of the psalms have been added in the margins of the Psalter, as on fos 9v, 11v, 16v etc., many of them clipped by the binder.

Colour and ornament: In the Calendar, blue is used for the **KL** and for **A** in the weekly series of letters, while red is used for rubrics and some of the (more important) saints. In the main part containing devotional texts, blue and red initials alternate to indicate divisions in the content, such as the verses of the psalms. Red is also used for rubrics, and red shading marks the beginning of sentences. Ornate calligraphic capitals use blue, red, green and pink/mauve to mark important divisions in the content, occuring on fos 8r (Item 3; pl. 11.1), 29v (Ps 26), 44r (Ps 38), 57v (Ps 51), 58r (Ps 52), 72r (Ps 68), 90r (Ps 80), 107r (Ps 97), 109r (Ps 101), 125v (Ps 109), 163r (Item 4), 176r (Item 5), 185r (Item 6), 187r, 187v (2), 189v, 198v, 200r, 206r, 207r, 207v (2), 211r, 211v, 213v, 214r, 225v, 228r, 243r, 243v, 257r, 273r, 307r, 308r, 308v, 309r, 309v, 310v, 311r, 312r (2), 312v, 313r, 313v. Some of these are major initials and have stem borders (with leaves and fruit) that extend down the side of the page and into the bottom margin, as fos 8r, 29v, 44r, 57v, 58r, 72r, 90r, 107r, 109r, 125v, 163r, 187r, 189v, 213v, 228r, 243r, 257r, 273r.

COLLATION

All quires have an outer bifolium of membrane with internal leaves of paper except as otherwise stated.

Booklet A: **I**⁸ fos 1–7, lacks 8, all membrane), **II**⁶ fos 8–13, **III**⁶ fos 14–19, **IV**⁶ fos 20–5, **V**⁶ fos 26–31, **VI**⁶ fos 32–7, **VII**⁶ fos 38–43, **VIII**⁶ fos 44–9, **IX**⁶ fos 50–5, **X**⁶ fos 56–61, **XI**⁶ fos 62–7, **XII**⁶ fos 68–73, **XIII**⁶ fos 74–9, **XIV**⁶ fos 80–5, **XV**⁶ fos 86–91, **XVI**⁶⁺¹ fos 92–8, a paper leaf added without visible stub, **XVII**⁶⁺¹ fos 99–105, a paper leaf added without visible stub, **XVIII**² fo 106, lacks 2 (membrane), **XIX**⁶ fos 107–13, **XX**⁶ fos 114–19, **XXI**⁶ fos 120–5, **XXII**⁶ fos 126–31, **XXIII**⁶ fos 132–7, **XXIV**⁶ fos 138–43, **XXV**⁶ fos 144–8, lacks 5 after fo 147 (no apparent loss of text), **XXVI**⁶ fos 149–53, lacks 2 after fo 149 (no apparent loss of text), **XXVII**⁶ fos 154–8 lacks a leaf (no apparent loss of text), **XXVIII**⁴ fos 159–62;

Booklet B: **XXIX**⁶ fos 163–8, **XXX**⁶ fos 169–74, **XXXI**⁶ fos 175–80, **XXXII**⁶ fos 181–6;

Booklet C: **XXXIII**⁶ fos 187–92, **XXXIV**⁶ fos 193–8, **XXXV**⁶ fos 199–204, **XXXVI**⁶ fos 205–10, **XXXVII**⁶ fos 211–16, **XXXVIII**⁶ fos 217–22, **XXXIX**⁶ fos 223–8, **XL**⁶ fos 229–34, **XLI**⁶ fos 235–40, **XLII**⁶ fos 241–6, **XLIII**⁶ fos 247–52, **XLIV**⁶ fos 253–8, **XLV**⁶ fos 259–64, **XLVI**⁶ fos 265–70, **XLVII**¹⁰ fos 271–

80, **XLVIII**⁶ fos 281–6, **XLIX**⁶ fos 287–92, **L**⁶ fos 293–8, **LI**⁶ fos 299–304, **LII**⁶ fos 305–10, **LIII**⁶ fos 311–16, **LIV**²⁺¹ fos 317–19, leaf 2 added and glued in, all paper.

There are occasional quire signatures in the centre of the bottom margin of the recto page at the beginning of the relevant quire: Quire **VI** fo 32r 'e' (suggesting that the first alphabetical series began at Quire **II** with an 'a' on fo 8), Quire **XXXIX** fo 223r 'k', Quire **LIV** fo 317r 'g'; and at Quire **XLVII** fo 271 perhaps an 'e'.

Hair/Flesh: The membrane is generally well prepared, and sometimes it is difficult to tell the flesh side from the hair side. Quire **I** HFHF, Quires **II–III, VI–VIII, X–XI, XIV–XVI, XX–XXIV, XXXII, XXXIV, XXXIX–XL** flesh outside, Quires **IV–V, IX, XII–XIII, XVII–XIX, XXV–XXXI, XXXIII, XXXV–XXXVIII, XLI–LIII** hair outside.

CONTENTS

Booklet A

1. Fos 1r/1–6v/32: Calendar. Begins '**KL Ianuari\<us\> h\<abe\>t dies xxxi. luna xxx**'. Ends '**Siluestri pape et co\<n\>f\<essori\> ixl**'.

2. Fo 7r/1–30: Computistical table for calculating liturgical dates. Begins in Dutch '**Die iare\<n\> ons here\<n\>**'. Ends 'vii. .v. .i. .x.' fo 7v/1–30: blank.

3. Fos 8r/1–162r/19: Psalter. Begins '**BE**atus vir | qui non a|biit in con|silio impio|ru\<m\>:' (Ps 1.1) (pl. 11.1). Ends 'om\<n\>is sp\<irit\>us laudet d\<omin\>um **Gl**\<ori\>a' (Ps 150.5). Fo 162v/1–19 blank.

Booklet B

4. Fos 163r/1–176r/12: Canticles. Begins '**CO**nfitebor tibi | d\<omi\>ne q\<uonia\>m irat\<us\> | es michi:' (Is 12.1). Ends '\<et\> glo|riam plebis tue israel **Gl**\<ori\>a p\<atri\>' (Lk 2.32).

5. Fos 176r/13–184r/14: Litany (follows without a break). Begins '**Kyri**[e] eleyson Christe | audi nos'. Ends 'Ihesu\s/ | et **Maria** sint uobiscu\<m\> in om|ni vita Amen.' fo 184r/15–19 and 184v/1–19 blank.

6. (a) Fo 185r/1–185v/16: A Series of Meditations on the Passion. Begins '**O Domine** ih\<es\>u christe | adoro te in cruce pe\<n\>|dentem'. Ends 'egressa est | miserere a\<n\>i\<m\>e mee in egressu suo | Amen. **p**\<ate\>**r n**\<oste\>**r. Aue maria.'** fo 185v/17–19 blank.

(b) fo 186r/2–16, on a page left blank by the scribe, an addition in a hand
of s.xvi. Begins '[D]Eus qui nos concepcionis | natiuitatis presentatacio<n>is
[*sic*] | Anunciacionis Visitacionis purify|cacionis Co<m>passionis
Assumpcionis | Et glorificacionis b<ea>te et glori[o]se | virg<in>is marie
gaudia et solempnita|tes recolendo letificas'. Ends 'gaudere mereamur in
celis | Per d<omin>um n<ost>r<u>m ih<esu>m <Christu>m filiu<m> |
tuu<m> qui tecu<m> viuit et[c]'. As *CO* 1875. Fo 186v/1–19 blank.

Booklet C
7. Fos 187r/1–319v/19: The Office of the Blessed Virgin Mary. "**Incipit
officiu<m> b<ea>tissi<m>e Marie v<ir>g<in>is**". Begins 'DIgnare | me lau|dare
te v<ir>|go sacra|ta' [As Anselm, *Orationes* in PL 158, 962D]. Ends apparently
incomplete 'p<er> crudelem | mortem tua<m> <et> p<er> o<m>nis passiones'.
Sometimes the scribe left blank space before the office for another day, possibly
because he was following the layout of an exemplar, as fos 227v, 242v/7–19,
256v/8–19, 272v/13–19, 290v/17–19.

Canon law, doctrine and theological discourse

IN THIS NEXT GROUP OF MANUSCRIPTS, the first is an unpretentious little paper manuscript (RB29) whose appearance belies its interest. Like the previous two manuscripts it also comes from France, written probably in the third quarter of the fifteenth century and, being a small manuscript, is typical of Franciscan pocket-books – small books that were carried by friars in the pockets of their robes. It seems to have been compiled around a collection of papal decretals and has an intriguing name at the end of Item 3: 'Scheuez' signed with a notarial flourish. Added to this are some compositions in verse, more decretals and a metrical digest of Peter Lombard's *Sentences*, which is a Franciscan work. At the beginning a quire of miscellaneous extracts, including some from Virgil, has been added.

By contrast, RB71 is a well-produced manuscript on good quality membrane containing genuine works by St Augustine, and written by a single scribe in the second half of the fifteenth century. This manuscript was owned by Frederick W. Conway (1782–1853), the Irish bibliophile, who had it bound in red morocco by James Adams of Dublin. When Conway died, his books were auctioned in 1854 and this one was acquired for Maynooth College library for 13s.

12 RB29
Miscellaneous works

Extracts, including two from Virgil • Papal Decretals • *Decreta Versificata*
• *Petri Lombardi Sententiae Metrice Digestae*

Latin

HISTORY

THIS IS A WORKADAY LITTLE PAPER manuscript mainly containing Canon Law, probably from France. The main part, Booklet B (pp 17–420), comprises a compilation of papal decretals (Item 2), written in a southern semi-textualis script by a single hand showing humanistic influence of s.xv[3] (pl. 12.1). Item 3 is a near-contemporary addition (at the end of Item 2) in a French gothic cursiva script that concludes with the name 'Scheuez' in a notarial flourish (pl. 12.2). Perhaps this booklet was owned (or even commissioned?) by a Maître Chevet. Booklet A, a single quire containing miscellaneous extracts, probably an afterthought added at the beginning, is mainly in a French semi-hybrida currens script of s.xv[3]. Booklet C contains two metrical compositions, the *Decreta Versificata*, and a metrical digest of the *Sentences* of Peter Lombard, which is Franciscan. The structure of the book suggests that all of it is a Franciscan

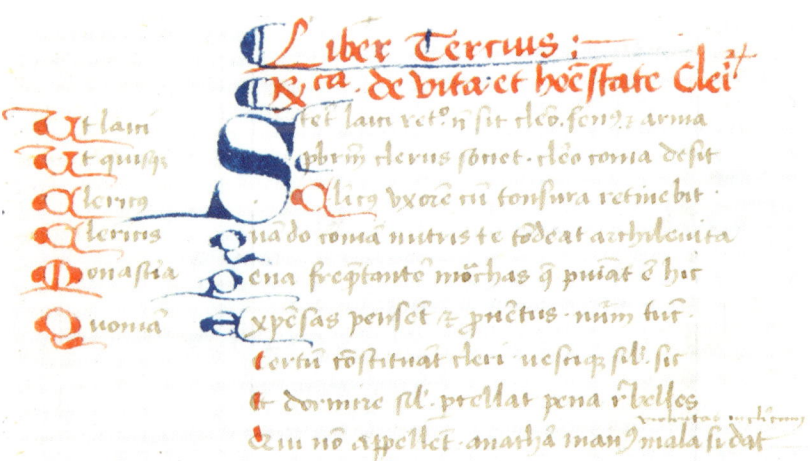

12.1 RB29, p. 121, the scribe of Booklet B, Item 2. Actual page dimensions 132 x 97mm.

compilation, as indeed its size and scope would tend to confirm (on small Franciscan books, see d'Avray 1980).

Two watermarks distinguish the two main parts of the manuscript (Booklets B and C). Booklet B shows a watermark Letter **P**, very similar in style and shape to Briquet's no. 8658, a gothic **P** surmounted by a quatrefoil, and showing a descender joining the letter to a two-pronged foot, the descender being traversed by a bar. This watermark is visible in Quires **II**, **IV–XI**, **XIII–XIV** and **XVI**. Briquet 1968 assigns it to Pontoise 1471 and Chalons-sur-Marne 1473, although it is also found in the Low Countries. Booklet C shows another watermark, unidentified from Briquet 1968, but probably a bird with an S-shaped neck or a snake, which is visible in Quires **XV**, **XVII–XVIII**, **XX–XXIII**.

Since the main scribe of Booklet B occurs also in Booklet C it would appear that the two scribes worked together at least to the extent that the main scribe of Booklet C took the work of the main scribe of Booklet B and incorporated it into his compilation, as is suggested by the brief statement added by the hand of the main scribe of Booklet C at the end of the last quire written by the main hand of Booklet B (Item 5(a); pl. 12.3). The compiler would also have added Booklet A at the beginning.

At some stage the manuscript, or part of it, probably became damp as there are damp marks centering around pp 349–61 in Item 4 (Quire **XVIII**).

Binding of s.xix in marbled paper on card with the corner guards missing, but provided with a membrane back over the spine. It was presumably at the time of this binding that the misplacement of Quire **XV** (pp 277–300), which should occur after **XVI**, became fixed.

Secundo folio (= p. 3): 'Rubrice q‹uar›ti libri su‹n›t xviii'.

CODICOLOGICAL DESCRIPTION

Fos iii [endleaves associated with the binding] + 240 + iii [endleaves associated with the binding], paper, measuring 132 x 97mm. Pp 2, 4, 6 and 8 have additional paper strips glued to the outer side of the page, and pp 475/6 and 477/8 each consist of two leaves that have been glued together. Written area in Quire **I** is 102 x 68mm; in Quires **II–XIV** and **XVI** it is 100 x 45mm (measured between the inner bounding lines); in Quire **XV** it is 115 x 48mm.

Pagination in pencil at the top right-hand corner of recto leaves first entered spasmodically with 287 etc. misnumbered 285 etc., augmented and corrected 1998.

Pricking: None visible.

Ruling: Booklet A: Quire **I** shows a frame rule in fine crayon divided into the main area on the inner side, showing a width of 52mm, with double vertical bounding lines, and a smaller area on the outer side showing a width of 16mm.

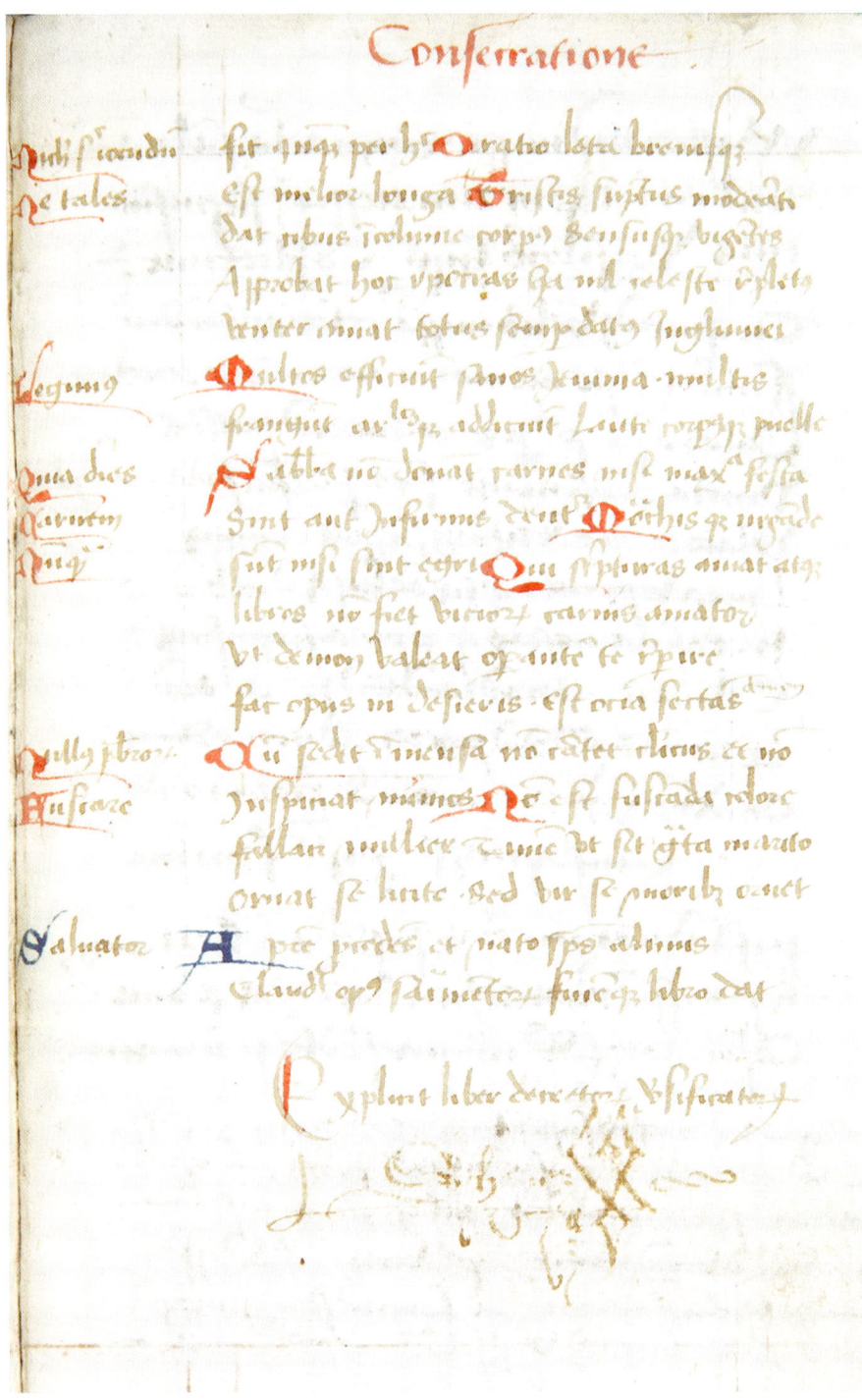

12.2 RB29, p. 419, the scribe of Booklet B, with the notarial name 'Scheuez'.
Actual page dimensions 132 × 97mm.

Booklets B and C: Quire **II** shows a frame rule in fine crayon with the main central area 50mm wide bordered by double vertical bounding lines and on both the inner and the outer side there is a narrower segment 16/17mm wide; this narrower segment is used for headings when the margin is on the left-hand side. When it is on the right-hand side some notes in a smaller script occur, perhaps added by a reader, but in Quire **XV** it is used for reference numbers. All rules extend to the outer edges of the leaves, and no lines are ruled for writing. The number of lines per page varies between twenty-four and twenty-nine. Quires **III, IV, V, VI, VII, VIII, IX, X, XI, XII, XIII, XIV, XVI** are similar. Quires **XV, XVII, XVIII, XIX, XX, XXI** show a similar frame rule, but the depth of the written area is greater, and there are 25–30 lines of writing. Item 6 shows a similar frame rule with the central frame measuring 102 x 49mm, and the number of lines varies from twenty-five to twenty-seven.

Colour and ornament: No colour in Booklet A. In Booklets B and C decorated initials in red and blue occur on pp 17, 21, 22, 24 etc., the last one occuring on p. 59. From the beginning of Quire **IV** (p. 57) there are also capitals in blue, and these then become the norm up to the end of Quire **XVI** (excluding Quire **XV**, which is bound in the wrong order). Decorated capitals in red and blue, with red flourishing, occur again in Quires **XV** (p. 277), **XVII** (pp 324, 328, 335, 339), **XVIII** (pp 342, 343, 345, 346, 348, 349, 351, 355, 359, 361, 363), **XIX** (pp 365, 370, 372, 373, 375, 376, 381, 386, 388), **XX** (pp 390, 392, 394, 396, 397, 399, 400, 403), and **XXI** (pp 405, 406, 407, 410, 411). Left-hand page headings (Work nos, up to p. 314) and paraph marks (and, later, header capitals) occur in blue, while rubrics, right-hand page headings (Book nos, up to p. 275, then pp 301–13) and capitals in red up to pp 339, 345 (after which they are in black), with the letter at the beginning of each line showing red shading. No headings in Quire **XV** (except on p. 277, probably added later); in Quire **XVII** there are no headings up to p. 324, and in Quires **XVII–XXI**, from pp 325–410, the 'Causa' and the relevant number form headings usually distributed over the left-hand and right-hand pages of an opening, often in red ink, but also in black ink, sometimes with the red inked over in black; from pp 411–19 (pl. 12.2) the heading is '[de] consecratione' in red or black. No colour in Item 6. Guide letters were written for later rubrication, but this was never done. Page headings in the hand of the scribe in the same colour of ink as the text.

COLLATION

Booklet A: **I**[8] pp 1–16;

Booklet B: **II**[10] pp 17–36, **III**[10] pp 37–56, **IV**[10] pp 57–76, **V**[10] pp 77–96, **VI**[10] pp 97–116, **VII**[10] pp 117–36, **VIII**[10] pp 137–56, **IX**[10] pp 157–76, **X**[10] pp 177–96,

XI[10] pp 197–216, **XII**[10] pp 217–36, **XIII**[10] pp 237–56, **XIV**[10] pp 257–76, **XV**[12] pp 277–300, **XVI**[8] pp 301–16, **XVII**[12] pp 317–40, **XVIII**[12] pp 341–364, **XIX**[12] pp 365–88, **XX**[8] pp 389–404, **XXI**[8] pp 405–20;

Booklet C: **XXII**[12] pp 421–44, **XXIII**[12] pp 445–68, **XXIV**[6] pp 469–80 (sewing at centre not visible, as two leaves have been glued together to make pp 475/6 and 477/8).

Note: Quire **XV** (pp 277–300) has been misplaced and should occur after **XVI**.

CONTENTS

Booklet A

1. (a) p. 1/1–3: Brief extract from Virgil, *Georgics*, Bk III, 66–8 beginning 'opti<m>a queq<ue> dies miser<is> mortali<bus> eui' and ending 'et dure rap<it> i<n>cleme<n>tia mort<is>'. As Mynors 1990: lvi. Lines 4–5 blank.

(b) p. 1/6–11: Brief extract from Virgil, *Aeneid*, Bk X, 467–72, beginning 'Stat sua cuiq<ue> dies b<re>ue et irrep<ar>ab<i>le te<m>p<us> | o<mn>ib<us> est vite' and ending 'fata voca<n>t'. As Mynors 1969: 348.

(c) p. 1/12–20: 'O p<re>clara<m> libro<rum> suppellectile<m> et o | iocu<n>dam familia<m>.', ending 'qua<n>tu<m> velis audias'.

(d) pp 2/1–3/8: 'Carmi<n>a Rubricar<um> p<ri>mi | libri Institu<t>ion<um> qui sunt nu<mer>o xxvi'. Ends 'Finis R<ubrica>ru<m> Institu<t>ionu<m> ciuiliu<m> qui | sunt numero no<na>genta Nouem'.

Pp 3/9–bottom, and 4 blank.

(e) pp 5/1–7/11: List of contents in a hand of s.xv. 'Ma<teria>m libror<um> q<ua>nd<oque> decretaliu<m>'. Ends 'Quinq<ua>ginta duos cleme<n>s nu<m>erat tibi qui<n>t<us> | Finis' (referring to Pope Clement V).

Pp 7/12–bottom, 8–16 blank.

Booklet B

2. Pp 17/1–276/29 and 301/1–316/20: Papal Decretals [by popes up to Clement III (d. 1191)], *Compilatio Prima* by Bernard of Pavia (d. 1213) in 5 books, with headings as follows: p. 17/1: "liber i. | ¶ R<ubri>ca de Constitutionibus [Ecclesiasticis]". (In the margin) 'Canonu<m>'. Begins 'CAnon seruetur p<ro>p<ri>o no<n> v<e>tere sensu | Culpa ferat da<m>nu<m>'; p. 67/8: "¶ **Liber Secundus:-** | ¶ R<ubri>ca de Iudicijs [et Processu Iudiciorum]:-"; p. 121/16: "¶ **Liber Tercius:-** | ¶ R<ubri>ca de vita et ho<n>estate Cle<r>i<corum>" (pl. 12.1); p. 183/12: "¶ **Liber Quartus:-** | ¶ R<ubri>ca de sponsalib<us> <et> mat<ri>monijs"; p. 213/9: "¶ **Liber Quintus:** | ¶ R<ubri>ca de Accusationibus". Ends p. 314/22–6 'si lup<us> | oues co<m>medit et pastor nescit | Indignu<m> est et a romane ecclesie co<n>|suetudine alienu<m> ut p<ro> spiritualib<us> |

fac<er>e q<ui>s omagiu<m> co<m>pellat<ur> | Finis'. Pp 315/1–316/18: Summaries of the books beginning "**De quibus tracte<n>t qui<n>q<ue> libri decre<ta>\liu<m>/ in g<e>n<er>ali**", and ending 'regula iuris. || finis **Laus . deo.**'. As analysed by Friedberg 1882: 1–65 (also 1897: 174–88). Discussed by Schulte 1875–7: III.78–82, §17.

3. P. 316/22–8: Addition in a near-contemporary French gothic cursiva hand, headed 'V<er>sus' and beginning 'Dec<re>tu<m> ce<n>tu<m> li <et> distinct<i>o<n>es et vna<m> | Trigi<n>ta causas et sex'.

Booklet C
Written by the scribe of Booklet B.
4. Pp 277/1–300/29, 317/1–419/21: *Decreta Versificata*.
p. 277/1: "Liber decretoru<m> versificator<um>" in 3 books. Bk 1 usually called 'Distinctiones' begins '**P**auper et incultus <con>textus v<er>sib<us>'; p. 324/17 "¶ **Incipit secu<n>d<us> Tractat<us>** [de causa]"; p. 410/26 "¶ **Tractatus de consecratio<n>e**". Ends 'q<uod> libro dat'. 'Explicit liber decreto<rum> v<er>sificator<um>' (pl. 12.2). Signed with a notarial flourish 'Scheuez'. Walther 1963–86: I, no. 13862.

5. (a) p. 420/1–17 (pl. 12.3): Added in the hand of the main scribe of Booklet C. Begins 'Misterioru<m> misse Signac<u>la salua|toris n<ost>ri agone<m> amarissi<mum> significa|tiua'. Ends 'Co<n>firmat<us> fide<m> minuit fo<m>ite<m>q<ue> remittit'.
   (b) p. 420/19–24: Added in another later hand. Begins 'Na<m> hoc sac<ra>m<en>tu<m> digne susceptu<m> caritate suscipiu<n>t'.

6. Pp 421/1–474/6: Anon. OFM (previously attrib. Bonaventura), *Petri Lombardi Sententiae Metrice Digestae*. "Libri 4or m<a>g<ist>ri S<um>maru<m> Carmi<n>e co<m>plexi". Lacks Proemium. Bk 1 begins '[I]N res et signa doct<ri>na<m> crede secari | Et dic p<er> signa nob<is> res significari'; Bk 2, pp 432/23–444/25, begins '[H]ic nequit errare dans vnu<m> cu<n>cta c<re>are'; Bk 3, pp 445/1–454/6, begins 'Constat q<uod> te<m>pus g<ra>tu<m> tu<n>c oriebat<ur>'; Bk 4, pp 454/9–474/6, begins 'Sacru<m> sig<na>tu<m> sac<ra> signa<n>s siue sac<ra>tum'. Ends 'Voto sincero te desidero volo quero A<men>', lacking the last five lines in the printed ed. 'Distinctiones libror<um> 4ᵒʳ | m<a>g<ist>ri S<um>ma<rum> familiari car|mi<n>e traducte Expliciunt'. As Bonaventura 1609: 205–23. Stegmüller 1947: 6, no. 14; Distelbrink 1975: 179–80, no. 198. Pp 474/7–bottom and 475 blank.

12.3 RB29, p. 420, the scribe of Booklet C, Item 5a. Actual page dimensions 132 × 97mm.

7. Pp 476/1–480/7: Notes in another hand of s.xv⁴.

(a) pp 476/1–477/21: On the Pentateuch, beginning 'Pentateu\con/ genes‹i›s exo^d‹us›', and ending 'affligere superbos. | 4'.

(b) pp 478/1–479/15: On the Gospels, beginning 'Nouu‹m› testa‹men›\tu‹m›/ | Eua‹n›\geliu‹m›/ matheus m‹ar›c‹usque› lucus‹que› [*recte* lucas‹que›] joh‹an›n‹is›'. Ends 'Est timor d‹omi›nj\alis/ filialis addit‹ur› illi'.

(c) p. 480/1–2: In verse: 'Cl‹er›icus ad bella p‹ro›mptus lasciua puella | Marcius in flore caret horu‹m› finis ho|nore'.

Lines 3–4 blank.

(d) p. 480/5–7: Possibly a truncated version of a dedicatory prayer (apparently corrupt, with perhaps a line missing after 'filium'): 'qua‹e›q‹ue› diuine volu‹n›tat‹i› b‹e›n‹e›placita ‹con›seque‹n›|t‹a› magne sc‹ri›psi i‹m›pleat nec filium | quod ibide‹m› no‹n› p‹er›mitto fieri'. Lines 8– bottom blank.

13 RB71

Augustine: *De diversis quaestionibus lxxxiii, Contra adversarium legis et prophetarum, De consensu evangelistarum, De pastoribus, De ovibus*

HISTORY

A WELL-PRODUCED MANUSCRIPT on good quality membrane containing works by St Augustine, and written s.xiii³/⁴ by a single scribe. Calligraphic initials mark the beginning of separate works (pl. 13.1). At the top of fo 2r there is an annotation (written over an erasure) which apparently reads 'ine<qua>l<ium> V<o>l<u>me<num> p<rimum> clii'; but if this is meant to be a reference to the parts of the first work the number is too high. Otherwise there are a few annotations by readers, as those on fos 24v, 26r (a doodle), 32r and 82r.

Bound 1834 in red goatskin morocco with gold-tooled ornament and gilt edging to the leaves by James Adams of Dublin (Ramsden 1954: 228 gives six addresses) for Frederick W. Conway (1782–1853), the Irish bibliophile and founder of the *Dublin Political Review*. It was sold to Maynooth College at the auction of Conway's books beginning 30 May 1854 for 13s. (as noted by Woods 1995: 31, 58, n. 9). Woods notes a similar binding for Dublin, Trinity College MS 42, an English Bible of s.xiii³/⁴ (Colker 1991: I.73–5). The binding of the present manuscript is so tight as to make collation difficult.

Secundo folio: 'Incipit liber Beati'.

CODICOLOGICAL DESCRIPTION

Fos i + ii + 89 + ii + i, membrane except for two paper endleaves (+ one leaf of thin card) front and back that belong with the binding, measuring 303 x 210mm, written area 226 x 164mm in double columns, the inner and outer columns being 71 and 75mm wide respectively. The membrane being of good quality there are hardly any holes in it (as fos 14, 49, 62, 85, 88), and the small hole on fo 14 has been written around by the scribe and circled by the rubricator. Fo 89 has been cut away below the bottom of the recto col. a (line 52) and below where the text finishes in col. b (line 14).

Pricking: None visible following cropping by a binder.

Ruling: In fine crayon. This is for a simple frame in double columns, and can be seen, more clearly on some folios than others, as on fos 7, 12 etc. The frame lines

Incipit liber beati Augustini epi̅ octu-
aginta trium qo̅m. In noie p̅ris · et fili̅
et sp̅s sancti Amen. Qo̅ p̅ma

Vtr̅ue vecu̅ a veritate ·
vocu̅ est Et di̅s dia̅ eo dia̅
est quo vera dia̅ est Om̅is
igitur dia̅ · a veri̅te h̅abet
vt om̅o dia̅ sit; Aliud aut dia̅ : aliud est
veritas; Nam veritas al̅is nu̅q̅ patitur
dia̅ ro̅ sepe fallit. Ro̅ igit̅ eu̅ a veri̅te
am̅a est · a seip̅a est Est aut veritas de̅s
deu̅ igit̅ h̅abet auctore̅ vt sit dia̅. Qo̅2·

Om̅e q̅ fit · ei a quo fit · par̅ esse no̅
pt̅ Alioqn iusti̅a q̅ sua cuiq̅ tribue̅
debet · d̅ reb̅ aufferat · necesse e̅ H̅oie2
ergo de̅s eu̅ feat̅ · q̅a̅ optimu̅ feat̅ : non
tn̅ id fe̅t q̅ erat ip̅e Melior aut homo
e̅ qui volu̅te q̅ qui bon̅ e̅ Voluntas igi̅
libera danda est h̅om̅ fuit Questio 3·

Nullo sapie̅te h̅oie auctore fit homo
detior No̅ em̅ p̅ua ist̅a culp̅a est
ymo talu̅ est q̅ in sapie̅ti̅ cu̅ius h̅oie2 culo̅
negat Est aut de̅s d̅ h̅oi̅ sapie̅ti p̅sta
tior Mlto mag̅ igit̅ deo auctore fit homo
detior Mlto em̅ p̅stantior dei volu̅tas
q̅ h̅ois sapie̅t̅ est Illo aut auctore eu̅ dicit̅
illo volete dicit̅ Est ergo vit̅iu̅ voli̅t̅e
q̅ est h̅o detior Qd̅ vit̅iu̅ si longe abest
a dei volu̅te ut ro̅ docet : i̅ quo sit quere̅
dum est · Questio quarta

generally extend to the outer edges of the leaves and across the centre. No horizontal lines were drawn and the number of lines written in each column varies from forty-eight on fo 2r/a to sixty on fo 25r/a, even on the same page (as on fo 2r col. a has forty-eight lines and col. b has fifty).

Scribal practice: The scribe of s.xiii$^{3/4}$ liked to add calligraphic flourishes to capitals (in the margins) and descenders in the bottom line of writing; sometimes these develop into doodles or drawings, as on fo 75r/b. Corrections (or annotations) by the scribe occasionally occur in the margin, as on fos 24r/b, 31v/b, 32r/b, 32v/b, 40r/a, 42v/b, 43r/b, 56r/b, 56v/b, 75v/b, 80v/a, 84v/a, 85r/b, and they are in red ink on fos 31r/b, 66r/a, 73r/a, 79v/a, 80v/a, 88r/b. Pointing hands are used apparently to indicate important subject matter, as on fos 2v (one in red), 3r (in red), 9v, 12r (in red), 14r, 14v, 15r (in red), 20v, 24v, 33v, 77v, 78r, 80v, 81r, 83r, 83v, 85r–86v, 87v, 88r, 89r. For the same purpose, triple points are found on fos 3r (in red), 5r, 12r (in red), 13r, 24v, 25r, 31r (in red, accompanying a marginal note), 34r (in red), 38r (in red), 48r (2, 1 in red), 50v, 63r (in red), 66r (2 in red), 67r, 68r (2 in red), 72r (in red), 73r (2 in red), 74v (in red), 75v/b, 77v/b, 78r/b, 79r/a (in red), 79v/a (in red), 79v/b, 80r/a, 82r/a, 84r/a (in red), 84v/a, 85r/a, 85r/b (in red), 85v/b, 86r/b, 86v/a, 87v/a, 87v/b, 88r/a, 88r/b (in red, accompanying a scribal note), 89r/a (2, 1 in red), some of them evidently used to reinforce the pointing hand. The same triple point (or triquetra) occurs at the end of the explicit in red on fo 75/a. Those in red are evidently the work of the scribe when doing the rubrication, and those in brown ink may be by the scribe too.

Colour: Larger, more calligraphic initials in blue and red, as **O** on fo 2r/a (with pen trails; pl. 13.1), **L** on fo 20r/b, **I** on fo 32v/b. A similar initial **V** in two shades of red occurs on fo 84r/b (with pen trails in red). All these initials mark the beginning of separate works. That at fo 78r/b/1 is marked only by an initial **Q** in metallic red. Red ink is also used for page headings, rubrics, explicits and initials, occasionally with metallic as on fo 6r/b. As noted above, some corrections and marks of *nota bene* by the scribe are in red ink, most notably that on fo 32r/b in the margin, partially cropped by a binder.

COLLATION

I^{12} (fos 1–12), **II**^{12} (fos 13–23, lacks 8 after fo 19), **III**^{12} (fos 24–35), **IV**^{14} (fos 36–49), **V**^{12} (fos 50–61), **VI**^{12} (fos 62–73), **VII**^{12} (fos 74–85), **VIII**^{4} (fos 86–9). No quire signatures or catchwords are visible.

Hair/Flesh: The quality of preparation for the membrane is such that even the hair side is usually smooth, so it is difficult to be categorical, but probably HFHFHF(H) and HF in Quire **VIII**; thus all quires show hair side outside.

CONTENTS

Fo 1r blank

Fo 1v/1–6: List of contents by the main hand in long lines, with spaces left above, between and below the entries. Begins 'Subscripta b‹ea›tis‹si›mi p‹at›ris Augustini op‹er›a: ‹con›tine‹n›t‹ur› i‹n› hoc libro'. Ends '**De** ouibus· liber vnus ; \ **Laus tibi d‹omi›ne ;**'.

1. Fos 2r/a/1–20r/a/8: Augustine, *De diuersis quaestionibus lxxxiii* (incomplete). "**Incipit liber Beati Augustini ep‹isco›pi oct|agintatriu‹m› q‹uaestioniu›m In no‹m›i‹n›e p‹at›ris . et filii | et sp‹iritu›s sancti Amen**". Begins 'OMne veru‹m› a veritate; | veru‹m› est Et o‹mn›is a‹n›i‹m›a eo a‹n›i‹m›a | est' (pl. 13.1). Ends '**Q.80.** Adu‹er›sus appollinaristas **Q.81.**', part of an (apparently incomplete) list of quaestiones presumably appended as a tabular guide at the end of the work. As Mutzenbecher 1975: 11–249; Migne, PL 40, 11–100 (some variant readings PL 47, 1222, and *RB57* (1947), 151). Dekkers no. 289.

Quaestio lviii (*recte* lix) beginning on fo 9r/b/24 is different from PL 40, no. LIX; Quaestiones lx–lxiv = PL LIX–LXIII, lacks PL LXIV; Quaestio lxvii lacks PL §§1–2 except for the quotation of Rom 8.19; Quaestio lxxx = PL LXXXII, and Quaestio lxxxi = PL LXXIX, given out of order.

There is a lacuna after fo 19v/60: quaestio lxxxi (PL LXXIX) ends incomplete 'Na‹m› n‹u›llo m‹od›o' (PL 40.92); fo 20r begins in the summary of quaestio lxxiv 'homo inanis qui‹a› fides sine op‹er›ib‹us› otiosa e‹st›' (= James 2.20 in the heading of Quaestio LXXVI in PL 40.37); as stated above the quaestiones are out of order.
Fo 20r/a/9–53: blank.

2. Fos 20r/b/1–32v/a/53: Augustine, *Contra adversarium legis et prophetarum libri duo*. "**Incipit liber Aurely Augustini p‹ri›m‹us› cont‹ra› | aduersariu‹m› legis et p‹ro›phetarum **". Begins 'LIbrum quem misistis fr‹atre›s dilectissi‹mi› | nescio cui‹us› he‹re›tici:'. Book 2 begins fo 26v/b/22. Ends 'Sed ut dixi i‹n› | fine p‹er›pauca su‹n›t que si d‹omi›n‹us› volu‹er›it q‹uan›toci‹us› | explicare curabo; ¶ Finit feliciter \'. As Daur 1985: 35–131; Migne, PL 42, 603–66. Dekkers no. 326.

3. Fos 32v/b/1–78r/a/24: Augustine, *De consensu evangelistarum libri quatuor*. "**Liber beati Augustini episcopi d‹e› con|sensu evva‹n›gelista‹rum› partit‹us› i‹n› libros | q‹ua›tuoR Incipit feliciteR ;**" Begins 'INter om‹n›es d‹iu›inas auctorita‹te›s q‹uae› | sanct‹is› l‹itte›ris ‹con›tine‹ntur› eua‹n›geliu‹m› merito | excellit'. Book 2 begins fo 38v/a/28. Book 3 begins fo 59v/a/20. Book 4 begins fo 75r/b/1. Ends 'qui eva‹n›gelista | ‹Christu›m longe ceteris alci‹us›

<com>me<n>dat ap<u>d eu<m> | et discipulis pedes lauat; **Explicit liber q<ua>rt<us> et vltim<us> b<ea>tis|simi p<at>ris Augustini yppone<n>sis e<pisco>pi | de <con>sensu evangelista<rum>** [followed by 7 lines now erased]'. As Weihrich 1904: 1–418; Migne, PL 34, 1041–230. Dekkers no. 273. Stegmüller no. 1467.

Fo 78r/a/32–52 blank.

4. Fos 78r/b/1–84r/b/32: Augustine, *De pastoribus* = Sermo 46 on Ezek 34.1–16. **"Incipit liber S<ancti> August<in>i d<e> pastorib<us>"**. Begins 'QUi pasto<rum> nomi<n>a audire volu<n>t: pa|sto<rum> officiu<m> i<m>plere nolu<n>t: q<ui>d ad eos'. Ends '**Aut** | si mag<is> vos delectat angariat<us> **Id** est q<ui> cogit<ur> | toll<er>e cruce<m> . recte ergo faciu<n>t i<m>p<er>atores catho|lici qui vos cogu<n>t ad vnitatem \'. As Lambot 1961: 529–70; Migne, PL 38, 270–95; Lambot 1953: 173–210. Dekkers no. 284.46.

5. Fos 84r/b/34–89r/b/14: Augustine, *De ovibus* = Sermo 47 on Ezek 34.17–31. **"Incipit liber d<e> ouib<us> ei<us>de<m>"**. Begins 'VErba q<uae> cantaui<mus> <con>tine<n>t p<ro>fessio<ne>s | n<ost>ras quia oues dei sum<us>'. Ends 'Sed t<ame>n qua di|stinc[t]io<n>e vos ho<m>i<n>es est<is> . ego d<omin>us de<us> vest<er> | dicit d<omin>us deus noster; \'. As Lambot 1961: 572–604; Migne, PL 38, 295–316. Dekkers no. 284.47. Fo 89v blank.

The Bible

BOUND IN RED SHEEPSKIN with gold tooling and gilt edging to the leaves by Gerald Bellew of Dublin around the middle of the nineteenth century (pl. C above), this manuscript presents extremely well on the inside too, with good illuminated initials. It is written on fine-quality membrane by a scribe probably from the south-east of France, but was probably made in Paris *c.* 1400. The thinness of the membrane allows a large book to be encompassed in one volume, and even to add another pertinent work probably by Stephen Langton, archbishop of Canterbury (d. 1228), who lived and worked in Paris for a time. The manuscript came to Maynooth College Library from Dr Laurence Renehan, president of St Patrick's College, Maynooth (1845–57).

Biblia Sacra, with Prefaces by Jerome and others • Stephen Langton (attrib.), *Interpretationes nominum Hebraicorum ordine alphabetico* (incomplete)

HISTORY

A WELL-PRESENTED BIBLE, with good illuminated initials (pl. 14.1), written on fine-quality membrane s.xiii/xiv by a scribe probably from the southeast of France; cp. BN lat. 12018, fo 1r (Cessoles, diocese of Aix, 1313–20), illustrated in Samaran and Marichal 1974, pl. lxxxvii and p. 265. The fact that the text is written on such fine-quality thin membrane suggests that the manuscript was made in Paris. If the last work is really by Stephen Langton its presence in a manuscript originating in France is no surprise, since he studied and wrote in Paris. Corrections/additions by the scribe occur relatively frequently, as on fos 1r, 17r, 23v, 24r, 27r, 29r, 29v, 30r etc., and, for example, on fos 78r, 108v, 290v, 461r, 493v, 494v, 496v, 500v; some in smaller writing on fos 30r, 30v, 44r etc. On fos 233v, 234r and 234v passages comprising comment by Jerome integrated into the text have been marked in red with a note in the margin '**Jeronim‹us›**'.

The particular importance of the Psalter is indicated through negative contrast by the lack of page headings (the only pages in the whole of the Bible not to have them) and by the fact that in addition to the first psalm six more are given importance (such as that given otherwise to the beginning of a biblical book) by the provision of illuminated initials, viz. Ps 1 Beatus vir, Ps 26 Dominus illuminatio mea, Ps 38 Dixi: Custodiam vias meas, Ps 52 Dixit insipiens in corde suo, Ps 68 Salvum me fac, Deus, Ps 80 Exultate Deo adiutori nostro, Ps 95 Cantate Domino canticum novum. These features suggest that the manuscript was made for use in a religious house. Annotations by a reader occur rarely, as on fos 62r, 244v.

At the bottom of fo 512v there is a pen trial 'nemo qui[?]', followed by a doodle in French (s.xvi/xvii), which is difficult to read, and the surname is illegible: 'Auant qu[']on puisse s[cr]ivere vytement | fault premierement sauoir tailler | La plume ainsy signe Gy M[?]as[?]'. Before one can write quickly it is first necessary to know how to trim the pen thus. Signed Guy M[(?)as(?)].

At the bottom of fo 1r 'Ex libris Rev adm L.F. Renehan D.D. Pres Collegii S. Patricii apud Maynooth 1845': Dr Laurence Renehan, president, St Patrick's College, Maynooth (1845–57).

The binding of s.xix^med is in red sheepskin with gold tooling and gilt edging to the leaves by Gerald Bellew of Dublin (Ramsden (1954: 28) gives two addresses: 21 S. King St., and 79 Grafton St.), signed at the bottom of the inside of the front

14.1 RB53, fo 4r, showing the beginning of Genesis with vignettes in initial capital **I** for the seven days of creation.

cover (pl. C). Some cropping by the binder is shown by the partial loss of text in marginal annotations, e.g., fo 244v.

Secundo folio: 'p<ro>ph<et>am int<er>rogat<us> a'.

CODICOLIGICAL DESCRIPTION

Fos ii + 512 + ii, membrane of very fine quality, thin and supple and showing no holes at all. Paper endleaves supplied with the binding of s.xix. The leaves measure 256 x 190mm, written area 165 x 120mm disposed in two columns (but 151mm wide in Quire **XLIII** where there are three columns), arranged in forty-three quires, but probably two quires are missing at the end. The bottom outer corner of fo 187 has been torn off. There are cuts in fos 188, 192, 210, 343, 428, 441, a tear in fo 293, and a discreet repair to a tear on the outer edge of fo 306. Some wormholes are visible at the end of the manuscript penetrating backwards from fo 512 to fo 494.

Pricking: Mostly not visible following cropping of the manuscript by a binder. In Quires **XXXV–XLII**, however, prick-marks in the bottom margin for the vertical bounding lines can be seen near the bottom edges of the leaves.

Ruling: In fine crayon. Quires **I–XLII** show a frame ruling for double columns with single outer bounding lines and in the middle a central line plus one to each side of it to mark the boundary of each column. The vertical bounding lines extend to the outer edges of the leaves. There are forty-eight horizontal lines for writing ruled between the outer vertical bounding lines, including across the central blank column in between the columns for writing; the top line does not receive writing. In the top margin two extra horizontal lines are ruled to receive the page headings. In Quire **XLIII** four double bounding lines are ruled to provide a written area of three columns with provision for initials, and there are forty-eight horizontal lines ruled between the outer vertical bounding lines to receive forty-seven lines of writing, with the top line not receiving writing. There is no provision for a heading in this quire.

Colour and ornament: Incipits/explicits and shading of appropriate letters in red, also some marginal reference marks on fo 268v.

Illuminated initials using blue, magenta, green, brown and white occur on fos 1r (F), 4r (I, with gold; pl. 14.1), 15v (H), 33v (U), 46r (L), 62v (H), 77r (E), 86v (P), 97r (I), 99v (F), 114v (F), 126r (E), 139v (P), 153v (A), 165r (C), 180v (I), 184v (E), 191r (E), 197r (E), 209r (U), 220r (T), 224r (A), 230r (I), 235v (B), 239v (D, Ps 26), 242r (D, Ps 38), 244v (D, Ps 52), 246v (S, Ps 68), 250r (E, Ps 80), 252v (C, Ps 95), 260r(P), 269r (U), 272r (O), 273v (D), 280r (O), 296v (U), 315v (U), 341r (E), 361v (A), 369v (U), 372v (U), 373v (U), 376r (U),

376v (E), 377v (U), 379r (O), 381v (U), 382v (I), 383r (I), 386v (O), 387v (E),
399v (F), 408r (B, with gold), 409r (L), 421r (I), 428v (F), 441v (I), 451r (P),
455v (P), 460v (P), 463v (P), 465v (P), 467r (P), 468r (P), 469r (P), 469v (P),
471r (P), 471v (P), 472v (P, M), 476v (P), 489v (I), 491r (P), 492r (S), 493r (Q),
494r (S), 494v (S, I), i.e., to mark the beginning of prefaces, books, important
psalms, gospels or epistles as appropriate. Gold is reserved for the beginning of
the Old and New Testaments. The letter F on fo 1r shows a figure, presumably
Jerome, sitting at a writing desk, and the letter I on fo 4r shows seven vignettes
of God on the various days of creation (pl. 14.1). The other letters show various
grotesques, animal forms and plant foliage.

Illuminated capitals sometimes appear in reflection on the facing page; e.g.,
I on fo 4r reflected on fo 3v, **L** on fo 46r reflected on fo 45v, **C** on fo 165r reflected
on fo 164v, **E** on fo 184v reflected on fo 185r, **E** on fo 191r reflected on fo 190v,
D on fo 244v reflected on fo 245r, **S** on fo 246v reflected fo 247r, **E** on fo 250r
reflected on fo 249v, **C** on fo 252v reflected on fo 253r, **P** on fo 260r reflected
on fo 259v, **P** on fo 465v reflected on fo 466r. Some reflections occur without
their source being apparent, e.g., **P** on fo 50v (probably a reflection of fo 86v,
both leaves being on the outside of a quire), (?)**S** on fo 74v, and **D** (prob. Ps 109)
on fo 255r, **A** on fo 495r (Revelations); in the last two cases a leaf is missing
beforehand.

Page headings occur in red and blue capitals (but none for the psalms, fos
236–59), occasionally red script as on fo 269r, and chapter numbers in red or
red and blue are entered in the margins, the central column, or in spaces on the
line between the end of one chapter and the beginning of the next, as on fos 4r/a,
4v/a, 5r/a etc. There are guide numbers entered in the margin by the scribe, as
on fos 6r, 7r, 8r etc., some trimmed or cut off by the binder. Throughout there
are calligraphic initials in red with blue flourishing or blue with red flourishing,
generally alternating with each other. On fos 76v, 296r, 361r there are larger
calligraphic initials in red and blue with flourishing also in both colours.

COLLATION

I¹² (fos 1–12), II²⁺¹² (fos 13–26), III¹² (fos 27–38), IV¹² (fos 39–50), V¹² (fos 51–
62), VI¹² (fos 63–74), VII¹² (fos 75–86), VIII¹² (fos 87–98), IX¹² (fos 99–110),
X¹² (fos 111–22), XI¹² (fos 123–34), XII¹² (fos 135–46), XIII¹² (fos 147–58),
XIV¹² (fos 159–70), XV¹² (fos 171–82), XVI¹² (fos 183–94), XVII¹² (fos 195–
206), XVIII¹² (fos 207–18), XIX¹² (fos 219–30), XX¹² (fos 231–42), XXI¹² (fos
243–54), XXII¹² (fos 255–64, lacks 1 and 3), XXIII¹² (fos 265–76), XXIV¹²
(fos 277–88), XXV¹² (fos 289–300), XXVI¹² (fos 301–12), XXVII¹² (fos 313–
24), XXVIII¹² (fos 325–36), XXIX¹² (fos 337–48), XXX¹² (fos 349–60), XXXI¹²
(fos 361–72), XXXII¹² (fos 373–84), XXXIII¹² (fos 385–96), XXXIV¹² (fos 397–

408), **XXXV**[12] (fos 409–20), **XXXVI**[12] (fos 421–32), **XXXVII**[12] (fos 433–44), **XXXVIII**[12] (fos 445–56), **XXXIX**[12] (fos 457–67, lacks 9), **XL**[12] (fos 468–79), **XLI**[12] (fos 480–91), **XLII**[12] (fos 492–500, lacks 4, 11, 12), **XLIII**[12] (fos 501–12).

Note 1: In Quire **XXXII** fo 380 has had its outer column cut off.
Note 2: In Quire **XLI** leaves 5, 6, 7, 8, fos 484–7, have some damage at the hinge at the bottom.
There are no quire signatures or catchwords visible.

Hair/Flesh: All quires FHFHFH, except Quire **II** FH+FHFHFH, so always flesh-side outside.

CONTENTS

1. Fos 1r/a/1–500v/a/16: Biblia Sacra, Vulgatae Editionis, with prefaces by St Jerome and others.

(i) fos 1r/a/1–3v/a/37: Jerome's Prologue to Paulinus. "**Incipit ep‹isto›la s‹an›c‹t›i iero|nimi p‹res›b‹ite›ri ad pauli|num p‹res›b‹ite›r‹u›m. de omni|b‹us› ystorie libris:**" Begins 'FRATER ambrosi‹us› [x for s expuncted] | tua michi munus|cula p‹er›ferens detulit | simul:'. Stegmüller no. 284.

(ii) Fos 3v/a/37–4r/a /32: Jerome's Prologue to the Pentateuch ad Desideratum. "**Incipit ep‹istu›la p‹ro›logus s‹an›c‹t›i yero‹n›imi | in librum genesi.**" Begins 'DEsid‹er›ii m‹e›i desid‹er›atus accepi ep‹isto›la‹s›?'. Stegmüller no. 285.
Fo 4r/a/33–46 blank.

(iii) Fos 4r/a/47–15v/b/11: Genesis. "**Incipit liber p‹raepo›sit[us] i‹d est› genesis?**". Begins 'IN PRINCIPIO? creauit | d‹eu›s celum ‹et› t‹er›ram.' (pl. 14.1).

(iv) Fos 15v/b/12–33v/b/25: Exodus. "**Incipit | textus exodi.**" Begins 'Hec sunt nomi‹n›a fi|lio‹rum› isr‹ae›l'.

(v) Fos 33v/b/25–46r/a/34: Leviticus. "**Incipit | liber leuitici.**" Begins 'UOcauit autem | moysen??'.

(vi) Fos 46r/a/34–62v/a/18: Numbers. "**Inci|pit liber numeri?**". Begins 'LOcutusq‹ue› est domin‹us› ad moy|sen'.

(vii) Fos 62v/a/18–76v/a/40: Deuteronomy. "**In|cipit lib‹er› deut‹eronim›o nomini**". Begins 'HEC su‹n›t u‹er›ba'.

(viii) Fos 76v/a/40–77r/a/11: Jerome's Prologue to Joshua. "**Incipit p‹ro›logus | s‹an›c‹t›i yeronimi p‹res›b‹ite›ri i‹n› libr‹i› iosue:**". Begins 'TANDEM finito pentate|uco moysi'. Stegmüller no. 311.

(ix) Fos 77r/a/11–86v/b/31: Joshua. "**Incip‹it› | lib‹er› iosue.**" Begins 'ET factum e‹st› p‹ost› | morte‹m› moysi'.

(x) Fos 86v/b/32–97r/b/27: Judges. "**Incip‹it› lib‹er› Iudic‹um›.**" Begins 'POst morte‹m› iosue꞉'.

(xi) Fos 97r/b/27–98v/b/26: Ruth. "**Incipit liber | Ruth.**" Begins 'IN DIEBUS uni‹us› iudicis'.

(xii) Fos 98v/b/27–99v/a/37: Jerome's Prologue to Kings. "**Incipit p‹ro›emiu‹m› s‹an›c‹t›i yero‹n›imi p‹res›b‹ite›ri in li|bros regum.**" Begins 'VIginti ‹et› duas e‹ss›e litt‹er›as ap‹ud› | hebreos'. Stegmüller no. 323.

(xiii) Fos 99v/a/39–114v/a/1: I Kings [= 1 Sam]. "**Incipit p‹ri›mus | liber regum.**" Begins 'FVIT uir unus'.

(xiv) Fos 114v/a/2–126r/a/32: II Kings [= 2 Sam]. "**Incipit liber s‹e›c‹un›d‹u›s꞉**". Begins 'FACTVM est aut‹em›'.

(xv) Fos 126r/a/33–139v/b/23: III Kings [= 1 Kgs]. "**Incipit liber t‹er›tius.**" Begins 'ET rex dauid senue‹r›at꞉'.

(xvi) (xvi) Fos 139v/b/23–152v/b/10: IV Kings [= 2 Kgs]. "**I‹n›cip‹it› iiii.**" Begins 'PREVARICATVS | est aut‹em›'.

(xvii) (a) Fos 152v/b/10–153r/a/42: Jerome's Prologue to Chronicles. "**Inci|pit p‹ro›logus s‹an›c‹t›i ieronimi p‹res›b‹ite›ri in libros p‹ar›a|lipomenon.**" Begins 'SI septuagi‹n›ta int‹er›p‹re›tum | pura.' Stegmüller no. 328.

  (b) Fos 153r/a/42–153v/a/25: Jerome's Prologue to Chronicles ad Domnionem, et Rogatianum. "**Incip‹it› arg‹umentum›꞉**". Begins 'Evsebius hieronim‹us› domnioni ‹et› roga|tiano suis in ‹Christ›o ih‹es›u꞉ salute‹m›. Quom‹od›o | g‹rae›co‹rum› ystorias'. Stegmüller no. 327.

(xviii) Fos 153v/a/26–165r/b/1: I Paralipomenon [= 1 Chr]. "**Incipit lib‹er› p‹ri›mus pa|ralipomenon꞉**". Begins 'ADAM. seth. enos ca|inan'.

(xix) Fos 165r/b/2–180r/a/27: II Paralipomenon [= 2 Chr]. "**Incipit liber s‹e›c‹un›-d‹u›s.**" Begins 'COnfortatus e‹st› ‹er›g‹o› sal‹am›on'.

(xx) (a) Fo 180r/a/28–180r/b/13: Preface to Esdras (= Oratio Manasse). "**Incip‹it› p‹rae›fatio i‹n› lib‹ro›s esd‹ras›.**" Begins 'D‹omi›Ne om‹ni›p‹oten›s d‹eu›s patru‹m› n‹ost›ro‹rum› abraham. y|saac. iacob.' Stegmüller no. 93,2.

  (b) Fo 180r/b/13–180v/b/8: Jerome's Prologue to Esdras. "**I‹n›cip‹it› p‹ro›l‹ogus› i‹n› libr‹o› | esdre .I.**" Begins 'Utrum difficilius sit'. Stegmüller no. 330.

(xxi) Fos 180v/b/8–184v/b/39: I Esdras [= Ezra]. "**Incipit liber es|dre p‹ri›mus.**" 'IN ANNO p‹ri›mo cyri regis p‹er›sa‹rum›'.

(xxii) Fos 184v/b/40–191r/a/4: II Esdras [= Nehemiah]. "**Incipit s‹e›c‹un›d‹u›s.**" Begins 'verba ne‹he›mie filii elchie: | ET factu‹m› e‹st› \in/ m‹en›se casleu'.

(xxiii) Fos 191r/a/5–197r/a/46: III Esdras [= I Esd]. "**Incipit .iij.**" 'ET fecit iosias pasca'.

(xxiv) Fo 197r/a/47–197r/b/8: Preface to Esdras IV. "**Incipit p‹re›fatio. in q‹ua›rtum.**" Begins 'LIber esdre p‹ro›ph‹et›e s‹e›c‹un›d‹u›s. filii sarei filii a|zarei'. Stegmüller no. 96.

(xxv) Fos 197r/b/9–208r/b/25: IV Esdras [= II Esd]. "**Incip‹it› lib‹er› | esdre?**". Begins 'ET factu‹m› e‹st› u‹er›bu‹m› | d‹omi›ni ad me dice‹n›s.'

(xxvi) (a) Fo 208r/b25–208v/b/30: Jerome's Prologue to Job. '**Incip‹it› p‹ro›l‹ogus› i‹n› libru‹m› iob.**" Begins 'COgor p‹er› sing‹u›los script‹ur›e diuine libros | adu‹er›sario‹rum›'. Stegmüller no. 344.

(b) Fos 208v/b/31–209r/a/20: Jerome's second Prologue to Job. "**Item alius p‹ro›logus.**" Begins 'SI aut fiscella‹m› | iu‹n›cto texere‹m›.' Stegmüller no. 357.

(c) Fo 209r/a/21–37: Preface to Job. "**Incip‹it› p‹re›fatio in libr‹um› iob?**". Begins 'IN t‹er›ra quide‹m› habitasse | iob'. Stegmüller no. 349.

(xxvii) Fos 209r/a/38–219v/b/29: Job. "**Incipit li|ber iob.**" Begins 'UIR ERAT in t‹er›|ra hus?'.

(xxviii) Fos 219v/b/30–220r/a/6: Jerome's Prologue to Tobias. "**Incipit p‹ro›logus s‹an›c‹t›i yer‹onimi› p‹res›b‹ite›ri. i‹n› libru‹m› tobie:**". Begins 'CHromatio ‹et› heliodoro ep‹iscop›is? iero‹n›imus | p‹res›b‹ite›r i‹n› domino salute‹m›. Mirari no‹n› de|sino'. Stegmüller no. 332.

(xxix) Fos 220r/a/6–224r/a/25: Tobias. "**Incipit | liber tobie?**". Begins 'TOBIAS ex tribu ‹et› ci|uitate neptalim'.

(xxx) Fo 224r/a/25–224r/b/2: Jerome's Prologue to Judith. "**Incipit p‹ro›logus in librum iudith.**" Begins 'APud hebreos lib‹er› iudith | int‹er› agiographa legit‹ur›'. Stegmüller no. 335.

(xxxi) Fo 224r/b/2–229v/b/9: Judith. "**Incip‹it› liber iudith:**". Begins 'ARFAXAT itaq‹ue› rex | medo‹rum›'.

(xxxii) (a) Fo 229v/b/9–35: Jerome's Prologue to Esther, "**Incip‹it› p‹ro›l‹ogus› s‹an›c‹t›i ier‹onimi› i‹n› lib‹rum› hest‹er›.**" Begins 'LIbru‹m› hest‹er› uariis tra‹n›slatorib‹us› co‹n›stat | e‹ss›e uitiatu‹m›?'. Stegmüller no. 341.

(b) Fo 229v/b/35–43: Jerome's Preface, "**Incipit | argum‹en›tum?**". Begins 'RVrsum in libro | hest‹er› alfabetu‹m›'. Fo 229v/b/44–46 blank. Fo 229v/b/47 "**Explic‹it› argum‹en›tum.**" Stegmüller no. 343.

(xxxiii) Fos 229v/b/47–235r/a/43: Esther. "**Incip‹it› lib‹er› hest‹er›?**". Begins 'IN dieb‹us› assueri regis'. Fo 235r/a/44 blank.

(xxxiv) (a) Fo 235r/a/45–235r/b/28: Jerome's Preface to Psalms. "**Incip‹it› p‹re›fatio ieronimi p‹res›b‹ite›ri i‹n› lib‹ro› psalt‹er›ij.**" Begins 'PSalt‹er›ium rome dudu‹m› po‹s›itus em‹en›da‹rum›ꝫ'. Stegmüller no. 430.
(b) Fo 235r/b/28–235v/a/24: Ps.Bede's Preface, "**Incipit p‹ro›logus.**" Begins 'DAuid filius iesse | cum e‹ss›et in regno suo'. Stegmüller no. 1665.

(xxxv) Fos 235v/a/24–259r/b/47: Psalms. "**Incip‹it› lib‹er› | psalt‹er›ii. ps‹almus› p‹ri›mus.**" Begins 'BEATVS uir qui n‹on› | abiit'.

A textual lacuna between fos 254 and 255 is indicated, although no stub is visible: the outside leaves of the quires are glued together at the hinge as part of the binding. Fo 254v/47 ends '‹et› de neccessitatib‹us› eo‹rum›' = Ps 106.13. Fo 255r/1 begins 'in domo. matre‹m› filio‹rum› letante‹m›.' = Ps 112.9. An illuminated capital from the missing leaf is reflected on fo 255r.
  A textual lacuna between fos 255 and 256 is indicated by a leaf missing. Fo 255v/47 ends 'in equitate tua uiuifi|ca me.' = Ps 118.40. Fo 256r/1 begins 'tua‹m› d‹omi›ne. ‹et› s‹e›c‹un›d‹u›m iudiciu‹m›' = Ps 118.149.

(xxxvi) (a) Fo 259v/a/1–47: Jerome's Prologue to the Books of Solomon. "**Incip‹it› p‹ro›lo‹gus› s‹an›c‹t›i yer‹onimi› p‹res›b‹ite›ri sup‹er› tres libros sal‹am›onis.**" Begins 'IVngat ep‹isto›la quos iungit sac‹er›dotiu‹m›'. Stegmüller no. 457.
(b) Fo 259v/a/47–260r/a/4: "**Ite‹m› alius p‹ro›logus.**" Begins 'Trib‹us› nominib‹us› uocatu‹m› Salomone‹m›'. Stegmüller no. 456.
(c) Fo 260r/a/4–30: Preface, "**Incip‹it› argum‹en›tum.**" Begins 'TRes libros salomo‹n›is .i. p‹ro›u‹er›bia ecc‹lesi›asten. | ‹et› canticu‹m› cantico‹rum›'. Stegmüller no. 455.

(xxxvii) Fos 260r/a/30–269r/a/4: Proverbs. "**Incipiu‹n›t p‹ro›u‹er›bia salo‹monis›.**" Begins 'PARABOLE sal‹om›onis | filii dauid regis isr‹ae›l'.

(xxxviii) Fos 269r/a/4–24: Prologue to Ecclesiastes. Added in top margin "**Incip‹it› p‹ro›logus in ecc‹lesi›asten?**". Begins 'MEmini me an‹te› hoc fer|me'. Stegmüller no. 462.

(xxxix) Fos 269r/a/24–272r/a/38: Ecclesiastes. "**Incipit | liber ecc‹lesi›astes?**". Begins 'UERBA eccl‹es›iastes filii | dauid regis ier‹usa›l‹e›m'.

(xl) Fo 272r/a/38–272r/b/4: Prologue to Song of Songs. "**Inci|pit p‹ro›logus in cantica cantico‹rum›**". Begins 'CAntica cantico‹rum› eo q‹uo›d s‹empe›r o‹mn›ia | cantica'.

(xli) Fos 272r/b/4–273v/b/33: Song of Songs. "**Incipit lib‹er› cant‹ica canticorum› | vox ecc‹lesi›e. ad ‹Christu›m.**" Begins 'OSCVLETVR me osculo'.

(xlii) Fos 273v/b/33–41: Prologue to Wisdom. "**Incip‹it› p‹ro›log‹us› in libru‹m› sapi‹enti›e.**" Begins 'LIber sapi‹enti›e ap‹ud› hebreos nusqua‹m› e‹st›'. Stegmüller no. 468.

(xliii)	Fos 273v/b/41–280r/a/22: Wisdom. "**Incipit lib‹er› sapie‹n›tie⁊**". Begins 'DILIGITE iustitia‹m›⁊ o‹mne›s | qui iudicatis t‹er›ram.'

(xliv)	Fo 280r/a/23–280r/b/10: Prologue to Ecclesiasticus. "**Incipit p‹ro›logus sup‹er› ecc‹lesi›asticum⁊**". Begins 'MVltor‹um› nob‹is› ‹et› magno‹rum› p‹er› lege‹m›'. Stegmüller no. 26.

(xlv)	Fos 280r/b/10–296r/b/30: Ecclesiasticus. "**In|cipit liber ecc‹lesi›asticus⁊**". Begins 'OMNIS sapie‹n›tia a d‹omi›no |deo e‹st›.'

(xlvi)	Fo 296r/b/30–296v/a/44: Jerome's Preface to Isaiah. "**Incip‹it› p‹re›fatio s‹an›c‹t›i yer‹onimi› i‹n› ysaia‹m› p‹ro›ph‹et›a‹m›**". Begins 'NEMO cum p‹ro›ph‹et›as u‹er›sib‹us› uid‹er›it e‹ss›e'. Stegmüller no. 482.

(xlvii)	Fos 296v/a/44–315r/b/2: Isaiah. "**Incip‹it› liber | ysaie p‹ro›ph‹et›e:**". Begins 'UISIO ysaie | filii amos'.

(xlviii)	(a) Fo 315r/b/3–315v/a/10: Jerome's Prologue to Jeremiah. "**Incip‹it› p‹ro›lo‹gus› i‹n› y‹er›emia‹m›**". Begins 'IEremias | p‹ro›ph‹et›a cui h‹ic› p‹ro›logus scribit‹ur›.' Stegmüller no. 487.

	(b) Fo 315v/a/10–19: Preface, "**Incip‹it› argum‹en›tum.**" Begins 'IEremias anathochites [*recte* Anatholites]'. Stegmüller no. 486.

(xlix)	Fos 315v/a/19–337v/a/10: Jeremiah. "**In|cip‹it› liber ieremie p‹ro›ph‹et›e.**" Begins 'UERBA yeremie filii | helchie'.

(l)	Fos 337v/a/10–339r/b/43: Lamentations. "**Incipiunt lam‹en›tatio‹n›es yeremie p‹ro›ph‹et›e. | Aleph.**" Begins 'QVom‹odo› sedet sola ciuitas plena | p‹o›p‹u›lo.'

(li)	Fo 339r/b/43–339v/a/3: Prologue to Baruch. "**In|cipit p‹ro›logus in librum baruch⁊**". Begins 'LIber iste q‹ui› baruch nomine p‹re›notat‹ur›'. Stegmüller no. 491.

(lii)	Fos 339v/a/3–341r/b/11: Baruch. "**Incipit liber baruch.**" Begins 'ET h‹ic› lib‹er› q‹ue›m sc‹ri›psit baruch | filius nerie'. Ends at ch. 5 'q‹uae› e‹st› ab ip‹s›o.', i.e., lacks ch. 6.

(liii)	Fo 341r/b/12–39: Jerome's Prologue to Ezechiel. "**Incipit p‹ro›logus in ezechielem**". Begins 'EZechiel p‹ro›ph‹et›a cu‹m› ioachi‹m› | rege iuda captiuus duct‹us› e‹st› i‹n› babylo‹n›e‹m›⁊'. Stegmüller no. 492.

(liv)	Fos 341r/b/39–361r/a/33: Ezechiel. "**Incipit lib‹er› ezechielis | p‹ro›phete ſ**". Begins 'ET factu‹m› e‹st› in t‹re›tesimo [*recte* trigesimo]'.

(lv)	Fo 361r/a/33–361v/a/36: Jerome's Prologue to Daniel. "**Inci|p‹it› p‹ro›logus i‹n› daniele‹m› p‹ro›ph‹et›a‹m›.**" Begins 'DANIELEM p‹ro›ph‹etam› iux‹ta› sep|tuagi‹n›ta int‹er›p‹re›tes'. Stegmüller no. 494.

(lvi) Fos 361v/a/36–369r/b/46: Daniel. "**Incip<it> lib<er> danielis p<ro>ph<et>e:**". Begins 'ANNO t<er>tio regni ioachi<m>'.

(lvii) Fo 369r/b/46–369v/a/15: Jerome's Prologue to the books of twelve prophets.
   (a) "**Incipit | p<ro>logus in librum .xii. p<ro>ph<et>arum:**". Begins 'NOn ide<m> ordo e<st> .xii. p<ro>ph<et>a<rum> ap<ud> heb<re>os:'. Stegmüller no. 500.
   (b) Fo 369v/a/15–33: "**Item alius p<ro>logus.**" Begins 'REgule s<un>t hec: sub quib<us> significatio<n>ib<us> | nominum'. Stegmüller no. 501.
   (c) Fo 369v/a/33–9: Preface to Hosea. "**Incipit** argum<en>tum:". Begins 'OSee crebro nominat eph<ra>im.' Stegmüller no. 506.

(lviii) Fos 369v/a/39–372r/b/11: Hosea. "**Incip<it> osee:**". Begins 'UERBUM d<omi>ni q<uo>d f<a>c<tu>m | e<st>. ad osee'.

(lix) (a) Fo 372r/b/11–41: Prologue to Joel. "**Incipit p<ro>|logus in iohel.**" Begins 'SAnctus iohel ap<ud> heb<re>os'. Stegmüller no. 511.
   (b) Fo 372r/b/42–372v/a/16: Jerome's Preface, "**Incipit argum<en>tum:**". Begins 'IOhel filius fatuel | desc<ri>bit t<er>ram'. Stegmüller no. 510.

(lx) Fos 372v/a/16–373v/a/25: Joel. "**Incipit iohel p<ro>ph<et>a.**" Begins 'UERBUM domini | q<uo>d f<a>c<tu>m est'.

(lxi) (a) Fo 373v/a/25–373v/b/2: Jerome's Prologue to Amos. "**Incipit p<ro>logus in amos | p<ro>ph<et>am.**" Begins 'AMos pastor <et> | rusticus'. Stegmüller no. 512.
   (b) Fo 373v/b/2–23: Preface to Amos. "**Incip<it> p<re>fatio.**" Begins '[O]zias rex cum d<e>i religione<m> sollicite emu|laret<ur>:'. Stegmüller no. 515.

(lxii) Fos 373v/b/23–375v/b/43: Amos. "**Incipit | amos p<ro>ph<et>a:**". Begins 'UERBA amos q<ui> fuit i<n> | pastoralib<us> thecui.'

(lxiii) (a) Fos 375v/b/44–376r/a/34: Prologue to Obadiah. "**Incipit p<ro>logus i<n> abdia<m> p<ro>ph<et>a<m>.**" Begins 'IAcob pat<ri>archa fr<atr>em h<ab>uit esau:'. Stegmüller no. 519.
   (b) Fo 376r/a/34–7: Jerome's Preface. "**Incip<it> arg<umentum>.**" 'Begins 'ABdias q<ui> int<er>p<re>tat<ur> s<er>uus d<omi>ni.' Stegmüller no. 516.

(lxiv) Fo 376r/a/38–376v/a/7: Obadiah. "**I<n>cip<it> abdias p<ro>ph<et>a.**" Begins 'UISIO abdie. H<aec> dic<it> dominus d<eu>s ad edo<m>.'

(lxv) (a) Fo 376v/a/7–42: Prologue to Jonah. "**Incip<it> p<ro>logus in | ionam p<ro>ph<et>am.**" Begins 'IOna<m> s<e>c<undu>m heb<re>i affirma<n>t filiu<m> fuisse'. Stegmüller no. 524.
   (b) Fo 376v/a/42–6: Jerome's Preface. "**Incip<it> | ar<gumentum>.**" Begins 'IOnas colu<m>ba pulch<er>ima. naufragio | suo passione<m> d<omi>ni p<re>figura<n>s.' Stegmüller no. 522.

(lxvi)   Fos 376v/a/47–377r/b/34: Jonah. "**Incipit iona p<ro>ph<et>a.**" Begins 'ET f<a>c<tu>m e<st> u<er>bum d<omi>ni ad | iona<m>'.

(lxvii) (a) Fo 377r/b/34–377v/a/3: Prologue to Micah. "**Incip<it> p<ro>logus | i<n> michea<m>.**" Begins 'TEmp<or>ib<us> ioathe <et> achac <et> ezechie | regum iuda.' Stegmüller no. 526.
         (b) Fo 377v/a/3–7: Jerome's Preface. "**Incip<it> ar<gumentum>.**" Begins 'MIcheas de morasthi coheres'. Stegmüller no. 525.

(lxviii) Fos 377v/a/7–379r/a/12: Micah. "**Incipit micheas p<ro>ph<et>a?**". Begins 'UERBUM d<omi>ni q<uo>d f<a>c<tum> | e<st> ad michea<m>'.

(lxix)   (a) Fo 379r/a/13–379r/b/8: Prologue to Nahum. "**Incip<it> p<ro>lo<gus> i<n> naum p<ro>ph<et>am.**" Begins 'NAum p<ro>ph<et>am an<te> adue<n>tum regis assyrio<rum>'. Stegmüller no. 528.
         (b) Fo 379r/b/9–13: Jerome's Preface. "**Incipit argum<en>tu<m>.**" Begins 'NAum <con>solator orb<is>'. Stegmüller no. 527.

(lxx)   Fo 379r/b/13–379v/b/46: Nahum. "**Incip<it> nau<m> p<ro>ph<et>a?**". Begins 'ONVS niniue: lib<er> ui|sionis naum helchese|i.'

(lxxi)   Fos 379v/b/47–380r/a/47: Prologue to Habakkuk. "**Incipit p<ro>logus. in abacuc p<ro>ph<et>am?**". Begins 'QVatuor p<ro>ph<et>e i<n> xii. p<ro>ph<et>a<rum> uolumine <con>ti|nent<ur>?'. Ends incomplete 'babylone<m> <et> nabucho. a q<ui>b<us> iudas <et> ierl<usalem>'. Fo 380r/b and 380v/a have been cut out. Stegmüller no. 531.

(lxxii) Fos 380v/b/1–381r/b/14: Habakkuk: ch. 1 begins imperfectly '<et> taces deuora<n>te impio iustiore<m> se [= Hab 1.13]'.

(lxxiii) (a) Fo 381r/b/14–42: Prologue to Zephaniah. "**Inci|p<it> p<ro>log<us> i<n> sopho<n>iam?**". Begins 'TRadunt heb<re>i c<ir>cumq<ue> [*recte* cuiusque] | p<ro>ph<et>e'. Stegmüller no. 534.
         (b) Fo 381r/b/42–381v/a/1: Jerome's Preface. "**Incipit | argum<en>tum.**" Begins 'SOphonias speculator <et> | achano<rum> d<omi>ni cognitor?'. Stegmüller no. 532.

(lxxiv) Fos 381v/a/2–382r/b/9: Zephaniah. "**Incip<it> sopho<n>ias p<ro>ph<et>a.**" Begins 'UERBUM d<omi>ni q<uo>d f<a>c<tum> | e<st> ad sopho<n>iam'.

(lxxv)   (a) Fo 382r/b/10–382v/a/17: Prologue to Haggai. "**Incip<it> p<ro>lo<gus> i<n> aggeu<m>?**". Begins 'IEremias p<ro>ph<et>a | ob c<aus>am'. Stegmüller no. 538.
         (b) Fo 382v/a/17–24: Jerome's Preface. "**Incip<it> argum<en>tu<m>.**" Begins 'AGgeus festiuus'. Stegmüller no. 535.

(lxxvi) Fos 382v/a/24–383r/a/38: Haggai. "**Incipit aggeus p<ro>ph<et>a.**" Begins 'IN ANNO s<e>c<un>do darii regis p<er>sa<rum>'.

(lxxvii) (a) Fo 383r/a/39–383r/b/36: Prologue to Zacharias. "**Incip‹it› p‹ro›lo‹gus›
i‹n› zacharia‹m›.**" Begins 'IN anno s‹ecund›o darii regis'. Stegmüller no.
539.

(b) Fo 383r/b/36–46: Jerome's Preface. "**Incip‹it› argum‹en›tu‹m›.**" Begins
'ZAcharias | memor d‹omi›ni sui multiplex'. Stegmüller no. 540.

(lxxviii) Fos 383r/b/46–386v/a/17: Zacharias. "**Incip‹it› zacharias p‹ro›ph‹et›a.**".
Begins 'IN m‹en›se oct‹av›o | i‹n› anno s‹ecund›o darii:'.

(lxxix) (a) Fo 386v/a/17–386v/b/2: Prologue to Malachi. "**Incip‹it› i‹n› malachia‹m›.**"
Begins 'D‹eu›S p‹er› moysen p‹o›p‹u›lo isr‹ae›l'. Stegmüller no. 543.

(b) Fo 386v/b/2–9: Jerome's Preface. "**Incip‹it› argum‹en›tu‹m›.**" Begins
'MAlachias ap‹er›te ‹et› i‹n› fine'. Stegmüller no. 544.

(lxxx) Fos 386v/b/10–387v/a/38: Malachi. "**Incip‹it› malachias p‹ro›ph‹et›a.**"
Begins 'ONus u‹er›bi d‹omi›ni ad isr‹ae›l. in | manu malachie.'

(lxxxi) Fo 387v/a/38–387v/b/15: Prologue to Maccabees. "**Incipit | p‹ro›logus in
libros machabeo‹rum›.**" Begins 'MAchabeo‹rum› lib‹ri› duo p‹re›notant'.
Stegmüller no. 551.

(lxxxii) Fos 387v/b/15–399v/b/22: Maccabees I. "**Incipit p‹ri›|mus lib‹er› machabeo-
‹rum›.**" Begins 'ET f‹a›c‹tu›m e‹st› postq‹uam› p‹er›cussit a|lexander'.

(lxxxiii) Fos 399v/b/23–408r/a/1: Maccabees II. "**Incipit s‹e›c‹un›d‹u›s?**". Begins
'FRATRIB‹us› qui su‹n›t p‹er› egyptu‹m›'.

(lxxxiv) Fo 408r/a/1–408v/a/35: Jerome's Prologue to the New Testament addressed to
Pope Damasus. "**Incipit | p‹ro›logus beati ieronimi i‹n› eu‹a›ngelio.**" Begins
'BEato pape damaso iero|nimus. Nouum opus | facere me cogis'. As PL 29, 525–30.

Fo 408v/a/36–47 and 408v/b/1–47 blank.

(lxxxv) Fo 409r/a/1–35: Prologue to Matthew. "**Incip‹it› p‹ro›logus in matheum
euang‹e›liam?**". Begins 'MAtheus ex iudea sic‹ut› in ordine p‹ri›mus po‹n›i|tur'.
Stegmüller no. 590.

(lxxxvi) Fos 409r/a/35–421r/a/17: Matthew. "**Inci|pit liber mathei euang‹e›liste.**"
Begins 'LIBER generatio‹n›is ih‹es›u ‹Christ›i filii dauid.'

(lxxxvii) Fo 421r/a/17–421r/b/7: Prologue to Mark. "**Incip‹it› p‹ro›logus | in marcum
euangelistam.**" Begins 'MArcus eua‹n›g‹e›lista electus d‹e›i. ‹et› pet‹ri› i‹n›
baptis|mate filius'. Stegmüller no. 607.

(lxxxviii) Fos 421r/b/8–428v/a/13: Mark. "**Incipit marcus euang‹e›lista.**" Begins
'INITIVM euang‹e›lia [*recte* -ii] ih‹es›u ‹Christ›i filii | d‹e›i'.

(lxxxix) (a) Fo 428v/a/13–21: Prologue to Luke. "**Incip‹it› p‹ro›lo‹gus› | beati luce
i‹n› eua‹n›g‹e›l‹iu›m ei‹us›de‹m›.**" Begins 'Q‹uonia›M quide‹m›
multi | conati s‹un›t [= Lk 1.1]'.

(b) Fo 428v/a/21–428v/b/15: Ps.Jerome, Prologue to Luke. "**Ite<m> alius p<ro>logus b<ea>ti yero<n>imi.**" Begins 'LVcas syr<us> nat<i>o<n>e anthiochen<us>. arte medic<us>.' Stegmüller no. 621.

(xc) Fos 428v/b/16–441r/b/19: Luke. "**Incip<it> lib<er> euang<e>lii s<ecundum> luca<m>.**" Begins 'FVIT in dieb<us> h<er>odis regis [= Lk 1.5]'.

(xci) Fo 441r/b/19–441v/a/5: Prologue to John. "**Incipit p<ro>log<us> | b<ea>ti yeronimi i<n> euang<e>l<iu>m s<ecundu>m ioh<ann>em.**" Begins 'HIc e<st> ioh<ann>es eu<a>ng<e>lista un<us> ex discipul<is> d<omi>ni'. Stegmüller no. 624.

(xcii) Fos 441v/a/5–451r/a/25: John. "**Incipit | euang<e>lium beati iohannis?**". Begins 'IN p<ri>ncipio erat u<er>bum.'

(xciii) Fo 451r/a/26–32: Prologue to Romans. "**Incipit p<ro>logus sup<er> ep<isto>lam. Ad romanos.**" Begins 'ROmani s<un>t i<n> | p<ar>tes ytalie.' Stegmüller no. 676.

(xciv) Fos 451r/a/32–455v/a/41: Romans. "**Incip<it> | ep<isto>la. ad romanos?**". Begins 'PAulus s<er>uus ih<es>u <Christ>i uocat<ur> ap<osto>l<u>s seg<re>gatus in eu<a>ng<e>l<ium> | d<e>i'.

(xcv) Fo 455v/a/42–455v/b/3: Prologue to 1 Corinthians. "**Incipit p<ro>logus in p<ri>mam | ep<isto>lam. ad corinthios.**" Begins 'COrinthii su<n>t achaici. Et hii si<milite>r ab ap<osto>lo audieru<n>t u<er>bum u<er>itatis: <et> subu<er>si s<un>t m<u>l|tipharie a falsis ap<osto>lis.' Stegmüller no. 684.

(xcvi) Fos 455v/b/3–460v/a/1: 1 Corinthians. "**Incip<it> | ep<isto>la p<ri>ma ad corinthios.**" Begins 'PAulus uocatus ap<osto>l<u>s | ih<es>u <Christ>i p<er> uoluntate<m> d<e>i.'

(xcvii) Fo 460v/a/2–6: Prologue to 2 Corinthians. "**Incip<it> p<ro>log<us> in s<ecund>am ep<isto>la<m>.**" Begins 'POst actam peni<tenti>am <con>solatoria<m> ep<isto>lam | sc<ri>bit eis a troiade <et> collauda<n>s hortat<ur> ad | meliora: <con>t<ri>statos quide<m> eos. s<ed> em<en>datos | ostende<n>s.' Stegmüller no. 700.

(xcviii) Fos 460v/a/6–463v/a/32: 2 Corinthians. "**Incipit ep<isto>la se|cunda ad corunthios.**" Begins 'PAVLVS ap<osto>l<u>s ih<es>u <Christ>i p<er> uo|luntate<m> dei. <et> timothe<us> | fr<ater>.'

(xcix) Fo 463v/a/33–9: Prologue to Galatians. "**Incip<it> p<ro>log<us> in ep<isto>la<m> ad galathas.**" Begins 'GAlathe su<n>t greci. hii u<er>bu<m> u<er>itatis p<ri>mu<m> | ab ap<osto>lo accep<er>unt: s<ed> p<ost> discessu<m> eius te<m>p|tati su<n>t a falsis ap<osto>lis.' Stegmüller no. 707.

(c)   Fos 463v/a/39–464v/b/47: Galatians. "**Incipit ep‹isto›la | ad galathas.**" Begins 'PAulus ap‹osto›l‹u›s no‹n› ab ho‹min›ib‹us› | n‹eque› p‹er› homine‹m›. Ends incomplete at ch. 5.20: ‹con›tentio‹n›es emu[lationes]. A leaf is missing after fo 464.

(ci)   Fo 465r/a/1–465v/b/13: Ephesians. Begins imperfectly at ch. 4.7 '[secundum] m‹en›sura‹m› donat‹i›o‹n›is ‹Christ›i'.

(cii)   Fo 465v/b/13–17: Prologue to Philippians. "**Incip‹it› p‹ro›logus i‹n› ep‹istola›m ad ph‹ilippenses›.**" Begins 'Philippe‹n›ses su‹n›t macedones. Hii accepto | u‹er›bo u‹er›itatis p‹er›stiterunt in fide: n‹on› receper‹unt› | falsos ap‹osto›los.' Stegmüller no. 728.

(ciii)   Fos 465v/b/17–466v/b/43: Philippians. "**Incipit | ep‹isto›la ad philippenses:**". Begins 'PAulus ‹et› timoth‹eu›s s‹er›ui ih‹es›u | ‹Christ›i:'.

(civ)   Fos 466v/b/43–467r/a/4: Prologue to Colossians. "**Incipit p‹ro›logus | in ep‹isto›lam ad colosenses.**" Begins 'COlosenses ‹et› hii | sic‹ut› laodice‹n›ses: s‹un›t asiani.' Stegmüller no. 736.

(cv)   Fos 467r/a/4–468r/a/19: Colossians. "**Incipit ep‹isto›la ad colo|senses:**". Begins 'PAulus ap‹osto›l‹u›s ‹Christ›i ih‹es›u p‹er› uo|luntate‹m› dei ‹et› timoth‹eu›s | fr‹ater›.'

(cvi)   Fo 468r/a/19–26: Prologue to 1 Thessalonians. "**Incip‹it› p‹ro›log‹us› | in ep‹isto›lam ad thesalo‹n›ice‹n›s‹es›.**" Begins 'Thesallonice‹n›ses | s‹un›t macedones. Qui accepto u‹er›bo u‹er›itati‹s› | p‹er›stiteru‹n›t in fide: ‹et› in p‹er›secut‹i›one ciuiu‹m› su|o‹rum›. P‹rop›t‹er›ea nec recep‹er›unt falsos ap‹osto›los n‹on› | ea q‹ue› falsis ap‹osto›lis dicebant‹ur›.' Stegmüller no. 747.

(cvii)   Fos 468r/a/26–469r/a/30: 1 Thessalonians. "**Incipit ep‹isto›la. ad thesasa|loni-censes. p‹ri›ma.**" Begins 'PAulus ‹et› siluanus ‹et› ti|motheus. ecc‹lesi›e thesalo|nicensiu‹m›'.

(cviii)   Fo 469r/a/31–6: Prologue to 2 Thessalonians. "**Incipit p‹ro›logus in ep‹isto›la ad thesalonice‹n›s‹es› .ii.**" Begins 'AD thesalonice‹n›ses s‹ecund›am ep‹isto›lam sc‹ri›bit ap‹osto›l‹u›s'. Stegmüller no. 752.

(cix)   Fo 469r/a/36–469v/a/42: 2 Thessalonians. "**Incipit ep‹isto›la ad | thesaloni-censes .ij.**" Begins 'PAulus ‹et› siluan‹us› ‹et› timoth‹eus› | ecc‹lesi›e thesalonice‹n›siu‹m›'.

(cx)   Fo 469v/a/42–6: Prologue to 1 Timothy. "**Incipit p‹ro›logus in ep‹isto›lam | ad timoth‹eu›m p‹rim›am.**" Begins 'Tymoth‹eu›m instruit ‹et› | docet de ordinat‹i›o‹n›e epis‹copa›t‹us› ‹et› diaconii ‹et› o‹mn›is | ecc‹lesi›astice discipline: scribe‹n›s ei ab athenis | ab urbe rome.' Stegmüller no. 765.

(cxi)   Fos 469v/a/46–471r/a/2: 1 Timothy. "**Incipit ep\<isto\>la ad timo|theum p\<ri\>ma?**". Begins 'PAulus ap\<osto\>l\<u\>s \<Christ\>i ih\<es\>u s\<e\>c\<un\>d\<u\>m i\<m\>|p\<er\>ium dei saluatoris'.

(cxii)   Fo 471r/a/2–6: Prologue to 2 Timothy. "**Incip\<it\> p\<ro\>log\<us\> i\<n\> ep\<isto\>la ad timot[h]e|um .ij.**" Begins 'ITem timotheo sc\<ri\>bit de exhorta|tione'. Stegmüller no. 772.

(cxiii) Fo 471r/a/7–471v/b/38: 2 Timothy. "**Incip\<it\> ep\<isto\>la ad timoth\<eum\> .ij**". Begins 'PAVLVS ap\<osto\>l\<u\>s \<Christ\>i ih\<es\>u p\<er\> uo|luntate\<m\> dei s\<ecundu\>m p\<ro\>mis|sione\<m\> uite.'

(cxiv)   Fo 471v/b/38–42: Prologue to Titus. "**Incip\<it\> p\<ro\>logus i\<n\> ep\<isto\>la\<m\> ad tituz?**". Begins 'TYtu\<m\> comonefac\<it\> \<et\> instruit'. Stegmüller no. 9124.

(cxv)   Fos 471v/b/42–472v/a/5: Titus. "**Incip\<it\> | ep\<isto\>la ad titum?**". Begins 'PAulus s\<er\>uus d\<e\>i. | ap\<osto\>l\<u\>s aut\<em\> ih\<es\>u \<Christ\>i s\<ecundu\>m fide\<m\> | electo\<rum\>'.

(cxvi)   Fo 472v/a/5–7: Prologue to Philemon. "**Incip\<it\> p\<ro\>lo\<gus\> i\<n\> ep\<isto\>la\<m\> ad phi|l\<em\>onez.**" Begins 'PHilemoni familiares litt\<er\>as fac\<it\>'. Stegmüller no. 783.

(cxvii) Fo 472v/a/8–472v/b/5: Philemon. "**Incip\<it\> | ep\<isto\>la ad philemonez?**". Begins 'PAulus ui\<n\>ct\<us\> \<Christ\>i ih\<es\>u \<et\> timo|theus fr\<ater\> philemoni di|lecto'.

(cxviii) Fo 472v/b/5–20: Prologue to Hebrews. "**Incip\<it\> p\<ro\>logus i\<n\> ep\<isto\>lam ad heb\<re\>os.**" Begins 'IN p\<ri\>mis dice\<n\>du\<m\> e\<st\> cur ap\<osto\>l\<u\>s paulus i\<n\> hac | ep\<istu\>la sc\<ri\>benda no\<n\> s\<er\>uau\<er\>it more\<m\> suu\<m\>: ut | u\<e\>l uocabulu\<m\> nominis sui. u\<e\>l ordinis | describ\<er\>et dignitate\<m\>.' Stegmüller no. 794.

(cxix)   Fos 472v/b/20–476v/a/7: Hebrews. "**Incipit ep\<isto\>la ad | hebreos?**". Begins 'MVltipharie multisq\<ue\> | modis olim d\<eu\>s loq\<ue\>ns'.

(cxx)   Fo 476v/a/7–33: Prologue to Acts. "**Incip\<it\> p\<ro\>lo|g\<us\> i\<n\> actus ap\<osto\>lo\<rum\>**". Begins 'LVcas antioce\<n\>sis nat\<i\>o\<n\>e | syrus'. Stegmüller no. 637.

(cxxi)   Fos 476v/a/33–489v/a/29: Acts. "**Incipit lib\<er\> | actus ap\<osto\<lo\<rum\>?**". Begins 'PRIMVM quide\<m\> s\<er\>mo|ne\<m\> feci de om\<n\>ib\<us\>'.

(cxxii) Fo 489v/a/29–489v/b/13: Prologue to Catholic Epistles. "**Incip\<it\> p\<ro\>logus in | ep\<isto\>las canonicas?**". Begins 'NOn ita e\<st\> ordo | ap\<ud\> g\<re\>cos'. Stegmüller no. 809.

(cxxiii) Fos 489v/b/14–491r/a/6: James. "**Incipit ep\<isto\>la b\<ea\>ti iacobi.**" Begins 'IACOBVS dei \<et\> d\<omi\>ni n\<ost\>ri ih\<es\>u \<Christ\>i s\<er\>uus'.

(cxxiv) Fos 491r/a/6–492r/b/9: 1 Peter. "**Incip‹it› ep‹isto›la beati petri .j. | prima.**" Begins 'PEtrus | ap‹osto›l‹u›s ih‹es›u ‹Christ›i: dilectis adue|nis disp‹er›sionis ponti.'

(cxxv) Fos 492r/b/10–493r/a/23: 2 Peter. "**Incip‹it› s‹ecund›a?**". Begins 'SYMON petrus s‹er›uus ‹et› ap‹osto›l‹u›s | ih‹es›u ‹Christ›i.'

(cxxvi) Fos 493r/a/23–494r/b/25: 1 John. "**Incip‹it› p‹rim›a ep‹isto›la | b‹eat›i ioh‹anni›s.**" Begins 'QVOD fuit ab initio.'

(cxxvii) Fo 494r/b/26–494v/a/12: 2 John. "**Incip‹it› s‹ecund›a ep‹isto›la b‹ea›ti ioh‹ann›is.**" Begins 'SENIOR electe d‹omi›ne ‹et› na|tis eius.'

(cxxviii) Fo 494v/a/13–44: 3 John. "**Incip‹it› t‹er›tia ep‹isto›la b‹ea›ti ioh‹ann›is**". Begins 'SEnior gaio k‹arissi›mo q‹uem› ego | diligo in u‹er›itate.'

(cxxix) Fo 494v/a/45–494v/b/47: Jude. "**Incipit ep‹isto›la iude.**" Begins 'IVDAS ih‹es›u | ‹Christ›i s‹er›uus. fr‹ater› a‹u›t‹em› iacobi?'. Ends incomplete at verse 18 'nouissimis t‹em›p‹o›rib‹us› uenie‹n›t illusores s‹ecundum› [desideria sua]'. A leaf is missing after fo 494.

(cxxx) Fos 495r/a/1–500v/a/16: Revelation. Begins imperfectly at ch. 2.13 '[testis] m‹eu›s fidel‹is› qui occisus e‹st› ap‹ud› uos: u‹bi› satha|nas h‹ab›itat'. Ends 'Dic‹it› q‹ui› testimo‹n›ium p‹er›hibet istorum. [Rev 22.20] | Etiam. Venio cito. Am‹en› Veni domine | ih‹es›u. Gratia domini n‹ost›ri ih‹es›u ‹Christ›i cum | omnib‹us› uobis. amen'.

Fo 500v/a/17–47 blank; fo 500v/b/1–47 blank.

2. Fos 501r/a/1–512v/c/47: Ps.Bede, Ps.Remigius of Auxerre, attrib. Stephen Langton (d. 1228), "Interpretationes nominum Hebraicorum ordine alphabetico" (incomplete), based on a list of proper names in the Bible, and arranged in three columns, beginning 'A. ac. app‹re›hende‹n›s u‹el› app‹re›hensio. | A ad testificans u‹e›l testimo‹n›ium. | A ad har dep‹re›catio. | A alma uirgo abs‹con›dita u‹e›l absco‹n›|sio u‹ir›ginitatis.' Ends incomplete 'Euffrates cresce‹n›s ‹ue›l frugif‹er› siu‹e› hu|mus aut pulue[rul]‹en›tus.' Evidently one quire or more is missing at the end, and up to two quires would have been required to complete the work. As *Bedae Opera* 1612, III, cols 371–480, here 371–413. Stegmüller 1940–80, no. 7708, see also 7192,1.

From Aix-en-Provence to Maynooth

A S STATED IN THE INSCRIPTION on fo 1v, the very fine manuscript described next is the Benedictional used by Armand de Narcès, archbishop of Aix-en-Provence.[1] This Benedictional is based on the collection of episcopal blessings brought together and organized by Guillaume Durand (bishop of Mende, 1285–96). It was written throughout in a handsome large somewhat Italianate book-script, almost certainly in south-east France, if not in Aix itself, and is datable by external criteria between 1329 and 1348, the period of Armand's tenure of his see (1329–48). The inscription is written in a rather showy French hand of the second half of the fourteenth century, i.e., fairly soon after Armand de Narcès's death of the plague on 21 July 1348. It records that the book was bequeathed by the archbishop to the chapter of Aix Cathedral. Research on Armand de Narcès revealed two references of special importance. First, there was a reference to his will, and secondly, there was a reference to a manuscript made for him and still preserved in Aix-en-Provence. The will survives in the Vatican and has been published. In it the archbishop left *tres libros meos* to the cathedral of St Sauveur (Aix-en-Provence): 'videlicet, [A1] Bibliam in duobus voluminibus, [A2] Pontificale et [A3] Librum Benedictionum, qui quidem libri sunt de una et eadem manu scripti'.[2] These three books written in the same hand were evidently part of a plan on the part of Armand de Narcès to provide himself with books necessary to the carrying out of his duties as archbishop. The last of these books [A3] is the Benedictional at Maynooth (RB74), previously presumed lost.[3] This Benedictional is not the only one of the three to survive. Its beautiful handwriting matches that of Aix-en-Provence, Bibliothèque Méjanes, cod. 13 (Rey 75),[4] a copy of the Pontifical by Guillaume Durand, the second work made for Armand that occurs in the list in his will [A2]. Indeed it is the form of the Pontifical that was adopted officially by the Church at the Council of Trent (1545–63) and remained in use until the Second Vatican Council (1962–5). There are also various other codicological features that the two manuscripts have in common. And that is not all: the hand of the inscription at the beginning of the Maynooth Benedictional is matched by the hand of the inscription in the Aix Pontifical, thus confirming that both manuscripts went to the cathedral chapter in Aix on the archbishop's death.[5]

1 Albanés, *Gallia Christiana Novissima*, 1, pp 83–6; Jullien de Pomerol, *Bibliothèques ecclésiastiques*, p. 247.   2 Albanés, 'Deux archevêques d'Aix', 120; Jullien de Pomerol, *Bibliothèques ecclésiastiques*, p. 248, whose labelling is adopted in square brackets.   3 Samaran and Marichal, *Catalogue des manuscrits*, 7.   4 For a description, see Leroquais, *Les pontificaux manuscrits*, 3–7; Andrieu, *Le pontifical romain au moyen-age* 3, 23–35; and, for a facsimile of part of fo 27, Samaran and Marichal, *Catalogue des manuscrits*, pl. xlviii (with a notice at p. 7).   5 See Lucas, 'Un nouveau manuscrit daté', 210–16.

What happened to these manuscripts after that? The manuscript of the Benedictional probably stayed in St Sauveur's Cathedral in Aix until the French Revolution, when the goods belonging to the cathedral chapter became the property of the state in 1791, allegedly 'restant à vendre'.[6] It is possible that the Bible was lost about this time. The manuscript of the Pontifical was acquired in 1830 by Monsignor Claude Rey, vicar-general at the cathedral at Aix, who took it with him while he was bishop of Dijon (1831–8), but it returned to Aix because Bishop Rey bequeathed it to the municipal library there, the Bibliothèque Méjanes, where it remains as cod. 13 (Rey 75), his generosity thus explaining the significance of the present subsidiary catalogue designation. The later history of the Benedictional until it came to Maynooth in the nineteenth century is unattested.

6 E. Marbot, *Catalogue historial des sanctuares & établissements religieux d'Aix depuis l'évangelisation jusqu'à l'an 1900* (Aix, 1913), p. 14.

Benedictional (by Guillaume Durand the Elder) made for Armand de Narcès, archbishop of Aix-en-Provence

(containing 166 benedictions). Datable by external criteria to between 1329 and 1348

HISTORY

ACCORDING TO THE INSCRIPTION on fo 1v this Benedictional, based on the collection brought together and organized by Guillaume Durand the Elder (bishop of Mende, 1285–96), was that used by Armand de Narcès, archbishop of Aix-en-Provence (1329–48; Albanés 1899: 1:83–6; Jullien de Pomerol 2001: 247), a canon lawyer by training who had a personal collection of some seventy books (Albanés 1883¹: 122–5; Coulet 1996: 211; Jullien de Pomerol 1996: 314; idem 2001: 248–54). The French provenance is confirmed by the inclusion of benedictions pertaining to the crown of thorns (fos 36v/18, 42v/15 and 43r/7), which was transferred from Constantinople to Paris by Louis IX (1214–70), who built the Sainte Chapelle to house it. The manuscript is written throughout in a handsome large somewhat Italianate book-script of s.xiv², almost certainly in the south-east France, if not in Aix itself (pl. 15.1). There are some corrections by the scribe, e.g., on fo 42r. The hand is the same as that of Aix-en-Provence, Bibliothèque Méjanes, cod. 13 (Rey 75), a copy of the Pontifical (properly the *Pontificalis Ordinis Liber*) of Guillaume Durand (a work compiled 1292–5), for a description of which, see Leroquais 1937: 3–7; Andrieu 1940²: 23–35 (pl. 15.2). Both were written during the archepiscopacy of Armand de Narcès (pl. 15.3), i.e., between 1329 and 1348, at his behest, and were evidently part of a plan to provide himself with a coherent set of well-organized books pertaining to the duties of his office (Lucas 2010). In his will he left *tres libros meos* to the cathedral of St Sauveur: 'videlicet, [A1] Bibliam in duobus voluminibus, [A2] Pontificale et [A3] Librum Benedictionum, quiquidem libri sunt de una et eadem manu scripti' (Albanés 1883¹: 120; Jullien de Pomerol 2001: 248, whose labelling is adopted in square brackets). The latter two of these books are A2 the Pontifical at Aix and the present manuscript, A3, the Benedictional at Maynooth, formerly presumed lost as the Bible [A1] still is (Samaran and Marichal 1968: 7). At Armand's death on 21 July 1348 they both went to the cathedral chapter. They are recorded there in the three inventories of the cathedral possessions of 1380, 1404 and 1407 (Chalandon 1993: 48, B.64 and B.65). According to the inventory of 1404, the present manuscript then had a binding with silver clasps. In it there are some marginal additions, e.g., on fos 11r, 18v (e.g., 'Benedictionem sancte trinitatis quere in dominica xxvii'), added to aid a reader s.xv; on fo 31r the remainder of the final word of a prayer and 'Amen' have been added at the bottom from the top of the following verso, to provide more convenient continuity without having to turn the page. The folios were given roman numbers at the top centre of the recto leaf probably s.xv, beginning with 'i' on fo 2r, now partially cropped. Fo 1, with its inscription on the verso, was added later, s.xiv. The manuscript may have been still in the collection of St Sauveur's Cathedral in 1533, when there occurs in an inventory dated 13 December at no. 284 'liber benedictionum pontifficalium. De pergameno, descriptum a la man' (Albanés 1883²: 173), but this entry could also apply to another manuscript. It probably stayed in Aix until the French Revolution, when the goods belonging to the cathedral chapter were 'nationalized' in 1791, allegedly 'restant à vendre' according to Marbot (1913: 14), but its history until it came to Maynooth s.xix is unattested. There is now a binding of s.xix$^{1/2}$ in white vellum with blind-stamped covers, some gold tooling (notably on the spine, which is labelled at the base 'M.S. | A.D. 1348') and gilt edging to leaves, by Gerald Bellew of Dublin [Ramsden (1954: 28) gives two addresses: 21 S. King St., and 79 Grafton St.], signed at the bottom right hand of the inside front cover. This binding would have been relatively expensive, though it is not impossible that the manuscript was already in the library at Maynooth when it was provided.

Modern foliation in pencil in the top right-hand corner of recto pages entered 1999. Earlier numbering of quires in pencil towards the bottom right corner starting with '2' on fo 2r.

Secundo folio: '**hic incipiu<n>t b<e>n<e>dict<i>ones**'.

CODICOLOGICAL DESCRIPTION

fos ii + 80 + ii, membrane with paper endleaves, measuring 256 x 190mm, framed area 202 x 125mm, written area 179 x 125mm (145 x 123mm on fo 1^v), with the two endleaves (front and back) added with the binding. The text is disposed in a single column of twenty-one long lines.

Pricking: Very little trace survives. In Quire **I** (fos 2–13) the prick-mark for the inner vertical frame-line can be seen at the bottom of most leaves, but in Quire **II** only on the last leaf, fo 25. Also in Quires **I** and **II** prick-marks for the top horizontal frame line can be seen near the inner and outer edge of leaves, but only on the last leaf of Quire **III** (fo 37). Thereafter no prick-marks are visible, except that on fos 78–80 prick-marks for horizontal lines of writing can be seen along the outer vertical frame line (double prick-marks on fo 79), apparently an addition to facilitate the addition of material on fos 78v–80r.

15.1 RB74, fo 43v, showing text of the Benedictional with illuminated capital **O** and calligraphic capitals. Actual page dimensions 256 x 190mm.

15.2 Aix 13, fo 148r, showing the same hand and illuminator/decorator in the Pontifical. By permission of the librarian, Bibliothèque Méjanes, Aix-en-Provence.

Ruling: Very fine, in crayon. There is a double vertical line for the outer side of the frame (continued as a single line after fo 14), and a double horizontal line for the bottom of the framed area, drawn on most pages in Quire **I**, on the first two leaves of Quire **II**, on the first leaf of Quire **III**, but it is not to be seen thereafter. The top horizontal line of the framed area (which never carries writing) extends, as do the other frame lines, to the edges of the leaves, and on verso pages the first line ruled for writing also extends to the outer edge, with some omissions, especially towards the end of the book, as fos 47, 57–8, 65–6, 68–72, 74–5, 78–80. After the discontinuation of the double horizontal frame line at the bottom of the framed area only one page, fo 19v, shows the bottom line of writing extended to the outer edge. There is no ruling on fo 80v.

Hair/Flesh: Quire **I**, H + FHFHFH, Quires **II–VI** FHFHFH, Quire **VII** FHFH.

Script: A very good example of Italianate Mediterranean-style book-script of s.xiv^med (see pl. 15.1). Note especially the ampersand, the **g**, the **d** well turned over on itself, the abbreviation **-bus** with the **us**-sign sitting on the line, the **-orum**, the **a** with its bowl, which is not much more than a little sketched loop at the foot of the ascender.

Colour: Illuminated initials (with trail borders, straight stemmed on fo 2r, with trefoil-shaped 'flowers' on branching stems) in blue, purple, magenta, white and gold on fos 2r, 29v, 43v (see pl. 15.1) to mark major divisions in subject matter. Calligraphic initials alternating between blue with red ornament and red with blue ornament throughout.

COLLATION

I^{1+12} fos 1–13, II^{12} fos 14–25, III^{12} fos 26–37, IV^{12} fos 38–49, V^{12} fos 50–61, VI^{12} fos 62–73, VII^8 fos 74–80 (lacks 8).
Catchwords are present at the bottom right-hand corner on fos 13v, 25v, 37v, 49v, 61v, and 73v.
Note: fo 1 is a later addition.

CONTENTS

Fo 1r blank.
Fo 1v/1–11: Inscription in the same French hand of s.xiv^{3/4} as that in Aix-en-Provence, Bibliothèque Méjanes, MS 13, fo 214r/1–10. 'Hic liber Benedictionum est | aquensis met<ro>politane ecclesie | quem scribi fecit: et eidem ecclesie in suo testa|mento legauit bone memorie: Armandus | Archiep<iscop>us aquen<sis>

qui tempore mortalita|tis magne: Anno d‹omi›ni .m.ccc.xlviii. obiit | et in eadem eccl‹es›ia requiescit: quem [altered to 'quam'] sicut hoc ‹et› | aliis plurib‹us› libris et iocalib‹us› suis d‹i›c‹t›am ecc‹lesi›a‹m› | honorauit. Sic bonorum retributor om‹n›i‹um› | honorare dignetur cum beatissimis sp‹irit›ib‹us› in | excelsis: Amen.' Apart from the first words this inscription is identical to that in the Pontifical at the Bibliothèque Méjanes 13, fo 214r (the last), beginning 'Hic liber qui pontificalis dicitur' (Albanés 1894: 16; Leroquais 1937: 6–7; Andrieu 1940²: 34; Lucas 2010: 210–16). That manuscript, having been left by Archbishop Armand de Narcès to the cathedral chapter, was subsequently sold to a later archbishop, Avignon Nicolaï (1406–34). Around 1830 it was presumably still in Aix, when it came into the possession of Monsignor Claude Rey, vicar general to the Aix chapter, who apparently took it with him while he was bishop of Dijon (1831–8), but retired to Aix and on his death in 1858 left it to the Bibliothèque Méjanes.

15.3 Aix 13, fo 1r, the beginning of the Pontifical, showing a bishop (presumably Armand de Narcès) and his entourage. By permission of the librarian, Bibliothèque Méjanes, Aix-en-Provence.

In what follows, wherever possible, each benediction is usually identified by reference to its Durand number in Moeller 1968, an edited text of the Benedictional of Guillaume Durand, whose Pontifical was used by Armand de Narcès (see above), and by reference to the *Corpus Benedictionum* by Moeller 1971–9.

1. Benedictiones Temporale

1.1. Fos 2r/1–3r/6: 'hic incipiu<n>t b<e>n<e>dict<i>ones pontificales in | d<omi>nicis dieb<us> per circulum anni. <cum> primo | b<e>n<e>dictio i<n> d<omi>nica p<ri>ma de adue<n>tu.'. 'OMnipotens deus cuius unige|niti aduentum <et> preteritum creditis' with musical notation in staves. Durand 1. As Moeller 1971–9: II.633, no. 1544.

1.2. Fo 3r/7–18: "b<e>n<e>d<ictio> in .ii. d<omi>nica | de aduentu d<omi>ni." 'Dominus ih<es>us <Christ> | qui sacracissimo | aduentu suo subuen<ir>e dignatus est'. Durand 2, otherwise generally assigned to Advent Sunday. As Moeller 1971–9: II.539, no. 1307.

1.3. Fo 3r/18–3v/8: "b<e>n<e>d<ictio> in .iii. do<mini>c<a> de aduentu." 'O<m>nip<otens> deus uos placato uultu res|piciat:'. Durand 3. As Moeller 1971–9: II.706, no. 1722.

1.4. Fo 3v/8–21: "b<e>n<e>d<ictio> in do<mi>nica quarta | de aduentu." 'Deus qui uos i<n> prioris | adue<n>tus gr<ati>a repa<ra>uit'. Durand 4. As Moeller 1971–9: II.494, no. 1200.

1.5. Fos 3v/21–4r/9: "b<e>n<e>d<ictio> in sabb<at>o quatuor tempo<rum>". 'Ihesu fili dauid qui duob<us> cecis clama<n>|tib<us> [*ed.* clinantibus] lumen oc<u>lorum reddidisti'. Specific to Durand 5. As Moeller 1971–9: II.577–8, no. 1405.

1.6. Fo 4r/10–19: "b<e>n<e>d<ictio> in do<mini>c<a> .i. p<os>t | natiuitatem | d<omi>ni." 'Deus qui unige<n>itu<m> | suu<m> misit i<n> terris'. Durand 6, which uniquely shows the reading 'misit in terris'. As Moeller 1971–9: II.480, no. 1168.

1.7. Fo 4r/19–4v/8: "b<e>n<e>d<ictio> i<n> do<mini>c<a> .i. post epiphaniam." 'Deus qui filii sui temporale<m> | puericia<m> fecit', Durand 7. As Moeller 1971–9: II.375, no. 926.

1.8. Fo 4v/8–19: "b<e>n<e>d<ictio> in d<omi>nica .ii. post | epyphania<m>." 'Deus qui sua mirab<i>li | potestate aq<ua>m u<er>tit i<n> uinu<m>'. Durand 8. As Moeller 1971–9: II.468–9, no. 1143.

1.9. Fos 4v/19–5r/8: "b<e>n<e>d<ictio> i<n> d<o>m<ini>c<a> | .iii. post epiphania<m>." 'O<m>nip<otens> deus uos | a p<e>cc<at>oru<m> o<mn>ium mac<u>lis dignet<ur> emu<n>|dare'. Durand 9, which uniquely shows the reading 'maculis dignetur emundare'. As Moeller 1971–9: II.702, no. 1711.

1.10. Fo 5r/8–17: "b‹e›n‹e›d‹ictio› in d‹omi›nica .iiii. post | epyphania‹m›." 'Temptat‹i›onu‹m› o‹mn›ium | a uob‹is› d‹omin›us p‹er›icula remoueat.' Durand 10. As Moeller 1971–9: II.823, no. 2019.

1.11. Fo 5r/17–5v/5: "b‹e›n‹e›d‹ictio› in do‹mini›c‹a› .v. | post epyphania‹m›." 'Deus qui seme‹n› bonu‹m› | i‹n› sua eccl‹es›ia no‹n› desinit ser‹er›e.' Durand 11, which uniquely shows the reading 'non desinit serere'. As Moeller 1971–9: I.342–3, no. 855.

1.12. Fo 5v/5–13: "b‹e›n‹e›d‹ictio› in d‹o›m‹ini›c‹a› .vi. post | epyphan‹iam›." 'Deus qui mare suis pedib‹us› | fecit esse calcabile.' Durand 12. As Moeller 1971–9: II.409, no. 1005.

1.13. Fos 5v/13–6r/2: "b‹e›n‹e›d‹ictio› in septuagesima." 'Ipse uos i‹n› eccl‹es›ia sua fructificare faciat.' Durand 13. As Moeller 1971–9: II.599–600, no. 1459.

1.14. Fo 6r/2–12: "b‹e›n‹e›dict‹i›o alia." 'O‹m›nip‹otens› deus ita stadium dirig‹er›e | dignet‹ur›.' Durand 14. As Moeller 1971–9: II.649–50, no. 1584.

1.15. Fo 6r/12–6v/1: "b‹e›n‹e›dictio in sexagesima." 'Sator o‹mn›ium bonoru‹m› ‹Christus› semen i‹n› cordi|bus u‹est›ris seminare.' Durand 15. As Moeller 1971–9: II.810, no. 1983, a variant of no. 612.

1.16. Fo 6v/1–10: "Item alia benedictio." 'Det uob‹is› d‹omi›n‹u›s nosc‹er›e misteria regni dei.' Durand 16. As Moeller 1971–9: I.250, no. 632.

1.17. Fo 6v/10–21: 'bened‹ictio› in .‹quinquagesima›." 'Lumen i‹n›deficiens deus. qui ad ill‹um›ina|tionem n‹ost›ram.' Durand 17. As Moeller 1971–9: II.604, no. 1471.

1.18. Fos 6v/21–7r/10: "Item alia b‹e›n‹e›dict‹io›." 'O‹m›nip‹otens› deus sua uos b‹e›n‹e›d‹i›c‹t›ione co‹n›fir|met.' Durand 18. As Moeller 1971–9: II.694, no. 1694.

1.19. Fo 7r/11–19: "b‹e›n‹e›dictio in fer‹ia› .iiij. | i‹n› capite ieiunioru‹m›." 'Saluator mu‹n›di | qui de celo desce‹n›|dens ad terras.' This Benediction is exclusive to Durand 19. As Moeller 1971–9: II.793, no. 1940.

1.20. Fo 7r/19–7v/16: "b‹e›n‹e›d‹ictio› | in do‹mini›c‹a› .i quad‹ra›-gesime." 'Benedicat uos | o‹m›nip‹otens› deus qui q‹ua›dragenarium | numeru‹m› i‹n› moyse.' The opening conforms to the variant found in Durand 20 (as well as others). As Moeller 1971–9: I.83–4, no. 192.

1.21. Fos 7v/16–8r/10: "b‹e›n‹e›d‹ictio› | i‹n› triduano q‹ua›|tuor tempor‹um› . i‹n› die .j‹ejunio›." 'Deus qui op‹er›atur | i‹n› sanctis suis ‹et› uelle ‹et› p‹er›fic[er]e pro bo|na uolu‹n›tate deuot‹i›o‹n›em u‹est›ram ad exeq‹uen›|dam salutatis abstine‹n›cie medicinam | sua‹m›:.' Durand 21.

1.22. Fo 8r/10–8v/4: "b‹e›n‹e›d‹i›c‹t›io | in die secunda. R‹ubr›ica." 'O‹m›nip‹otens› deus qui | niniuitaru‹m› c‹u›lpas ita ferire disposu|it.' Durand 22. As Moeller 1971–9: II.674–5, no. 1646.

1.23. Fo 8v/4–20: "b‹e›n‹e›dict‹i›o | i‹n› die tercia." 'Misericors ‹et› mis‹er›ator d‹omin›us benignissi|mus'. Durand 23. As Moeller 1971–9: II.614–15, no. 1497.

1.24. Fos 8v/20–9r/17: "b‹e›n‹e›d‹ictio› | in do‹mini›c‹a› .ii. quadrages-‹ime›." 'Abducat uos de finib‹us› uicioru‹m›'. Durand 24, to which the opening word 'Abducat' rather than 'educat' is specific. As Moeller 1971–9: II.548, no. 1331; cf. also no. 5.

1.25. Fo 9r/17–9v/16: "b‹e›n‹e›d‹ictio› in do‹mi›nica tercia | quadragesime." 'O‹m›nip‹otens› deus ieiunio‹rum› | u‹est›roru‹m› uictimas clement‹er› accipiat.' Durand 26. As Moeller 1971–9: II.647, no. 1577.

1.26. Fos 9v/16–10r/5: "b‹e›n‹e›dict‹i›o i‹n› do‹mini›c‹a› .iiii. qua|dragesime." 'Deus qui uos ad p‹re›sentiu‹m› | q‹ua›dragesimaliu‹m› dieru‹m› medietate‹m› di|gnatus est'. Durand 28. As Moeller 1971–9: II.490–1, no. 1193.

1.27. Fo 10r/6–16: "**Item alia b‹e›n‹e›dictio. R‹ubr›ica.**" 'Auferat a uob‹is› d‹omin›us uelame‹n› litt‹er›e [*recte* litteris] occi|dentis.' Durand 29. As Moeller 1971–9: I.23, no. 48.

1.28. Fo 10r/16–10v/4: "b‹e›n‹e›d‹ictio› | in do‹mini›c‹a› de passione do‹mini›." 'Accendat i‹n› uob‹is› d‹omin›us uim sui amoris'. Durand 30. As Moeller 1971–9: I.3–4, no. 8.

1.29. Fo 10v/5–17: "b‹e›n‹e›dict‹io› in ramis | palmaru‹m›." 'Benedicat uos o‹m›nip‹oten›s | deus. cui ‹et› ieiunioru‹m› | mac‹er›at‹i›o‹n›e. ‹et› p‹re›sentium dieru‹m› obs‹er›uat‹i›one | plac‹er›e studetis.' The reading 'Benedicat uos' not 'nobis' conforms to that found in Durand 32 (as well as others). As Moeller 1971–9: I.78, no. 180.

1.30. Fos 10v/17–11r/4: "b‹e›n‹e›d‹ictio› | in fer‹ia› .iiii. ma|ioris ebdomade." 'Dominus deus n‹oste›r | uos p‹er›ducat ad arborem uite qui uos | extraxit de lacu miserie.' Durand 35.

1.31. Fo 11r/4–16: "b‹e›n‹e›dictio in cena d‹omi›ni." 'Benedicat uos deus qui p‹er› unige‹n›iti | filii sui passionem uetus pascha in | nouu‹m› uoluit'. Durand 36. As Moeller 1971–9: I.100–1, no. 233.

Added in hand of s.xv in bottom margin of fo 11r:

> 'Quod ipse p‹re›stare dignetur cuius | regnum et imperium sine fine per|manet⁊ in secula seculo‹rum›. Amen | Et benedictio dei omnipote‹n›tis p‹at›ris | et filii et sp‹irit›us sancti⁊ descendat | super vos et maneat semp‹er›. ame‹n›.'

1.32. Fo 11r/16–11v/3: "**Item alia b‹e›n‹e›d‹ictio›.**" 'O‹m›nipotentis d‹e›i et d‹omi›ni n‹ost›ri ih‹es›u ‹Christ›i be|nedictionib‹us› repleamini'. Durand 37, which shows the fuller version of the opening represented here 'dei et domini nostri ihesu Christi'. As Moeller 1971–9: II.743, no. 1815.

1.33. Fo 11v/3–19: "b‹e›n‹e›dictio in | sabbato s‹an›c‹t›o." 'Deus qui de ecc‹lesi›e sue | i‹n›temerato ut‹er›o nouos p‹o›p‹u›los produ|cens'. Durand 39. As Moeller 1971–9: I.353, no. 879.

1.34. Fos 11v/19–12r/10: "b‹e›n‹e›d‹ictio› i‹n› | die s‹an›c‹t›o pasche". 'Benedicat uos o‹m›nipotens | deus. hodierna int‹er›ue‹n›iente pascha||li sollempnitate'. Durand 40. As Moeller 1971–9: I.124–5, no. 292.

1.35. Fo 12r/10–19: "b‹e›n‹e›dict‹i›o in fer‹ia› | s‹e›c‹un›da in albis." 'Deus qui int‹er› mu‹n›di | primordia s‹u›bducto fluctu'. Normally this benediction was used for Easter Sunday but the usage here for Feria II in albis follows that of Durand 41. As Moeller 1971–9: II.404–5, no. 995.

1.36. Fo 12r/20–12v/9: "**Item alia b‹enedictio›**." 'Illustret dei filius corda | u‹est›ra ad credenda‹m› sue resurrectionis || u‹er›itatem'. Durand 42. As Moeller 1971–9: II.582–3, no. 1419.

1.37. Fos 12v/9–13r/1: "b‹e›n‹e›d‹ictio› in feria | .iii. in albis." 'Concede mis‹er›icors deus | huic plebi tue salutifera'. Durand 43, otherwise normally assigned to Easter Sunday. As Moeller 1971–9: I.226–8, no. 575 or 576.

1.38. Fo 13r/2–12: "**alia b‹e›n‹e›d‹ictio›**." 'Dei filius qui ostensione | membro‹rum› suo‹rum›'. Specific to Durand 44. As Moeller 1971–9: I.245, no. 620.

1.39. Fo 13r/12–21: "b‹e›n‹e›d‹ictio› in feria | .iiii. in albis." 'Deus qui de diu‹er›sis | florib‹us›'. Durand 45, otherwise normally assigned to Easter Sunday. As Moeller 1971–9: I.352, no. 877.

1.40. Fo 13r/21–13v/10: "**Item alia b‹e›n‹e›d‹ictio›**." 'Deus qui tercia manifestatione sue re|surrectionis'. Durand 46. As Moeller 1971–9: II.473–4, no. 1154.

1.41. Fo 13v/10–19: "b‹e›n‹e›d‹ictio› in feria .v. in albis. R‹ubrica›." 'Deus qui peccatrici conu‹er›se post re|surrectione‹m› suam uoluit'. Durand 47. As Moeller 1971–9: II.426–7, no. 1047.

1.42. Fos 13v/19–14r/10: "b‹e›n‹e›d‹ictio› in fe|ria .vi. in albis". 'Det uob‹is› d‹omin›us uiciis | ad uirtutes'. Specific to Durand 48. As Moeller 1971–9: I.248, no. 628.

1.43. Fo 14r/10–21: "b‹e›n‹e›d‹ictio› in sabb‹at›o in albis. R‹ubrica›." 'Deus qui p‹er›acto senario numero die | sacro sabbati'. Durand 49. As Moeller 1971–9: II.439–40, no. 1076.

1.44. Fo 14r/21–14v/11: "**Item alia b‹e›n‹e›dictio.**" 'O‹m›nip‹otens› deus det uob‹is› sp‹irit›ualis sabb‹at›i ueri|tatem'. Specific to Durand 51. As Moeller 1971–9: II.638–9, no. 1559.

1.45. Fos 14v/11–15r/4: "b‹e›n‹e›d‹ictio› in octav‹e› | pasche." 'Deus cui‹us› unige‹n›itus | hodierna die discipul‹is› suis'. Durand 52. As Moeller 1971–9: I.268–9, no. 679.

1.46. Fo 15r/4–12: "b‹e›n‹e›dict‹i›o i‹n› do‹mini›c‹a› .i. p‹os›t oct‹aue› pasch‹e›." 'Benedicat uos o‹m›nip‹otens› deus qui uos gratuita mis‹er›atione creauit'. Durand 53. As Moeller 1971–9: I.132, no. 314.

1.47. Fo 15r/12–15v/1: "alia b‹e›n‹e›d‹ictio›." 'Protegat uos d‹omin›us a morsib‹us› lupi i‹n›ui|sibilis:'. Durand 54. As Moeller 1971–9: II.770, no. 1884.

1.48. Fo 15v/1–12: "b‹e›n‹e›d‹ictio› in do‹mi›nica .ii. p‹os›t oct‹aue› | pasch‹e›." 'Det uob‹is› d‹omin›us longanimitate‹m› | i‹n› p‹er›-egrinat‹i›o‹n›e p‹re›senti.' Specific to Durand 55. As Moeller 1971–9: I.248–9, no. 630.

1.49. Fo 15v/12–21: "b‹e›n‹e›d‹ictio› i‹n› do‹mini›c‹a› .iii. post | oct‹aue› pasche." 'Benedictionu‹m› suaru‹m› | sup‹er› uos d‹omin›us ymbrem i‹n›fundat.' Durand 57. As Moeller 1971–9: I.157–8, no. 380. Normally this benediction was used for Ascension Eve but the usage here for Dominica III post octave Pasce follows that in Durand.

1.50. Fos 15v/21–16r/10: "**Item alia benedictio**". 'Deus qui tristitia‹m› discip‹u›loru‹m› ue‹n›turi.' Durand 58. As Moeller 1971–9: II.475, no. 1159.

1.51. Fo 16r/10–18: "b‹e›n‹e›d‹ictio› in do‹mini›c‹a› .iiii. post oct‹aue› pasche." 'Donet uob‹is› saluator saluti u‹est›re ‹con›grua | fiducial‹ite›r postulare'. Durand 59. As Moeller 1971–9: II.547, no. 1329.

1.52. Fo 16r/18–16v/6: "b‹e›n‹e›dict‹io› i‹n› rogati|onib‹us›." 'O‹m›ni-p‹otens› deus deuotione‹m› u‹est›ram | dignant‹er› intendat.' Durand 127 Dominica XXVI post Pentecost. As Moeller 1971–9: II.510, no. 1236. The attribution to Rogationtide seems to be unique. Cf. 1.107.

1.53. Fo 16v/7–14: "**Item alia in feria .ii. [rogationum]**" 'O‹m›nip‹otens› deus sua | uos cleme‹n›tia b‹e›n‹e›dicat'. The attribution to Feria II Rogationum is specific to Durand 61. As Moeller 1971–9: II.695, no. 1696. Cf. 3.14 below.

1.54. Fos 16v/14–17r/1: "**In feria .iiii. [rogationum]** b‹e›n‹e›d‹ictio›." 'INclinet dominus aure‹m› sua‹m› ad preces u‹est›re humilitatis.' Durand 62 assigned to Feria III Rogationum. As Moeller 1971–9: II.589, no. 1433.

1.55. Fo 17r/1–11: "b‹e›n‹e›dict‹i›o in ascensione". 'Benedicat uos o‹mni›p‹oten›s deus cui‹us› unige|nitus hodierna die celoru‹m› alta pe|netrauit.' Durand 63. As Moeller 1971–9: I.118, no. 281.

1.56. Fo 17r/11–18: "b‹e›n‹e›d‹ictio› in do‹mini›c‹a› .i. post as|censionem". 'INsere d‹omi›ne ac firma | p‹o›p‹u›li tui sensib‹us› i‹n›spirame‹n›ta | salutis et‹er›ne'. Durand 64 with the distinctive reading 'inspiramenta salutis eterne'. As Moeller 1971–9: II.594–5, no. 1447.

1.57. Fo 17r/18–17v/10: "b‹e›n‹e›dict‹io› in uigilia | penthec‹osten›." 'Benedicat uos o‹m›nip‹otens› deus | ob cui‹us› p‹ar›acliti sp‹iritus› aduentu‹m› me‹n›tes:'. Durand 65. As Moeller 1971–9: I.80, no. 186.

1.58. Fo 17v/10–21: "b‹e›n‹e›dict‹i›o in die pent|thecosten." 'Deus qui hodierna die | discip‹u›loru‹m› me‹n›tes'. Durand 67. As Moeller 1971–9: II.385, no. 948.

1.59. Fo 18r/1–9: "**Item alia b‹e›n‹e›d‹ictio›**". 'Deus pat‹er› o‹m›nip‹otens› qui | exaltato ‹Christ›o filio suo'. Durand 68, otherwise assigned to Pentecost Eve. As Moeller 1971–9: II.302–3, no. 757.

1.60. Fo 18r/10–17: "b‹e›n‹e›d‹ictio› in .ii. die p‹os›t | penthec‹osten›." 'Deus qui ap‹ostu›los ‹Christ›i filii sui eius recessu'. Durand 69, otherwise generally assigned to Pentecost. As Moeller 1971–9: I.314–15, no. 787. The reading 'sui eius' is specific to Durand.

1.61. Fo 18r/17–18v/7: "b‹e›n‹e›d‹ictio› in die .iii. post | penthec‹osten›". 'Benedicat uos o‹m›nip‹oten›s deus qui cu‹n›c|ta ex nichilo creauit.' Durand 70, who alone assigns it to Wednesday after Pentecost. As Moeller 1971–9: I.80–1, no. 187.

1.62. Fo 18v/7–17: "b‹e›n‹e›dict‹io› in oct‹aue› penthec‹osten›." 'Domine ih‹es›u ‹Christ›e qui discipul‹is› tuis | tuu‹m› dedisti sp‹iritu›m.' Durand 71. As Moeller 1971–9: II.521, no. 1258. The reading 'dedisti' rather than 'tribuisti' is favoured by Durand.

1.63. Fos 18v/17–19r/5: "b‹e›n‹e›dictio in do‹mini›c‹a› .ii. post penthe-c‹osten›". 'CAritate sua uos d‹omin›us reple|re dignet‹ur›.' Durand 72 assigned to first Sunday after Pentecost. As Moeller 1971–9: I.161, no. 388.

1.64. Fo 19r/5–19: "**Item alia benedictio.**" 'Deus qui purpuratu‹m› diuite‹m› pro sua | ‹con›demnauit i‹n›iquitate.' Durand 73, who alone assigns it to the second Sunday after Pentecost. As Moeller 1971–9: II.455–6, no. 1110.

1.65. Fo 19r/19–19v/6: "b‹e›n‹e›dictio in do‹mini›c‹a› .iii. post | penthec‹osten›." 'Deus pater o‹m›nip‹otens› qui uos | ad suam uocauit cena‹m›:.' Durand 74, who assigns it to the second Sunday after Pentecost. As Moeller 1971–9: I.303–4, no. 760.

1.66. Fo 19v/6–16: "**Item alia b‹e›n‹e›d‹ictio›.**" 'Deus ‹et› homo ‹Christus› qui fecit [cenam magnam] id est sacie|tatem.' Durand 75, otherwise assigned to the second Sunday after Pentecost. As Moeller 1971–9: I.275, no. 695.

1.67. Fos 19v/16–20r/3: "b‹e›n‹e›dictio | in do‹mini›c‹a› .iiii." 'O‹m›-nip‹otens› deus qui unige‹n›itu‹m› | suum ad ove‹m›.' Durand 76, otherwise assigned to the third Sunday after Pentecost. As Moeller 1971–9: II.685, no. 1673.

1.68. Fo 20r/3–17: "**Item alia.**" 'MEdicus a‹n›i‹m›arum› ‹Christus› qui p‹e›cc‹a›tores n‹on› | solu‹m› recip‹er›e.' Durand 77, otherwise assigned to the third Sunday after Pentecost. As Moeller 1971–9: II.608, no. 1481.

1.69. Fo 20r/18–20v/3: "b‹e›n‹e›dictio in do‹mini›c‹a› | quinta." 'Misericors deus mise|ricordes uos faciat.' Durand 78, otherwise assigned to the fourth Sunday after Pentecost. As Moeller 1971–9: II.613, no. 1494.

1.70. Fo 20v/3–17: "**Ite‹m› alia.**" 'Pater u‹este›r mis‹er›icors qui pro uob‹is› in | mu‹n›du‹m› misit filiu‹m›.' Durand 79, usually assigned to the fourth Sunday after Pentecost. As Moeller 1971–9: II.750–1, no. 1836.

1.71. Fos 20v/17–21r/9: "b‹e›n‹e›d‹ictio› in do‹mini›c‹a› .vi." 'Deus qui p‹er› suos piscatores id est | doctores eccl‹es›ie.' Durand 81, usually assigned to the fifth Sunday after Pentecost. As Moeller 1971–9: II.437, no. 1071.

1.72. Fo 21r/9–16: "b‹e›n‹e›d‹ictio› in do‹mini›c‹a› .vii." 'Baptisma q‹uo›d accepistis i‹n› ‹Christ›o.' Durand 82, generally assigned to the sixth Sunday after Pentecost. As Moeller 1971–9: I.25, no. 54.

1.73. Fo 21r/16–21v/2: "**Item alia.**" 'Multiplicet i‹n› uob‹is› d‹omin›us copiam sue be|nedictio‹n›is.' Durand 83, who alone assigns it as an alternative benediction for the seventh Sunday after Pentecost. As Moeller 1971–9: II.615–16, no. 1499.

1.74. Fo 21v/2–8: "b‹e›n‹e›d‹ictio› i‹n› do‹mini›c‹a› | .viii. p‹os›t penth‹ecosten›." 'Ab om‹n›i p~~e‹ccat›o~~ emu‹n›datos | p‹e›cc‹at›o efficiat uos d‹omin›us sanctificatos.' Durand 84, often otherwise assigned to the seventh Sunday after Pentecost. As Moeller 1971–9: I.1–2, no. 3.

1.75. Fo 21v/9–21: "**Item alia b‹e›n‹e›d‹ictio›.**" '‹Christ›us fons m‹isericord›ie qui | turbam q‹uonda›m docuerat'. Durand 85, generally assigned to the seventh Sunday after Pentecost. As Moeller 1971–9: I.213, no. 540.

1.76. Fos 21v/21–22r/16: "b‹e›n‹e›d‹ictio› i‹n› do‹mini›c‹a› .xi. [*recte* .ix.]" 'ITa uos o‹m›nip‹ot›e‹ns› deus tribuat facta carnis | mortificare'. Durand 86, usually assigned to the eighth Sunday after Pentecost. As Moeller 1971–9: II.600–1, no. 1461.

1.77. Fo 22r/16–22v/2: "b‹e›n‹e›dictio | i‹n› do‹mini›c‹a› | .x." 'AB om‹n›ib‹us› co‹n›cupisce‹n›tiis | mal‹is› euacuatos:'. Durand 88, usually assigned to the ninth Sunday after Pentecost. As Moeller 1971–9: I.2, no. 4.

1.78. Fo 22v/2–14: "b‹e›n‹e›d‹ictio› in dominica .x." 'DEus o‹m›nip‹otens› qui om‹n›es diuitias h‹abe›t in | sua potestate'. Durand 89, who alone assigns it to the tenth Sunday after Pentecost. As Moeller 1971–9: I.295–6, no. 741.

1.79. Fo 22v/14–21: "b‹e›n‹e›dictio in dom[i]nica .xi." '[A] Blasphematorib‹us› ‹Christ›i sec‹er›nens:'. Durand 90, generally assigned to the tenth Sunday after Pentecost. As Moeller 1971–9: I.1, no. 1.

1.80. Fos 22v/21–23r/13: "b‹e›n‹e›dictio in dominica .xii." 'Dominus ih‹es›us ‹Christus› qui p‹er› affectu‹m› com|passionis'. Durand 91 (11th Sunday), generally assigned to the 10th Sunday after Pentecost. As Moeller 1971–9: II.536, no. 1299.

1.81. Fo 23r/13–20: "b‹e›n‹e›d‹ictio› in dominica .xii." 'PEr passione‹m› ‹Christ›i iustificatos'. Durand 92, who alone assigns it to the twelfth Sunday after Pentecost. As Moeller 1971–9: II.753, no. 1843.

1.82. Fo 23r/20–23v/9: "**Item alia.**" 'DEus qui pro p‹e›cc‹at›oribus | ue‹n›it'. Durand 93, who alone assigns it to the twelfth Sunday after Pentecost. As Moeller 1971–9: II.452, no. 1101.

1.83. Fo 23v/10–18: "b‹e›n‹e›dictio in do‹mini›c‹a› | .xiii. 'REdemptoris u‹est›ri ih‹es›u | ‹Christ›i b‹e›n‹e›dictionib‹us› repleamini'. Durand 95, who alone assigns it to the thirteenth Sunday after Pentecost. As Moeller 1971–9: II.776, no. 1899.

1.84. Fos 23v/18–24r/9: b‹e›n‹e›dict‹i›o in dom‹ini›ca .xiiii." 'BEenedictionis [*sic*] sue oculos ‹Christus› sup‹er› uos | dignetur'. Durand 97, who alone assigns it to the fourteenth Sunday after Pentecost. As Moeller 1971–9: I.153, no. 369.

1.85. Fo 24r/9–15: "b‹e›n‹e›d‹ictio› in do‹mini›c‹a› .xv." 'TRibuat uob‹is› d‹omi›n‹u›s carnis desid‹er›ia'. Durand 98, who alone assigns it to the fifteenth Sunday after Pentecost. As Moeller 1971–9: II.826, no. 2025.

1.86. Fo 24r/16–24v/3: "**Item alia b‹e›n‹e›d‹ictio›**" 'O‹m›nip‹otens› deus qui decem | uiros ad se clama‹n›tes mu‹n›dauit'. Durand 99, who alone gives it as an alternative benediction for the fifteenth Sunday after Pentecost. As Moeller 1971–9: II.663, no. 1618.

1.87. Fo 24v/4–10: "**b‹e›n‹e›dictio in dom‹in›ica | .xvi. R‹ubr›ic‹a›**" 'PRestet uo‹bis› d‹omi›n‹u›s | sup‹er›are cenodoxia‹m›'. Durand 100, who alone assigns it to the sixteenth Sunday after Pentecost. As Moeller 1971–9: II.763, no. 1867.

1.88. Fo 24v/10–20: "**Item alia b‹e›n‹e›d‹ictio›.**" 'Conditor celi et terre'. Durand 101, who alone gives it as an alternative benediction for the sixteenth Sunday after Pentecost. As Moeller 1971–9: I.230–1, no. 582.

1.89. Fos 24v/21–25r/6: "**bened‹ictio› i‹n› d‹o›m‹ini›ca .xvii. Rubrica.**" 'IN tribulatione faciat uos d‹omi›n‹u›s pacie‹n›tes'. Durand 102, who alone assigns it to the seventeenth Sunday after Pentecost. As Moeller 1971–9: II.586, no. 1427.

1.90. Fo 25r/7–19: "**Item al‹ia›**" 'Deus qui filiu‹m› uidue delatu‹m› | extra portu‹m› [*recte* porta‹m›] uoluit suscitare'. Durand 103, who alone gives it as an alternative benediction for the seventeenth Sunday after Pentecost. As Moeller 1971–9: I.376, no. 929.

1.91. Fo 25r/19–25v/6: "**b‹e›n‹e›dictio in .iiii. fer‹ia›.**" 'Det uob‹is› d‹omi›n‹u›s munus sue b‹e›n‹e›dict‹i›o‹n›is'. Durand 104, otherwise usually assigned for general use. As Moeller 1971–9: I.249, no. 631.

1.92. Fo 25v/7–14: "**Item alia b‹enedictio›.**" 'Concedat uob‹is› om‹n›i-pote‹n›s | deus munus sue b‹e›n‹e›dict‹i›o‹n›is'. Durand 105, who alone gives it as an alternative benediction for Feria IV following the seventeenth Sunday after Pentecost. As Moeller 1971–9: I.225, no. 571.

1.93. Fos 25v/14–26r/1: "**b‹e›n‹e›d‹ictio› in feria .vi. Rubrica.**" 'O‹m›nip‹otens› deus celesti uos protectione | circumdet'. Durand 106, who alone assigns it as here. As Moeller 1971–9: II.626–7, no. 1528.

1.94. Fo 26r/1–9: "**Item alia**" 'O‹m›nip‹otens› sempit‹er›ne deus dext‹er›e sue p‹er›petu|o uos circu‹m›det'. Durand 107, otherwise usually assigned for general use. As Moeller 1971–9: II.640, no. 1562.

1.95. Fo 26r/9–17: "**b‹e›n‹e›d‹ictio› in sabb‹at›o**" 'Purificet uos o‹m›nip‹otens› deus u‹est›rorum cor|dium'. Durand 108, otherwise usually assigned for general use. As Moeller 1971–9: II.771, no. 1886.

1.96. Fo 26r/17–26v/5: "**Item alia b‹e›n‹e›dictio.**" 'O‹m›nip‹otens› deus uniu‹er›sa a uob‹is› adu‹er›sa exclu|dat'. Durand 109, who alone assigns it as here. As Moeller 1971–9: II.698–9, no. 1703. Cf. 3.16 below.

1.97. Fo 26v/5–11: "b‹e›n‹e›dictio i‹n› do‹mini›c‹a› .xviii." 'IN unitate sp‹iritus› faciat uos d‹omin›us amb‹u›lare'. Durand 110, otherwise usually assigned to the seventeenth Sunday after Pentecost. As Moeller 1971–9: II.586, no. 1428.

1.98. Fos 26v/11–27r/1: "**Item alia**" 'Salus et medicus a‹n›i‹m›aru‹m› ih‹esus› qui i‹n› do|mo principis phariseoru‹m› ydropicu‹m› | dignatus e‹st› curare'. Durand 111, who alone gives it as an alternative benediction for the eighteenth Sunday after Pentecost. As Moeller 1971–9: II.792, no. 1936.

1.99. Fo 27r/1–7: "b‹e›n‹e›d‹ictio› in do‹mini›c‹a› .xix." 'Dignos uos d‹omin›us efficiat suo sac‹er›docio'. Durand 112, who alone assigns it as here. As Moeller 1971–9: II.512, no. 1242.

1.100. Fo 27r/8–17: "b‹e›n‹e›dictio. in do‹mini›c‹a› .xx." '‹Christ›us ih‹es›us qui | pa[ra]liticu‹m› curauit'. Durand 115, where it is given as an alternative benediction for the twentieth Sunday after Pentecost. As Moeller 1971–9: I.215–16, no. 546.

1.101. Fo 27r/17–27v/8: "b‹e›n‹e›dictio in do‹mini›c‹a› .xxi." 'Pater o‹m›nip‹otens› rex s‹an›c‹t›orum. [*recte* caelorum] qui per i‹n›carna|tionis sue misteriu‹m› nupcias fecit fi|lio suo:' Durand 117, who alone assigns it to the twenty-first Sunday after Pentecost. As Moeller 1971–9: II.750, no. 1835.

1.102. Fo 27v/8–18: "**Item alia b‹e›n‹e›dictio.**" 'Deus qui filiu‹m› reguli p‹er› diuinitatis'. Durand 119, who, unlike here, gives it as an alternative benediction for the twenty-second Sunday after Pentecost. As Moeller 1971–9: I.375–6, no. 927. The fact that no Benedictio in dominica xxii is present here suggests that it has been assigned to the wrong date.

1.103. Fos 27v/19–28r/10: "b‹e›n‹e›dictio in do‹mini›c‹a› .xxiii." 'Deus et homo rex | celestis gl‹or›ie sic uob‹is› cum s‹er›uis suis'. Durand 121, who alone assigns it as here (albeit as an alternative). As Moeller 1971–9: I.275–6, no. 696. The reading with 'vobis' after 'sic' is unique to Durand.

1.104. Fo 28r/11–28v/1: "b‹e›n‹e›dictio in do‹mini›c‹a› | .xxiiii. R‹ubr›ica" 'Magister uerax ‹Christus› co‹n›|siliu‹m›'. Durand 123, who alone assigns it as here (albeit as an alternative). As Moeller 1971–9: II.605–6.

1.105. Fo 28v/1–8: "b‹e›n‹e›d‹ictio› in d‹omini›c‹a› .xxv." 'IMpleat uos d‹omin›us agnit‹i›o‹n›e uolu‹n›tatis sue'. Durand 124, who alone assigns it as here. As Moeller 1971–9: II.585–6, no. 1426.

1.106. Fo 28v/8–21: "b‹e›n‹e›d‹ictio› i‹n› d‹omini›c‹a› **eadem.**" 'Dator [*recte* Factor] o‹m›nium bonoru‹m› ‹et› resuscitator | mortuo‹rum›'. Durand 125, who alone gives it as an alternative benediction for the twenty-fifth Sunday after Pentecost. As Moeller 1971–9: II.563–4, no. 1366.

1.107. Fo 29r/1–8: "b‹e›n‹e›dictio i‹n› d‹omini›c‹a› | .xxvi." 'DEuotio-ne‹m› u‹est›ram do‹minus› | digna‹n›ter inte‹n›dat'. Durand 127, who alone assigns it as here (albeit as an alternative). As Moeller 1971–9: II.510, no. 1236. Cf. 1.52.

1.108. Fo 29r/9–16: "b‹e›n‹e›dictio i‹n› d‹omini›c‹a› | .xxvii." 'Benedicat uos deus | ex quo o‹mn›ia. b‹e›n‹e›dicat uos'. Durand 128, where it is assigned to Trinity Sunday. As Moeller 1971–9: I.96, no. 221

1.109. Fo 29r/16–29v/6: "**Item alia b‹e›n‹e›d‹i›c‹t›io.**" 'O‹m›nip‹otens› trinitas unus et uerus deus. | pat‹er› ‹et› filius ‹et› sp‹iritus› s‹an›c‹t›us det uob‹is›'. Durand 129, where it is assigned to the Octave of Pentecost. As Moeller 1971–9: II.738–9, no. 1804.

2. Benedictiones Sanctorale

2.1. Fo 29v/6–18: "**bened‹ictio› i‹n› festiuitati|bus s‹an›c‹t›o‹rum›. b‹e›n‹e›d‹icti›o. ‹prima›. i‹n› | uigil‹ia›. nat‹iuitatis› d‹omi›ni. R‹ubrica›.**" [24 Dec.] 'DEus qui in filii | sui d‹omi›ni n‹ost›ri ih‹es›u | ‹Christ›i humilitate [sic] mu‹n›du‹m› iacente‹m› | dignatus est'. Durand 130. As Moeller 1971–9: I.374–5, no. 925.

2.2. Fos 29v/18–30r/12: "**b‹e›n‹e›d‹ictio› in natiuitate d‹omi›ni.**" [25 Dec.] 'O‹m›nip‹otens› sempit‹er›ne | deus qui incarnat‹i›o‹n›e unigeniti sui | mu‹n›di tenebras effugauit'. Durand 131. As Moeller 1971–9: II.673–4, no. 1643.

2.3. Fo 30r/12–30v/7: "**b‹e›n‹e›d‹ict‹i›o | i‹n› secunda | missa.**" 'O‹m›nip‹otens› deus. qui om‹n›e genus humanu‹m› tenebris infideli|tatis'. Durand 133. As Moeller 1971–9: II.676, no. 1650.

2.4. Fo 30v/8–19: "**ad missa maiore‹m›**" 'Benedicat uos o‹m›nip‹otens› | deus. u‹est›ramq‹ue› ad sup‹er›na excitet in|tent‹i›o‹n›em'. Durand 134. As Moeller 1971–9: I.134–5, no. 321.

2.5. Fos 30v/19–31r/10: "**b‹e›n‹e›d‹ictio› in festo | sancti steph‹an›i protho|martiris:**" [26 Dec.] 'DEus qui b‹ea›t‹u›m | stephanu‹m› p‹ro›thomartire‹m›'. Durand 135. As Moeller 1971–9: I.341–2, no. 854.

2.6. Fo 31r/10–31v/1: "**b‹e›n‹e›d‹ictio› i‹n› festo s‹an›c‹t›i ioha‹n›|nis ap‹osto›li et eu‹a›nge|liste.**" [27 Dec.] 'O‹m›nip‹otens› deus dignet‹ur› | uob‹is› per int‹er›cessione‹m› b‹ea›ti ioh‹ann›is'. Durand 136. As Moeller 1971–9: II.642–3, no. 1566.

2.7. Fo 31v/1–13: "**b‹e›n‹e›d‹ictio› in festo i‹n›ocenti|um.**" [28 Dec.] 'O‹m›nip‹otens› deus pro cuius unige‹n›iti | uen‹er›anda infantia'. Durand 137. As Moeller 1971–9: II.656, no. 1600.

2.8. Fos 31v/13–32r/7: "**b‹e›n‹e›d‹ictio› in oct‹aua› nat‹iuitatis› d‹omi›ni.**" 'O‹m›nip‹otens› deus cuius unige‹n›itus hodierna | die ne lege‹m› solu‹er›et'. Durand 138. As Moeller 1971–9: II.633–4, no. 1545.

2.9. Fo 32r/7–21: "**b‹e›n‹e›d‹ictio› i‹n› | in apparitione d‹omi›ni.**" [6 Jan.] 'Deus qui lume‹n› | ueru‹m› es. qui unige‹n›itu‹m› suu‹m› hodierna | die stella duce'. Durand 139, but the wording of the opening phrase here differs. As Moeller 1971–9: I.291, no. 732.

2.10. Fo 32v/1–17: "b‹e›n‹e›dict‹i›o i‹n› oct‹aua› epipha|nie." 'DEus mirabiliu‹m› | et uirtutu‹m› auctor'. Durand 141. As Moeller 1971–9: I.294, no. 738. Normally assigned to Epiphany Eve.

2.11. Fos 32v/17–33r/7: "b‹e›n‹e›dictio in conu‹er›sione s‹an›c‹t›i | pauli. R‹ubr›ic‹a›." [25 Jan.] 'Deus qui per gra‹tia›m suam | b‹ea›t‹u›m paulu‹m›'. Cf. fo 40v/21. Unique to Durand 142. As Moeller 1971–9: II.432. Similar to Moeller 1971–9: I.381, no. 940.

2.12. Fo 33r/7–18: "b‹e›n‹e›d‹ictio› in purificat‹i›one | beate marie" [2 Feb.] 'O‹m›nip‹otens› deus qui unige‹n›itu‹m› | suum hodierna die in assumpta car|ne'. Durand 143. As Moeller 1971–9: II.685–6, no. 1674.

2.13. Fo 33r/18–33v/6: "b‹e›n‹e›d‹ictio› | in cathedra sa‹n›cti | petri." [22 Feb.] 'O‹m›nip‹otens› deus dignet‹ur› | uos sua b‹e›n‹e›dict‹i›o‹n›e ditare'. Durand 144. As Moeller 1971–9: II.1643, no. 1568.

2.14. Fo 33v/6–15: "b‹e›n‹e›dictio i‹n› an|nu‹n›ciati|one d‹omi›ni." [25 Mar.] 'O‹m›nip‹otens› deus | qui hodierna die | ang‹e›l‹u›m gabriele‹m› direxit'. Durand 145. As Moeller 1971–9: II.667, no. 1629.

2.15. Fos 33v/15–34r/2: "b‹e›n‹e›d‹i›c‹t›io i‹n› inuentione sancte | crucis." [3 May] 'O‹m›nip‹otens› d‹omin›us qui per sangui‹n›em | crucis sue cuncta pacificauit'. Specific to Durand 146. As Moeller 1971–9: II.720, no. 1759.

2.16. Fo 34r/2–18: "b‹e›n‹e›d‹ictio› i‹n› festo s‹an›c‹t›oru‹m› gerua|su ‹et› prothasu." [19 June] 'Deus cui‹us› dictioni | subiecta su‹n›t cuncta'. Specific to Durand 147. As Moeller 1971–9: I.263, no. 664.

2.17. Fo 34r/18–34v/12: "bened‹ictio› i‹n› | festo sancti ioha‹n›nis | baptiste." [24 June] 'Benedicat uos | o‹m›nip‹otens› deus beati ioh‹ann›is | baptiste int‹er›cessione | cui‹us› hodie solle‹m›nia || natalicia celebratis'. Durand 148. As Moeller 1971–9: I.77, no. 179. Here the addition of the word 'sollemnia' is apparently unique.

2.18. Fos 34v/12–35r/1: "b‹e›n‹e›dictio i‹n› festo | ap‹osto›lorum petri et pau|li Rubrica." [29 June] 'Benedicat uos o‹m›nip‹otens› deus. qui uos beati | petri ap‹osto›li salub‹er›ima co‹n›fessione'. Durand 149 gives the reading 'qui nos' but 'nos' and 'uos' are indistinguishable in this manuscript. As Moeller 1971–9: I.84, no. 193.

2.19. Fo 35r/2–8: "b‹e›n‹e›d‹ictio› in festo b‹eat›e ma|rie magdalene." [22 July] 'Benedicat uos d‹omin›us per m‹er›itu‹m› b‹eat›e marie | magdalene. protegatq‹ue› assidue'. As Moeller 1971–9: I.110–11, no. 258. Not found in other sources of Durand.

2.20. Fo 35r/8–16: "b‹e›n‹e›dict‹i›o ad uin|cula sancti pet‹ri›." [1 Aug.] 'Deus qui ap‹osto›l‹u›m petru‹m› | eduxit de carcere'. Specific to Durand 152. As Moeller 1971–9: I.329, no. 820.

2.21. Fo 35r/16–35v/4: "b‹e›n‹e›dictio i‹n› inuent‹i›o‹n›e | sancti stephani." [3 Aug.] 'Sui dilecti protho|martiris steph‹an›i meritis uos d<omin>us deui|are dignetur'. Specific to Durand 153. As Moeller 1971–9: II.817, no. 2004.

2.22. Fo 35v/4–16: "**b<e>n<e>d<ictio> i<n> festo | sancti dom|inici.**" [4 Aug.] 'Deus qui in b<eat>o dominico | officium ap<osto>licu<m> dignatus e<st> | suscitare.' Specific to Durand 154. As Moeller 1971–9: II.396, no. 975.

2.23. Fos 35v/16–36r/4: "**b<e>n<e>dict<i>o in festo sancti | laurentii.**" [10 Aug.] 'Tribuat uob<is> d<omin>us tempta|tionu<m> carnaliu<m> incentiua deuinc<er>e'. Durand 157. As Moeller 1971–9: II.826–7, no. 2027.

2.24. Fo 36r/4–19: "**b<e>n<e>d<ictio> i<n> uigil<ia> assu<m>p|tionis b<eat>e marie**" [15 Aug.] 'IMmense magnitud<in>is | i<n>estimabilis potencie ac et<er>ne deus.' Durand 158, otherwise usually assigned to the Assumption itself. As Moeller 1971–9: II.584–5, no. 1424. The wording with 'ac' is apparently unique to this manuscript.

2.25. Fo 36r/19–36v/18: "**In | festo assu<m>pt<i>o<n>is b<eat>e m<arie>.**" [15 Aug.] 'O<m>nip<otens> sempit<er>ne | deus | qui unige<n>itu<m> [filium] tuu<m> d<omin>um n<ost>r<u>m || ih<esu>m <Christu>m que<m> om<n>es celi t<er>raq<ue>.' Durand 159, to whom the reading with 'quem' is specific. As Moeller 1971–9: II.737, no. 1801.

2.26. Fos 36v/18–37r/9: "**b<e>n<e>dict<i>o i<n> t<ra>nslat<i>o<n>e sancte co|rone d<omi>ni.**" [19 Aug.] 'Benedicat uos o<m>nip<otens> d<eu>s | b<e>n<e>d<i>cione celesti qui pro uob<is> i<n> pas|sione sua spinis uoluit coronari'. Specific to Durand 160. As Moeller 1971–9: I.116, no. 276. Cp. 2.50 at fo 42v/15.

2.27. Fo 37r/9–18: "**b<e>n<e>dict<i>o | de sancto aug|gustin<o>.**" [28 Aug.] 'INstruat d<omin>us corda u<est>ra fidei sue u<er>itate'. Durand 161. As Moeller 1971–9: II.596, no. 1450.

2.28. Fo 37r/18–37v/8: "**b<e>n<e>dictio in decollatione | s<an>c<t>i ioh<ann>is bapt<iste>.**" [29 Aug.] 'Deus qui nos beati | ioh<ann>is baptiste concedit'. Durand 162, where the reading with 'nos' is confirmed. As Moeller 1971–9: II.491–2, no. 1194.

2.29. Fo 37v/8–16: "**b<e>n<e>dict<io> i<n> nati|uitate b<eat>e marie uirg<in>is**" [8 Sept.] 'O<m>nip<otens> deus | sua | uos dignet<ur> p<ro>tectione b<e>n<e>dic<er>e | qui | hunc diem p<er> natiuitate[m] b<eat>e marie fecit cla|rescere'. As Moeller 1971–9: II.696, no. 1697. Not previously assigned to Durand.

2.30. Fos 37v/16–38r/4: "**b<e>n<e>d<ictio> i<n> festiuitate om<n>ium | s<an>c<t>oru<m>.**" [1 Nov.] 'Benedicat uos | o<m>nip<otens> deus b<e>n<e>d<i>c<t>ione p<er>petua'. As Moeller 1971–9: I.116–17, no. 277. Not previously assigned Durand.

2.31. Fo 38r/4–12: "**b<e>n<e>dictio de s<an>c<t>o martino.**" [11 Nov.] 'Conferat uob<is> d<omin>us s<an>c<t>a dona sinc<er>e cari|tatis.' As Moeller 1971–9: I.231, no. 583. Attributed to Durand but not previously authenticated. Moeller reads 'Conferat vobis dominus viscera sincerae caritatis'.

2.32. Fo 38r/12–20: "**b<e>n<e>dict<i>o de sa<n>cto | andrea."** [30 Nov.] 'Det uob<is> d<omin>us gloriam crucis | agnosc<er>e'. Specific to Durand 178. As Moeller 1971–9: I.248, no. 629.

3. Benedictions for the Common of the Saints: Commune

3.1. Fo 38r/20–38v/9: "**b<e>n<e>dictio de s<an>c<t>is ang<e>lis."** 'DEus qui ad salutem u<est>ram ang<e>lo<rum> || suoru<m> utit<ur> minist<er>io'. Durand 168, where it is assigned to St Michael (29 Sept.). As Moeller 1971–9: I.311, no. 779.

3.2. Fo 38v/10–19: "**benedict<i>o pl<ur>imo<rum> | ap<osto>lorum."** 'Deus qui uos in | ap<osto>licis tribuit consist<er>e'. Durand 180. As Moeller 1971–9: II.495–6, no. 1203.

3.3. Fos 38v/19–39r/8: "**b<e>n<e>d<ictio> de s<an>c<t>is eu<a>ngelistis."** 'Precib<us> beati .ill<ius>. | eu<a>ng<e>liste s<upe>r uos d<omin>us copiam sue be||nedictionis i<n>fundat:'. As Moeller 1971–9: II.765–6, no. 1875. Attributed to Durand's compilation but not previously authenticated.

3.4. Fo 39r/8–15: "**b<e>n<e>dictio unius martiris."** 'Beati m<arti>ris sui .ill<ius>. int<er>cessione uos do<minus> | b<e>n<e>dicat. <et> ab o<mn>i malo defendat'. Durand 182. As Moeller 1971–9: I.26, no. 57.

3.5. Fo 39r/15–39v/3: "**b<e>n<e>d<ictio> pl<ur>imorum | m<arti>r<u>m."** 'Benedicat uos d<omin>us | b<ea>torum m<arti>r<u>m suo<rum> ill<orum> suf|fragiis.' Durand 183. As Moeller 1971–9: I.66–7, no. 153.

3.6. Fo 39v/4–12: "**b<e>n<e>dict<io> unius confes|soris."** 'O<m>nip<otens> deus det | uob<is> copiam sue b<e>n<e>d<i>c<t>ionis | qui b<eatu>m ill<um> asciuit uirtute confessionis.' Durand 184. As Moeller 1971–9: II.710, no. 1733.

3.7. Fo 39v/12–19: "**b<e>n<e>dictio pl<ur>imoru<m> confes|sorum."** 'S<an>c<t>orum co<n>fessorum ill<orum> m<er>itis | uos d<omin>us faciat b<e>n<e>dici. <et> co<n>tra omnia | adu<er>sa eoru<m> int<er>cessione mu<n>iri'. Durand 185. As Moeller 1971–9: II.804–5, no. 1968.

3.8. Fos 39v/19–40r/11: "**b<e>n<e>d<ictio> | uni<us> uirginis et martiris."** 'Benedicat | uos qui b<eat>e uirgini .ill<i>. co<n>cessit et de||corem uirginitatis. <et> gl<or>iam passion<n>is'. Durand 186, here with 'vos' rather than 'vobis'. As Moeller 1971–9: I.75–6, no. 175.

3.9. Fo 40r/11–40v/4: "**b<e>n<e>dict<i>o unius uirginis non | martiris."** 'Deus qui sacris uirginib<us> | centesimi fructus celestia confert | p<re>mia uob<is> m<er>itis s<an>c<t>e uirg<in>is ill<i> cu<m> sup<er>na | b<e>n<e>dict<i>o<n>e di<ui>na co<n>ferat gaudia'. Durand 187.

3.10. Fo 40v/5–21: "**b<e>n<e>dictio i<n> dedica|tione eccl<es>ie."** 'Benedicat et custo|diat uos o<m>nip<otens> d<omin>us | domu<m>q<ue> h<a>nc sui luminis p<re>sencia illu|strare.' As Moeller 1971–9: I.54–5, no. 123. The variant 'luminis' instead of usual 'muneris' occurs in Paris 733 and Utrecht, both of which reflect the Durand tradition.

3.11. Fos 40v/21–41r/11: "b<e>n<e>dict<i>o in co<n>u<er>sione s<an>c<t>i **pauli.**" [25 Jan.] 'Deus fons et origo b<e>n<e>dict<i>o<n>is uos in | hac domo co<n>gregatos pro a<n>niuer|saro festo sue dedicat<i>onis om<n>i<um> repleat | i<n>tellectu sacre erudit<i>o<n>is'. Abridged form of Moeller 1971–9: I.278–9, no. 703. Associated with the Durand tradition in other manuscripts, and now possibly to be included in his compilation. Cf. fo 32v/17.

3.12. Fo 41r/11–41v/6: "b<e>n<e>dict<i>o i<n> ordi<n>at<i>one ep<iscop>i." 'Deus qui p<o>p<u>lis tuis i<n>dulge<n>do <con>sulis'. As Moeller 1971–9: II.441–2, no. 1081. Associated with the Durand tradition by its use for episcopal ordination.

3.13. Fo 41v/6–19: "b<e>n<e>dict<io> in co|ronat<i>one regis." 'Benedicat tibi d<omin>us | <et> custodiat te. <et> sic<ut> uoluit sup<er> p<o>p<u>l<u>m | suu<m> te <con>stitu<er>e regem.' Durand 205. As Moeller 1971–9: I.62–3, no. 143.

3.14. Fos 41v/19–42r/5: "b<e>n<e>dict<i>o i<n> ordi|natione pre[s]biteri." 'O<m>nip<otens> deus sua uos | clemencia b<e>n<e>dicat'. Durand 61, who restricted the use of this benediction to the ordination of a priest. As Moeller 1971–9: II.695–6, no. 1696. The same as 1.53 at fo 16v/7–14.

3.15. Fo 42r/5–16: "b<e>n<e>dict<i>o i<n> conse|cratione altaris." 'O<m>-nip<otens> deus | qui uos | hodie<r>na die ad co<n>secrat<i>o<n>em istius \altaris/'. Durand 190, who alone used 'altaris' as an alternative for usual 'aulae'. As Moeller 1971–9: II.689, no. 1681.

3.16. Fo 42r/17–42v/6: "bened<ictio> i<n> reco<n>cilia|t<i>one ecc<lesi>e." 'O<m>nip<otens> deus uniu<er>sa | a uob<is> <et> ab hoc templo ad|u<er>sa excludat.' Durand 109, reflecting here the English tradition of assigning it 'in reconciliatione ecclesiae'. As Moeller 1971–9: II.698–9, no. 1703. The same as 1.96 at fo 26r/17–26v/5.

3.17. Fo 42v/6–15: "b<e>n<e>dictio i<n> sy|nodo." 'O<m>nipotentis dei filius | qui est initiu<m> <et> finis <com>plementu<m> tri|buat uob<is> caritatis'. Durand 204, for the end of a synod. As Moeller 1971–9: II.623, no. 1519, variant of no. 417.

3.18. Fos 42v/15–43r/7: "benedictio in | festo corone d<omi>ni." [?19 Aug.] 'BEnedicat uos | o<m>nip<otens> deus b<e>n<e>dict<i>o<n>e celesti. qui pro | uob<is> i<n> passione sua spinis uoluit corona|ri'. Specific to Durand 160. As Moeller 1971–9: I.116, no. 276. The same as 2.26 at fo 36v/18.

3.19. Fo 43r/7–17: "Item alia benedictio." 'Deus qui unige<n>iti sui passionis insi|gnia uoluit'. Specific to Durand 193, normally used for the blessing of relics. As Moeller 1971–9: II.478, no. 1163.

3.20. Fo 43r/17–43v/7: "**b‹e›n‹e›dict‹i›o pl‹ur›imaru‹m› uirginu‹m›.**" 'O‹m›nip‹otens› deus int‹er›cedentib‹us› uirginib‹us› | suis uos dignetur b‹e›n‹e›dic‹er›e'. Durand 189. As Moeller 1971–9: II.713, no. 1742.

3.21. Fo 43v/7–16: "**b‹e›n‹e›|dictio gen‹er›alis in o‹m›ni | te‹m›pore.**" 'O‹m›nip‹otens› deus sua | uos b‹e›n‹e›dictione dignet‹ur› | locupletare. ‹et› sensu‹m› in uob‹is› sap‹ient›ie salutaris | per sp‹iritu›m s‹an›c‹tu›m i‹n›fund‹er›e'. Durand 197; cf. Moeller 1971–9: II, 695–6, no. 1696. The wording with 'benedictione dignetur locupletare' instead of 'clementia benedicat' and with 'per spiritum sanctum infundere' instead of 'infundat' is apparently unusual.

4. Benedictions with Liturgical Forms: Ordinale

4.1. Fos 43v/16–48v/13: "**Incip‹it› | ordo ad cathecuminu‹m› faciendu‹m›. R‹ubr›ica.**" 'ORdo ad cathecuminu‹m› faciend‹um› stans i‹n› | eccl‹es›ie limine sac‹er›dos' (pl. 15.1). Begins: 'Ioh‹ann›es quid petis ad eccle||siam dei R[esponsio] Fidem'; fo 46v/19 'Exorcizo te i‹m›mu‹n›de | sp‹iritus› in no‹m›i‹n›e pa+tris'; fo 47r/13 'Ingred‹er›e in ecc‹lesi›am dei. ut accipias bene|dictione‹m› celestem a d‹omi›no n‹ost›ro ihesu ‹Christ›o; fo 47r/16 'Credo | i‹n› unu‹m› deu‹m›. ad hec eleuatus asportat‹ur›. Explic‹it› | cathecumin‹us› s‹ed› si statim debeat baptizari | dicat‹ur›', and continues "**Sequencia s‹an›c‹t›i eu‹a›ngelii secundu‹m› | matheu‹m›.**", 'IN illo t‹em›p‹o›re: Oblati sunt ih‹es›u | paruuli. ut manus eis impon‹er›et ... Et cu‹m› imposuiss‹et› manus: | abiit inde: [Mt 19.13–15]', followed by the section of the Ordo Romanus X in Sabbato Sancto dealing with baptism 'Postea tenens manu‹m› s‹upe›r caput | i‹n›fantis sac‹er›dos dicat simbolu‹m›'. Ends: 'ut cu‹m› d‹omin›us uenerit ad nupcias po\s/|sis ei occurr‹er›e in aula celesti. ame‹n›'. Up to Explicit as Martène 1763: I.17–18, Ordo VII, a form not found in the Pontifical of Guillaume Durand; then (with slight variations) as PL 78, 1015A–1016D.

4.2. Fos 48v/14–52r/21: "**ORdo pro nupciis celebrandis . ac spo‹n›so | et sponsa b‹e›n‹e›dicendis**". Begins at fo 49r/4: 'Creator et cons‹er›uator humani gen‹er›is | dator gr‹ati›e sp‹irit›ualis. largitor et‹er›ne salu|tis'. Ends: 'ut h‹ab›eatis uita‹m› et‹er›na‹m› adiuuante | d‹omin›o n‹ostro› ih‹es›u ‹Christ›o qui cu‹m› p‹at›re ‹et› s‹piritu› s‹ancto› ui‹uit› ‹et› re‹gnat› d‹eus›. ame‹n›'. Begins as Andrieu 1940[2]: 385–6, but this form is used for a different purpose in the Pontifical of Guillaume Durand.

4.3. Fos 52v/1–78r/8: "**ORdo minoru‹m› fratru‹m› s‹ecundu›m co‹n›-sue\tu/di‹n›em Ro|mane ecc‹lesi›e ad uisitand‹um› i‹n›firmu‹m›.**" Begins 'Miserere mei deus. | Et intrantes domu‹m› dicat sac‹er›dos Pax huic domui. R Et om‹n›ib‹us› h‹ab›itantib‹us› i‹n› ea. ame‹n›'. Ends: '‹et› p‹e›cc‹at›a que per fragilitatem mun|dane ‹con›uersationis co‹m›misit. Tu ue‹n›ia mi|sericordissime pietatis absterge. per ‹Christum› do‹minum› n‹ostrum›. Amen.' Begins as Andrieu 1940¹: 486. This form is not used for this purpose in the Pontifical of Guillaume Durand; compare Andrieu 1940²: 462. With litany on fo 56. Musical settings indicated with neums and staves on fos 62r–75v. Fo 78r/9–21: no text.

5. Additional Benedictions

5.1. Fos 78v/1–79r/12: Begins 'Humiliate uos ad benedictionem. | Et cho|rus res|po‹n›det'. Ends 'Humili uoce | clamantes atq‹ue› dicentes de|o gracias semper agamus:' Musical setting indicated with neums and staves. Fo 79r/13–21: no text.

5.2. Fo 79v/1–13: "**B‹e›n‹e›dict‹i›o pastoral‹is› seu po‹n›tifical‹is› i‹n› festo corporis .‹Christ›i.**" [Corpus Christi, Thursday after Trinity Sunday] 'DEscendat sup‹er› uos gr‹ati›e celestis i‹n›unda‹n›s | b‹e›n‹e›dict‹i›o. ut qui hodierna die sacratis|sime Eucharistie solle‹m›pnitate‹m› ex‹u›ltantibus | a‹n›imis celebratis. uirtute‹m› eius in uob‹is› iugit‹er› | senciatis Amen. Uiuat in uobis iugis | memoria d‹omi›nice passionis. qui se ip‹su›m dat | uobis in cibum sacre co‹mmun›ionis donec ip‹s›e ue|niens. se ip‹su›m prebeat in eduliu‹m› esue [*recte* sue] finitio|nis. Amen Quatinus que‹m› nu‹n›c sub | reru‹m› specie fiteliter sumitis in uia. inmedia|ta uisione cernatis in patria. Amen.' Not found elsewhere.

5.3. Fos 79v/13–80r/8: "**De transfigurat‹i›o‹n›e d‹omi›ni.**" [6 Aug.] 'DOmine ih‹es›u ‹Christ›e cui se transfiguranti | celu‹m› \per/ paternam uoce‹m›. t‹er›ram p‹er› discip‹u›los. | Petrum. Ioh‹ann›em. et Iacobu‹m›. paradisu‹m› et In|fernu‹m›. uiuos et mortuos. lege‹m› ‹et› p‹ro›ph‹et›\i/am. per | moysen et heliam p‹ro›uisu‹m› e‹st› as[s]istere. da uob‹is› utriusq‹ue› testame‹n›ti no‹n› deficientib‹us› testimo|niis. ad tante uirtutis gaudia p‹er›uenire. Amen. Et qui fidem in rem. co‹n›te‹m›pla||tione‹m› in spem transfigurat‹i›one subita co‹m›|mutasti. da nob‹is› utque su‹m›mo desiderio | co‹n›templa‹tione›m in et‹er›na b‹ea›titudine specie ten‹us› assequam‹ur›. Amen. Et qui presentem | diem tanti‹s› priuilegiis fecisti celebrem. da | nobis ut de malo ad bonu‹m›. de uiciis ad uir|tutes. de labore perueniamus ad requiem. | Amen.' Not found elsewhere.

5.4. Fo 80r/8–16: "**De s‹an›c‹t›o uince‹n›cio.**" [22 Jan.] 'O‹m›nipotens deus uos dignetur b‹e›n‹e›|dicere. qui b‹ea›t‹u›m m‹arty›rem suu‹m› | et leui|tam uincenciu‹m› dignatus est coronare.' Ends 'in eterna p‹at›ria meream‹ur› esse felices. Ame‹n›.' As Moeller 1971–9: II.705, no. 1719. Fo 80r/17–21: no text; fo 80v blank.

Note: Further images of Aix-en-Provence, Bibliothèque Méjanes MS 13 are currently available via the internet at: www.enluminures.culture.fr.

The Venetian naval commander's 'Commissione'

WRITTEN IN A SINGLE CALLIGRAPHIC hand at Venice in 1481, this manuscript is a fair copy, unique in its survival, of a 'Commissione' given by the Doge of Venice to Niccolò da Pesaro, Captain of the Gulf. Its history thereafter is not known until it appears in Ireland, where it was provided with its binding of green goatskin during the nineteenth century. Intriguingly, the binding is very similar to that of the oldest Irish manuscript in Maynooth's collection (C110). It was owned by Dr Daniel McCarthy, professor of scripture (Hebrew) and vice-president of Maynooth College (1854–, 1872–81), who gave it to St Patrick's College, Maynooth, on St Patrick's Day 1871.

16 RB52
'Commissione' given by the Doge of Venice to Niccolò da Pesaro, 1481

HISTORY

THE MANUSCRIPT WAS written in a single hand (corrections by the scribe in red on fo 2r, in gold on fo 12r, and in black on fo 16v) at Venice 1481, being the *copia di pregio*, i.e., a fair copy prepared to order for preservation in a noble family, of a 'Commissione' given by the Doge of Venice to Niccolò da Pesaro, Captain of the Gulf (i.e., the fleet that guarded the Adriatic), the only extant copy of this 'Commissione' (pl. 16.1). Members of the Pesaro family were leading naval commanders at the time. Its history thereafter is not known until it turned up in Ireland.

From the incorporation of the third front endleaf with annotation by James Henthorn Todd (1805–69; on whom, see Simms 1969), Regius Professor of Hebrew in the University of Dublin and librarian of Trinity College (1852–69), in the binding it would seem that he owned it, but it does not occur in the sale of his manuscripts (Todd 1869).

The binding of green goatskin on boards with an ornamental border blind-stamped on both covers and 'MS. | 1481' in gold leaf on the spine, was provided in Ireland s.xix. Our attention has been drawn by Aoibheann Nic Dhonnchadha (DIAS), with information from Paul Hoary, to a similar binding on the oldest Irish manuscript owned by Maynooth College (s.xv), MS C110, previously in the possession of Eugene O'Curry before coming via the Catholic University of Ireland to Maynooth in 1900 (Corish 1995: 324). This manuscript was also bound in green goatskin but has been handled much more or kept in less propitious storage conditions, with the result that it looks so dark that Ó Fiannachta (1965–73: fasc. 6, p. 69) was misled into thinking it was black ('dubh'). Features in common between the two bindings (apart from the green goatskin covers and the ornamental blind-stamped border) include pastedowns and flyleaves of the same Spanish marble pattern and endleaves of the same coarse paper. It seems probable that both manuscripts were bound by the same binder. Both Todd and O'Curry were in Dublin, and in touch with each other, up to O'Curry's death in 1862, so it is reasonable to conclude that the bindings were done in Dublin *c.*1850–60. It is a curiosity that Todd wrongly thought RB52 contained fragments of medical manuscripts (see below) and C110 does actually contain medical texts.

Shortly after Todd's death in 1869, RB52 was owned by Dr Daniel McCarthy, professor of scripture (Hebrew) and vice-president of Maynooth College (1854–,

1872–81). Given to St Patrick's College, Maynooth, 17 March 1871 (i.e., St Patrick's Day) by Dr McCarthy, as recorded on fo 27v.

Secundo folio: 'suam i‹n› p‹ri›mo'.

CODICOLOGICAL DESCRIPTION

Fos iii + 27 + ii, membrane, with two paper endleaves (part of the binding, the outer ones marbled matching the backing on the boards) front and back, and a third (lilac) paper endleaf at the front, measuring 222 x 159mm. Written area 150 x 95mm, top line not written on.

Pricking: Prick-marks generally not visible, but occasionally one for the outer vertical frame line can be seen at the bottom of the leaf, e.g., fos 3, 4, 10.

Ruling: In crayon with the single vertical frame lines extending to the edges of the leaves and twenty-eight long horizontal lines between the verticals for twenty-seven lines of writing.

Script: A moderately competent littera antiqua with round (not tall) **s** at the ends of words, a single-compartment **a**, elisions of ligatures such as **be**, **bo**, **ho**, a knot-like ending to descenders (unlike the serifs on ascenders), and there are two forms of ampersand (cp. fo 3r/22 with fo 3r/26 on pl. 16.1); it is not always entirely regular on the line, e.g., fo 3r/22 'tollendum'. Capital **G** and **I** look slightly old-fashioned for the date: e.g., fo 3r/2 'MOCENIGO'.

Ornament: Fo 3r, the first page of the main text (pl. 16.1), shows a continuous illuminated border in gold leaf, decorated with black, blue, green, mauve, red and silver. The border contains two mottoes, written by the illuminator (not the scribe), on the left 'Si priora parua nouissima multiplicentur nimis', and on the right 'CHUPIO RENOVARI'. At the foot of the page there is a section showing two mermen holding the heraldic shield of the noble family to which Pesaro belonged (per pale indented or and azure) on a blue ground surmounted by the motto 'DEDISTI LETITIAM I‹N› CORDE MEO'. The first letter of the text, N in 'NOS' in gold on a blue ground, is illuminated with a crowned figure playing the lyre and the circular motto 'RECTE IVDICATE FILIOS HOMINVM', again, written by the illuminator. Chapter initials alternating in gold with mauve flourishing, and blue with red flourishing, up to fo 15r; on fos 13v, 14r, 14v and after fo 15r paraphs in blue.

COLLATION

I¹² fos 1–12, **II**¹⁶ fos 13–27 (lacks 16).

RECTE IVDICATE FILIOS HOMINVM

NOS IOANNES MOCENIGO DEI GRA DVX VENETIARV &C. COMIT TIMVS tibi NOBILI VIRO NICOLAO DE CHA DE PE SARO DILEC TO CIVI & FIDELI NRO

ituro in bona gratia Capitanee trium galearz ad uiagi um Barbarie. Vt illas mercatores homines & mercinas in eis existentes eundo stando & redeun[do] regere & gub nare debeas. Sicuti pro honore nro & conseruatione r iparum galearum mercatoru & hominu earz ac mer cationum videbis conuenire

Capitolo primo

RAtionem & iustitiam facies inter gente tibi comissa secundum tua discretione bona fide & sine fraude aliquam ad tollendam audatiam & materiam delinqndi homib; galearu tibi comissarum. Comittimus tibi qt quotiens casus aduenerit aliquem de gentib; tibi com issis in aliquib; terris uel locis nre iurisdicioni sub positis & in quib; president nri rectores aliquos ex cessus comittere debeas omne opam dare efficacie ad

DEDISTI LETITIAM I CORDE MEO

Sipriorum parua nouissima

mutaplicentur nimis a

CRVPIO PERO

16.1 RB52, fo 3r, the beginning of the *Commissione*.
Actual page dimensions 222 x 159mm.

CONTENTS

1. Fo iii^r: Note (s.xix), preceded by the number '1069', saying erroneously as far as the contents are concerned: 'These are fragments of Medical | MSS— the penmanship of very | remarkable elegance & beauty. | JHTodd'; James Henthorn Todd (1805–69), Regius Professor of Hebrew, University of Dublin, librarian of Trinity College (1852–69); see above. The lilac paper shows a watermark of Britannia in a three-line oval frame surmounted by a crown.

Fo 1r blank.

2. Fos 1v/1–24r/10: 'Commissione' given by Giovanni Mocenigo (Doge of Venice, 1478–85) to Niccolò da Pesaro 1481 in two parts. Part I, preface and chapters 1–12, 14–24, 26, 28–31, 33–8 in Latin, chapters 13, 25, 27, 32 and part II in Italian (Venetian).

(a) Fos 1v/1–2v/20: List of chapters in red ink begins '1 Q<uod> d<omin>us capetaneus face<re> debeat iustitia<m> i<n>gente<m> S<ib>i <com>missam & o<mn>es | diligentes cu<m> o<mn>i dilige<n>tia assignare'. Ends '38 Q<uod> nullus portare possit de rebus prohibitis p<er> eccl<esia>z | ad infidelium p<ar>tes & de pena illo<rum> q<ui> <con>tra feceri[n]t·'.

(b) Fos 3r/1–24r/10: Main text begins 'NOS IOANNES | MOCENIGO | DEI GR<ATI>A DVX | VENETIAR<UM> | &C. CO<M>MIT|TIMVS TIBI | NOBILI VIR° | NICOLAO DE | CHA DE PE|SARO DILEC|TO CIVI & | FIDELI N<OST>RO | ituro in bona gratia Capitaneo trium galear<um>' (pl. 16.1). Part II begins fo 15r/9 **Mccclxxx. die primo febr<uar>ij In rogatis** | IN Nomine iesu <Christ>i <et> in bona gra<tia> al viago | de barbaria el siano deputade tre galie'. Ends 'Tertia galea deliberata fuit uiro nobili s<ignore> francisco | pizamano <filiu>s petri pro £11 duc<ato> j°. | Finis'.

Fo 24r/18–19 in another hand: 'Dat<um> In m<e>o Ducali palatio Die Secundo m<ensi>s Maij | Indictione xiiij'. Mcccc l xxx^{mo} primo'.

Fos 24r/20–27v/3 no text.

Discussion, with quotations printed by Soave-Bowe and Meek 1978: 28, 30.

3. Fo 27v/4–6: Inscription recording the gift of the manuscript by Dr McCarthy to Maynooth College. 'Presented by Danl MacCarthy | to Maynooth College | March 17 / 1871'.
Fo 27v/7–27 no text.

FRAGMENTS

17 Fragment RB523/1
Image of a Martyr

HISTORY

THIS IMAGE OF A MARTYR (pl. 17.1) is Italian dating from s.xiv[4], probably from Tuscany or Bologna (*ex informatione* Stella Panayotova). It was probably cut from a liturgical manuscript or a Book of Hours. Formerly pasted to a piece of cream cardboard with a typewritten label saying (misleadingly) 'Original leaf from an illuminated manuscript Book of Hours executed in England about 1380'. After the word 'Hours', someone has added in ink '(The Ascension)'. The label looks as though it might date from the 1940–50s, in which case the date of acquisition would probably be s.xx[med]. This date would fit with the date of the donation by Fr Au(gu)stin Hurley mentioned above (p. 86).

CODICOLOGICAL DESCRIPTION

A single membrane fragment measuring (as cut down) 88 x 56mm.

CONTENTS

The martyr shows a golden halo and wears a green robe with fur trim. He is holding a book in his right hand and a palm branch in his left hand, typically representing a martyr. There is no text. No text or image is visible on the verso.

17.1 RB523/1, single fragment of a leaf, showing a martyr.

18 Fragment RB523/2
Book of Hours (extract)

HISTORY

WRITTEN IN A TEXTUALIS semi-quadrata script of s.xv^med in France (pl. 18.1). Probably acquired s.xx^med.

CODICOLOGICAL DESCRIPTION

A single membrane leaf measuring (as trimmed) 184 x 133mm. The written area is 174 x 121mm.

Pricking: None visible as the leaf has been cropped.

Ruling: Very faint in crayon. Twenty lines of text.

Colour and ornament: Ornamental initial letter **D** in pink trimmed with brown and with a brown centre on a blue square ground. The centre shows filigree work in blue and white with flower heads in pink and white, and the outer areas of the blue square ground shows white ornamental frame and scroll work. Two other smaller ornamental capitals in blue, brown and pink. The text area is framed on the three outer sides by a border of fine trailing stems in brown on a natural ground with flowers and leaves in blue, green, red, gold, pale pink and purple.

CONTENTS

1. Fo 1r/1–1v/20: Extract from a Book of Hours, beginning at Prime of the Blessed Virgin Mary, "**Ad prima<m>.**" Begins 'DEus in | adiutoriu<m> meu<m> | intende' [Ps 69]; fo 1r/9 '**ymn<us>** | MEmento salutis auctor'; fo 1r/16 '**an<tiphona>**. Assumpta.'; fo 1r/16 '**p<salmus>** [53] DEus in no<m>i<n>e tuo saluu<m> me fac: et | in virtute tua iudica me'; fo 1r/20 [Ps 53.5] Quonia<m> alieni insurrexeru<n>t', continuing on fo 1v/1 adu<er>sum me'; fo 1v/9 '**psalm<us>** [84] | BEnedixisti d<omi>ne t<er>ram tua<m>', ending incomplete at v.9 'Et sup<er> sanctos'.

19 Fragment RB523/3
Liturgical Psalter (extract)

HISTORY

WRITTEN IN A SOUTHERN textualis formata script s.xiv[3/4], probably from southern France (pl. 19.1). This leaf was probably acquired s.xx[med].

CODICOLOGICAL DESCRIPTION

A single membrane leaf measuring 332 x 238mm. The written area is 256 x 170mm, divided into two columns, each 78mm wide.

Pricking: Single prick-marks are visible at the top for the outer frame rules.

Ruling: Hardpoint in double columns, with thirty-two lines per column.

CONTENTS

1. Fo 1r/a/1–1v/b/32: Extract from a Liturgical Psalter or Breviary. Begins imperf. Ps 118.142 'Iustitia tua iustitia i<n> et<er>|num <et> lex tua u<er>itas'; fo 1r/b/32 Ps 118.166 'ex|pectaba<m> salutare tuu<m>', continued on fo 1v/a/1 'd<omi>ne <et> mandata tua di|lexi'; fo 1v/a/29 Ps 118 ends 'n<on> su<m> oblit<us>'; fo 1v/a/29 'ant<iphona> | Gressus meos d<omi>ne dirige s<ecundum> | eloquiu<m> tuu<m>' [Ps 118.133]; fo 1v/a/31 '**Capitulu<m>** | Alt<er> altius onera portate. | <et> sic adimplebitus lege<m> <Christ>i' [Gal 6.2]; fo 1v/b/2 '**R<esponsa>** Redime me d<omi>ne <et> | mis<erere> mei.' [Ps 25.11]; fo 1v/b/3 '**V<ersus>** Pes m<eu>s stetit in | uia recta' [Ps 25.12]; fo 1v/b/4 '**V<ersus>** Ab occultis m<e>is | munda me d<omine>' [Ps 18.13]; fo 1v/b/5 '**R<esponsa>** Et ab alienis | pa[r]ce s<er>uo tuo.' [Ps 18.14]; fo 1v/b/6 '**a<ntiphona>** Clamaui.'; fo 1v/b/7 Ps 119 (complete) 'AD d<omin>um cum tri|bularer clamaui. <et> exav|diuit me.', ending fo 1v/b/23 'impugnaba<n>t me gra|tis.'; fo 1v/b/23 '**a<ntiphona>** Clamaui <et> exaudiuit | me'; fo 1v/b/24 '**a<ntiphona>** Auxiliu<m> meu<m>' [Ps 120.2]; fo 1v/b/25 Ps 120.1 'LEuaui oculos meos in | montes.', ending incomplete at v.4 'Ecce n<on> dor|mitabit neq<ue> dormiet'.

dne. 7 mandata tua di
lexi. Custodiuit aia mea
testimonia tua. 7 dilexit
ea uehemet. Seruaui man
data tua 7 testimonia tu
a. q2 oes uie mee i ospectu
tuo.
Appropinquet deprecatio
mea i ospectu tuo dne.
iuxta eloquiu tuu da mi
chi intellectu. Intret po
stulatio mea i ospectu tu
o. sedm eloquiu tuu eripe
me. Eructabut labia
mea ymnu. cu docueris
me iustificationes tuas.
Pronuntiabit lingua
mea eloquium tuu: quia
oia mandata tua equita.
Fiat manus tua ut sal
uet me. qm madata tua
elegi. Concupiui saluta
re tuum dne. 7 lex tua me
ditatio mea e. Viuet aia
mea 7 laudabit te. 7 iudi
cia tua adiuuabt me. Er
raui sicut ouis q piit. q
re seruum tuum qz man
data tua ñ su oblit. ant.
Gressus meos dne dirige s3
eloquiu tuu Capitulu.
Si altius onera portate.

7 sic adimplebitis lege
xpi. R. Redime me dne 7
miserere mei. V. Pes mis stetit in
uia recta. V. Ab occultis mis
muda me d. R. Et ab alienis
parce seruo tuo. a. Clamaui.
Ad dñm cum tri
bularer clamaui. 7 exau
diuit me. One libera aia
mea a labiis iniquis. 7 a li
gua dolosa. Quid det ti
bi aut quid apponat ti
bi. ad lingua dolosa. Sa
gitte potentis acute. cu
carbonib; desolatoriis.
Heu michi qa icolatus ms
prolongatus e. habitaui
cum habitantibz cedar. mul
tum incola fuit aia mea.
Cum his qui oderat pace
eram pacificus. cu loqueba
illi impugnabat me gra
tis. a. Clamaui 7 exaudiuit
me. a. Auxiliu meu.
Leuaui oculos meos in
montes. unde ueniet auxi
liu m. Auxiliu meu a
dño. qui fecit celu 7 tra.
Non det i omotioe pedes
tuum. neqz dormiet q
custodit te. Ecce ñ dor
mitabit neqz dormiet

19.1 RB523/3, single leaf from a Liturgical Psalter, showing the verso.

Fragments in bindings

URING THE LATE SIXTEENTH and the seventeenth centuries, if printed books were to be bound, they were often provided with bespoke bindings as required by the purchaser/recipient. In these bindings, 'waste' material such as unwanted manuscript leaves from an earlier period was 'recycled' to lend strength to the binding, or even to provide the cover, membrane being stronger and more durable than paper. Searches for manuscript fragments in the bindings/wrappers of the Russell Library's printed books have taken place from time to time, notably under the auspices of the project called 'Unique to the Book' carried out by Elizabeth Murphy, who succeeded in covering about 60 per cent of the books in the collection, giving priority to the theological volumes. The Russell Library collection is particularly rich in books printed in Spain or having Spanish provenance, following the transfer of the collections in the Irish College at Salamanca to Maynooth in 1951 (Richardson 1995; Woods 1995, p. 59, n. 28), that college itself having acquired many of the books in the other Irish colleges in Spain that had closed previously.

The following books have been identified to date as having bindings containing such fragments of manuscript material, most of such material dating from the fifteenth century. Details of the relevant books are given below under their library class-mark, together with any bibliographical notice of the books concerned in square brackets, so as to provide a platform for analysis. Indications of size (folio etc.) are also given, and of provenance in so far as they are available. There follows a brief description of the nature of the fragment(s), how they are attached to each book, and images are provided to show their scope and content as far as possible. These images also cast incidental light on some early modern binding practices.

20.1 CL.G.6.35a, upper spine.

20 CL.G.6.35a

Pollux, Julius of Naucratis (s.ii), ΙΟΥΙΟΥ ΠΟΛΥΔΕΥΚΟΥΣ ΟΝΟΜΑΣΤΙΚΟΝ ΕΝ ΒΙΒΛΙΟΙΣ ΔΕΚΑ. Julii Pollucis Onomasticon, decem libris constans: ... variis doctorum vivorum lucubrationibus emendatum; Adjecta interpretatio Latina Rudolphi Gualtheri, & Notae, Studio atque opere Wolfgangi Seberi. Frankfurt am Main, Claude de Marne and the heirs of Johann Aubry I of Hanau, 1608. Quarto. [*BLG* P853]

   Two small fragmentary strips of manuscript around the top and bottom of the spine inside a loose white vellum cover (pl. 20.1).

21 F138 (Furlong collection)

Archdekin (= Archdeacon), Richard, SJ, alias McGillacuddy (1619–90),
   Theologia Tripartita Universa. Dillingen, Johann Kaspar Bencard, 1694.
   Quarto. [*BLG* A784]
Thin strip of manuscript material along the inside of the spine (pl. 21.1).

22 H.Sc.7.1.a.b

Buchanan, George (1506–82), *Rerum Scoticarum Historia libris XX*. Frankfurt,
   Johann Wechels, 1582. Octavo. [Adams B3057; CLC B2584]
Bound with:
*Georgii Buchanani Franciscanus et fratres. Elegiarum Liber I. Silvarum Liber
   I. HendecasyllabΩn Liber I. EpigrammatΩn Liber III. De sphaera
   fragmentum.* [Attrib. by BL to Geneva, Pierre de Saint-André], 1584.
   Octavo. [Adams B3053; *CLC* B2578]

22.1 H.Sc.7.1.a.b, back pastedown.

Provenance: Title-page inscribed 'Ed[ward] Reynolds of Braunston [Northants] 1643', who became bishop of Norwich in 1661.

Part of a manuscript leaf or leaves used as a pastedown on the inside of the front and back board covers (pl. 22.1).

23 NT.1.20

Burgos, Pablo de, known as Paul de Santa Maria (*c*.1351–1435), ed. C. Sanctotisius. *Scrutinium Scripturarum*. Burgos, Phelippe Junta, 1591. Folio. [Adams P508; Pettas 2005: no. 570]

23.1 NT.1.20, lower back spine.

24.1 Ph.2.264, upper spine front.

24.2 Ph.2.264, upper spine front, reverse side.

Provenance: Spanish inscription dated 1598.

A fragment of manuscript material (much rubbed) used to strengthen the attachment of the boards to the spine (pl. 23.1).

24 Ph.2.264

Niphus, Eutychius Augustinus (1473–1538), *Augustini Niphi Medicis Philosophi Suessani Expositiones in Omnes Aristotelis Libros*. Venice, Hieronymus Scotus, 1546. Folio.

Provenance: Spanish inscription.

Small fragmentary strips of a manuscript leaf at the top and middle of the spine to hold the book together and attach it to the board covers (pls 24.1, 24.2).

25 Ph.4.223

Francisco de Toledo, SJ (1532–96), *D. Francisci Toleti Societatis Iesu Commentaria una cum Quæstionibus in Tres Libros Aristotelis De Anima*. Cologne, Heirs of Arnold Birckmann, 1576. Quarto.

Provenance: Title-page inscribed 'Es del Colegio Irlandes de Salamanca'.

Four fragmentary strips of manuscript leaf around the spine to hold the book together and strengthen its attachment to the white vellum wrapper (pls 25.1, 25.2).

25.1 Ph.4.223, front endpaper (complete).

25.2 Ph.4.223, back endpaper (mid-section).

26 Ph.4.226

Agricola, Rudolf Huysman, called Rodolphus (1443–85), *Rodolphi Agricolae Phrisii, de inventione dialectica libri tres, cum scholijs Ioannis Matthæi Phrissemij*. Paris, Michel de Vascosan and Pierre Gaudoul, 1533. [Renouard IV (1992), p. 197, no. 558]

Thin strip of a manuscript leaf visible between the spine and the back cover (pl. 26.1).

27 PP.7b

Petramellarius, Joannes Antonius (d. 1623), *Io. Antonii Petramellarii Bononiensis, SS. Mauritij, & Lazari Hierosolymit. Equitis. Ad librum Onuphrii Panuinii De Summis Pontif. et S.R.E. Cardinalibus. A Paulo Quarto ad Clementis Octaui Annum Pontificatus Octauum. Continuatio*. Bologna, Heirs of Giovanni Rossi, 1599. Quarto. [Adams P772; *CLC* P645]

Provenance: Title-page inscribed 'Es del seminario yrlandes de Salamanca'.

Three fragmentary strips of manuscript around the top, the bottom and the lower middle sections of the spine inside a loose white vellum cover (pl. 27.1).

28 RB2

Boniface VIII, Pope (1294–1303), *Liber Sextus Decretalium*. Ed. Giovanni d'Andrea (1270–1348). Strassburg, Johann Reinhard Grüninger, 1491. Folio. [ISTC ib01005000]
Bound with:
Clement V, Pope (1305–14), *Constitutio<n>es Clementinarum*. Ed. Giovanni d'Andrea. Strassburg, Johann Reinhard Grüninger, 1491. Folio. [ISTC ic00735000]

Leaves pasted and bound in to the binding, as follows:

26.1 Ph.4.226/3, inner spine.

27.1 PP.7b, back endpaper.

28.1 RB2, front bifolium.

1. A bifolium pasted on to the inside of the front cover, each leaf measuring 225 x 150/160mm (pl. 28.1)

2. The lower part of a leaf written in two columns pasted on to the inside of the front cover, measuring 157 x 218mm. The leaf has been cut so that some text is lost from the left side of the first column, as well as from the top of the page.

2a. Another leaf, post-medieval, containing a papal letter, inserted at the front, of which there is a typed transcript at the back.

3. A bifolium pasted at the bottom to the inside of the back cover, each leaf measuring 210 x 161mm (pl. 28.2)

4. A leaf containing musical notation pasted at the top of the inside of the back cover, partly under no. 3.

5. Another bifolium on the inside of the back cover, much rubbed, also partly under no. 3.

28.2 RB2, back bifolium.

29 RB8a

Duns Scotus, Johannes (1265–1308), *Questiones subtilissime Scoti in metaphysicam Aristotelis*. Ed. Mauritius de Portu Hibernicus. Venice, Johannes Hamman, for Andreas Torresanus de Asula, 1499. Quarto. [ISTC id00373000]

Provenance: Ecclesiastical armorial bookplate of Sergius Sersale.
    Part of a manuscript leaf used for the outside binding glued to a card backing (pl. 29.1).

29.1 RB8a, front cover.

31.1 TD.3.20, lower spine.

30 Sc.17.46.1.2

Gemma, Frisius, Reinerus (1508–55), *Arithmeticae Practicae Methodus facilis.* Ed. Jacques Peletier (1517–82). Paris, Guillaume Cavellat, 1550. Octavo.

Strips of manuscript to hold the boards to the spine, plus parts of leaves glued to the insides of the board covers (pl. 30.1).

30.1 Sc.17.46.1.2, back cover.

31 TD.3.20

Francisco à Christo Eremita (*fl.* 1561–81), *Praelectionum, sive Enarrationum Admirabilis Divini Verbi Incarnationis. Libri sex.* Coimbra, Johannes Alvares, 1564. [Thomas 1940, p. 9]

Impressions of strips of a manuscript leaf used to hold the book together (pl. 31.1).

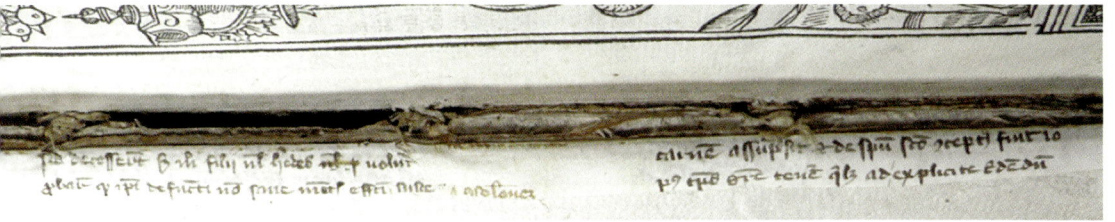

32.1 Th.5.1173, inner spine (front).

32.2 Th.5.1173, inner spine (back).

32 Th.5.1173

Richard of St Victor (d. 1173), *Omnia Opera in unum volumen congesta ... diligentia emendata ... nunc primum parrisiis impressa*. Paris, Jean Petit 1501? Folio. [*CLC* R393]

Bound with:

Thomas de Perseigne (d. *c.*1190) and Jean Algrin (1180–1237), *Cantica canticorum cum duobus Co<m>mentariis plane egregiis, altero venerabilis patris F. Thome Cistertien<sis> Monachi: altero lo<n>ge reuerendi Cardinalis M Ioa<n>nis Halgrini ab Abbatisuilla*. Paris, Josse Bade, 1521 (explicit on fo clxxx^r). Folio. [Renouard 1969, II.198, no. 469]

And:

Mercurius, Johannes, Corigiensis [lacks tp: *Exhortationes in Barbaros, Thurcos, Scithas Johannis Mercurii corigiensis perornate*]. Lyon, Claude Davost, 1501. Folio. [Gültlingen 1993, p. 15, no. 2]

Provenance: Title-page inscribed 'Ex libris Antonij Pinati'.

Very thin strips of manuscript along the inside of the front and back covers of the binding of white vellum on card (pls 32.1, 32.2).

33 Th.5.1274 (vol. I)

Thomas Aquinas, St (1225–74), *Scriptum Sancti Thome de Aquino super Primo Sententiarum*. Ed. Cornelio Sambuco Veronensis OP. Venice, Heirs of Ottaviano Scoto of Monza, 1514. Folio.
Bound with:
Thomas Aquinus, St, *Scriptum Sancti Thome de Aquino super secundo Sententiarum*. Ed. Cornelio Sambuco Veronensis OP. Venice, Heirs of Ottaviano Scoto, 1520. Folio.
And:
Thomas Aquinas, St, *Quodlibetales questiones Sancti Thome*. Venice, Heirs of Ottaviano Scoto, 1525. Folio.

Provenance: Title-page inscribed 'Es de la Comp‹añi›a de Jh‹esu›s de Sal‹amanc›a'.

Th.5.1274 (vol. II):

Thomas Aquinus, St, *Divi Thome Aquinatis in tertio sententiaru‹m›*. Ed. Timotheus Maffei Veronensis (1400–70). Venice, Heirs of Ottaviano Scoto, 1518. Folio.
Bound with:
Thomas Aquinus, St, *Sanctus Thomas de Aquino super quartum librum magistri sententia‹rum› nouissime recognitus*. Venice, Giorgio Arrivabene for the heirs of Ottaviano Scoto, 1514.

Provenance: Title-page inscribed 'Es del collegio [*sic*] de la Comp‹añi›a de Jesus de Sal‹amanc›a'.
[Dates of publication are stated on vol. I, pt i, fo 147v, pt ii, fo 150v, pt iii, fo 60r, and on vol. II, fo 264.]
   Manuscript fragments in strips 5 cm wide attached to the spine along the inside of the covers of the white vellum binding (pls 33.1, 33.2).

34 Th.5.1549

Bunderius, Joannes OP (1482–1557), *Compendium Concertationis, huius seculi sapientium ac theologorum, super erroribus moderni temporis*. Paris, Vivant Gaulterot, 1549. Octavo. [*CLC* B2726]
   A single strip from a manuscript leaf inside the back cover with writing on both sides (pl. 34.1).

33.1 Th.5.1274, front endpaper (vol. I).

33.2 Th.5.1274, upper spine (vol. 2).

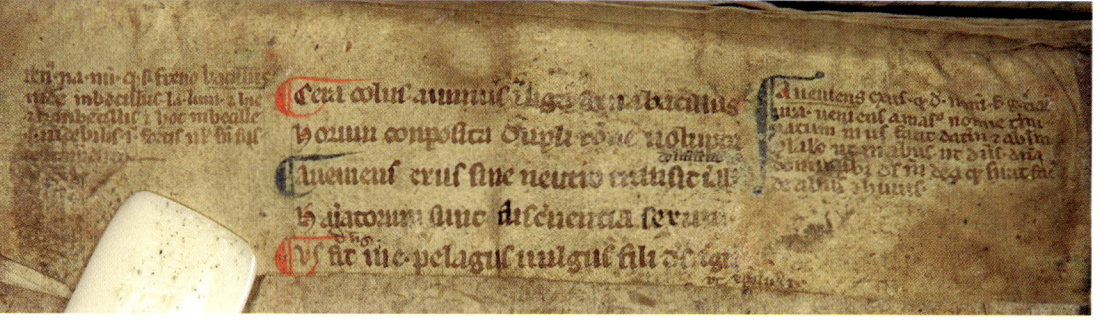

34.1 Th.5.1549, back endpaper (verso).

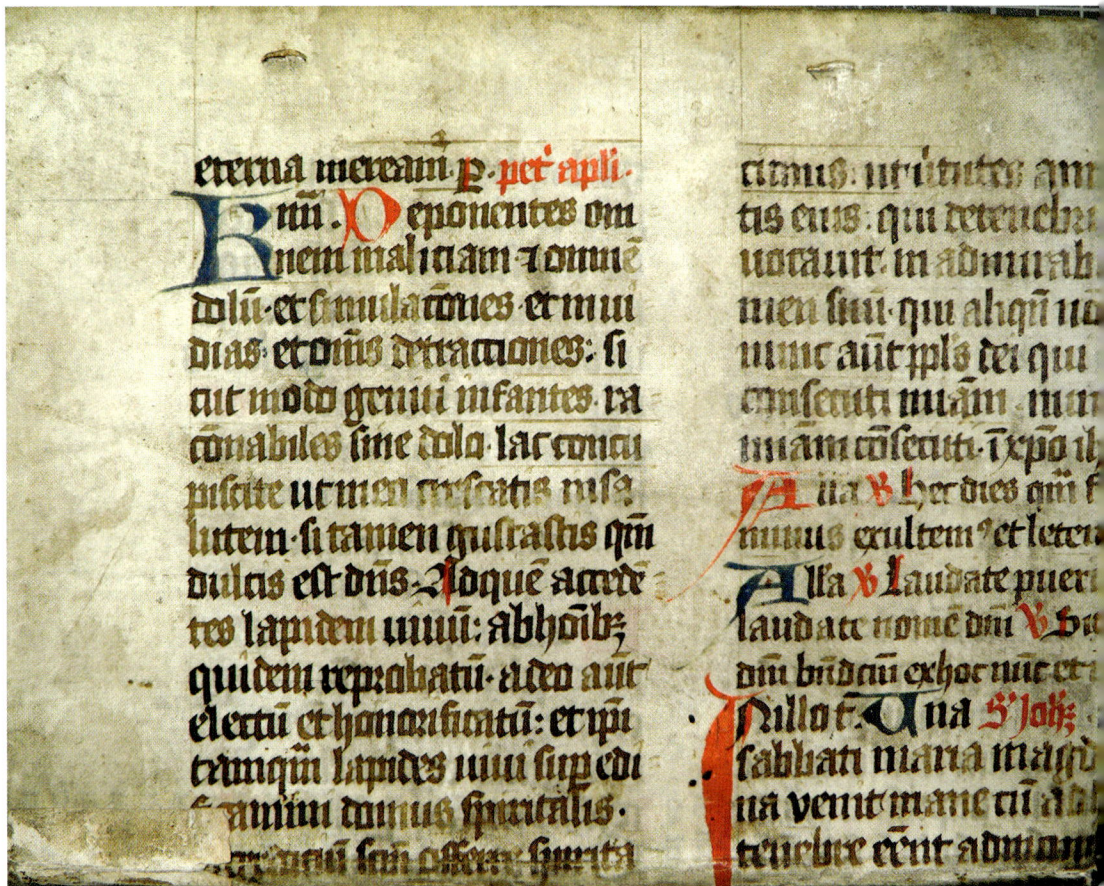

35.1 Th.5.1601, front cover.

35 Th.5.1601

Thyraeus, Petrus (1546–1601), *Daemoniaci cum Locis Infestis et terriculamentis nocturnis*. Cologne, 'Materni' Cholinus and Goswin Cholinus, 1604. [*BLG* T455]

Provenance: Title-page inscription dated 1696.
    Part of a manuscript leaf has been used for the binding on card (pl. 35.1).

36 Th.5.1603

Gregorius de Valentia SJ (1550–1603), *De Reali Christi Praesentia in Eucharistia, et de transubstantiatione Panis et Vini in Corpus et Sanguinem Christi, Libri Tres*. Ingolstadt, David Sanctorius, 1587. Quarto.

Provenance: Title-page inscribed 'Pro. Conv. Salisburg FF. Min. Strict. Observ.', i.e., the Franciscan house at Salzburg (Austria).
    Part of a manuscript leaf (backed with paper) used for the binding (pl. 36.1).

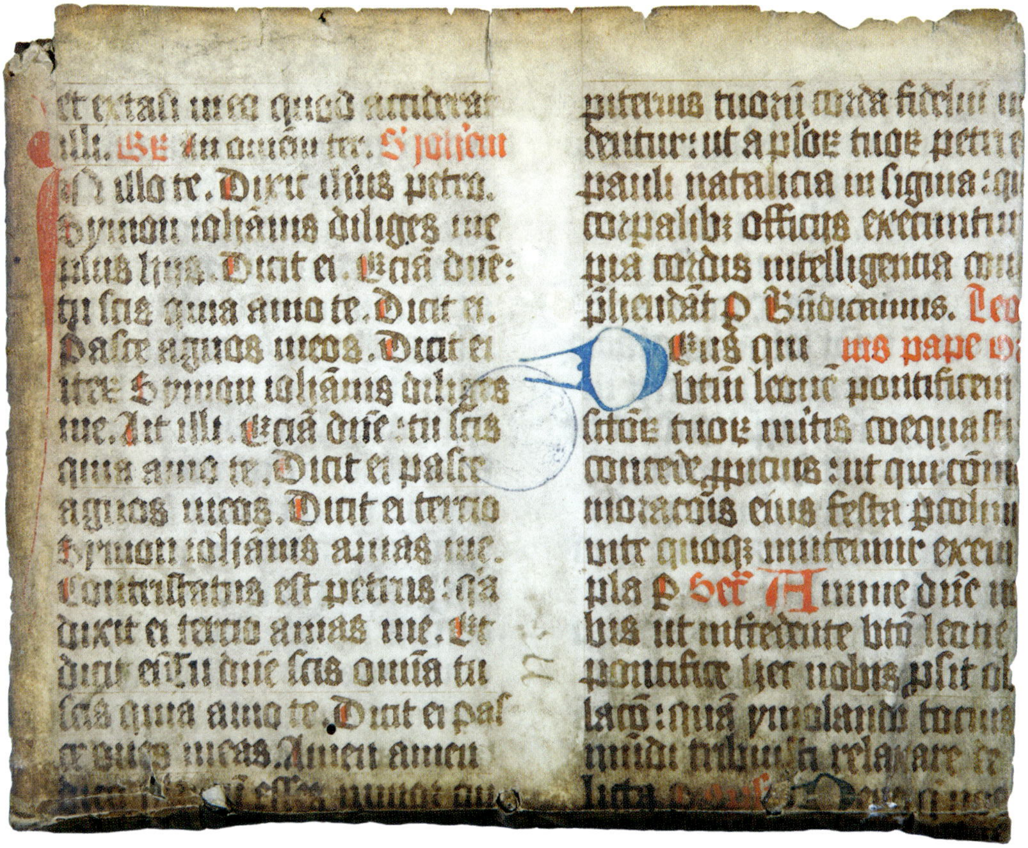

[manuscript leaf image — Latin liturgical/theological text in Gothic script, two columns, with coloured initials]

37 TM.6.1546

36.1 Th.5.1603, front cover.

Codex de penitentia per doctorem de Medina sacre Theologie professorem, in Complutensi Universitate editus. Alcalá de Henares (= Complutum), Juan de Brocar for Athanasius a Salzedo, 1547. Folio.
Bound with:
Codex de Restitutione et co‹n›tractibus. Ed. Juan de Medina (1490–1546). Alcalá de Henares, Juan de Brocar, 1546. Folio.
And:
Pizarro, Diego, *Tratado nueuamente hecho sobre los ce‹n›sos al quitar a manera de glosa de las extravagantes de los po‹n›tifices Martino quinto y Calixto tertio.* Guadelupe, Francisco Diaz Romano, 1548. Folio.

Provenance: Title-page inscribed 'Colegio de Nobles Irlandeses Salamanca'.
    Five small scraps of manuscript material (3 with writing at the front, only 2 at the back) inside the front and back covers of white vellum (pls 37.1, 37.2).

37.1 TM.6.1546, front endpaper (complete).

37.2 TM.6.1546, front endpaper (detail).

38 TP.2.128

Vincent Ferrer OP, St (1350–1419), vol. I: *Beati Vincentii … Sermones Æstiuales, eisdem … per Damianum Diaz … Adnotationes in margine accesserunt*. Vol. II: *Beati Vincentii … Sermones Hyemales Eisdem … per Damianum Diaz … Adnotationes in margine accesserunt*. Antwerp, Philip Nutius, 1570. Octavo. [*BT* no. 7114]

Strips of manuscript material along the spine inside the front and back covers of white vellum on card; both vols (pl. 38.1).

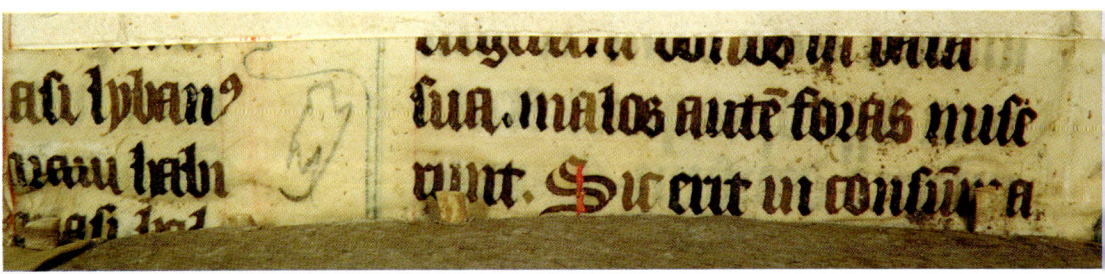

38.1 TP.2.128, back binding (vol. 1).

Appendix

EXTRACTS FROM THE WILL of the Very Reverend Dr Laurence Renehan (1797–1857), president of Maynooth College

> 'I bequeath to the Trustees of the College of Maynooth the sum of one hundred pounds sterling to be applied in the purchase of manuscripts, or books treating or illustrative of the history of the Roman Catholic Church in Ireland, for the use of the Library of said College, or in lieu thereof, at the option of said Trustees, I bequeath to them my set of manuscripts known as 'The O'Renehan MSS' together with such other of my manuscripts and rare books illustrative of the history of the Roman Catholic Church in Ireland as the Revd Dr Russell of Maynooth College may select, so however that the manuscripts and books selected by him shall not together with the said O'Renehan MSS exceed in the estimation of the said revd Dr Russell the value of two hundred pounds.'

The list includes: Item 42 'Breviarum Romanum M.S. Saec XV'. See the entry for no. 6 (RB31) above, pp 87–96. When he died, after the relevant selections had been made, Dr Renehan's books were put in an auction sale:

Bibliotheca Renehaniana: Catalogue of the rare, valuable and extensive library of the late Very Reverend Dr Renehan ... which will be sold by auction, by H. Lewis ... 31 Anglesea Street ... November 2nd, 1857. Dublin, 1857. Copy in TCD at Gall.6.k.29, another copy in the Russell Library with prices and buyers written in by hand.

Of the 1,842 lots, none were manuscripts. Some of his printed books may have found their way back into the college library, but identification can be difficult because he did not always inscribe his books.

Bibliography

[Adam of Adersback (Alderspacensis)], *Summula clarissimi iuris consultissimique viri Raymundi* [de Peñafort] *demum reuisa ac castigatissime correcta breuissimo compendio sacramentorum alta complectens mysteria*. [Paris, Jean Poitevin, n.d. *c.*1500]. Proctor 1898: no. 8376. [RB47]

Adams, H.M., *Catalogue of books printed on the continent of Europe, 1501–1600, in Cambridge libraries* (Cambridge, 1967).

Ainsworth, Sir John, 'Report on the non-Gaelic MSS in Maynooth College', unpublished typescript, 1973, on deposit in the Russell Library, St Patrick's College Collection, Maynooth.

Albanés, [J.H.], 'Deux archevêques d'Aix qui n'en font qu'un seul et un autre archevêque qui en fait deux', *Bulletin du Comité des Travaux Historiques et Scientifiques* (Section Histoire et Archéologie) 1883¹, 87–132. [RB74]

Albanés, [J.H.], 'Inventaire du trésor de l'église métropolitaine d'Aix au commencement du XVIe siècle', *Bulletin du Comité des Travaux Historiques et Scientifiques* (Section Histoire et Archéologie) 1883², 149–76. [RB74]

Albanés, [J.H.], *Aix*, in *Catalogue général des manuscrits des bibliothèques publiques de France*, n.s. xvi (Paris, 1894). [RB74]

Albanés, J.H., *Gallia Christiana Novissima: histoire des archevêchés, évêchés & abbayes de France*, vol. 1 (Montbéliard, 1899). [RB74]

Andrieu, Michel, *Le pontifical romain au moyen-age* I : *Le pontificale romain du XIIe siècle*, Studi e Testi 86 (Città del Vaticano, 1938). [RB36]

Andrieu, Michel, *Le pontifical romain au moyen-age* II : *Le pontificale de la curie romaine au XIIIe siècle*, Studi e Testi 87 (Città del Vaticano, 1940¹). [RB74]

Andrieu, Michel, *Le pontifical romain au moyen-age* III : *Le pontifical de Guillaume Durand*, Studi e Testi 88 (Città del Vaticano, 1940²). [RB74]

Andrieu, Michel, *Les ordines romani du haut moyen âge*, Spicilegium Sacrum Lovaniense 11 (Louvain, 1931). [RB36]

Attwater, Donald, *The Penguin dictionary of saints*, 3rd ed. with Catherine Rachel John (London, 1995).

Augustinus, Antonius, *Opera Omnia*, 8 vols (Lucca, Joseph Rocchius, 1769). Vol. IV contains *Antiquae Collectiones Decretalium* with Augustinus' notes. [RB29]

Balau, Sylvain, 'La bibliothèque de l'abbaye de Saint-Jacques, à Liège', *Bulletin de la Commission Royale d'Histoire de Belgique* 71 (1902), 1–61, 226.

Barraclough, Geoffrey, *Public notaries and the papal curia* (London, for the British School at Rome, 1934. [RB47]

Becdelièvre, Comte de, *Biographie Liègeoise*, 2 vols (Liège, Imprimerie de Jeunehomme Frères, 1836–7).

Bede: *Venerabilis Bedae Presbyteri Anglo-Saxonis viri sua ætate doctissimi Opera*, 8 vols (Cologne, Sumptibus Anton. Hierati et Ioan. Gymnici, 1612). [*Bedae Opera* 1612]

Beichner, P.E., CSC, 'Cantica Canticorum B. Marie', *Marianum* 21 (1959), 6–15. [RB47]

Berlière, Dom Ursmer, 'La sécularisation de l'abbaye de Saint-Jacques a Liège (1785)', *RB*, 33 (1921), 173–89, 34 (1922), 46–66, 109–18. [Account of sale of Liège books at pp 55–61]

Berlière, Dom Ursmer, *Monasticon Belge*, II : *Province de Liège* (Abbaye de Maredsous, 1928).

Biblia Sacra Vulgatae Editionis Sixti V Pont. Max. iussu recognita et Clementis VIII auctoritate edita (Vatican, 1965).

Bischoff, Bernhard, 'Über gefaltete Handschriften, vornehmlich hagiographischen Inhalts' in his collected *Mittelalterliche Studien: ausgewählte Aufsätze zur Schriftkunde und Literaturgeschichte*, 3 vols (Stuttgart, 1966–81), I.93–100. [RB47F]

Bohatta, Hanns, *Bibliographie der Livres d'Heures ... des XV. und XVI. Jahrhunderts* (Vienna, 1924). [RB39]

Bollandists, Society of, *Bibliotheca Hagiographica Latina*, 2 vols + 2 supplements (latest by Hendrik Fros), Subsidia Hagiographica 6 (2 vols), 12, and 70 (Brussels 1900–1, 1911, 1986). BHL

Bollandus, Joannes, *Acta Sanctorum*, 68 vols (Antwerp, 1643–1940). [*ActaSS*]

Bonaventura, St, *Legenda Maior et Legenda Minor S. Francisci*, Analecta Franciscana 10.5, Coll. S. Bonaventurae (Quaracchi-Firenze, 1941).

Bonaventura, St, *Opera ... diligentissime emendata*, vol. VI (Mainz, 1609). [RB29]

Bouxhon, Nicolas, 'Summa Omnium quae in Inferiori Bibliotheca Sti Jacobi continentur ordine quidem alphabetico', unpublished handwritten catalogue of books *c.*1667 from St Jacques, Liège, in: Brussels, Bibliothèque Royale, Collection Générale, MS no. 13993.

Briquet, C.-M., *Les filigranes: dictionnaire historique des marques du papier dès leur apparition vers 1282 jusqu'en 1600*, ed. Allan Stevenson (Amsterdam, 1968). [RB29]

Burke, Sir Bernard, *A genealogical and heraldic history of the landed gentry of Ireland* (London, 1899). [RB38]

Burke, Sir Bernard, *The general armory of England, Scotland, Ireland and Wales* (London, 1884, repr. 1961). [RB31]

Burn, A.E., *The hymn Te Deum and its author* (London, 1926). [RB36]

Cabié, Robert, 'Le pontifical de Guillaume Durand l'ancien et les livres liturgiques languedociens', *Cahiers de Fanjeaux* 17 (1982), 225–37. [RB74]

Capelli, Adriano, *Cronologia, Cronografia e Calendario Perpetuo dal Principio dell'Èra Cristiana ai nostri Giorni*, 6th ed. (Milan, 1988).

Capelli, Adriano, *Dizionario de Abbreviature Latine ed Italiane* (Milan, 1961). Supplemented by Pelzer 1964.

Chalandon, Anne, 'La bibliothèque de la cathédrale d'Aix à la fin du moyen-âge à travers trois inventaires inédits (1380, 1404 et 1407)', *Provence Historique*, 43 (1993), 35–60. [RB74]

Chevalier, Ulysse, *Repertorium Hymnologicum*, 6 vols, Subsidia Hagiographica 4 (Louvain and Brussels, 1892–1920).

Colker, M.L., *Trinity College Library Dublin, descriptive catalogue of the mediaeval and Renaissance Latin manuscripts*, 2 vols (Aldershot, for TCD Library, 1991).

Corish, P.J., *Maynooth College, 1795–1995* (Dublin, 1995).

Cottineau, L.H., OSB, *Répertoire topo-bibliographique des abbayes et prieurés*, 3 vols (Macon, 1939–70).

Coulet, Noël, 'Bibliothèques aixoises du XVᵉ siècle (1433–1488)' in *Livres et Bibliothèques (XIIIᵉ-XVᵉ Siècle)*, Cahiers de Fanjeaux 31 (Toulouse, 1996), pp 209–39. [RB74]

Culot, Paul, and Claude Sorgeloos, *Quatre siècles de reliure en Belgique, 1500–1900*, 3 vols (Brussels, 1989–98). [Includes many examples of Belgian bindings, including some from eighteenth-century Liège, but none match the RB16, 45, 46 group.]

Daris, Joseph, *Notices sur les églises du diocèse de Liège*, 4:2 (Liège, 1871).

D'Avray, D.L., 'Portable vademecum books containing Franciscan and Dominican texts' in *Manuscripts at Oxford: an exhibition in memory of Richard William Hunt on themes selected and described by his friends*, ed. A.C. de la Mare and B.C. Barker-Benfield (Oxford, 1980), pp 60–4. [RB29, 31]

Daur, K.-D., *Sancti Aurelii Augustini Contra Adversarium Legis et Prophetarum*, CCSL 49 (Turnhout, 1985). [RB71]

De Hamel, C.F.R., *Glossed books of the Bible and the origins of the Paris booktrade* (Woodbridge, 1984).

De Hamel, C.F.R., *A history of illuminated manuscripts* (Oxford, 1986, 2nd ed. 1994).

Dekkers, Eligius, *Clavis Patrum Latinorum*, Sacris Erudiri 3 (Bruges, 1961).

Deshusses, Jean, *Le sacramentaire grégorien*, Spicilegium Friburgense 16 (Freiburg, 1971). [RB36]

Distelbrink, Balduinus, *Bonaventurae Scripta Authentica Dubia vel Spuria Critice Recensita*, Subsidia Scientifica Franciscalia 5 (Rome, 1975). [RB29]

Dove, Mary (trans.), *The Glossa Ordinaria on The Song of Songs* (Kalamazoo, MI, 2004). [RB47]

Dove, Mary, *Glossa Ordinaria Pars 22 In Canticum Canticorum*, CCCM 170 (Turnhout, 1997). [RB47]

Dreves, G.M., Clemens Blume and Henry M. Bannister, *Analecta Hymnica Medii Aevi*, 55 vols (Leipzig, 1886–1922). *Register*, ed. Max Lütolf, 3 vols (Bern, 1978). [AH]

[Edwards, Thomas], *A catalogue of the splendid and valuable collection of books, manuscripts and missals, the property of Thomas Edwards, esq. (late of Halifax,*

Yorkshire) ... : which will be sold by auction ... on Thursday, May 15th, 1828, and five following days (Sunday excepted) (London, 1828). [RB31]

Eizenhöfer, Leo, and Herman Knaus, *Die Liturgischen Handschriften der Hessischen Landes- und Hochschulbibliothek Darmstadt*. Vol. 2 of *Die Handschriften der Hessischen Landes- und Hochschulbibliothek Darmstadt* (Wiesbaden, 1968). [Includes Liège MSS now at Darmstadt]

Eubel, Conrad, *Hierarchia Catholica Medii Aevi*, vols 1–3 (Münster, 1913). [RB16]

Fairbairn, James, *Fairbairn's crests of the families of Great Britain and Ireland* (Rutland, Vermont, 1968). [RB31]

Falletti, L., 'Guillaume Durand', *Dictionnaire de Droit Canonique*, 5 (1953), cols 1014–75, with a notice of the Pontifical at cols 1060–1. [RB74]

Fischer, Bonifatius, *Novae Concordantiae Bibliorum Sacrorum iuxta Vulgatam Versionem critice editam*, 5 vols (Stuttgart-Bad Cannstatt, 1977).

Fowler, G.B., 'A new dedicatory preface to the commentary on Ps 118 by Engelbert of Admont', *RTAM*, 29 (1962), 306–12. [RB16]

Fowler, G.B., 'Additional notes on manuscripts of Engelbert of Admont (*c*.1250–1331)', *RTAM* 28 (1961), 269–82, esp. 275–6, no. 19, where other MSS (possibly) containing the text are listed. [RB16]

Fowler, G.B., 'Manuscript Admont 608 and Engelbert of Admont (*c*.1250–1331)', *Archives d'Histoire Doctrinale et Littéraire du Moyen Age* 44 (1977), 149–242. [RB16]

Fowler, G.B., 'Manuscripts of Engelbert of Admont (chiefly in Austrian and German libraries)', *Osiris* 11 (1954), 455–85, esp. 484–5, no. 73, where nine other MSS and two fragments are listed. [RB16]

Fowler, G.B., 'Some autographs of Engelbert of Admont' in *Festschrift W. Sas-Zaloziecky* [= Vladimir Romanovitch Zalozetsky] *zum 60. Geburtstag* (Graz, 1956), pp 60–7, esp. pp 61–2, 64. [RB16]

Fowler, G.B., *Intellectual interests of Engelbert of Admont* (New York, 1947, repr. 1967), esp. pp 202–3, no. 30, where six other MSS are listed. [RB16]

Friedberg, E.[A.], *Quinque Compilationes Antiquae nec non Collectio Canonum Lipsiensis*. Leipzig, Tauchnitz 1882, pp 1–65. [RB29]

Friedberg, E.A., *Die Canonen-Sammlungen zwischen Gratian und Bernhard von Pavia* (Leipzig, 1897). [RB29]

Froehlich, Karlfried, and M.T. Gibson (intr.), *Biblia Latina cum Glossa Ordinaria: Facsimile reprint of the Editio Princeps by Adolph Rusch of Strassburg, 1480/1*, 4 vols (Turnhout, 1992).

Giordano, Céline, 'Autour des cathédrales provençales: les livres et les bibliothèques (fin XIIIᵉ siècle–1530)', PhD, Université Aix-Marseille 1 (Université de Provence) 2005. [RB74]

Grégoire, Réginald, *Bruno de Segni: exégète médiéval et théologien monastique*, Centro Italiano de Studi sull'alto medioevo 3 (Spoleto, 1965). [RB46]

Griggs, William, *147 examples of armorial book plates: from various collections*, 2nd ser. (London, 1892).

Gültlingen, Sybille von, *Bibliographie des livres imprimés à Lyon au seizième siècle*, vol. II, Bibliotheca Bibliographica Aureliana CXLI (Baden-Baden, 1993). [FB32]

Gy, P.-M., OP, *Guillaume Durand, évêque de Mende (v.1230–1296) canoniste, liturgiste et homme politique* (Paris, 1992). [RB74]

Hamell, P.J., *Maynooth students and ordinations: index, 1795–1895* (Birr, Co. Offaly, 1982).

Harris, B.E., C.P. Lewis and Alan Thacker, *A history of the county of Chester*, Victoria County History of England (London, 1987–). [RB31]

Hauréau, B., *Notices et extraits de quelques manuscrits latins de la Bibliothèque Nationale*, 6 vols (Paris, 1890–3), repr. in 3 vols (Farnborough, 1967).

Healy, John, *Maynooth College: its centenary history* (Dublin, 1895).

Herscher, Irenneus, OFM, 'A bibliography of Alexander of Hales', *Franciscan Studies*, 26 (= n.s. 5, 1945), 435–54. [RB16]

Hoyaux, J., *Inventaire des manuscrits de la bibliothèque de l'université de Liège. Manuscrits acquis de 1886 à 1960* (Liège, 1970).

Hughes, Andrew, *Medieval manuscripts for Mass and Office: a guide to their organization and terminology* (Toronto, 1995 ed.).

Jähnig, Bernhart, *Johann von Wallenrode OT*. Quellen und Studien zur Geschichte des deutschen Ordens 24 (Bonn-Godesberg, 1970). [RB16]

Janssens, Herman, 'Notice sur un manuscrit de Saint Augustin provenant de l'ancienne abbaye de Saint-Jacques à Liège', *Le Musée Belge* 30 (1926), 137–44.

Jiroušková, Lenka, 'Textual evidence for the transmission of the *Passio Olavi* prior to 1200 and its later literary transformations' in *Saints and their lives on the periphery: Veneration of saints in Scandinavia and eastern Europe (c.1000–1200)*, ed. Haki Antonsson and I.H. Garipzanov (Turnhout, 2010), pp 219–39. [RB519]

Jullien de Pomerol, M.-H., 'Les livres dans les Dépouilles des Prélats Méridionaux' in *Livres et Bibliothèques (XIIIe–XVe siècle)*, Cahiers de Fanjeaux 31 (Toulouse, 1996), 285–314. [RB74]

Jullien de Pomerol, M.-H., *Bibliothèques ecclésiastiques au temps de la papauté d'Avignon*, vol. 2, Documents, Études et Répertoires publiés par l'Institut de Recherche et d'Histoire des Textes 61 (Paris, 2001), no. 348.54 at pp 247–54. [RB74]

Kelly, J.N.D., *The Athanasian Creed* (London, 1964).

Kelly, J.N.D., *The Oxford dictionary of popes* (Oxford, 1986).

Kennedy, Máire, 'Foreign language books, 1700–1800' in Raymond Gillespie and Andrew Hadfield (eds), *The Irish book in English, 1550–1800* (Oxford, 2006), pp 368–82.

Kennedy, Patrick, *Kennedy's Book of arms*, originally published as *Sketches collected chiefly from the records in Ulster's Office and other authentic documents* (1816) (Canterbury, 1967). [RB38]

Knaus, Hermann, *see* Staub.

Korteweg, A.S., 'The masters of Otto van Moerdrecht and followers, *ca.* 1420–55' in H.L.M. Defoer, A.S. Korteweg and W.C.M. Wüstefeld, *The golden age of Dutch manuscript painting*, intr. James H. Marrow (New York, 1990), pp 75–88. [RB37]

Kuttner, Stephan, *Repertorium der Kanonistik (1140–1234)*, Studi e Testi 71 (Città del Vaticano, 1937). [RB47]

Lacombe, Paul, *Livres d'heures imprimés au XVᵉ et au XVIᵉ siècle conservés dans les bibliothèques publiques de Paris : catalogue* (Paris, 1907). [RB39]

Lambot, Cyril, 'Le Sermon XLVI de Saint Augustin *De Pastoribus*', *RB* 63 (1953), 165–210. [RB71]

Lambot, Cyrillus, OSB, *Sancti Aurelii Augustini Sermones De Veteri Testamento id est Sermones I–L*, CCSL 41 (Turnhout, 1961). [RB71]

Lapière, M.-R., *La lettre ornée dans les manuscrits mosans d'origine bénédictine (XIe–XIIe siècles)*, Bibliothèque de la Faculté de Philosophie et Lettres de l'Université de Liège 229 (Paris, 1981). [RB46]

Lépine, André, *600 Devises ecclésiastiques belges* (Cerfontaine, 1973).

Leroquais, V[ictor], *Les bréviaires manuscrits des bibliothèques publiques de France* (Paris, 1934).

Leroquais, V[ictor], *Les livres d'heures manuscrits de la Bibliothèque Nationale et supplément*, 4 vols (Paris, 1927–43).

Leroquais, V[ictor], *Les pontificaux manuscrits des bibliothèques publiques de France*, vol. 1 (Paris, 1937). [RB74]

Liège: St Jacques, Benedictine abbey at; for list of books, see Bouxhon, Montfaucon, Mortiaux-Denoël, Paquot.

Little, A.G., *Initia Operum Latinorum quae saeculis xiii. xiv. xv. attribuuntur* (Manchester, 1904).

Lucas, A.M., and P.J. Lucas, 'Lost and found: some manuscripts from Liège now in Maynooth', *Scriptorium* 58 (2004), 83–99.

Lucas, P.J., 'Un nouveau manuscrit daté : le Bénédictionnaire d'Armand de Narcès, archevêque d'Aix-en-Provence (1329–48), retrouvé à Maynooth en Irlande', *Scriptorium* 64 (2010), 120–6. [RB74]

Macaulay, Ambrose, *Dr Russell of Maynooth* (London, 1983).

Marbot, E., *Catalogue historial des sanctuares & établissements religieux d'Aix depuis l'évangelisation jusqu'à l'an 1900* (Aix, 1913). [RB74]

Marbot, E., *La liturgie aixoise: étude bibliographique et historique* (Aix, 1899). Description of Aix Bibliothèque Méjanes MS 13 at pp 38–41. [RB74]

Martène, Edmond, and Ursin Durand, *Voyage Littéraire de deux religieux bénédictins de la congrégation de Saint-Maur*, 2 vols (Paris, 1717–24).

Martène, Edmond, *De Antiquis Ecclesiæ Ritibus Libri Tres*, 2 vols (Antwerp, 1763–4). [RB74]

Moeller, Edmond, *Corpus Benedictionum Pontificalium*, 4 vols, CCSL 162, 162A, 162B, 162C (Turnhout, 1971–9). [RB74]

Moeller, Eugène (Edmond), 'Liber Benedictionum Pontificalium de Guillaume Durand évêque de Mende (composé entre 1280 et 1290)', *Questions Liturgiques et Paroissiales* 49 (1968), 12–42, 115–36. [RB74]

Mohan, G.E., 'Initia operum Franciscalium (XIII–XV S.)', *Franciscan Studies* 38 (1978), 377–498. [RB31]

Montfaucon, Bernardus de, *Bibliotheca Bibliothecarum Manuscriptorum Nova* (Paris, 1739), II, 1348–50. [Select list of books at Liège, St Jacques]

Moody, T.W., and W.E. Vaughan, *A new history of Ireland*, IV: *Eighteenth-century Ireland, 1691–1800* (Oxford, 1986).

Mortiaux-Denoël, Christine (with Étienne Guillaume), 'Le fonds des manuscrits de l'abbaye (de) Saint-Jacques de Liège', *RB*, 101 (1991), 154–91, and 107 (1997), 352–80.

Mutzenbecher, Almut, *Sancti Aurelii Augustini De Diversis Quaestionibus Octoginta Tribus*, CCSL 49A (Turnhout, 1975). [RB71]

Mynors, R.A.B., ed., *P. Vergili Maronis Opera* (Oxford, 1969). [RB29]

Mynors, R.A.B., ed., *Virgil Georgics* (Oxford, 1990). [RB29]

Neligan, Agnes, 'The library: looking back, 1995–1800' in Neligan, *Maynooth Library*, pp 3–28.

Neligan, Agnes, *Maynooth Library: treasures from the collections of Saint Patrick's College* (Dublin, 1995).

Newman, Jeremiah, *Maynooth and Georgian Ireland* (Galway, 1979).

Ó Fiannachta, Pádraig, *Lámhscribhinni Gaeilge Choláiste Phádraig, Má Nuad*, fasc. 2–8 (Maynooth, 1965–73). Continuation of Walsh, *Catalogue of Irish manuscripts*.

Oliver, Judith, 'The *Crise Bénédictine* and revival at the abbey of St Jacques in Liège, *c.*1300', *Quaerendo* 8 (1978), 320–36.

Pächt, Otto, and J.J.G. Alexander, *Illuminated manuscripts in the Bodleian Library, Oxford*, 3 vols (Oxford, 1966–73). [RB52]

Papworth, J.W., *An alphabetical dictionary of coats of arms belonging to families in Great Britain and Ireland* (London, 1874, repr. [1961]). [RB31]

Paquot, J.-N., 'Catalogue de livres de la bibliothèque de la célèbre ex-abbaye de St-Jacques à Liège, dont la vente se fera publiquement au plus offrant, sur les cloitres de laditte ex-abbaye, le 3 mars 1788 et jours suivans, à 2 heures précises de relevée', unpublished printed sale catalogue prepared prior to sale of books from St Jacques, Liège, beginning 3 Mar. 1788, in: Brussels, Bibliothèque Royale, Fonds Van Hulthem, MS no. 22595. See also Liège.

Pearson, David, *Provenance research in book history: a handbook* (London, 1994).

Pe[t]z, Bernardus, and Philibertus Hueber, *Codex Diplomatico-Historico-Epistolaris* VI (Augsburg and Graz, 1729). Pt III, pp 6–8, item ix. (The printing of

Engelbert's Dedicatory Preface (shorter version) in this book is superseded by Fowler 1962.) [RB16]

Pelzer, Auguste, *Abréviations latines médiévales* (Louvain and Paris, 1964). Supplement to Capelli, *Dizionario de Abbreviature.*

Peremans, Nicole, 'Une bibliothèque, reflet d'une culture et d'une personnalité', *Bulletin de l'Institut Archéologique Liégeois* 84 (1972), 87–106. [On Stoupy and his library, re. RB54]

Pertz, G.H., *Auspiciis societatis Aperiendis Fontibus* [Annales, chronica et historiae aevi Saxonici], MGH, Scriptores 3 (Hannover, 1839). [RB47]

Pettas, William, *A history & bibliography of the Giunti (Junta) printing family in Spain, 1526–1628* (New Castle, DE, 2005). [FB4]

Pine, L.G., *A dictionary of mottoes* (London, 1983).

Pollard, Mary, *A dictionary of members of the Dublin book-trade* (London, 2000). [RB519]

Proctor, Robert, *An index to the early printed books in the British Museum: from the invention of printing to the year MD. With notes of those in the Bodleian Library*, vol. II (London, 1898).

Ramsden, Charles, 'Bookbinders of the United Kingdom (outside London), 1780–1840' (privately printed, 1954).

Réau, Louis, *Iconographie de l'art chrétien*, vols I–VI (Paris, 1958).

[Renehan, Laurence], *Bibliotheca Renehaniana: Catalogue of the rare, valuable and extensive library of the late Very Reverend Dr Renehan ... which will be sold by auction, by H. Lewis ... 31 Anglesea Street ... November 2nd, 1857* (Dublin, 1857).

Renouard, Philippe, *Inventaire chronologique des éditions parisiennes du XVIe siècle*, III 1521–30 (Abbeville, 1985). [RB39]

Renouard, Philippe, *Inventaire chronologique des éditions parisiennes du XVIe siècle*, IV 1531–5 (Abbeville, 1992). [FB7]

Reynolds, L.D., L. *Annaei Senecae ad Lucilium Epistulae Morales*, 2 vols (Oxford, 1965). [RB47]

Richardson, Regina Whelan, 'The Salamanca Archives' in Neligan, *Maynooth Library*, pp 112–47.

Rose, Valentin, *Verzeichniss der Lateinischen Handschriften der Königlichen Bibliothek zu Berlin*, Bd II (Berlin, 1901), pp 521–2, no. 578. [RB16]

Samaran, Charles, and Robert Marichal, *Catalogue des manuscrits en écriture latine portant des indications de date, de lieu ou de copiste*, vol. III (2 parts) (Paris, 1974). [RB53]

Samaran, Charles, and Robert Marichal, *Catalogue des manuscrits en écriture latine portant des indications de date, de lieu ou de copiste*, vol. VI (Paris, 1968). [RB74]

Sammarthanus, Dionysius [Denis of St-Marthe], OSB, *Gallia Christiana, in provincias ecclesiasticas distributa; qua series et historia archiepiscoporum,*

episcoporum et abbatum Franciæ vicinarumque ditionum, vol. III (Paris, 1725). [List of abbots of St Jacques le Mineur, Liège, cols 980–88; St Laurence, Liège, cols 988–96]

Schaller, Dieter, and Ewald Künsgen, *Initia Carminum Latinorum saeculo undecimo antiquiorum* (Göttingen, 1977). [SK]

Schmidt, Adolf, 'Ein Evangeliar aus St. Jakob in Lüttich', *Zentralblatt für Bibliothekswesen* 42 (1925), 265–8.

Schnitzler, Hermann, *Die Sammlungen des Baron von Hüpsch Ein Kölner Kunstkabinet um 1800* (Cologne, 1964).

Schulte, J.F. von, *Die Geschichte der Quellen und Literatur des canonischen Rechts von Gration bis auf die Gegenwart*, 3 vols (Stuttgart, 1875–77). [RB29]

Sharpe, Richard, *Irish manuscript sales* (Dublin, forthcoming).

Silvestre, L.-C., *Marques typographiques: ou Recueil des monogrammes, chiffres, enseignes, emblèmes, devises, rébus et fleurons des libraires et imprimeurs qui ont exercé en France depuis l'introduction de l'imprimerie en 1470 jusqu'à la fin du seizième siècle*, published in 9 parts (Paris, 1853–65). [RB39]

Simms, G.O., 'James Henthorn Todd', *Hermathena* 109 (1969), 5–24. [RB52, 519]

Smalley, Beryl, 'Gilbertus Universalis, bishop of London (1128–34) and the problem of the Glossa Ordinaria', *RTAM* 7 (1935), 235–62, and 8 (1936), 24–64. [RB45]

Smalley, Beryl, *The study of the Bible in the Middle Ages* (Oxford, 1952 ed.).

Soave-Bowe, Clotilde, and Christine Meek, 'A voyage to Barbary in the fifteenth century', *Hermathena* 124 (1978), 24–41. [RB52]

Sodi, Manlio, and Alessandro Toniolo, *Concordantia et Indices Missalis Romani*, Monumenta Studia Instrumenta Liturgica 23 (Vatican, 2002).

St George, Richard, *Pedigrees made at the visitation of Cheshire, 1613*, Harleian Society 59 ([London], 1909). [RB31]

Staub, K.H., *Die Handschriften der Hessischen Landes- und Hochschulbibliothek Damstadt*, vol. 5.1 (Wiesbaden, 2001).

Staub, K.H., and Herman Knaus, *Bibelschriften und Ältere Theologische Texte*, vol. 2 of *Die Handschriften der Hessischen Landes- und Hochschulbibliothek Darmstadt*, vol. 4 (Wiesbaden, 1979). [Includes Liège MSS now in Darmstadt]

Stegmüller, Fridericus, *Repertorium Biblicum Medii Aevi*, 11 vols (Madrid, 1940–80).

Stegmüller, Fridericus, *Repertorium Commentariorum in Sententias Petri Lombardi* (Würzburg, 1947). [RB29]

[Stoupy, E.S. de], *Catalogue des livres de la bibliothèque de feu M. de Stoupi* (Liège, 1786). [RB54]

Thomas, Henry, *Short-title catalogue of Portuguese books printed before 1601 now in the British Museum* (London, 1940). [FB12]

Thompson, John, 'William Reeves and the medieval texts and manuscripts at Armagh', *Peritia* 10 (1996), 363–80. [RB519]

Thorndike, Lynn, and Pearl Kibre, *A catalogue of incipits of medieval scientific writings in Latin*, rev. ed. (London, 1963).

[Todd, J.H.], *Catalogue of the valuable library of the late Rev. James H. Todd, comprising select biblical literature; the history, antiquities, and language of Ireland; ... and an important collection of patristic, Irish and other manuscripts ...; to be sold by auction by John Fleming Jones ... 8 d'Olier Street ... November 15th 1869* (Dublin 1869). Probably compiled by William Reeves (on whom see Thompson 1996). [RB52, 519]

[Troy, J.T.], *Catalogue of the very choice and valuable library of the late Most Rev. Doctor Troy, Roman Catholic archbishop of Dublin ... Catalogues may be had of ... Charles Sharpe, auctioneer, 33 Anglesea Street* (Dublin, Richard Grace [1823]).

Valentine, Lucia, *Ornament in medieval manuscripts: a glossary* (London, 1965).

Vattasso, Marcus, *Initia Patrum diorumque Scriptorum Ecclesiasticorum Latinorum*, 2 vols, Studi e Testi 16–17 (Rome, 1906–8).

Vervliet, H.D.L., 'Early sixteenth-century Parisian roman types', *De Gulden Passer* 83 (2005), 1–88. [RB39]

Vervliet, H.D.L., *The palaeotypography of the French Renaissance: selected papers on sixteenth-century typefaces*, 2 vols (Leiden, 2008). [RB39]

Vincent of Beauvais, *Speculum Maius*, 4 vols (Venice, Dominicus Nicolinus, 1591); vol. IV = *Speculum historiale*. [RB47]

Vincentius Bellovacensis, *Speculum historiale* (Venice, Hermann Liechtenstein, 1494). [RB47]

Volk, Paulus, OSB, 'Baron Hüpsch und der Verkauf der Lütticher St. Jakobsbibliothek (1788)', *Zentralblatt für Bibliothekswesen*, 42 (1925), 201–17.

Volk, Paulus, OSB, *Der liber ordinarius des Lütticher St Jakobs-Klosters*, Beiträge zur Geschichte des alten Mönchtums und des Bendiktinerordens 10 (Münster, 1923).

Vulgate: see Biblia, Fischer.

Walsh, Paul, *Catalogue of Irish manuscripts in Maynooth College Library*, part 1 (Maynooth, 1943). Continued by Ó Fiannachta 1965–73.

Walther, Hans, *Carmina Medii Aevi Posterioris Latina*, 9 vols (Göttingen, 1963–86). [RB29]

Weber, Robertus, OSB, *Ambrosii Autperti Opera*, pars III, CCCM 27B (Turnhout, 1979). [RB47]

Weihrich, Franciscus, *Sancti Aureli Augustini De Consensu Evangelistarum Libri Quattuor*, CSEL 43 (Vienna and Leipzig, 1904). [RB71]

Wheeler, W.G., 'Libraries in Ireland before 1855: a bibliographical essay', 2 vols, unpublished minor thesis for Dip. Lib., University of London, 1957. Copy in TCD Early Printed Books room (no class-mark) revised by hand to May 1965. [Vol. II is a check-list of auction sale catalogues.]

Wichner, [Père] Jacob, *Kloster Admont und seine Beziehungen zur Wissenschaft und zum Unterricht* (Graz, 1892), pp 46–7 [not seen]. [RB16]

Wilmart, André, *Auteurs spirituels et textes dévôts du moyen age latin* (Paris 1932, repr. 1971).

Woods, Penelope, 'Books rich, rare and curious' in Neligan, *Maynooth Library*, pp 29–63.

Woolnough, C.W., *The art of marbling* (London, 1853). [RB36]

Yvard, Catherine, 'Minute masterpieces: study of a late fifteenth-century book of hours from Rouen and Tours (Dublin, Chester Beatty Library, WMs 89): vol. IV: Catalogue of illuminated books of hours in Irish libraries'. PhD, TCD, 2005. [RB37, 38, 39]

Index of former manuscript owners

Index of incipits

Note: Items starting with lower-case letters are imperfect at the beginning.

Index of contents

References are to the manuscript class-mark and item number where appropriate. For short extracts see the Index of Incipits.

General Index

References in *italics* are to illustrations in the manuscripts

Abdon, St, martyr (fd 30 July), mass for 75

Achilleus, St, martyr (fd 12 May), mass for 73

Adam, 1st man *136*

Adam of Adersback, work by(?) 49

Adams, James, Dublin bookbinder s.xix² 10–11, 152, 160

Adauctus, St, martyr (fd 30 Aug.), mass for 76

Adela of Flanders, wife of Canute IV, king of Denmark 146

Adoration of the Magi, The *138*

Advent, benedictions for 190, masses for 60, office for 94

Agapitus, St, martyr (fd 18 Aug.), mass for 76

Agatha, St, virgin martyr (fd 5 Feb.), mass for 72

Agnes, St, virgin martyr (fd 21 Jan.), masses for 71–2, office for 94

Aherne, Revd Maurice, first professor of dogmatic theology SPCM 3

Airvaux, St Peter's abbey, abbot of, *see* Stoupy

Aix-en-Provence, Bibliothèque Méjanes 8, 182–3, 188–9, 205; cathedral of St Sauveur 7, 182; manuscript from 3, 6, 7, 11, 182–5, 189; *see also* Manuscripts. For abp of *see* Armand, Nicolaï

Alexander, St, martyr (fd 3 May), office for 95

Alexander of Hales OFM (*c*.1185–1245), work erron. attrib. to 20–6

All Saints' Day (1 Nov.), benediction for 201, mass for 59, 78, office for 95, prayers for 82

All Souls' Day (2 Nov.), mass for 78

Amalberge, St (fd 10 July), mother of St Gudula 103, 146

Ambrose, St (*c*.339–97; fd 7 Dec.), patristic author 4, 5, 38, 43–4; mass for 72, office for 94

Amiens 3

Anacletus, *see* Cletus

Anastasius, St, martyr (fd 22 Jan.), office for 94

Andrew the apostle, St (fd 30 Nov.), benediction for 202, mass for 71, office for 94

Anicetus, St, pope (*c*.157–*c*.168; fd 17 Apr.), office for 95

Anne, St, mother of the Blessed Virgin Mary (fd 26 July) *125*, *132*, *144*; mass for 59, 75, 81, prayers for 82

Anniversary of a death, masses for 68

Annunciation, The (25 Mar.) *107*, *109*, *111*, *118*, *126*, *137*; benediction for 200, office for 95

Annunciation to the Shepherds, The *138*

Anselm of Canterbury 151, work attrib. to 114